Chernobyl!

It was the stuff bad dreams are made of. But it was entirely predictable. In fact, Chernobyl was...

- prophesied nineteen centuries ago in the Bible by John the Revelator
- recorded by the French seer Nostradamus in the 16th century
- written in the astrological configurations that slowly, yet inexorably, were lining up, ticking off the minutes, waiting to trigger the release of an ages-old karma.

For the first time, Elizabeth Clare Prophet brings together these three prophecies of the worst industrial catastrophe in history and demonstrates that Chernobyl was no freak accident.

She reveals the karma of the explosion, details the precise astrological configurations that set it off, and outlines the consequences of the disaster, including a stunning prophecy by Nostradamus—of vital importance to everyone on earth—about the future of the Soviet empire.

Chernobyl is just the beginning.

The Messenger of Saint Germain reinterprets Nostradamus' predictions for the 20th century misconstrued by others. Against the backdrop of current economic and military trends she pierces the ___ ns the signs of the I ___ ny accuracy.

"Can anything or anyone come between a people and this handwriting on the wall?" asks Mrs. Prophet.

"Is there an intercessor who can turn the tide of Darkness and invoke the oncoming tide of Light to devour the karma...of a nation?

"Must this prophesied economic debacle followed by war and the nuclear nightmares come to pass?"

The answer, she says, is "Yes, Yes, and No."

And that is the essence of Saint Germain's message: that a nation united under God can, indeed must, change prophecy—if nuclear war and economic debacle are to be turned back.

In the capstone of this volume—the dictations of Saint Germain delivered by Elizabeth Clare Prophet—the Lord of the Seventh Ray gives his prophecies on cataclysm, the economy, the cocaine curse, nuclear confrontation between the superpowers and war in Europe. His analysis of world affairs highlights the interplay of the forces of Light and Darkness. His final sobering message is the great quickening of America to the trials ahead that will be surmounted only through Divine Intervention.

Saint Germain does not leave his readers comfortless. He tells them what they can do to avert, or at least mitigate, personal and planetary karma that hangs as a sword of Damocles over the nations—before it devastates the earth.

Saint Germain On Prophecy—four books in one you dare not be without.

Saint Germain

On PROPHECY

Coming World Changes

Nostradamus on U.S./U.S.S.R. Confrontation
War in Europe • Earthquakes • Chernobyl

Recorded by
Elizabeth Clare Prophet

SUMMIT UNIVERSITY 🍃 PRESS®

To the diligent and the wise ones
who are the builders of a new age and
a new civilization I remain committed
unto the end of the prophecy of your karma

Saint Germain

SAINT GERMAIN ON PROPHECY
Coming World Changes
Recorded by Elizabeth Clare Prophet

Copyright © 1986 Summit University Press
All rights reserved.

Library of Congress Catalog Card Number: 86-63286
International Standard Book Number: 0-916766-74-8

This book is set in 11 point Electra with 1.5 points lead.
Printed in the United States of America
First Printing: December 1986

SUMMIT UNIVERSITY 🦢 PRESS®

Contents

Book One

The Count Saint Germain
The Wonderman of Europe

The Man Who Would Not Die
(And Knows Everything)

And Samuel grew, and the LORD was with him, and did let none of his words fall to the ground.

And all Israel from Dan even to Beer-sheba knew that Samuel was established to be a prophet of the LORD.

I Samuel

But in the days of the voice of the seventh angel, when he shall begin to sound, the mystery of God should be finished, as he hath declared to his servants the prophets.

Revelation

The Count
Saint Germain

He lived to make men free.

That, in a phrase, sums up Saint Germain's many embodiments. Although he has played many parts, in each life he has brought the Christ/Light in prophecy and the alchemy of freedom to liberate the people of earth.

Enter Saint Germain January 1, 1987.

He comes to the fore as the Lord of the Seventh Ray and Age. He comes to initiate us in the gift of *prophecy* and the gift of the *working of miracles*—that we might foresee by the Spirit of the prophets what is coming upon us and turn the tide by the miracle violet flame.

More than fifty thousand years ago, a golden-age civilization thrived in a fertile country with a semitropical climate where the Sahara Desert now is. It was filled with great peace, happiness and prosperity and ruled with supreme justice and wisdom by this very Saint Germain.

The majority of his subjects retained full, conscious use of the wisdom and power of God. They possessed abilities that today would seem

superhuman or miraculous. They knew they were
extensions of the Central Sun—Life-streams issu-
ing from the Great Hub of the Spirit/Matter cosmos.

For their wise ruler had charted for them on a
great mural in the center of the capital city, "the
City of the Sun," their cosmic history—that they
should not forget the Source whence they had
come nor their reason for being: To become sun-
centers in this distant galaxy they now called home,
extensions of the Law of the One. For they were
part of an expanding universe. And their sense of
co-measurement with the One sustained an ever-
present cognition of the I AM THAT I AM.

Saint Germain was a master of the ancient
wisdom and of the knowledge of the Matter spheres.
He ruled by Light every area of life; his empire
reached a height of beauty, symmetry and perfection
unexceeded in the physical octave. Truly the heavenly patterns were outpictured in the crystal chalice of the earth. And elemental life served to
maintain the purity of the Matter quadrants.

The people regarded their hierarch as the
highest expression of God whom they desired to
emulate, and great was their love for his presence.
He was the embodiment of the archetype of universal Christhood for that dispensation—to whom
they could look as the standard for their own
emerging Godhood.

Guy W. Ballard, under the pen name of
Godfre Ray King, recounted in *Unveiled Mysteries*
a soul journey in which Saint Germain conducted

him through the akashic record of this civilization and its decline.[1]

Saint Germain explained to him that "as in all ages past, there was a portion of the people who became more interested in the temporary pleasures of the senses than in the larger creative plan of the Great God Self. This caused them to lose consciousness of the God-Power throughout the land until it remained active in little more than the [capital] city itself. Those governing realized they must withdraw and let the people learn through hard experience that all their happiness and good came from the adoration to the God within, and they must come back into the Light if they were to be happy."

Thus, the ruler (the embodied representative of the spiritual hierarchy of the earth under Sanat Kumara) was instructed by a cosmic council that he must withdraw from his empire and his beloved people; henceforth their karma would be their Guru and Lawgiver, and free will would determine what, if any, of his legacy of Light they would retain.

According to plan, the king held a great banquet in the Jeweled Room of his palace, with his councillors and public servants in attendance. Following the dinner, which had been entirely precipitated, a crystal goblet filled with "pure electronic essence" appeared to the right of each of the 576 guests. It was the communion cup of Saint Germain, who, with the mantle and sceptre of the ancient priest/kings, gave of his own Light-essence to those who had faithfully served the realm to the glory of God.

As they drank to the "Flame of the most High Living One," they knew they could never completely forget the divine spark of the inner God Self. This soul-protection, afforded them through the ever-grateful heart of Saint Germain, would be sustained throughout the centuries until once again they should find themselves in a civilization where the cosmic cycles had turned and they would be given the full knowledge to pursue the Divine Union—this time nevermore to go out from the Golden City of the Sun.

Now a Cosmic Master from out the Great Silence spoke. His message was broadcast from the banquet hall throughout the realm. The resplendent being, who identified himself solely by the word *Victory* written upon his brow, brought warning of crisis to come, rebuked the people for their ingratitude to and neglect of their Great God Source, and reminded them of the ancient command to obey the Law of the One—Love. Then he gave them the following prophecy of their karma:

"A visiting prince approaches your borders. He will enter this city seeking the daughter of your king. You will come under the rule of this prince but the recognition of your mistake will be futile. Nothing can avail, for the royal family will be drawn into the protection and care of those whose power and authority are of God, and against whom no human desire can ever prevail. These are the great Ascended Masters of Light from the golden etheric city over this land. Here your ruler and his beloved children will abide for a cycle of time."

The king and his children withdrew seven days later. The prince arrived the next day and took over without opposition.

As we study the history of Saint Germain's lifestream we shall see that time and time again the Master and his way of God-mastery have been rejected by the very ones he sought to help; notwithstanding the fact that his gifts of Light, Life and Love—fruits of his adeptship freely given— his alchemical feats, elixir of youth, inventions and prognostications have been readily received.

The goal of his embodiments extending from the golden-age civilization of the Sahara to the final hour of his life as Francis Bacon was always to liberate the children of the Light, especially those who in their carelessness in handling fiery principles of the Law had been left to their own karmic devices—in whose vices they were often bound. His aim was to see the fulfillment of his prayer offered at the final banquet of his reign:

> If they must have the experience that consumes and burns away the dross and clouds of the outer self, then do Thou sustain and at last bring them forth in Thy Eternal Perfection. I call unto Thee, Thou Creator of the Universe—Thou Supreme Omnipotent God.

As the High Priest of the Violet Flame Temple on the mainland of Atlantis thirteen thousand years ago, Saint Germain sustained by his invocations and his causal body a pillar of fire, a fountain of violet singing flame, which magnetized people from near and far to be set free from every binding condition of body, mind and soul. This they achieved by self-effort through the offering of invocations and the practice of Seventh Ray rituals to the sacred fire.

An intricately carved marble circular railing enclosed the shrine where supplicants knelt in adoration of the God flame—visible to some as a physical violet flame, to others as an 'ultraviolet' light and to others not at all, though the powerful healing vibrations were undeniable.

The temple was built of magnificent marble ranging in hue from brilliant white, shot through with violet and purple veins, to deeper shades of the Seventh Ray spectrum. The central core of the temple was a large circular hall lined in ice-violet marble set upon a rich purpled marble floor. Three stories in height, it was situated midst a complex of adjacent areas for worship and the various functions of priests and priestesses who ministered unto the Flame and mediated its voice of Light and Prophecy unto the people. Those who officiated at this altar were schooled in the universal priesthood of the Order of Melchizedek at Lord Zadkiel's retreat, the Temple of Purification, in the locale of the West Indies.

Through the heights and depths of the ages that have ensued, Saint Germain has ingeniously used the Seventh Ray momentum of his causal body to secure freedom for keepers of the flame who have kept alive 'coals' from the violet flame altar of his Atlantean temple. He has extolled and exemplified freedom of the mind and spirit. Endowing the four sacred freedoms with an identity of their own, he has championed our freedom from state interference, kangaroo courts, or popular ridicule in matters ranging from scientific investigation to the healing arts to the spiritual quest.

Standing on a platform of basic human rights for a responsible, reasoning public educated in the principles of liberty and equal opportunity for all, he has ever taught us to espouse our inalienable divine right to live life according to our highest conception of God. For the Master has said that no right, however simple or basic, can long be secure without the underpinning of the spiritual graces and the Divine Law that instills a compassionate righteousness in the exercise thereof.

Returning to the scene of the karma of his people as Samuel, prophet of the LORD and judge of the twelve tribes of Israel (c. 1050 B.C.), Saint Germain was the messenger of God's liberation of the seed of Abraham from bondage to the corrupt priests, the sons of Eli, and from the Philistines by whom they had been defeated. Bearing in his heart the special sign of the blue rose of Sirius, Samuel delivered to the recalcitrant Israelites a

prophecy parallel to his twentieth-century dis-
courses—both inextricably linked with God's covenants concerning karma, free will and grace:

"If ye do return unto the LORD with all your
hearts, then put away the strange gods and Ash-
taroth from among you, and prepare your hearts
unto the LORD and serve him only: and he will
deliver you out of the hand of the Philistines."
Later, when King Saul disobeyed God, Samuel
freed the people from his tyranny by anointing
David king.

True to the thread of prophecy that runs
throughout his lifetimes, Saint Germain was Saint
Joseph of the lineage of King David, son of Jesse,
chosen vessel of the Holy Ghost, father of Jesus in
fulfillment of the word of the LORD to Isaiah—
"There shall come forth a rod out of the stem of
Jesse, and a Branch shall grow out of his roots. . . ."

We see, then, in each of Saint Germain's
embodiments that there is present the quality
of alchemy—a conveyance of Godly power. So
ordained the instrument of the LORD, Samuel
transferred His sacred fire in the anointing of
David and just as scientifically withdrew it from
King Saul when the LORD rejected him from
being king over Israel. This unmistakable sign of
the Seventh Ray adept, often in humble garb, was
also present as the Holy Spirit's power of the
conversion of souls and the control of natural
forces in his life as the third-century Saint Alban,
first martyr of the British Isles.

A Roman soldier, Alban hid a fugitive priest, was converted by him, then sentenced to death for disguising himself as the priest and allowing him to escape. A great multitude gathered to witness his execution—too many to pass over the narrow bridge that must be crossed. Alban prayed and the river parted—whereupon his executioner, being converted, begged to die in Alban's place. His request was denied and he was beheaded that day alongside the saint.

But Saint Germain was not always to be counted in the ranks of the Church. He fought tyranny wherever he found it, including in false Christian doctrine. As the Master Teacher behind the Neoplatonists, Saint Germain was the inner inspiration of the Greek philosopher Proclus (c. A.D. 410–485). He revealed his pupil's previous life as a Pythagorean philosopher, also showing Proclus the sham of Constantine's Christianity and the worth of the path of individualism (leading to the individualization of the God flame) which Christians called "paganism."

As the highly honored head of Plato's Academy at Athens, Proclus based his philosophy upon the principle that there is only one true reality—the "One," which is God, or the Godhead, the final goal of all life's efforts. The philosopher said, "Beyond all bodies is the essence of soul, and beyond all souls the intellectual nature, and beyond all intellectual existences the One."[2] Throughout his incarnations Saint Germain demonstrated tremendous breadth of knowledge in the Mind of God; not surprising was the range of his pupil's awareness. His writings extended to almost every department of learning.

Proclus acknowledged that his enlightenment and philosophy came from above—indeed he believed himself to be one through whom divine revelation reached mankind. "He did not appear to be without divine inspiration," his disciple Marinus wrote, "for he produced from his wise mouth words similar to the most thick-falling snow; so that his eyes emitted a bright radiance, and the rest of his countenance participated of divine illumination."[3]

Thus Saint Germain, white-robed, jeweled slippers and belt emitting star-fire from far-off worlds, was the mystery Master smiling just beyond the veil—mirroring the imagings of his mind in the soul of the last of the great Neoplatonic philosophers.

Saint Germain was Merlin. The unforgettable, somehow irretrievable figure who haunts the mists of England, about to step forth at any moment to offer us a goblet of sparkling elixir. He the 'old man' who knows the secrets of youth and alchemy, who charted the stars at Stonehenge, and moved a stone or two, so they say, by his magical powers—who would astonish no one if he suddenly appeared on a Broadway stage or in the forests of the Yellowstone or at one's side on any highway anywhere.

For Saint Germain *is* Merlin.

Enter Merlin January 1, 1987, with his final prophecy to heroes, knights, ladies, crazies, and villains of the Aquarian Camelot.

Merlin, dear Merlin, has never left us—his spirit charms the ages, makes us feel as rare and unique as his diamond and amethyst adornments. Merlin is the irreplaceable Presence, a humming vortex about whose science and legends and fatal romance Western civilization has entwined itself.

It was the fifth century. Midst the chaos left by the slow death of the Roman Empire, a king arose to unite a land splintered by warring chieftains and riven by Saxon invaders. At his side was the old man himself—half Druid priest, half Christian saint—seer, magician, counselor, friend, who led the king through twelve battles to unite a kingdom and establish a window of peace.

At some point, the spirit of Merlin went through a catharsis. The scene was one of fierce battle, the legend says. As he witnessed the carnage, a madness came upon him—of seeing all at once past/present and future—so peculiar to the lineage of the prophets. He fled to the forest to live as a wild man, and one day as he sat under a tree, he began to utter prophecies concerning the future of Wales.

"I was taken out of my true self," he said. "I was as a spirit and knew the history of people long past and could foretell the future. I knew then the secrets of nature, bird flight, star wanderings

and the way fish glide."⁴ Both his prophetic
utterances and his "magical" powers served one
end: the making of a united kingdom of the tribes
of the old Britons. His pervasiveness is recalled in
an early Celtic name for Britain, "Clas Myrddin,"
which means "Merlin's Enclosure."⁵

By advising and assisting Arthur in establishing his kingship, Merlin sought to make of Britain
a fortress against ignorance and superstition where
Christ achievement could flower and devotion to the
One could prosper in the quest for the Holy Grail.
His efforts on this soil were to bear fruit in the nine-
teenth century as the British Isles became the place
where individual initiative and industry could
thrive as never before in twelve thousand years.

But even as Camelot, the rose of England,
budded and bloomed, nightshade was twining
about its roots. Witchcraft, intrigue and treachery
destroyed Camelot, not the love of Launcelot and
Guinevere as Tom Malory's misogynistic depiction suggests. Alas, the myth he sowed has ob-
scured the real culprits these long centuries.

'Twas the king's bastard son Modred by his
half sister Margawse⁶ who, with Morgana le Fay
and a circle of like sorceresses and black knights,
set out to steal the crown, imprison the queen,
and destroy for a time the bonds of a Love that
such as these (of the left-handed path) had never
known nor could—a Reality all of their willing,
warring and enchantments could not touch.

Thus it was with a heavy heart and the spirit of

a prophet who has seen visions of tragedy and desolation, fleeting joys and the piercing anguish of
karmic retribution endlessly outplayed, that Merlin
entered the scene of his own denouement, to be
tied up in spells of his own telling by silly, cunning
Vivien—and sleep. Aye, to err is human but to pine
for the twin flame that is not there is the lot of many
an errant knight or king or lonely prophet who
perhaps should have disappeared into the mists
rather than suffer sad ignominy for his people.

Some say he still sleeps but they grossly under-
estimate the resilient spirit of the wise man re-
bounded, this time in thirteenth-century England
disguised as Roger Bacon (c. 1214–1294). Reenter
Merlin—scientist, philosopher, monk, alchemist
and prophet—to forward his mission of laying the
scientific moorings for the age of Aquarius his
soul should one day sponsor.

The atonement of this lifetime was to be the
voice crying in the intellectual and scientific wilderness that was medieval Britain. In an era in
which either theology or logic or both dictated the
parameters of science, he promoted the experimental method, declared his belief that the world
was round, and castigated the scholars and scientists of his day for their narrow-mindedness. Thus
he is viewed as the forerunner of modern science.

But he was also a prophet of modern technology. Although it is unlikely he did experiments to
determine the feasibility of the following inventions, he predicted the hot-air balloon, a flying

machine, spectacles, the telescope, microscope, elevator, and mechanically propelled ships and carriages, and wrote of them as if he had actually seen them! Bacon was also the first Westerner to write down the exact directions for making gunpowder, but kept the formula a secret lest it be used to harm anyone. No wonder people thought he was a magician!

However, just as Saint Germain tells us today in his *Studies in Alchemy* that "miracles" are wrought by the precise application of universal laws, so Roger Bacon meant his prophecies to demonstrate that flying machines and magical apparatus were products of the employment of natural law which men would figure out in time.

From whence did Bacon believe he derived his amazing awareness? "True knowledge stems not from the authority of others, nor from a blind allegiance to antiquated dogmas," he said. Two of his biographers write that he believed knowledge "is a highly personal experience—a light that is communicated only to the innermost privacy of the individual through the impartial channels of all knowledge and of all thought."[7]

And so Bacon, who had been a lecturer at Oxford and the University of Paris, determined to separate himself and his thoughts from the posing and postulating residents of academe. He would seek and find his science in his religion. Entering the Franciscan Order of Friars Minor, he said, "I will conduct my experiments on the magnetic forces of the lodestone at the selfsame shrine where my fellow-scientist, St. Francis, performed his experiments on the magnetic forces of love."[8]

But the friar's scientific and philosophical world view, his bold attacks on the theologians of his day, and his study of alchemy, astrology and magic led to charges of "heresies and novelties," for which he was imprisoned in 1278 by his fellow Franciscans! They kept him in solitary confinement for fourteen years,[9] releasing him only shortly before his death. Although the clock of this life was run out, his body broken, he knew that his efforts would not be without impact on the future.

The following prophecy which he gave his students shows the grand and revolutionary ideals of the indomitable spirit of this living flame of freedom—the immortal spokesman for our scientific, religious and political liberties:

> I believe that humanity shall accept as an axiom for its conduct the principle for which I have laid down my life—the right to investigate. It is the credo of free men—this opportunity to try, this privilege to err, this courage to experiment anew. We scientists of the human spirit shall experiment, experiment, ever experiment. Through centuries of trial and error, through agonies of research...let us experiment with laws and customs, with money systems and governments, until we chart the one true course— until we find the majesty of our proper orbit

as the planets above have found theirs.... And then at last we shall move all together in the harmony of our spheres under the great impulse of a single creation—one unity, one system, one design.[10]

To establish this freedom upon earth, Saint Germain's lifestream took another turn—as Christopher Columbus (1451–1506). But over two centuries before Columbus sailed, Roger Bacon had set the stage for the voyage of the three ships and the discovery of the New World when he stated in his *Opus Majus* that "the sea between the end of Spain on the west and the beginning of India on the east is navigable in a very few days if the wind is favorable."[11]

Although the statement was incorrect in that the land to the west of Spain was not India, it was instrumental in Columbus' discovery. Cardinal Pierre d'Ailly copied it in his *Imago Mundi* without noting Bacon's authorship. Columbus read his work and quoted the passage in a 1498 letter to King Ferdinand and Queen Isabella, saying that his 1492 voyage had been inspired in part by this visionary statement.

Columbus believed that God had made him to be "the messenger of the new heaven and the new earth of which He spake in the Apocalypse of St. John, after having spoken of it by the mouth of Isaiah."[12]

His vision went back as far as ancient Israel, perhaps even further. For in discovering the New

World, Columbus believed that he was the instrument whereby God would, as Isaiah recorded around 732 B.C., "recover the remnant of his people. . . . and shall assemble the outcasts of Israel, and gather together the dispersed of Judah from the four corners of the earth."[13]

Twenty-two centuries passed before anything visible happened that seemed to be the fulfillment of this prophecy. But late in the fifteenth century, Christopher Columbus was quietly preparing to set the stage for the fulfillment of this prophecy, certain that he had been divinely selected for his mission. He studied the biblical prophets, writing passages relating to his mission in a book of his own making entitled *Las Proficias* or *The Prophecies*—in its complete form, *The Book of Prophecies concerning the Discovery of the Indies and the Recovery of Jerusalem*. Although the point is seldom stressed, it is a fact so rooted in history that even *Encyclopædia Britannica* says unequivocally that, "Columbus discovered America by prophecy rather than by astronomy."[14]

"In the carrying out of this enterprise of the Indies," he wrote to King Ferdinand and Queen Isabella in 1502, "neither reason nor mathematics nor maps were any use to me: fully accomplished were the words of Isaiah." He was referring to Isaiah 11:10–12.

Thus we see that lifetime by lifetime, Saint Germain, whether his outer mind was continuously cognizant of it we know not, was re-creating that golden pathway to the Sun—a destiny come full circle to worship the God Presence and re-establish a lost golden age.

As Francis Bacon (1561–1626), the greatest mind the West has ever produced, his manifold achievements in every field catapulted the world into a stage set for the children of Aquarius. In this life he was free to carry to its conclusion the work he had begun as Roger Bacon.

Scholars have noted the similarities between the thoughts of the two philosophers and even between Roger's *Opus Majus* and Francis' *De Augmentis* and *Novum Organum*. This is made even more astounding by the fact that Roger's *Opus* was never published in his lifetime, fell into oblivion, and not until 113 years after Francis' *Novum Organum* and 110 years after his *De Augmentis* did it appear in print!

The unsurpassed wit of this immortal soul, this philosopher/king, this priest/scientist, might easily have kept its humor with the stubborn motto drawn from tyrants, tortures and tragedy: If they beat you in one life, come back and beat them in the next!

Francis Bacon is known as the father of inductive reasoning and the scientific method which, more than any other contributions, are responsible for the age of technology in which we now live. He foreknew that only applied science could free the masses from human misery and the drudgery of sheer survival in order that they might seek a higher spirituality they once knew. Thus, science and technology were essential to Saint Germain's plan for the liberation of his Lightbearers and through them all mankind.

His next step was to be nothing less bold than universal enlightenment!

"The Great Instauration" (restoration after decay, lapse, or dilapidation) was his formula to change "the whole wide world." First conceived when Bacon was a boy of 12 or 13 and later crystallized in 1607 in his book by the same name, it did indeed launch the English Renaissance with the help of Francis' tender, caring person. For over the years, he gathered around himself a group of illuminati who were responsible among other things for almost all of the Elizabethan literature— Ben Jonson, John Davies, George Herbert, John Selden, Edmund Spenser, Sir Walter Raleigh, Gabriel Harvey, Robert Greene, Sir Philip Sidney, Christopher Marlowe, John Lyly, George Peele, and Lancelot Andrewes.

Some of these were part of a "secret society" that Francis had formed with his brother, Anthony, when the two were law students at Gray's Inn. This fledgling group, called "The Knights of the Helmet," had as its goal the advancement of learning by expanding the English language and by creating a new literature written not in Latin but in words which Englishmen could understand.

Francis also organized the translation of the King James Version of the Bible, determined that

the common people should have the benefit of
reading God's Word for themselves. Furthermore,
as was discovered in the 1890s in two separate
ciphers—a word-cipher and a bi-literal cipher embedded in the type of the original printings of the
Shakespearean Folios[15]—Francis Bacon *was* the
author of the plays attributed to the actor from
the squalid village of Stratford-on-Avon. He *was*
the greatest literary genius of the Western world.

So, too, was Bacon behind many of the political ideas on which Western civilization is based.
Thomas Hobbes, John Locke and Jeremy Bentham
took Bacon as their ideological starting point. His
revolutionary principles are the engine that has
driven our nation. They are the very essence of the
can-do spirit. "Men are not animals erect," Bacon
averred, "but immortal Gods. The Creator has
given us souls equal to all the world, and yet
satiable not even with a world."[16]

Francis Bacon also continued the task he had
begun as Christopher Columbus, promoting the
colonization of the New World, for he knew that it
was there that his ideas could take deepest root and
come to fullest flower. He convinced James I to
charter Newfoundland and was an officer in the
Virginia Company, which sponsored the settle-
ment of Jamestown, England's first permanent
colony in America. And he founded Freemasonry,
dedicated to the freedom and enlightenment of
mankind, whose members played a large part in
founding the new nation.

Yet he could have been an even greater boon to England and the whole world had he been allowed to fulfill his destiny. The same ciphers which run throughout the Shakespearean plays also run through Francis Bacon's own works and those of many of his circle of friends. Both ciphers contain his true life story, the musings of his soul, and anything he wished to bequeath to future generations but could not publish openly for fear of the queen.[17]

Its secrets reveal that he should have been Francis I, King of England. He was the son of Queen Elizabeth I and Robert Dudley, Lord Leicester, born four months after a secret wedding ceremony. But she, wishing to retain her "Virgin Queen" status and afraid that if she acknowledged her marriage, she must give power to the ambitious Leicester, also lest the people prefer her male heir to herself and demand the queen's premature withdrawal from the throne, refused to allow Francis, on pain of death, to assume his true identity.

The queen kept him dangling all his life, never giving him public office, never proclaiming him her son, never allowing him to fulfill his goals for England. No, she would not allow her son to bring in the golden age of Britannia that was meant to be but never was. What cruel fate— a queen mother unbending, contemptuous before her golden age prince!

He was raised the foster son of Sir Nicholas and Lady Anne Bacon and at age fifteen heard the truth of his birth from his own mother's lips in the same breath with which she barred him forever from the succession. In one night his world was in a shambles. Like young Hamlet, he pondered over and over the question, "To be or not to be?" That was *his* question.

In the end, he determined not to rebel against his mother or later, against her ill-fitted successor, James I. This despite the great good he knew he could bring to England, despite his vision of the land "as she might be, if wisely governed."[18] He knew he had within himself the power to be a monarch such as the land had never known, a true father of the nation. He wrote of the "impulses of the godlike patriarchal care for his own people" he would exercise[19]—shades of the golden age emperor of the Sahara.

Fortunately for the world, Francis determined to pursue his goal of universal enlightenment in the avenues of literature and science, as adviser to the throne, supporter of colonization, and founder of secret societies, thereby reestablishing the thread of contact with the ancient mystery schools. The outlet of his wounded spirit was his cipher writing into which he poured out his longings to a future age.

Thus from a celestial visitation he took his lead as he was led to achieve his immortality by Truth's rhyme not by kingly fame. AthenA, the original "spear shaker," was his Muse and Patroness. The double A, his signet, revealed his source and hers in the works he accomplished out of

the vision he described in a poem written in 1576 at
age fifteen:

> And now, it is time for us to tell you
> *How we found the way to conceal these ciphers.*

One night, when a youth, while we were reading
In the holy scriptures of our great God...

That passage of Solomon, the King, wherein he
Affirmeth "That the glory of God is to conceal
A thing, but the glory of a King is to find it out."

As we read and pondered the wise
Words and lofty language of this precious
Book of love, there comes a flame of fire which
Fills all the room and *obscures our eyes with its*
Celestial glory. And from its swells a heavenly
Voice, that, lifting our minds above her
Human bounds, ravisheth our soul with its sweet
Heavenly music. And thus it spake:

"My son, fear not, but take thy fortunes and
Thy honours up. Be that thou knowest thou art,
Then art thou as great as that thou fearest,
Thou are not what thou seemest. At thy birth
The front of heaven was full of fiery shapes;
The goats ran from the mountains, and the herds
Were strangely clamorous to the frighted fields.
These signs have marked thee extraordinary,
And all the courses of thy life will show,
Thou art not in the roll of common men.

"Be thou not, therefore, afraid of greatness,
Some men become great by advancement, vain
And favour of their prince; some have greatness
Thrust upon them by the world, and some achieve

Greatness by reason of their wit; for there is
A tide in the affairs of men, which taken at the
Flood, leads on to glorious fortune.
   Omitted, all the
"Voyage of their life is bound in shallows
And miseries. In such a sea art thou now afloat,
And thou must take the current when it serves,
Or lose thy ventures. Thy fates open their hands
   to thee.
"Decline them not, but let thy blood and spirit
Embrace them, and climb the height of virtue's
Sacred hill, where endless honour shall be made
Thy mead. Remember that what thou hast just
Read, that the Divine Majesty takes delight
   to hide
His work, according to the innocent play of
   children,
To have them found out; surely for thee to
Follow the example of the most high God cannot
Be censured. Therefore put away popular
   applause,
"And after the manner of *Solomon* the king,
compose
A history of thy times, and fold it into
Enigmatical writings and cunning mixtures of the
Theatre, mingled as the colours in a painter's shell,
And it will in due course of time be found,

"For there shall be born into the world
(Not in years, but in ages) a man whose pliant and
Obedient mind we, of the supernatural world,
   will take

Special heed, by all possible endeavour, to frame
And mould into a pipe for thy fingers to sound
What stop thou please; and this man, either led or
Driven, as we point the way, will yield himself a
Disciple of thine, and will search and seek out thy
Disordered and confused strings and roots
    with some
Peril and unsafety to himself. For men in
    scornful and
Arrogant manner *will call him mad*, and point
    at him
The finger of scorn; and yet they will,
Upon trial, practice and study of thy plan,
*See that the secret, by great and voluminous
    labour,
Hath been found out.*"

    And then the Voice we heard
    Ceased and passed away.[20]

By the time of his death in 1626, persecuted
and unrecognized for his manifold talents, Francis
Bacon had triumphed over circumstances which
would have destroyed lesser men, but which for
him proved the true making of an Ascended Master.

Enter Saint Germain May 1, 1684,
God of Freedom to the earth.
Draped with a cloak of stars,
He stands with his twin flame,
The Goddess of Justice,
Against the backdrop of Cosmos.

He is come to ignite the fires
  of world transmutation
In hearts attuned to the cosmic cyphers
And to avert personal and planetary cataclysm.
He pleads the cause of God-Freedom
Before the councils of men
And presents his case before
The world body of Lightbearers.
He offers a ransom for the oppressed—
Gift of his heart—and of his mind,
Rarest jewel of all our earthly souvenirs—
And of his causal body:
Sphere upon sphere of the richness of himself
Harvested from the divine, and the human,
  experience.

All this he offers.
Like a beggar with his bowl piled high,
He plies the streets of the world
Eyeing passersby
Hopeful that even one in every million
Might take the proffered gift
And hold it to his heart in recognition
Of the Source, of the Sun,
And of the alchemy of the age so close.
Yes, as close as free will and the Divine Spark
Is our extrication from the dilemma
Of doubt and deleterious concepts and death.
And as far, as far as the toiler's envy
Of our Love tryst is from grace,
So, without him, is the morning of our deliverance
From tangled entanglements of karmic crisscrosses

Of our doodling and dabbling for centuries'
  boredom
With personalities far less, oh yes, than his.

Enter Saint Germain
Into our hearts forever, if we will only let him.

May 1, 1684, was Saint Germain's Ascension
Day. From heights of power well earned and
beyond this world's, he still stands to turn back
all attempts to thwart his 'Great Instauration'
here below.

Desiring above all else to liberate God's people,
whether they would or no, Saint Germain sought
and was granted a dispensation from the Lords of
Karma to return to earth in a physical body. He
appeared as "le Comte de Saint Germain," a
"miraculous" gentleman who dazzled the courts
of eighteenth- and nineteenth-century Europe
where they called him "The Wonderman." And
with good reason. Never had anyone so captured
the attention of an entire continent quite like this
Monsieur. He was, as Voltaire described him, the
"man who never dies and who knows everything."

But that was incomplete. He was also the
man who could play the violin "like an orchestra."
The man who spoke flawless French, English,
Italian, Spanish, and Portuguese—who was an
expert in Latin, Greek, Chinese, Sanskrit, and
Arabic. The man who was a poet, painter and
artisan; scholar, statesman, and raconteur.

He was no mythical figure spun out of salon gossip. Frederick the Great, Voltaire, Horace Walpole and Casanova mentioned him in their letters. Newspapers of the day—*The London Chronicle* of June 1760, *Le notizie del Mondo*, a Florentine newspaper in July of 1770, and *The Gazette of the Netherlands*—took note of him.

Madame du Hausset, *femme de chambre* to Madame de Pompadour, wrote of him at some length in her memoirs. She tells how in 1757 he undertook to remove a flaw from a medium-sized diamond for Louis XV. After weighing the diamond, she wrote, "his Majesty said to the Comte: 'The value of this diamond as it is, and with the flaw in it, is six thousand livres; without the flaw it would be worth at least ten thousand. Will you undertake to make me a gainer of four thousand livres?'

"Saint Germain examined it very attentively, and said, 'It is possible; it may be done. I will bring it to you again in a month.'

"At the time appointed the Comte de St. Germain brought back the diamond without a spot, and gave it to the King. It was wrapped in a cloth of amianthos, which he took off. The king had it weighed immediately, and found it very little diminished. His Majesty then sent it to his jeweller...without telling him of anything that had passed. The jeweller gave him nine thousand six hundred livres for it. The King, however, sent for the diamond back again, and said he would keep it as a curiosity."

The King, of course, was astonished. He made the remark that "M. de St. Germain must be worth millions, especially if he possessed the secret of making large diamonds out of small ones."

The sources of the Wonderman's income and his net worth were never discovered. Clearly he was a man of extraordinary means. One countess wrote that even though he dressed plainly, he wore an abundance of diamonds—on every finger, on his watch, on his shoe buckles. The finest diamonds even adorned his snuff box. But as for making diamonds grow, Madame du Hausset tells us that "the Comte neither said that he could or could not, but positively asserted that he knew how to make pearls grow, and give them the finest water."

There seemed, in fact, no end to the things he could do. The Marquis de Valbelle reported seeing him change a silver six-franc piece into gold. In a letter dated 1763, Count Karl Cobenzl asserted that the Count Saint Germain had performed "under my own eyes. . .the transmutation of iron into a metal as beautiful as gold."

How did he do it? Many would have liked to have known the Count's secrets—kings, ministers, diplomats, mystics, and savants. Some, no doubt, desired to enrich themselves. Others sought his ruin—for the Wonderman had his enemies. But whatever their purpose, no one ever discovered anything about him he did not wish them to know. The Count was a man of mystery.

No one knew quite where he came from nor

how old he was, although there was a great deal of speculation about the matter. For the 112 years, beginning in 1710, that European society reported seeing him, the Wonderman appeared to be about 45 years of age. But when asked, he would graciously decline to reveal his date of birth. To one countess he would admit only that he was very old.

Sometimes he appeared to be jesting. Or was he reading from *akasha?* Madame de Pompadour wrote that he would describe scenes from the court of Valois [fourteenth to sixteenth century] in such precise and minute detail as to give the unmistakable impression that he had been there.

The Wonderman was reputed to have concocted medicines which prolonged his life and to know the secret of the elixir of life. One memoir-writer said that he gave such an elixir to Madame v. Georgy "which for fully a quarter of a century preserved unaltered the youthful charms she possessed at 25."

Nor were these the end of the Count's wonders. His manners were exquisite and he was a brilliant, although sometimes enigmatic, conversationalist. Madame d'Adhémar, confidante of Marie Antoinette, reported seeing him vanish outside the royal quarters at Versailles. Cornelius van Sypesteyn wrote that he could "tame bees and make snakes listen to music." Such feats known to Indian yogis alike, nevertheless did not detract from his remarkableness.

But to what end were the Count's labors? A

man with infinite wealth and eternal life has no
need to impress. The truth of the matter is, he had
a number of goals, including dispersing the gathering storm that eventually burst forth on Europe as
the French Revolution.

The Count had the ability to describe the
future with the same precision with which he
recalled the past. He saw the French Revolution
coming long before the reign of terror and the
guillotine when blood flowed in the streets of Paris.

But he certainly did not think it was an
unalterable event. No, indeed. "A gigantic conspiracy is being formed, which as yet has no
visible chief, but he will appear before long," he
told Madame d'Adhémar some years before the
revolution when the French throne was the most
splendid institution in Europe. She recorded his
prophecy in her diary: "The aim is nothing less
than the overthrow of what exists, to reconstruct it
on a new plan. There is ill-will towards the royal
family, the clergy, the nobility, the magistracy.
There is still time, however, to baffle the plot;
later, this would be impossible."

Apparently, the Wonderman had it in mind
to help effect a smooth transition from monarchi-
cal to republican forms of government. He knew
the old order was passing and labored to establish a
United States of Europe before the French Revolution would ultimately leave nothing good nor
bad of her royal houses.

The Count Saint Germain tried to warn

Louis XVI of the webs of intrigue being woven around the monarchy, Madame d'Adhémar reported. First he explained to Marie Antoinette what would take place. He then begged her to tell the king and arrange a meeting between the two of them without the presence of the king's chief adviser, Monsieur de Maurepas.

Madame d'Adhémar, present at the meeting between the Wonderman and Marie Antoinette, recorded his words: "Some years yet will pass by in a deceitful calm; then from all parts of the kingdom will spring up men greedy for vengeance, for power, and for money; they will overthrow all in their way.... Civil war will burst out with all its horrors; it will bring in its train murder, pillage, exile. Then it will be regretted that I was not listened to."

Alas, it is not only in his own country that a prophet may be without honor. Maurepas, a bitter enemy of the Count Saint Germain, intervened. King and Count never met. The rest is history.

There is much more to tell, of course. But many of the things that could be said are already included in the opening section of *Saint Germain On Alchemy*, entitled "The Wonderman of Europe." They also appear in *The Comte de Saint Germain* by Isabel Cooper-Oakley. The latter, for the most part, is a collection of eyewitness accounts of the Count Saint Germain's amazing works drawn from letters and diaries, family archives, and state papers, including the secret diplomatic correspondence files of the British National Record Office.

Through the eyes of his contemporaries, you can read about the Wonderman's secret diplomatic missions for Louis XV, his retreat in the Himalayas, his efforts to change the outcome of some of his own prophecies. And you may also read about his enemies.

The Count Saint Germain has been remembered by some as a rogue, a charlatan, a swindler, a revolutionary in league with those who overthrew the French monarchy and various other epithets. Some of these are the result of a case of mistaken identity—the comte was occasionally confused with Count Claude Louis St. Germain (1707–1778), who served for a time as Minister of War to Louis XVI. There was also at least one impostor who made his way through the salons of Paris *claiming* to be the illustrious Count.

Those who called him a charlatan or a swindler were naturally never able to produce even a shred of evidence and with good reason: the Wonderman spent his time enriching others—hardly the behavior of a swindler. "Many a poor father of a family, many a charitable institution, was helped by him in secret," Cornelius van Sypesteyn wrote in *Historische Herinneringen*. "Not one bad, nor one dishonourable action was ever known of him, and so he inspired sympathy everywhere."

"Thus clearly stands out the character of one who by some is called a 'messenger' from that

spiritual Hierarchy by whom the world's evolution
is guided," Cooper-Oakley concluded. "Such is
the moral worth of the man whom the shallow
critics of the earth called 'adventurer.'"

The charge of charlatanry was no doubt born
as often of jealousy of his powers as disbelief in his
miracles. The Count Saint Germain was accused
in his own time, without foundation, by an un-
named group of Jesuits of "immorality, infidelity,
anarchy" and, because of his work with alchemists
and the Masons, by Abbé Barruel and later Nesta
Webster, of being a magician in league with various nefarious secret societies seeking the overthrow of France, including the Bavarian Illuminati
founded in 1776 by Adam Weishaupt.

Since 1786 when the Illuminati were exposed
and suppressed by the Bavarian government, it has
been well known that it was a subversive organization which was deceptively grafted onto the body
of Masonry by Weishaupt and Baron von Knigge,
that it was anti-religious and anti-monarchical in
outlook, that it desperately opposed the goals and
philosophy of Masonry. Furthermore, it was thought
by some to have played a crucial role in fomenting
the French Revolution. Barruel's and Webster's
accusations apparently rise from their general mis-
understanding of the history of secret societies and
the Count Saint Germain's mystical powers.

Such accounts of the work of the Count bear
no more relation to reality than the tales of contemporary novelist Chelsea Quinn Yarbro, whose

Hotel Transylvania (and its sequels) is taken from the life of the illustrious Count, with the exception that she has made him out to be a vampire! But unlike Abbé Barruel and Mrs. Webster, at least she knows when she is writing fiction and says so.

Nevertheless, we do not like to see so beloved a figure as the Hierarch of the Aquarian Age thus counterfeited in the minds of a public who so need his intercession. Nor do we care to see Mrs. Yarbro make the personal karma of so blackening the name of America's sponsoring Master.

Some criticism of the Count was spawned from nothing more than seeds of superstition born of fear. Case in point: Saint Germain has told us of how he walked through the streets of Paris healing children from a disease similar to poliomyelitis. At his touch, they would recover almost instantly— and yet their mothers would jerk them from his grasp and call him *diable*—devil.

But, as we have seen, the most painful denouement for the Wonderman was that he could not secure the necessary response from those who could have turned the tide in the affairs of men and nations. The royalty were willing to be entertained by the adept but not to relinquish their power and move with the winds of democratic change. They and their jealous ministers ignored his counsel and opened the door to the war and bloodshed that has resounded through the present century.

In a final attempt to unite Europe, Saint Germain backed Napoleon, who misused the

Master's power to his own demise. The opportunity to set aside the retribution due an age thus passed, Saint Germain was once again forced to withdraw from a karmic situation. In this episode, though clearly visible as the mediator, Saint Germain with his miracles *en main* and his prophecies fulfilled could still be ignored!

Well, as suddenly as the Count Saint Germain burst onto the stage of Europe he disappeared. Or perhaps it is more accurate to say that after 1822—the date of his last recorded appearance—he simply stopped appearing.

In the latter eighteenth century, he told Franz Gräffer and Baron Linden he would go to "rest" in the Himalayas. In 1875, Saint Germain helped the masters M. (El Morya), K.H. (Koot Hoomi), and Serapis Bey found the Theosophical Society. But that was not all.

Throughout the period of his labors as "the Comte," Saint Germain had been constantly in service in various "far-off lands," including one that became a hot-bed of revolution—a rustic land that would eventually be called the United States of America. After all, he has told us that "the American Revolution was the means of bringing freedom in all of its glory into manifestation from the East unto the West."

Even as Francis Bacon, he had seen America as his last hope. He wrote in cipher, "I trusteth all to the future and a land that is very far towards the sunset gate....I keep the future ever in my plan, looking for my reward, not to my times or countrymen, but to a people very far off, and an age not like our own, but a second golden age of learning."[21]

In "The Mystical Origins of the United States of America," an article which appears in *Saint Germain On Alchemy*, the role Saint Germain played behind the scenes in founding the United States of America—particularly how he inspired the Masons with the vision of a union of sovereign states in a new order of the ages—is described.

Now, once again, the earth is at a crossroads. Once again, the Hierarch of the Aquarian Age is trying to assist mankind to avoid catastrophes that could dwarf those that occurred when his warnings as the Count Saint Germain were not heeded.

As the decades have passed, the rate of increase in the return of mankind's karma has precipitated what is known as the Dark Cycle—the era of Chaos and old Night whose signs are foretold in Revelation, even as the hoof beats of the Four Horsemen can be heard throughout the land.

Let us listen to the prophet Samuel—dubbed Uncle Sam by his people—who has indeed begun to sound his prophecy to the chosen. He has warned that the I AM Race—those who have the seed of the name I AM THAT I AM within their hearts—"have not hearkened unto the LORD, nor have they fulfilled the wholeness of the Law."

Therefore, the Master says, "some among this people must be and become direct initiates of Sanat Kumara, for always there has been the requirement of the ransom. Let those who are the inner circle of the devotees, those who are the firstfruits who come and stand as the ensign of the people, raise up the banner of Christ as the one whom they serve, the one who by his very Communion promise at the Last Supper designated each and every son and daughter of God for the internalization of the Word. . . .

"Unfortunately, and this word is mild, but it is unfortunate indeed that the laws of Christ and his Teachings, so meticulously brought forth to the close initiates, are not fully known today, having been taken even from the holy people. Therefore, to obey the Christ becomes the challenge of the hour—to find the Person of that Christ, to find the Way and the Teachings.

"You have received the lost Word and the lost Teachings of Jesus Christ through our effort. . . . As a result of this, you have been strengthened and protected in that Word and Teaching. And some from among you have taken their leave at the conclusion of their embodiment and gone in the full resurrection with Jesus Christ. . . . Thus, the proof of the Teaching and the Path is that it leads one successively to that higher and higher consciousness whereunto the individual is assumed into the very heart of the I AM Presence [becoming indeed the pure Person of that Christ]."

Today, as we see the cycles of earth's returning karma reach a mounting crescendo wherein even the four sacred freedoms are threatened, the Brotherhood has set aside a place in America's Rocky Mountains for the pursuit of the Lost Teachings of Jesus to their fullest expression.

Saint Germain spoke of it in 1983 when he said that we have come "to a similar moment to that of that final hour of the golden age when I presided where the Sahara now is. My family is much larger than it was then, for I include every one of you who love me as my very own family. . . . In that hour, our family was taken to the golden etheric city of light. In this hour, we have summoned you to a higher place in the mountains of the north."

As the outpost of the Royal Teton Retreat, it is called the Royal Teton Ranch. Beloved Jesus announced on May 31, 1984, that to this Inner Retreat in southwestern Montana, to this "Place Prepared," Lord Maitreya had come again to reopen his Mystery School, which had been withdrawn from the physical octave just prior to the sinking of Lemuria.

Let us see what we may accomplish for our beloved Terra and our brothers and sisters on Earth with the renewed opportunity the Hierarchs of the Aquarian Age, our beloved Saint Germain and his twin flame, the Ascended Lady Master Portia, have given to us.

Let us study to show ourselves worthy of the gifts of prophecy and of the working of miracles which he brings. And most importantly, let us strive to the utmost to overcome personal and planetary karma through those invocations to the violet flame and Seventh Ray rituals of transmutation we once knew, that the prophecy of Saint Germain's Great Golden Age may be fulfilled.

The Keepers of the Flame have vowed to be victorious in this age. And they shall!

RULER OF A GOLDEN-AGE CIVILIZATION
over 50,000 years ago

Almost as large as the United States, the Sahara Desert encompasses 3.3 million miles. But it was not always arid. Science believes that it was inhabitable at least once in its geological past. "There is abundant evidence, both archaeological and geological," writes Henri Lhote in Reader's Digest's The World's Last Mysteries, "that once it was a green and fertile country in which a Negroid race of people hunted or tended a large variety of land and aquatic animals." The theory says that the region was desert prior to 10,000 B.C. but that then the monsoon rains moved north, bringing it to a period of fertility which ended about A.D. 500 when the land reverted to its former climate.

Only one quarter of the vast Sahara is sand dunes. Barren plains, mountains and valleys such as this one make up the rest.

Map of the Sahara Desert

An Idealistic Depiction of the Atlantean Mystery
Temple, *J. Augustus Knapp*

Map of Poseidonis

Atlantis before the final cataclysm which destroyed it 11,500 years ago. Astral clairvoyance, says A. P. Sinnett in the foreword to W. Scott-Elliot's Story of Atlantis, revealed the records of its civilization. Scott-Elliot's book is a compilation of the discoveries of a number of students who, Sinnett says, were "allowed access to some maps and other records. . .from the remote periods concerned" to promote the success of their work. These maps, he says, had been physically preserved by those other than the races presently occupying Europe—

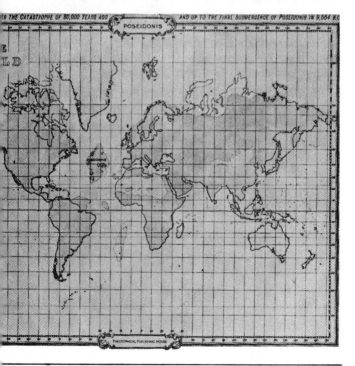

presumably by the Adepts who tutored students of Theosophy, although Sinnett does not specify. Scott-Elliot writes that the continent was destroyed in stages, with cataclysm occurring 800,000, 200,000 and 80,000 years ago. The last remnant of Atlantis was the continent-island Poseidonis, located near the Azores, which in 9564 B.C. was submerged in a catastrophe referred to in many ancient writings, including those of Plato, he says.

Atlantis, *Auriel Bessemer*

OVERLEAF:
*His first prophecy—the boy
Samuel delivers the word of
the LORD to the high priest
Eli, whose sons were corrupt
priests of Israel. They treated
the offerings made to the
LORD with contempt and
"lay with the women that assembled at the door of the
tabernacle of the congrega-
tion." So the LORD came to
Samuel and said to him, "In
that day I will perform
against Eli all things which
I have spoken concerning his
house: when I begin, I will
also make an end. For I have
told him that I will judge
his house for ever for the
iniquity which he knoweth;
because his sons made
themselves vile, and he re-
strained them not." Samuel
delivered this word to Eli,
who said, "It is the LORD:
let him do what seemeth
him good," and all Israel
"knew that Samuel was es-
tablished to be a prophet of
the LORD."* I Samuel 2, 3

Samuel and Eli, *detail, John Singleton Copley*

When Samuel was old, the children of Israel de-
manded a king, "like all the nations." He showed
the people how a king would tyrannize over them and
usurp the freedoms which they took for granted. But
they demanded a king. "They have not rejected thee,
but they have rejected me, that I should not reign over
them," God said to his prophet. Then the LORD led
Samuel to Saul and told him that "this same shall
reign over my people." Their free will became the
LORD's mandate—and their karma, as history records.

I Samuel 8, 9

Samuel Blessing Saul, *Gustave Doré*

*When the disobedient King Saul rejected the
word of the LORD and the LORD rejected him
from being king, "for rebellion is as the sin of
witchcraft, and stubbornness is as iniquity and
idolatry," the LORD sent Samuel to the house of
Jesse in Bethlehem to anoint the shepherd boy
David, youngest of Jesse's sons, to be king
of Israel.*   I Samuel 15, 16

Samuel Anointing David, *Jan Victors*

*After the death of Samuel, when Israel was
gathered for battle against the Philistines, Saul
sought out "a woman that hath a familiar spirit
at Endor," and told her to call up Samuel. "And
Samuel said to Saul, Why hast thou disquieted
me, to bring me up? And Saul answered, I am*

sore distressed; for the Philistines make war against me, and God is departed from me, and answereth me no more, neither by prophets, nor by dreams: therefore I have called thee, that thou mayest make known unto me what I shall do."

And Samuel delivered unto him a dire prophecy, ending with the words, "Moreover the LORD will also deliver Israel with thee into the hand of the Philistines: and tomorrow shalt thou and thy sons be with me." And the next day Saul fell upon his sword in battle, taking his own life, and the Philistines slew his three sons and all his men.

I Samuel 28–31

Saul and the Witch of Endor, *Gustave Doré*

The Marriage of the Virgin, *Raphael, 1504*

*Illustration of a passage from the Apocryphal
Gospel of James shows the wedding ceremony
which took place after the men of Judea gathered
for a sign from the Lord as to which of them
should be the husband of Mary. Joseph was chosen
and took Mary to his wife. A disappointed suitor
in the foreground breaks his rod over his knee.*

*The angel of the Lord had instructed Zacharias
the high priest to have each man bring his rod
and come to the temple.*

*After the high priest had received their rods,
he went into the temple to pray;*

*And when he had finished his prayer, he took
the rods, and went forth and distributed them,
and there was no miracle attended them.*

*The last rod was taken by Joseph, and behold
a dove proceeded out of the rod, and flew upon
the head of Joseph.*

Protevangelion 8:9–11

OVERLEAF:
The Vision of St. Joseph, *Philippe de Champaigne*

*"Behold, the angel of the Lord appeareth to
Joseph in a dream, saying, Arise, and take the
young child and his mother, and flee into Egypt,
and be thou there until I bring thee word: for
Herod will seek the young child to destroy him.
When he arose, he took the young child and his
mother by night, and departed into Egypt."*

Matthew 2:13, 14

The Flight into Egypt,
Gustave Doré, 1865

Rest on the Flight
into Egypt,
*Federico Barocci,
c. 1570*

The Holy Family with the
Lamb, *Raphael, 1507*

*St. Joseph Shrine in St. Joseph's
Grove at The Grotto,
Portland, Oregon*

Joseph, Jesus and Mary in the Workshop,
artist unknown

SAINT ALBAN
3rd century

Britain's first martyr, Alban has been revered by the people of the Isles since his death in A.D. 303. As the Reverend Alban Butler writes in his Lives of the Fathers, Martyrs and other Principal Saints, *"Our island for many ages had recourse to St. Alban as its glorious proto-martyr and powerful patron with God, and acknowl-edged many great favours received from God, through his intercession."*

Alban was a prosperous Roman, native of Verulam, which was for many years one of the most populous cities in Britain. Rev. Butler tells us he traveled to Rome in his youth *"to improve himself in learning and in all the polite arts. . . . Being returned home he settled at Verulam, and lived there with some dignity."* But Alban gave all this up when he became a Christian and was sentenced to die.

St. Alban, detail, White Friars, 1947, St. Alban's Episcopal Church, Washington, D.C.

St. Alban and the Executioner, *artist unknown*

The power of conversion delayed Alban's execution. After a river had parted in response to his prayer, "the executioner was converted at the sight of this miracle. . . and throwing away his naked sword, he fell at the feet of the saint, begging to die with him, or rather in his place. The sudden conversion of the headsman occasioned a delay in the execution. In the mean time the holy confessor, with the crowd, went up the hill." There Alban fell on his knees. "At his prayer a fountain sprang up, with the water whereof he refreshed his thirst. A new executioner being found, he struck off the head of the martyr."

An anonymous history of Britain written in the ninth century from still older sources tells the following story: Vortigern, usurper of Britain's throne, was unsuccessful in building himself an impregnable fortress. Each night, the stones and timber his men had gathered would vanish away. The king's magicians told him that the fortress could never be built unless the blood of a fatherless child were sprinkled upon it. His men, sent far and wide, returned with the boy Merlin, who was rumored to be the son of a virgin nun.

But Merlin, instead of submitting to be sacrificed, challenged the magicians to tell what was beneath the foundations of the fortress. As they could not say, he told the men to dig and while they did so, revealed that they would find an underground pool and in it two snakes, one red and one white.

When the pool was uncovered, the snakes began to fight, ending in the victory of the red snake. Merlin explained that the snakes represented two dragons, and that the red dragon was the Britons and the white the Saxons. Thus he prophesied the eventual demise of Vortigern and the yet unborn Arthur's triumph in driving out the Saxons. The legend was magnified over time, and in later romances the snakes became dragons as in the illustration to the left.

Protector of Britain's future: in exchange for arranging the union of Uther Pendragon and Ygerne of Corn-wall, Merlin requested that he should rear the child that would be born.

In boastful battle, Arthur nearly threw his life away by refusing to surrender to Sir Pellinore, who had beaten him in joust. Merlin appeared and by some accounts put Pellinore to sleep; by others, thundered the prophecy that the hope of Britain lived in Arthur and would die with him, shaming Pellinore into sparing the king's life.

Ever vigilant, Merlin watches from behind a pillar as his young charge proves his birthright by pulling the sword from its resting place—succeeding where all the nobles and fighting men of Britain had failed. "Whoso pulleth out this sword of this stone and anvil is rightwise king born of all England."

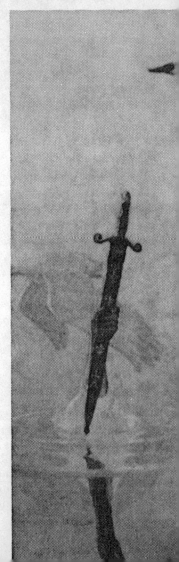

"And there I saw mage
  Merlin, whose vast wit

And hundred winters are
  but as the hands

Of loyal vassals toiling for
  their liege. . . .

"There likewise I beheld
  Excalibur

Before him at his crowning
  borne, the sword

That rose from out the
  bosom of the lake,

And Arthur row'd across
  and took it—rich

With jewels, elfin Urim,
  on the hilt,

Bewildering heart and eye—
  the blade so bright

That men are blinded by it."

Idylls of the King
Alfred Lord Tennyson

Dweller in the wild places, Merlin by legend asked his sister to build him a remote building "to which you will give me seventy doors and as many windows, through which I may see fire-breathing Phoebus with Venus, and watch by night the stars wheeling in the firmament; and they will teach me about the future of the nation." Sound like a description of Stonehenge? For centuries people believed that the ancient astrological observatory was built by Merlin himself. Scientists say it antedates the wizard by millennia. But who knows how old Merlin is anyway!

OVERLEAF:

*To pry from Merlin his secret
magic spell, a spell of woven
paces and of waving arms,
Vivien followed him into a
wild wood. The spell, if
wrought on anyone, would
make its victim seem to lie
closed in the four walls of a
hollow tower and none could
find that man forevermore.
As Tennyson recounts the
tale, there rested upon
Merlin a great melancholy,
for which he left Camelot...*

*He walk'd with dreams and
    darkness, and he found
A doom that ever poised
    itself to fall,
An ever-moaning battle
    in the mist,
World-war of dying flesh
    against the life,
Death in all life and lying
    in all love,
The meanest having power
    upon the highest,
And the high purpose broken
    by the worm.*

The Bard, *Thomas Jones, 1774*

The Beguiling of Merlin, *Sir Edward Burne-Jones*

*Vivien lay at his feet, kissed them, begged, pleaded,
sang, cajoled, wept, demanded that he prove his love
by telling her the spell: "Trust me not at all or all in
all." And so the night wore on and with it the will of
the old man until*

*What should not have been had been,
For Merlin, overtalk'd and overworn,
Had yielded, told her all the charm, and slept.*

*Then, in one moment, she put forth the charm
Of woven paces and of waving hands,
And in the hollow oak he lay as dead,
And lost to life and use and name and fame.*

*Then crying, "I have
  made his glory mine,"
And shrieking out,
  "O fool!" the harlot
  leapt
Adown the forest, and
  the thicket closed
Behind her, and the
  forest echo'd "fool."*

Vivien Bewitches Merlin,
Howard Pyle

Roger Bacon, *Gordon Ross*

Roger Bacon, *the Hope-Pinker statue,*
University Museum, Oxford

Roger Bacon, *Howard Pyle*

*The monk-scientist in his study, surrounded by
the collected occult and scientific wisdom of the
ages. His library contained many manuscripts—
from the ancient* Key of Solomon, *which was
supposed to contain the Hebrew king's magic formulas, to the Persian physician Avicenna's* Canon
of Medicine, *to works on Greek philosophy.*

OVERLEAF:

*Tradition attached Friar Bacon's name to this old
structure and bridge, which is called Folly Bridge
or sometimes Friar Bacon's Bridge. The tower has
been called "Friar Bacon's Study" although, as
Antony à Wood wrote around 1661, the "name
though meerly traditionall and not in any record
to be found; yet neverthelesse their might be
some matter of truth in it, being soe delivered
from one generation to another."*

*Working at a prodigious rate, Bacon produced
his three great works—Opus Majus, Opus
Minus, and the Opus Tertium—just fifteen to
eighteen months after the pope requested them.
Opus Majus fills 821 modern pages. Its seven
parts are entitled Causes of Error, Philosophy,
Study of Tongues, Mathematics, Optical Science,
Experimental Science, and Moral Philosophy.*

Bacon's Study at Oxford, *from a Gough print*

*A page of Bacon's Opus Majus,
from the Digby Manuscript*

His "outer person and bodily disposition" were thus described by Bishop Bartolomé de las Casas, 1474–1566: "He was tall more than average; his face long and of a noble bearing; his nose aquiline; his eyes blue; his complexion white, and somewhat fiery red; his beard and hair fair in his youth, though they soon turned white through hardships borne; he was quick-witted and gay in his speech and, as the afore-said Portuguese history says, eloquent and high-sounding in his business; he was moderately grave; affable towards strangers; sweet and good-humoured with those of his house...of a discreet conversation and thus able to draw love from all who saw him. Finally, his person and venerable mien revealed a person of great state and authority and worthy of all reverence."

The oldest known portrait of Columbus, this woodcut was made in the late sixteenth century by Swiss artist Tobias Stimmer.

Aliprando Capriolo, 1596

Attributed to Ridolfo Ghirlandaio, c. 1525

Three portraits of Christopher Columbus. Compare one at left with portraits of Roger Bacon, p. 70, Francis Bacon, p. 92, the Wonderman of Europe, p. 94, and Sindelar portrait of Saint Germain, front cover.

Artist unknown

Columbus, artist unknown

The Boy Columbus on the Wharf in Genoa, *N. C. Wyeth*

Prophetic vision of the New World? "At a very tender age I became a sailor, and I have continued until this day. The art of navigation incites those who follow it to learn the secrets of the world," wrote Columbus to King Ferdinand and Queen Isabella of Spain in 1501.

Columbus at Salamanca, *Nicolo Barabino*

Queen Isabella appointed a commission in 1486 to assess Columbus' proposed journey. Composed of professors of the university and representatives of the Catholic church, it sat at Salamanca, a great center of learning in Spain.

Many of the commissioners came with their minds already made up. They deliberated for four years,

grilling the navigator on theological and philosophical points. They cited Church Fathers such as Saint Augustine to prove that there could not be anyone living on the other side of the world. Augustine had declared that for people to be living on the other side of the world, they would have to have descended from someone other than Adam, which would contradict the Bible. Others argued that a voyage to the other hemisphere would be a downhill journey and if it were completed, a return trip could never be made as it would be entirely uphill.

During their years of deliberation, Columbus followed the queen around Spain as she waged war on the Moslems. The commission finally reached a verdict: it determined that the Spanish crown should not support his voyage.

But the indomitable Isabella, unhappy with their conclusion, appointed a new commission, which accepted Columbus' plan.

The Glorification of Columbus, *artist unknown*

Columbus' Discovery of America, *artist unknown, 1493*

Watling Island in the Bahamas was renamed San Salvador in 1926. Scholars believed it to be the original landing site of Columbus on October 12, 1492, which he had christened San Salvador. However, the National Geographic Society has recently concluded, based upon their five-year study, that he in fact landed on Samana Cay, 65 miles southeast of Watling.

Francis Bacon, *Nicholas Hilliard, 1578*

"Could I but paint his mind," famed miniaturist Nicholas Hilliard wrote on the border of his portrait of Francis at 18. At that age, Francis had already attended Cambridge for three years, become disillusioned with its stifling atmosphere, entered Gray's Inn to study law, and spent three years at the court of France.

He lamented the sorry state of education, where men "learn nothing but to believe" in authorities. "They are like a becalmed ship: they never move but by the wind of other men's breath," he wrote. It was as a youth that he planned his great intellectual revolution. Thomas Macaulay wrote of him that he had "an amplitude of comprehension such as has never yet been vouchsafed to any human being."

OVERLEAF:
Viewers of portraits of Bacon and his parents often comment on their dissimilarities. Lord Keeper Nicholas Bacon and his wife, Lady Anne Bacon, lady-in-waiting and confidante of Queen Elizabeth, have markedly different features from Francis; moreover their hair is fair while his is dark.

Was Francis the legitimate son of Queen Elizabeth and Robert Dudley, Lord Leicester? Cipher embedded in the type of the 1620 edition of Bacon's Novum Organum, which appears to have been written by Bacon himself, says that he was but that his mother did not acknowledge him as she would have been forced to reveal her secret marriage to Leicester.

Sir Nicholas Bacon,
artist unknown, 1579

Lady Anne Bacon,
attributed to
George Gower, 1580

The following conversation between Lady Bacon
and Francis is recorded in the cipher, discovered by
Elizabeth Wells Gallup in the 1890s.

"You need not fear dishonour, your father is a noble
gentleman who was properly married by law to the
queen..."

"Where was I born?"

Robert Dudley,
Earl of Leicester

Queen Elizabeth,
Nicholas Hilliard

*"In Windsor Castle. I will tell you the story of your
birth. I know it all, for from your infancy the queen
and I have conversed. I was made privy to the marriage of your mother, and when you were born I
secretly conveyed you out of the nuptial room in a
round, painted box, carried you to my house and
brought you up as my own."*

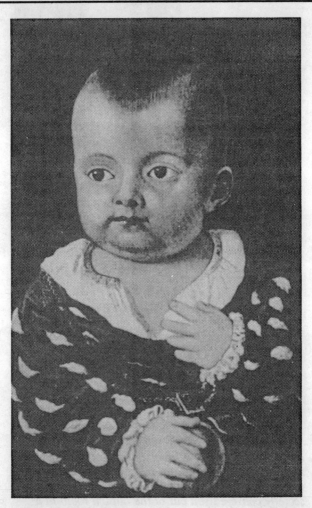

Francis Bacon as a Child

The Benchers of Gray's Inn commissioned this statue of Francis Bacon in 1908 in commemoration of the three-hundredth anniversary of his having been elected treasurer of the house. His memorable doings at the Inn included not only serving as its treasurer (1608–1617) and Dean of Chapel, but also planting trees in the walks and turning the back field into gardens which became celebrated for their beauty for hundreds of years. As a student, he had written, staged, and starred in plays for the enjoyment of all.

Portrait of Francis Bacon, *engraved by W. C. Edwards, after a Paul van Somer painting, c. 1616*

Britain's greatest intellect, Francis Bacon fathered inductive reasoning and the modern scientific method, conducted experiments of his own, shepherded a group of the Elizabethan era's greatest writers, oversaw the translation of the King James Version of the Bible, supported the colonization of the New World and Newfoundland and even, some say, authored the Shakespearean plays.

Francis Bacon took the Greek Goddess Pallas Athena to be the muse of his poetry. "Be thou the Tenth Muse, ten times more in Worth Than those Old Nine which Rhymers invocate," he wrote in a sonnet "To Athena." She was the Goddess of Wisdom and Knowledge, of Greek mythology, represented as the shaker of the Spear of Knowledge, shaking it at the Serpent of Ignorance. It has been conjectured that as the author of the Shakespearean plays, Bacon gave the name Shake-speare to the obscure British actor William Shaksper.

The Count Saint Germain, Wonderman of Europe

Notes to Book One

For an alphabetical listing of many of the philosophical and hierarchical terms used in *Saint Germain On Prophecy,* see the comprehensive glossary, "The Alchemy of the Word: Stones for the Wise Masterbuilders," in *Saint Germain On Alchemy.*

1. See Godfré Ray King, *Unveiled Mysteries,* 3d ed. (Chicago: Saint Germain Press, 1939), pp. 39-61.
2. Thomas Whittaker, *The Neo-Platonists: A Study in the History of Hellenism,* 2d ed. (Cambridge: Cambridge University Press, 1928), p. 165.
3. Victor Cousin and Thomas Taylor, trans., *Two Treatises of Proclus, The Platonic Successor* (London: n.p., 1833), p. vi.
4. Geoffrey of Monmouth, *Vita Merlini,* in Nikolai Tolstoy, *The Quest for Merlin* (Boston: Little, Brown & Co., 1985), p. 217.
5. Brendan LeHane et al., *The Enchanted World: Wizards and Witches* (Chicago: Time-Life Books, 1984), p. 34.
6. Sir Thomas Malory understood that King Arthur had at least two sisters. One Margawse married King Loth and bore him four sons, the oldest of whom was Gawain. She or another sister, alleges Malory, bore Modred to King Arthur. (Norma Lorre Goodrich, *King Arthur* [New York: Franklin Watts, 1986], p. 221.)
7. Henry Thomas and Dana Lee Thomas, *Living Biographies of Great Scientists* (Garden City, N.Y.: Nelson Doubleday, 1941), p. 15.
8. Ibid., p. 16.
9. Ibid., p. 17; David Wallechinsky, Amy Wallace, and Irving Wallace, *The Book of Predictions* (New York: William Morrow and Co., 1980), p. 346.
10. Thomas, *Living Biographies,* p. 20.
11. Wallechinsky and Wallace, *Book of Predictions,* p. 346.
12. Clements R. Markham, *Life of Christopher Columbus* (London: George Philip & Son, 1892), pp. 207-8.
13. Isa. 11:11, 12.
14. *Encyclopædia Britannica,* 15th ed., s.v. "Columbus, Christopher."
15. **Bacon's ciphers.** Francis Bacon's word-cipher was discovered by cryptographer Dr. Orville W. Owen, who published five volumes of *Sir Francis Bacon's Cipher Story* between 1893 and 1895. The story hidden in his word-cipher can be constructed by stringing together words, lines, and passages from the works of various Elizabethan writers. In contrast,

deciphering the bi-literal cipher is an exact, scientific process of grouping together the italic letters (printed in two different fonts of type) that appear with peculiar frequency in original editions of the Shakespearean plays and other of Bacon's works. This cipher was discovered by an assistant of Dr. Owen, Mrs. Elizabeth Wells Gallup, who first published the stories Bacon had concealed in his bi-literal cipher in 1899. To insure that his ciphers would eventually be discovered and his true life story revealed, Bacon had described in detail the bi-literal method of cipher writing in his Latin version of *De Augmentis* (1624), which some 270 years later Mrs. Gallup studied and applied. Ironically, Mrs. Gallup found that Bacon's bi-literal cipher contained complete directions on how to construct the word-cipher, which was actually discovered first by Dr. Owen.

16. Will Durant, *The Story of Philosophy: The Lives and Opinions of the Greater Philosophers* (Garden City, N.Y.: Garden City Publishing Co., 1927), p. 157.
17. The information detailed in the following paragraphs is taken from Margaret Barsi-Greene, comp., *I, Prince Tudor, Wrote Shakespeare* (Boston: Branden Press, 1973), pp. 56-75, and Alfred Dodd, *The Martyrdom of Francis Bacon* (New York: Rider & Co., n.d.), p. 25.
18. Barsi-Greene, *I, Prince Tudor*, p. 217.
19. Ibid., pp. 219-20.
20. Ibid., pp. 76-77.
    Much of the information on the Count Saint Germain recounted in this section is taken from Isabel Cooper-Oakley, *The Comte de St. Germain: The Secret of Kings* (London: The Theosophical Publishing House Ltd., 1912).
21. Barsi-Greene, *I, Prince Tudor*, pp. 239, 243.

Book Two

Nostradamus: The Four Horsemen

Signs of the Times
What the Seer Really Saw for the 20th Century

O ye hypocrites, ye can discern the face of the sky—but can ye not discern the signs of the times?

Jesus

CHAPTER I

Signs of the Times of Nostradamus

Jules Verne anticipated the submarine, Leonardo da Vinci the helicopter. But there was another more celebrated visionary who predicted not only the submarine and air travel, but also air battles, bombardments, nuclear warfare and fallout...*in the 1500s!* A man who wrote about wars, revolutions, betrayals, executions, and treaties long before they happened—some of them right to the date, others with precise and unmistakable detail.

In his day some thought he was writing gibberish. Others took him for a tool of the devil. Even after some of his remarkable predictions came true, there were still those who believed he was a fraud. But more recently he has been called such things as "the man who saw tomorrow" or "the man who saw through time." He is, without doubt, the best known and most illustrious (or notorious) of seers.

Born Michel de Nostredame, December 14, 1503,[1] at Saint-Rémy, in Provence, France, he is known by his Latinized name, Nostradamus. Michel

was the eldest of the five sons of Jacques and
Reynière de Nostredame, a family of Jewish con-
verts to Christ. At a young age he studied mathematics, Hebrew, Greek, Latin and the 'celestial
science' of astrology under his grandfather's tutelage. At nineteen he studied medicine at Mont-
pellier under the finest physicians. Taking time out
to minister to those afflicted of the plague, he
completed his doctorate and went on to study
under the philosopher Julius-César Scaliger.

He practiced medicine throughout his life,
delivered many of the plagues, but his wife and son
and daughter he could not. In their death he
experienced a profound grief, followed by travel
and study under the most learned minds of Europe.

The now-ripened prophet, who believed the
earth was round and revolved about the sun a
century before Galileo was prosecuted for pro-
pounding his theory, had also become a renowned
healer dispensing unorthodox cures, as well as a
student of white magic and the occult. He returned to Salon in 1554, married a widow of means
and there diligently wrote his Prophecies in four-
line verses called quatrains collected in groups of
one hundred called centuries.

His extraordinary fame traveled far and wide.
Before his death he was titled Physician in Ordinary by Queen Catherine de' Medici. But he had
left unfinished the seventh of his ten centuries
and barely begun an eleventh and a twelfth. His
vision had reached the year 3797, a time and space
most of us have never considered as some future

crossroad. Yet this the seer saw—the signs of times yet to be which for him were already outplayed in his eternal mind.

What sort of world did Nostradamus live in?

It was an age which had not seen the development of the steam engine, the locomotive or auto. The bicycle had not been invented. Yet he predicted safe travel "by air, land, sea and wave."[2]

In Nostradamus' day kings were absolute monarchs who ruled by divine right. In France, where he lived, there were no juries, much less trial by jury for a commoner. To try a monarch was unthinkable. Yet Nostradamus predicted "the queen sent to death by jurors chosen by lot"[3]—which is precisely what happened to Marie Antoinette.

The age of Nostradamus had barely seen the discovery of the New World. Yet the French seer mentions the "government of America" more than 200 years before the fact, when a mere fifty years before the American Revolution few in their wildest imagination would have guessed the colonies would rebel against the English Crown, much less *defeat* what was then the most powerful empire on earth. But, then, Nostradamus did what is humanly impossible.

Consider: Nostradamus' prophecies span a period of 2,242 years which begins in 1555, when he published his first set of predictions, and runs through the year 3797.[4] What would you say are the odds of "guessing" the month and year in which two nations make a treaty—and then naming the two nations, picking the winner, and specifying a major effect of the outcome? If there were only fifteen nations in the world in 1555, and there were more, the odds of a lucky guess would be 1 in 11,299,680.[5]

Yet Nostradamus did just that.

In October of 1727, Persia and Turkey terminated a conflict in which the Turks lost the war but signed a very favorable treaty and won the peace. Some 172 years earlier, Nostradamus described this event in a quatrain which reads:

> The third climate comprehended under Aries,
> The year thousand seven hundred twenty and
>   seven in October,
> The King of Persia taken by those of Egypt,
> Conflict, death, loss, great opprobrium to
>   the cross.[6]   III.77

Even the usually skeptical Edgar Leoni—a capable, yet largely incredulous authority on Nostradamus—had to concede that "there was indeed a peace concluded in October 1727 between the Turks and the Persians," as Nostradamus said there would be. "Ashraf," Leoni noted, "usurping Shah of Persia, had defeated the Turks, but in return for recognition of his dynasty, he gave back Erivan, Tauris and Hamadan, and recognized the Sultan as legitimate successor of the Caliph,"[7] and as such, the chief of the Moslems.

The quatrain, as you may have noticed, does not mention the Turks. But according to Stewart Robb, another authority on Nostradamus, "those of Egypt" is a synecdoche—a figure of speech where a part is used for the whole (or vice versa), such as Moscow for the Soviet Union—for the Turks. Egypt had been part of the Ottoman Empire since 1517. Robb points out that "Nostradamus does not say 'the Egyptians,' but 'those of Egypt,' the distinction being the simple one made between the people of a country and its rulers. In 1727, those of Egypt were the Turks, who were Mohammedans, and the extension of whose power was therefore opprobrious to Christianity."

Although the Shah was not captured nor killed, Robb argues plausibly that in consideration of the treaty he signed—in which he dismembered his nation by ceding western Persia to the Turks— the Shah was nevertheless "taken" or conquered. [8]

That was by no means the only time Nostradamus named, against all odds, the date of a future event. In one quatrain Nostradamus gives the date of the "Seventh War" (around 1580) and the "War of Spanish Succession" (1703). [9] And in his oracular Epistle to Henry II, he predicted that "the Christian Church will be persecuted more fiercely than it ever was in Africa, and this will last up to the year 1792, which they will believe to mark a renewal of time." [10]

France was a Catholic country. But in 1792 it was in the midst of the French Revolution and the Church was experiencing just the kind of savage persecution Nostradamus had predicted. Right after the National Convention abolished the monarchy, it threw out the Gregorian calendar because of its Christian associations, introduced its own secular "revolutionary calendar," and proclaimed the first day of "the Year I of the French Republic." This "renewal of time," as Nostradamus put it, took place, as predicted, in 1792.

Now, that little bit of prognostication did not go unnoticed by skeptics ancient or modern. The learned Edgar Leoni says that it is here that Nostradamus was "closest to a bull's-eye" and cites a reference in the February 1792 edition of the *Journal historique et littéraire* to a royalist newspaper, the *Journal de la ville*, that published this particular prophecy and informed readers that the "copy of Nostradamus, in which this prediction is found, will remain exposed in our office for eight days, so that the curious will be able to verify it for themselves."

"The editor of the magazine then goes on to explain," says Leoni, "how, though Nostradamus is generally conceded to be a fraud, he might have been divinely inspired for just this one marvelous prophecy."[11]

Nostradamus' accuracy was not restricted to dates. In fact, few of his predictions have them, although he said in his letter to Henry II that "if I had wanted to date each quatrain, I could have done so."[12] Rather, he couched his prophecies in terms so specific that the circumstances they fit are unmistakably related to one event, historical circumstance, or series of related events.

This quatrain illustrates his divine genius:

The husband, alone, afflicted, will be mitred
Return, conflict will take place at the
    Tuileries:
By five hundred, one betrayer will be titled
Narbon and Saulce, "we have oil with knives."[13]

                        IX. 34

    Narbon and Saulce. Two specific names. Suppose Nostradamus had written Simon and Garfunkel, Burns and Allen, or Rodgers and Hammerstein? The mere fact that he had mentioned their names centuries before the fact would have been impressive. Yet here he not only names Narbonne and Sauce (the eighteenth-century forms of Narbon and Saulce) but shows them to be key players in a sociopolitical drama that would ultimately change the course of history.

    The French seer was describing one of the great turning points in the French Revolution, a crucial scene in the tragedy of Louis XVI and Marie Antoinette—their ill-fated attempted escape from Paris made on the night of June 20, 1791.

    Louis XVI and Marie Antoinette were under virtual house arrest at the heavily guarded Tuileries in Paris and their situation was growing ever more desperate. They decided, therefore, to flee to a point on the border of Luxembourg where they were to be met by Austrian troops sent by Emperor Leopold II, the queen's brother. Disguised, the king and queen slipped out of Paris and the royal coach made it as far as Varennes, a town near the border.

In Varennes, the king and queen were recognized and then detained. Since their papers were in order, though there was still some question about their identity, Monsieur Sauce, a grocer and the mayor of the town, was at first inclined to let them pass. But he gave in under pressure, had them held in Varennes, and invited them into his combination grocery store/home until their identity could be verified.

Once positively identified, the king tore off his disguise and warmly embraced his captors. Sauce then forced them to remain there until word came from the Assembly and they were turned over to the guard, who brought them back to Paris—and ultimately their doom.

This critical turning point in the lives of the king and queen and the revolution sealed their fate and sounded the death knell for the monarchy and the monarchs.

Note, twice Sauce could have saved the king and queen by simply letting them go. Even while held in Sauce's home, Marie Antoinette pleaded with Mme Sauce to release them. "I would like to, Your Highness," she replied, "for I love my king, but I love my husband too and would not have him lose his head." Thus Sauce, as Nostradamus predicted, betrayed the king, who was forcibly returned (*return* is in the quatrain) to Paris.

While still on the subject of events that took place in the grocery store, let us note that Sauce sold oil in his shop. The cans were suspended from the rafters and the shop smelled of rancid oil. Thus, it seems as if Nostradamus actually recorded a line of dialogue spoken by the proprietor to a customer, more than two hundred years before the fact: "Sauce, 'we have oil.'"

Shortly after Louis XVI's return to Paris, Count Narbonne was made Louis' Minister of War. Narbonne was one among the nobility whose actions powerfully contributed to Louis' ruin. We have, therefore, two betrayers: Narbonne, who, as specified in the quatrain, was titled; and Sauce, a bourgeois who was given a 20,000 livre reward by the Assembly for his patriotic act, showered with praise, and later guillotined.

Once the king and queen were back at the Tuileries, the already ugly mood in Paris drifted rapidly towards the frenzy of violence known as "the reign of terror." On August 10, 1792, a carefully organized mob attacked the Tuileries, set it afire, and killed 600 or so of the Swiss Guard. Leading the mob were 513 Marseillais, who are generally called "The Five Hundred."[14]

Then, during the siege, precisely as Nostradamus had written, Louis (husband) was confronted by the mob (500) at the Tuileries (conflict will take place at the Tuileries) without his guards (alone) who forced him to put on the red cap of liberty used by the revolutionaries (will be mitred).

In short, quatrain IX.34, as Robb observes, is "a marvelous pen-picture."[15] Not only has Nostradamus described with great accuracy a future sequence of events in the life of a future king and queen at a turning point in French history, but also has he done it with an amazing economy of words. And in the process he has provided such precise detail that it could apply to no other set of historical circumstances.

Although Nostradamus seems to have written a good many predictions about the French Revolution, his interests varied widely. He named and described circumstances in the life of "the heroic [Marshal] de Villars," Louis XIV's ablest and most valiant general; chronicled the rise and fall of Napoleon; named and detailed events in the lives of Franco and Hitler; and, some 362 years in advance, described the Bolshevik Revolution.[16]

But it is his prophecies for our time that become the most fascinating. And frightening. With no less foresight and perspicacity than he demonstrated while penning the history of future events that have now passed us by, Nostradamus has given us a vivid description of the challenges our generation must soon face.

Let us bear in mind as we consider them that Nostradamus said his predictions were divinely inspired and supported by astrological calculation. I believe that the spirit of prophecy that was upon Nostradamus came through the heart of Saint Germain, a thesis supported by Nostradamus' own description of the setting in which he received his prophecies:

He is alone at night, seated in his secret

study, which he tells us is a specially built room in his attic, when "a small flame comes out of the solitude and brings things to pass which should not be thought vain." Then, when all is set, "divine splendour, divinity itself, sits beside him," in order (as Jean-Charles de Fontbrune, author of several books on the seer, understands it) "to dictate its message."[17]

Let us also bear in mind that Nostradamus' prophecies were obscure by design. The reasons for this are as complex as the quatrains themselves. He was writing at a time when one accused of witchcraft or black magic could be burned at the stake. Lee McCann, author of *Nostradamus: The Man Who Saw Through Time*, reminds us that "while Nostradamus was a boy preparing [to continue his education at] Avignon, five hundred of the piteous creatures accused of witchcraft were burned in Geneva."[18]

Not wanting to be summarily executed by potential adversaries in Church or State, nor to interfere with God's will by revealing it prematurely, Nostradamus therefore set his prophecies down in a deliberately hard-to-understand mystical prose. He nevertheless thought that they were too easy to decipher and rewrote them into the cryptic quatrains in chronologically organized centuries.

The quatrains contain a bewildering mixture of French, Latin, Greek, Italian, Provençal, symbols, astrological configurations, anagrams, synecdoches, puns and other literary devices. Still he thought they were too easy. Nostradamus mentions a number of times his concern about "the danger of the times" and "the calumny of evil men." Just to be sure, he scrambled the order prior to their publication in 1555.[19]

When Nostradamus' prophecies first appeared, they were enthusiastically received by those in the leisure classes who had read the earlier predictions he published in an annual almanac. But they were greeted with scorn and derision by a superstitious populace. According to Leoni, "the first half-dozen printed reactions to the prophetic efforts of Nostradamus were extremely negative."

He was accused of madness, impiety, ignorance of astrology, indiscriminate consumption of alcoholic beverages, and of advising a sick patient (Nostradamus was a physician of considerable fame) to "sleep with a little black woman."

He was criticized by physicians, astrologers, philosophers and poets. The less educated masses took Nostradamus, whose quatrains they believed were filled with infernal nonsense, for a tool of the devil. One taunting critic wrote, "Where do you get that stuff? You intolerable pest, leading people astray with your false teachings full of abomination...."[20]

When some of his prophecies came true, however, Catherine de' Medici, consort to Henry II, invited Nostradamus to court where he found favor. Even so, after he published several more centuries in 1558, his adversaries grew in number. Some even demanded that he be arraigned before the Holy Inquisition. But when Henry II died after a jousting accident on July 10, 1559, in the manner Nostradamus had predicted in quatrain 35 of the first century, his fame was assured.

The quatrain reads in part, "The young lion [Count de Montgomery, Captain of the Scottish Guard] will overcome the old one [Henry II] / On the field of battle in single combat: / He will put out his eyes in a 'cage of gold,'" taken to mean the king's gilded helmet. With an apparent medical diagnosis of his injury, "two fractures one," the predicted outcome was that Henry II would "die a cruel death."[21]

The fatal tournament was to celebrate the double wedding of Henry's sister Elisabeth to Philip II of Spain, and his daughter Marguerite to Emmanuel Philibert, Duke of Savoy. The tournament lasted for three days. Henry acquitted himself admirably in the lists and asked Gabriel Montgomery to ride against him in the last course of the day. He declined but Henry commanded him to obey.

Catherine pleaded with Henry not to participate in the joust. In his biography of the queen, Jean Héritier reports that Catherine "had expected for a long time that her husband would die a violent death. The *Centuries* of Nostradamus... had predicted such a death for him. The Queen was obsessed by the fatal quatrain."

Héritier goes on to say that "Nostradamus' prediction coincided exactly with that of Lucca Gaurico.

The Italian bishop-astrologer, who was world-famous, approved by the Popes—by Julius II and Leo X as well as Clement VII and Paul III—had told Henri II, three years before Nostradamus published his *Centuries*, to avoid all single combat, especially in his forties, as at that period of his life he would be in danger of a head wound which might lead to blindness or death.... She begged the King in vain not to take part in the tournament."[22]

Henry liked tournaments, ignored the prophecy and, as a result of a freak accident, was pierced in or above the eye by a splinter of Montgomery's broken lance which slipped under his visor, and he died a "cruel death" ten days later.

Word of Nostradamus' prophecy and Henry's death spread to all corners of Europe, and the French seer's fame never wavered thereafter. Ever since, Nostradamus has been praised by some and criticized by others.

It is often argued that Nostradamus' prophecies are so vague that they can be applied to virtually anything. "The style of the Centuries is so multiform and nebulous," wrote historian Jean Gimon, summarizing this line of criticism, "that each may, with a little effort and good will, find in them what he seeks."[23]

But that is not the case. Nostradamus intended his "enigmatic sentences," as he explained to Henry II, to have "only one sense and meaning, and nothing ambiguous or amphibological inserted."[24]

After much study of Nostradamus' work, including detailed consideration of the numerous prophecies that have already come true, Stewart Robb concluded that Nostradamus' prophecies are obscure until overtaken by events, at which time they are eminently clear and, owing to his precise use of language, allow only one possible interpretation for each quatrain or series of related quatrains.

The "Narbon and Saulce" quatrain can scarcely apply to anything other than previously described. In another quatrain Nostradamus stipulates certain events will occur "in the year that France has a one-eyed king,"[25] which, as we have seen by the ten days the wounded Henry II ruled France, was 1559.

No other one-eyed king has ever held the French throne; hence that is the only possible year for the prophecy. The quatrain predicting the treaty of October 1727 between the Persians and Turks can hardly refer to anything else, and so on.

I think we can also say that while Nostradamus described future events in concrete terms which limited his predictions to specific situations, the language he used added a mystical dimension to his prophecies that helps convey his meaning and intent and reveals the depth and breadth of his own perceptions.

CHAPTER 2

Nuclear War and a Golden Age

A mong the quatrains which the experts agree are due to be fulfilled in the next several decades, we note but one that includes a date— "the year 1999, seventh month." The other predictions we deduce by the subject matter to be the signs of our times. Where Nostradamus mentions air travel, for example, one can safely restrict the time frame to the twentieth century or beyond.

In many cases, the precise outcome of these prophecies is still unclear. Mindful that Nostradamus' predictions are obscure before the time of their fulfillment and clear after the fact, we approach with caution something of a middle ground, a period when part of the prophecy—a specific event or a broad trend—has come to pass. As for the quatrains we will be discussing, we are in this middle ground, a twilight, or penumbral, zone where enough has already happened to make valid, useful, even if sometimes tentative, interpretation possible.

This state of seeing through Nostradamus' glass somewhat darkly has led to differences of opinion among the best and most popular of Nostradamus' current commentators about what we should expect. Nevertheless, Saint Germain's pivotal date of January 1, 1987, signals events which have progressed far enough so that the clarity of Nostradamus' warning of the dangers that lie ahead cannot be denied.

These consist of the signs of the Four Horsemen: famine, cataclysm (probably earthquakes), plagues, economic turmoil, and wars—a very dark period of global conflict blackened by the use of nuclear and bacteriological weapons—followed by a period of regeneration when Nostradamus tells us "there will be almost renewed another reign of Saturn, and golden age."[26]

It appears there are a number of quatrains which deal with nuclear war and/or nuclear explosions. When contemplating these, bear in mind that Nostradamus had to describe technologies and effects his age could scarcely imagine and therefore had to resort to metaphorical devices. Further, Nostradamus had to hold back elements of what he knew because "some given to censure would raise difficulties"[27] and was therefore somewhat constrained in his descriptions. Notwithstanding, that which was obscure to readers in Nostradamus' time becomes crystal clear in ours:

> At sunrise one will see a great fire,
> Noise and light extending towards "Aquilon:"
> Within the circle death and one will hear
>   cries,
> Through steel, fire, famine, death awaiting
>   them.[28]

II.91

Note the vivid description, economy of words, and adept use of language of Nostradamus' style that characterize his 'painting' of "a great fire," a brilliant light extending towards "Aquilon" (literally the "north wind, north"), a name interpreters of Nostradamus take to stand for Russia and sometimes the United States, but in general the nations of the "north."[29]

The image of a nuclear blast is so clear that Leoni says, "This one might some day be applied to the explosion of U.S. H-bombs in Russia in World War III."[30] But since Aquilon can also be the United States, it could conceivably be the other way around. It is reasonable to suppose that if American nuclear weapons were exploding in Russia, Soviet warheads might be falling in the U.S.

After the fire, noise, and light, there will be cries heard "within the circle of death" and then additional loss of life from "steel" (as Leoni translates the French word *glaive*, or from a "two-edged sword," as is its literal translation) as well as from fire and famine.

Rene Noorbergen, author of *Nostradamus Predicts the End of the World*, takes "within the circle" to be the Arctic Circle.[31] But the blast radius of a nuclear warhead is the more reasonable interpretation.

If, on the other hand, the quatrain describes the north from the viewer's position, north could be anything north of Nostradamus' locale—the little town of Salon near Marseille where the seer set forth his visions.

But what about a mystical interpretation of the quatrain. Both it and other of Nostradamus' apocalyptic prophecies can be related to the Bible. In a spiritual sense, the north refers to the Father, or the I AM THAT I AM. This, combined with the two-edged sword, infers judgment or a divine wrath delivered, perhaps, by The Word of God and his armies. (Rev. 19:11–16)

Noise and light extending *towards* Aquilon may be interpreted as originating to the viewer's north and being spread toward the point of north or the point of origin of the north wind from which the winter wind reaches the prophet.

If the quatrain leads to only one conclusion, a nuclear explosion toward the north, it may be seen, as was the destruction of Sodom and Gomorrah, as a decision by higher powers—Nephilim gods or Karmic Lords, we know not—to let fly and no longer prevent the karma of the superpowers from bringing to naught mankind's betrayal of their gods or their God through the impersonal hand of Karma triggered by the warlords in the earth.

This could be a judgment not unlike the Flood, before which "it repenteth the LORD that he had made man on the earth...and the earth was corrupt before God,...for all flesh had corrupted his way...and every imagination of the thoughts of [man's] heart was only evil continually."

This quatrain with others that seem to predict nuclear holocaust could be the judgment by nuclear fire, for God promised Noah, and sealed his covenant with a rainbow, that the waters of a flood would nevermore destroy the earth or all flesh.

In addition, when considering this quatrain we ought to keep in mind that mystically speaking the time of sunrise is the time of the rising of the Sun of Righteousness (Jer. 23:6) within the individual or of Christ's Second Coming.

It is taught by the ancients that at the apocalyptic moment of a great enlightenment or the appearance of a Cosmic Christ, there is a corresponding fire, noise and light. This spiritual and physical chemicalization which occurs when God intensifies his Light for the transmutation of all Darkness, the purging of his holy people and the judgment of the seed of the Wicked One (even the straightening of the earth's axis) may very well manifest as nuclear explosion, whether triggered by God or man or fallen angel or cataclysm—all of which have as their antecedent personal and planetary karma come due.

There is always a physical reaction to such an influx of Light. Since the Son comes for the judgment, or realignment, of that which is gone out of the way, the earth experiences any or all of the following: chaos, cataclysm, economic upheaval, disruption of the normal cycles of life in society and nature, wars, plague and death.

Jesus, the representative of the Cosmic Christ, said, "I AM come to send fire on the earth; and what will I if it be already kindled?"

When the Son of man comes he will descend from the throne of the Father, the I AM Presence, the seat of the north wind, and with him "a great fire." But if the fire of nuclear war be already kindled, then there will be by his two-edged sword— even if his instrument be in the hand of opposing armies—"fire, famine, death awaiting" the people on that notable day of the Lord.

It is proverbial that God's judgments of his own—i.e., the return of their karma for their disobedience to him—is allowed to descend through the embodied fallen angels who are positioned East and West at the head of nations and their financial structures. Witness the destruction of Israel and Judah at the hand of the Assyrians and Babylonians. More than this we cannot say concerning Century II, quatrain 91.

The imagery of the next quatrain is likewise intense and fearsome:

> There will be unleashed live fire, hidden
>   death,
> Horrible and frightful within the globes,
> By night the city reduced to dust by the fleet,
> The city afire, the enemy amenable.   V. 8

Leoni tells us that "in this verse we find predicted a horrible 'new weapon,' a city burnt to the ground by it and by the action of a ship and an enemy convinced of the necessity of making peace. The quatrain thus probably fits nothing so well as the action of the United States against Japan, with ships and atom bombs, in the latter half of 1945." Leoni goes on to say, however, that "World War III may see a much better fulfillment."[32]

In the 1500s, the picture that emerges from the next quatrain must have seemed like the vision of someone in a delirium. But not to us. In the *mise-en-scène* we see a nuclear blast, air battles, and strange-looking creatures:

> They will think they have seen the Sun
>   at night
> When they will see the pig half-man:
> Noise, song, battle, fighting in the sky
>   perceived,
> And one will hear brute beasts talking.[33]
>
> I.64

In our time, "noise, song, battle, fighting in the sky perceived" is all too easy to imagine for anyone who reads the papers, watches television, or has sat through *Top Gun*. The brilliance of the "Sun at night" gives it a nuclear and—since the word *Sun* is capitalized—distinctly apocalyptic cast. While Leoni allows that "fighting in the sky sounds very modern," he wonders whether "Nostradamus had 'signs in the heavens' in mind."[34] Perhaps he had both—the dark night of nuclear warfare as a backdrop for the Second Coming of Christ.

It is nothing less than astonishing that in using the phrase "they will think they have seen the Sun at night," Nostradamus has closely paraphrased the actual words of the first civilians to unknowingly witness an atomic explosion.

Three weeks before an atomic bomb was dropped on Hiroshima, August 6, 1945, the world's first atomic bomb was detonated in a pre-dawn test in the desert at Alamogordo, New Mexico. Mrs. H. E. Weiselman, 150 miles away on the Arizona/ New Mexico state line, witnessed the flash, which she said "was just like the sun had come up and then suddenly gone down again."[35]

Then, in March of 1954, twenty-three Japanese fishermen aboard the *Lucky Dragon Number Five* inadvertently sailed into the testing area around Bikini Atoll in the central Pacific. They were 100 miles from the island when a nuclear test was conducted. The fishermen said the blast looked like a "second sun rising in the west early in the morning."[36]

But what about "the pig half-man"? This image has puzzled Nostradamians for some time. Erika Cheetham, author of a number of books on Nostradamus, says it "seems a clear picture of a pilot in silhouette wearing an oxygen mask, helmet and goggles. The oxygen breathing apparatus does look remarkably like a pig's snout.

"The battle is clearly described as being fought in the air; the screams may be the sound of dropping bombs as they whine to earth. The battle is clearly watched, 'aperçu,' by people on the ground.

"It is important to understand the wording of the last line. The aeroplanes, 'bestes brutes,' are heard talking to others. Could this be a forecast of radio communication? Certainly this quatrain helps to convince me that Nostradamus' visions were of two dimensions, both visual and aural."[37]

The prophet is not only clairvoyant but clairaudient—capable of reading the future already sketched in akasha: not as a handwriting on the wall, but as a videotape projected on a screen—of events that are yet to be.

And whether or not they do come to pass still depends upon the free will of enlightened sons and daughters of God who see in Saint Germain's violet flame, the alchemy of the Holy Spirit, the means God has provided for us to transmute that which our karma is prophesying will take place *unless* we intercede by invoking the sacred fire of God to transmute that karma in the name JESUS CHRIST—before it cycles into the physical!

CHAPTER 3

U.S./U.S.S.R.–
Aggressors Can Agree

While most, if not all, modern Nostradamian commentators believe he predicted nuclear conflict, they also entertain the notion that, contrary to current trends in international relations, in the next war the United States and the Soviet Union will be allies against an Arab or Asiatic conqueror—or a combination of forces from the Far and Middle East. In a less complex version of this theory, Arab forces will invade Europe.

The themes of the Asiatic conqueror and war in the Middle East are well developed in Nostradamus' writings. But the notion that the United States and the Soviet Union will be allies against some combination of forces from the East rests on just a few quatrains. One of the most important of these is the twenty-first quatrain of the sixth century:

> When those of the Arctic pole are united together,
> In the East great terror and fear:

The newly elected, sustained the great one
  trembles,
Rhodes, Constantinople stained with barbarian
  blood.   VI.21

"Those of the Arctic pole" are usually taken
to be the United States and the Soviet Union. In
his latest book, *Nostradamus and the End of Evils
Begun*, Stewart Robb approaches this quatrain
gingerly, but leaves no question about the direction of his thinking:

"With no intention of asserting that I know
its meaning," he says, "or whether or not it will
soon be fulfilled, it does look like a 'latter-day'
prophecy. The reader may tussle with it. . . . But if
Russia and the U.S.A. unite to constitute a world-
police-force for peace the picture could change
overnight.

"Such a police force, run by two giants with
atomic powers of persuasion would cause almost
uncontrollable consternation throughout the entire Middle East. This may happen at a time when
a newly-elected successor to Andropov or a successor's successor appears on the scene."[38]

Rene Noorbergen exercises none of Robb's caution when deciphering this quatrain. Instead, in
Nostradamus Predicts the End of the World he states
unambiguously that about the same time Greece
and Turkey are fighting a war and Turkey is invaded
by Arab forces "the two nations who share communication across the Arctic Ocean—the United
States and the Soviet Union—will announce or

conclude a military alliance against the Far Eastern power and the consolidated Arab forces. This will cause grave concern in the Far East, and the newly elected leader of the Far Eastern alliance will have much to fear."[39]

When considering this quatrain in light of the current geopolitical configuration, Cheetham admits to the difficulty of reading into Nostradamus a Soviet-American alliance but says, sounding as if she does not believe it herself, that "although at the moment it is geopolitically almost incredible that the Allies will be the U.S.A. and the U.S.S.R., the constant references to an Eastern antichrist make it more feasible."[40] But, as we shall see, she, like the others, is swayed by a world view which militates for certain interpretations.

The second and perhaps even more important of the two quatrains that are used to show that Nostradamus predicted a Soviet-American alliance reads:

One day the two great masters will be friends,
Their great power will be seen increased:
The new land will be at its high peak,
To the bloody one the number recounted.[41]

II.89

In this quatrain "the two great masters" are, of course, taken to be the United States and the Soviet Union; the "new land," the United States either "at its high peak" or, in a variant translation, "at the height of its power."[42]

Again, with great certainty, Noorbergen asserts

that "at the point in history when the United States will be the most powerful nation in the world, it will ally itself with the power of the Soviet Union." Perhaps telling us more about his own world view and personal expectations than Nostradamus' prediction, he says that the alliance "may be the result of a realization on both sides that neither can win a war against the other, and that a form of friendship and mutual assistance may be the only way to stop the arms race. Nostradamus appears to indicate that a war could mean mutual destruction, and that because of this an alliance will be forged."[43]

Noorbergen, Cheetham and Robb may see such an alliance. But did Nostradamus? In order to answer the question we must first determine whether "the two great masters" (or "those of the Arctic pole") are, in fact, the United States and the Soviet Union.

While that may indeed be the case, no one has presented any evidence to support such a thesis, much less bothered to present a persuasive argument to that effect. Rather, they seem to have assumed that that is what Nostradamus was talking about and that he placed the time for the fulfillment of these quatrains in the latter part of the twentieth century—something which is by no means self-evident either in the quatrains or in the signs of the times.

Therefore, for the moment let us treat "the alliance" as a working hypothesis or, better yet, a favorite assumption. And in so doing let us consider a second, but hidden, assumption which immeasurably assists, if not enables, these commentators to conclude that the United States and the Soviet Union will be allies—namely that friendship precludes simultaneous hostility between the two superpowers.

Unfortunately, power politics are not that simple. Competition and cooperation, the bywords for managed conflict in our time, have characterized East-West relations for many years. In 1973, for example, during the Nixon-Brezhnev period of détente, superpower rivalry brought the world to the brink of nuclear destruction.

In *The Secret Conversations of Henry Kissinger*, Matti Golan, chief diplomatic correspondent and columnist for the Israeli paper *Ha'aretz*, tells the story of the step-by-step diplomacy of the Yom Kippur War, presumably in such revealing detail that the government of Israel decided to ban the book "on the grounds of damage to the security of the state."[44] Golan argued that the book, which admittedly did contain a lot of restricted information, was more damaging to the reputation of Kissinger and other diplomats than Israel's security and it did finally see the light of day.

Without going into unnecessary detail, a quick reading of Golan's account makes it painfully obvious that the cynical exploitation of détente by both the secretary of state and the Kremlin so helped fuel the fires of war that on October 24, 1973, they nearly engulfed the world. That was the day, according to Golan, that reports "reached Washington of a high alert of Soviet units in

Eastern Europe, with seven Soviet airborne divisions on standby. Direct Soviet military intervention in the Middle East loomed as a real possibility."[45]

At this juncture, the diplomatic maneuverings of Henry Kissinger were, as usual, very complex. War had broken out on October 6. Israel, after initial military setbacks, had taken the offensive and by October 22 had nearly encircled Egypt's Second and, of greater importance, their elite Third Army. Egypt, then the Soviet Union's client, was faced with a military disaster.

On October 21, Henry Kissinger and his Soviet counterparts negotiated a cease-fire that went into effect the evening of the twenty-second and which was imposed on Israel before they could completely surround and destroy the Third Army. Israeli government and military officials were outraged.

When the war first broke out Kissinger had held up the delivery of desperately needed military equipment. Then, when the Israelis finally got the upper hand in the fighting, he negotiated a cease-fire when they believed they were only a couple of days away from finishing off the Third Army.

At a meeting with Israel's chief of staff and senior commanders, Kissinger, stung by criticism of his negotiations, made a remark that Golan says "sounded to [the Israelis] like an indirect go-ahead for the continuation of the fighting."[46]

Just a few hours after the cease-fire went into effect, the commander of the Egyptian forces tried to break out of the Israeli army's grip. The Israelis took this interruption of the cease-fire as an opportunity to take the city of Suez, a necessary prerequisite to destroying the Third Army. Suez, however, was better defended than the Israelis had anticipated and the fight for the city was taking longer than expected.

Whatever the Israelis' speed, the Kremlin was not prepared to see the destruction of Egypt's Third Army—a fact Kissinger was well aware of. By the morning of October 23 he was receiving threats of dire consequences from the Kremlin if he failed to restrain the Israelis.

There can be no doubt as to what Kissinger thought might happen if he did not do so. Golan tells us that Kissinger "called in [Israeli] Ambassador Dinitz and was blunt and brutal. 'You want the Third Army? We won't go to a third world war for you,' he warned."[47]

Events were fast reaching a boiling point. Israel's army was fighting house-to-house in Suez. The Soviets had activated seven airborne units. Diplomatic tempers were white hot.

Kissinger had repeatedly rejected a Soviet-Egyptian proposal for the United States and the Soviet Union to jointly police the cease-fire. The Soviets then said that "if the United States would not agree to a joint action," they might take unilateral action to stop the fighting. The Soviets were simultaneously "urging the Arabs to use the 'oil weapon' against the West."

At that time most people were aware that

the deepening crisis in the Middle East was serious, but just how serious was not generally known. Although this information is still highly classified and precise details are therefore sketchy, we do know that the Soviets were ready to intervene on behalf of Egypt and that they were on the verge of using nuclear weapons. While this is not stated explicitly in Golan's or similar accounts, one will not suffer eyestrain to read it between the lines.

According to Golan, on October 24, Kissinger "had to act simultaneously on two levels. To the Israelis there were more threats that they would lose the protection and support of the United States if the offensive continued. The Russians he answered in their own coin. With the concurrence of the president he ordered an alert of U.S. units, including the nuclear-supplied Strategic Air Command.

"In order to stress the determination of the United States 'to go to the brink' over a direct Soviet intervention in the Middle East, Kissinger went on TV [on October 25] and mentioned the possibility of nuclear war:

> We possess, each of us, nuclear arsenals capable of annihilating humanity. We, both of us, have a special duty to see to it that confrontations are kept within bounds that do not threaten civilized life.[48]

Both threats worked. A cease-fire was adhered to and the world came back from the brink without ever knowing just how far it had gone. In this case, senior U.S. officials diffused the threat. But if they had failed, it is easy to imagine a scenario of rapid escalation leading to a full-scale U.S.-Soviet nuclear exchange—*during the heyday of détente!*[49]

With friends like these...

Without attempting to show that this high-powered episode is the fulfillment of Nostradamian prophecy, it should be clear that under the same circumstances wherein the United States and the Soviet Union can be considered friends, they can also play the role of archenemies and rivals.

Above and beyond that, the phrase "When those of the Arctic pole are united together, / In the East great terror and fear" does not necessarily stipulate that if the United States and the Soviet Union became friends, those in China and/or the Middle East would be frightened. The reference to "in the East" could just as well be talking about grave anxiety in Moscow, the capital of the Eastern Bloc, as well as a number of other things.

If nothing else, the Yom Kippur War shows that there was a good deal of fear in Moscow on two separate occasions, the first being great anxiety over Egypt's near loss of their Third Army (which would have adversely affected Soviet standing in the Middle East—probably the then most important theater in the world), the second being the very real possibility of a nuclear exchange with the United States.

CHAPTER 4

The Friend/Enemy
Superpower Relationship

Those for whom Nostradamus wrote his grave warning, that they might prepare for and survive a nuclear war, have a right to hear interpretations based on the words Nostradamus used. For the correct knowledge of our "future history" can save the lives of millions if we act upon it while there is time.

My teacher always used to say, "Whenever you assume—instead of getting the facts first-hand—you make an "ass" out of "u" and "me." This little rule of Tom Thumb has saved many a chela from the donkey pen.

The future is in the eye of the beholder and the eyewitness account is that of a particular person's position. This x factor of every equation—quatrain—Nostradamus wrote cannot be discounted in the interpretation. He is locked in a grid of time and space. Moments of astrological time before or after happenings, as we know, make all the difference.

My view, then, of Nostradamus' view, is only as accurate as the Presence reveals to me the same scene through Nostradamus' eye. Only thus are my prophecies on Nostradamus revealed. Without the all-seeing eye of the Presence, I have but reason and conjecture, intuition and sixth sense— and the signs of the times—to pry his secrets.

What I do see is that Nostradamus' descriptions are a geometry of words that comprise a four-dimensional kind of Chinese puzzle. Only if you put the pieces together in order will they fit. They fit only one way. And if you strain them, they won't work.

The resolution that gives the revelation is a harmony of disciplines—from mysticism to pure mathematics, from the Kabbala to karma and the direct dictation of the Presence, at times without the seeing. For the word itself as formula is power and the power to unlock our future lies in the Word and it can be discovered and known. But it takes time and love and the freedom to contemplate the fohatic keys and signals that give rise to the worded formula.

These are not all revealed to me by any means, but as I am told, I will tell you, dear reader, for this is my only purpose...to bear the prophecy to your heart and mind that you may do with it what you will. Now let us use every means at our disposal to check and recheck our reading of what God writes in our hearts.

Let us pause to reexamine these two pivotal quatrains to see if "those of the Arctic pole" and "the two great masters" are indeed the United

States and the Soviet Union and whether it is reasonable to suppose they will become friends or form an alliance in our time.

> When those of the Arctic pole are united
>   together,
> In the East great terror and fear:
> The newly elected, sustained the great one
>   trembles,
> Rhodes, Constantinople stained with barbarian
>   blood.[50]   VI.21

> One day the two great masters will be friends,
> Their great power will be seen increased:
> The new land will be at its high peak,
> To the bloody one the number recounted.[51]
>   II.89

We have seen that Robb, Noorbergen, and Cheetham believe "those of the Arctic pole" and "the two great masters" to be the United States and the Soviet Union. Leoni takes a different approach. While considering "those of the Arctic pole" (VI.21), he notes that the "only 16th-century states with any parts in the Arctic Circle were Sweden and Denmark's Norway." Unsure of just when this prophecy should be fulfilled, he says, "Now, of course, we have the U.S. and the U.S.S.R."[52]

To that list we can also add Canada, Finland, Greenland (which is a protectorate of Denmark) and arguably Iceland—giving us a list of seven or eight nations to consider.

Nostradamus does not give a date for this

quatrain, nor does he describe any specific technology that would place it in the twentieth century. On the other hand, there is nothing to keep it from being fulfilled in the near future.

But even if this quatrain is a sign for our time, there is nothing that requires us to pick the United States and the Soviet Union from this group of seven or eight nations. It could just as well refer to the United States and Canada, who are united together by a 5,335-mile border of friendship and a common origin in the seed of Joseph, whose father Jacob passed on to him and to his sons, Ephraim and Manasseh, the birthright of the true seed of Abraham. Nor is there anything in this quatrain that indicates Nostradamus was talking about two nations rather than three or more.

It is easy to pick the United States and the Soviet Union from this list if you, like Noorbergen, have already concluded that in II.89 Nostradamus predicted that the two great masters would be friends.

But what about II.89? Does it really say that the United States and the Soviet Union are "the two great masters" who one day "will be friends"? Leoni says that the phrase "will be friends" can be translated "will be dismissed."[53] He nevertheless prefers "will be friends."

But is that reasonable? The answer is no. Upon close examination it appears that a key word in the quatrain has been mistranslated. The first line of II.89 reads in French, *"Un jour seront demis les deux grands maîtres."* Leoni translates it, "One day the two great masters will be friends," while Erika Cheetham offers a slightly different translation, rendering the first line, "One day the two great leaders shall become friends."[54]

Leoni thinks that "the two great masters" probably describes "the Anglo-American Entente of 1941, with the Atlantic Charter meeting of Churchill and Roosevelt, and American industry switching to heavy war production, the statistics of which seemed foolish boasting to the bloody Hitler."[55]

In trying to discover the meaning of this verse, Erika Cheetham noted in her 1973 work on the seer entitled *The Prophecies of Nostradamus* that "to solve this quatrain one must first decide on the translation of the word *demis* in the first line. Nearly all versions have the word *d'amis* (friends) which is how I have translated it here, because to understand *demis* as meaning halved would make nonsense of line two [Their great power will be seen to grow].

"The power of the leaders cannot be seen to increase if they are halved. The two great leaders sound as though they may be the great powers, and line 3 (the New Land) links this with America, as Nouvelle Lande was one of the contemporary names for America. If not, it may refer to the modern usage of the New World."[56]

What becomes apparent from her comment is that Nostradamus did use the word *demis* (halved) but nearly all translators have arbitrarily changed it to *d'amis* (friends) because *demis* made no sense. Leoni, for example, says *demis* is a variant of *damis* and conjectures, "Presumably *d'amis* [is] intended."[57] Everyone else seems to have followed suit.

By definition *demis*, or halved, means to divide into two equal parts, separate into halves, to reduce to one half, to share equally.

In the lexicon of international relations, the United States and the Soviet Union are locked in a global competition on all fronts—in other words, they are enemies. Thus *demis* makes perfect sense. Their forces are divided, not united as one, and they are divided ideologically as well as karmically, irreparably by an ancient polarization, a squaring off, if you will, which to this hour, try as they may, has neither sought nor found resolution.

This enmity—and the mutual fear of being destroyed or dominated by the other—has stimulated the arms race, including the building of huge nuclear arsenals.

There is, however, a bizarre twist in the friend/enemy superpower relationship—the transfer of technology from West to East that makes it possible for the Soviets to be an enemy by creating an enemy that had no power to be an enemy in the first place. It is as though the U.S. halved her potential power by giving it away—"I'll take half, you take half." So important is this trade that it has been suggested that East minus West equals zero. Yes, a half minus a half equals zero!

Some of this technology is stolen, of course.

But a great deal of it has simply been sold to the Soviets. And this has been going on for a long time, in fact as long as the Soviet Union has been a nation.

In his landmark study—*Western Technology and Soviet Economic Development* written in three volumes covering the years 1917 to 1930, 1930 to 1945, and 1945 to 1965—Professor Antony Sutton convincingly demonstrated with reams of factual data that the Soviet Union has virtually no indigenously developed technology. Ninety to ninety-five percent of its technology comes from the West— about two-thirds of it from the United States.[58]

At the outset, most of the trade and transfer of technology took place through concessions. It was always clear in Lenin's mind what this trade was for. "Concessions," he told the Russian Communist Party in 1920, "these do not mean peace with capitalism, but war upon a new plane."[59]

Professor Sutton points out that during the years that Lenin was proclaiming that "socialism is electrification," General Electric was heavily involved in schemes to promote the use of electrical systems throughout the Soviet Union. At the end of World War II Ambassador Averell Harriman reported that "Stalin said that about two-thirds of all the large industrial enterprises in the Soviet Union have been built with the United States' help or technical assistance."[60]

What is now readily apparent is that we have built the Soviet military-industrial complex, which builds armaments for the Soviet Union, in the same way that our military industrial complex builds aircraft, tanks, missiles for ours. "No army has a machine that churns out tanks," points out Professor Sutton. "Tanks are made from alloy steel, plastics, rubber and so forth. The alloy steel, plastics and rubber are made in Soviet factories to military specification. Just like in the United States.

"Missiles are not produced on missile-making machines. Missiles are fabricated from aluminum alloys, stainless steel, electrical wiring, pumps and so forth."[61] These, too, are made in Soviet factories—factories that came courtesy of Yankee know-how.

McKee Corporation built the largest steel and iron plant in the world—modeled after the U.S. Steel plant in Gary, Indiana—in the Soviet Union. The huge Gorki truck plant was built by Ford Motor Company and the Austin Company. The ZIL truck plant was built by Arthur J. Brandt Company of Detroit, Michigan. Both produce military trucks.

The Soviet T-54 tank used in Vietnam had a Christie suspension bought from the U.S. Wheel Track Layer Corporation. The Soviets bought the technology they needed to MIRV their missiles and bought computers they could not develop that have become the centerpiece of modern high-tech warfare. In short, as Professor Sutton observes, "we have built ourselves an enemy."[62]

In the 1980 presidential campaign Ronald Reagan took President Carter to task for his policy of open trade with the Soviets. But the Reagan administration has continued to expand trade with the Soviets, removing President Carter's wheat embargo—imposed in response to the invasion of Afghanistan—and other trade restrictions. Then, in May of 1985, they reactivated the U.S./U.S.S.R. Joint Commercial Commission which had not met since 1978.

In addition, the U.S./U.S.S.R. Trade and Economic Council, a private organization of about 300 members whose complete membership list is known only to Washington and Moscow, facilitates East/West trade. Although information about the council is difficult to come by, it appears to have some affiliation with the Department of Commerce—a fact they deny. In any case, according to Professor Sutton, the council has eight full-time engineers in New York City who select U.S. technology needed by the Soviet military and arrange to have it transferred.[63]

The net result of this trade is that it makes war between the superpowers far more likely. Oddly enough, while Cheetham places great emphasis on a global war beginning in the Middle East, she does not, as do Robb and Noorbergen, rule out nuclear war between the United States and the Soviet Union.

In fact, while discussing II.89 she says, "The present building up of Cruise missiles, Pershing

IIs, etc., does not seem to bode well for the West. Nostradamus implies that our arms build up is so great, so committed perhaps, that the West will force the East into a warlike position. This could well be the case."[64]

While I cannot say I find myself in total agreement with her analysis of the arms race, it is clear that she could not make such a statement if she did not think war possible between the superpowers.

Nevertheless, in 1985 Erika Cheetham expanded on the theme stated in her earlier work. While she still maintained the pivotal word should be *d'amis* (friends), she provided even stronger evidence for *demis*, explaining that "the key to this quatrain lies in the word 'demis' in line one. It is almost certainly a misprint for d'amis, which I have used. *To understand demis in its usual sense of hatred,* would make nonsense of the rest. [emphasis added] Powers of great leaders cannot be increased if they are halved."[65]

But, as we have just seen, she has it backwards. If we are to apply this quatrain to the United States and the Soviet Union, we must recognize that in this case "halved" implies "hatred" implies an increase in the military power of the two blocks implies conflict of just the kind we are experiencing yields a very different reading of the quatrain which heretofore has been the linchpin of the theories that Nostradamus predicted a Soviet-American alliance.

Thus, embedded in one of the quatrains on which turns the theory that Nostradamus did not predict war between the United States and the Soviet Union is a word that, when properly translated and understood, annihilates that theory even as it annihilates the peace its interpreters say it prophesies.

The significance of this fundamental error cannot be overstated. The general themes in Nostradamus' writings emerge from the interpretation of a number of quatrains which appear to be about the same subject and, when taken as a group, provide greater meaning than the sum of the parts. Conversely, as the big picture emerges from the group of quatrains, it influences the way the interpreter approaches each individual quatrain.

In other words, the interpreter's understanding of the theme influences the way he interprets the quatrains within the group. Likewise, the way these themes are thought to work together influences not only the way individual quatrains are interpreted, but also how the themes, and hence the events they describe, should work together.

If, for example, you accept the notion of an alliance between the Soviet Union and the United States, when you see that there are also general themes that seem to describe war coming out of the Middle or Far East, you may erroneously conclude, as did Rene Noorbergen, that "Nostradamus' scenario for World War III...will start quietly while peace is prevailing throughout the world. It will be the change in Russia from Communism to a more tolerable form of government that will be the catalyst. Nostradamus predicts that this change in Russia will open the way for friendship between the United States and Russia, nations he calls the 'two brothers of the Far North who will share communication across the Arctic Ocean.'

"A condition that looks like a blessing," he says, "will turn out to be a curse, for the developing friendship of the two super-nations will disturb the balance of power in the world, and shortly thereafter, when they combine their might with that of Western Europe, the peoples of the Far East and the Middle East will retaliate and get ready for an armed conflict supported by the nuclear and bacteriological/chemical arsenal of Red China."[66]

But when "the alliance" postulated by twentieth-century interpreters is taken out of the equation, we can regain some perspective. As it now stands, we still have the same basic themes—an Asiatic or Oriental conqueror, conflict in the Middle East, an Eastern attack on Europe, and nuclear war among them. But since we can soundly dispense with the notion that the "U.S. and U.S.S.R. will be allies," the way these themes interact dramatically changes.

CHAPTER 5

The "Conquering Oriental" Theme

In addition to the confusion over the relationship of Russia and America, a narrow interpretation of Nostradamus' nomenclature may have led some commentators to miss several quatrains that could apply to a Soviet-American or East-West conflict involving Europe. Robb, for example, believes "the city" always refers to Paris, and "the Church" the Catholic Church. He also warns his readers to "be careful of the word *Orient*. To Nostradamus, it means *Middle*, not *Far East*. For him the Far East is Asia. As for *barbare*, he pens it for Arabs on the war-path."[67]

In a set of quatrains that he believes describes an Arab invasion of Europe, he includes this one.

> The Oriental will leave his seat,
> He will pass the Appenine mountains, to see France;
> He will pierce through the sky, the waters and snow,
> And he will strike everyone with his rod.[68]

II.29

Leoni translates *"L'Oriental,"* which Robb renders "The Oriental," as "The Easterner," and says it is one of the "'conquering Orient' theme. The invader comes to France by way of Italy." He thinks that it is "probably intended for an Arab or Persian, the Turks being France's chief ally and friend in Nostradamus' day," but wonders whether "aerial navigation [is] intended in line 3" and declares that "in this age, the rod would suggest a 'secret weapon.'"[69]

Robb generally concurs, stating that the conquering Arab Prince "will have a mighty air force, and will probably attack [Europe, including England] in the white season." Cheetham also thinks the rod "could mean a weapon" and while she doesn't quite forecast an invasion, she notes "there is a curiously threatening quality in the last line, as though no one is expecting any harm to come from the visitor."[70]

If, however, one simply takes the "Oriental" or "Easterner" to mean the strong man in Moscow, the leader of the Eastern Bloc, you then have a very good description of the anticipated movement of Soviet or Warsaw Pact forces in an all-out attack on Europe. Note that it is not immediately apparent that the "Oriental" comes by way of Italy since the assertion "he will pass the Appenine mountains" suggests that he could travel to the north of the Apennines, which run the length of Italy's boot.

That would put the invading force into the strategic invasion routes moving east to west into

NATO's central region. Whereas aircraft or missiles are implied (and would unquestionably be part of an integrated attack on Europe), an invasion, by definition, implies the movement of armies—in this case possibly describing either a breakthrough on NATO's southern flank, the westward movement of an invasion force, fanning out along the three main corridors in NATO's central region, or both.

Such an interpretation is not unreasonable. The military logistics are consistent with modern doctrines of warfare. And the Soviet Union is an Eastern nation. In fact, much of the Soviet Union is located in Asia. No less of an authority on the matter than Mikhail Gorbachev recently declared that "the Soviet Union is also an Asian and Pacific country" and reminded the world that the "greater part of our territory lies east of the Urals, in Asia."[71]

Historians are divided over the degree to which the Golden Hordes that swept out of Mongolia into the steppes in the thirteenth century influenced Russian culture. But there was certainly some influence and whether it came from the period of the Mongol invasion or earlier, the Russian (and now Soviet) mentality has a distinctly Oriental cast.

Russia was not only a home to the Eastern Orthodox Church, but by the fifteenth century it also conceived of itself as the heir of Byzantium and the spiritual leader of the Orthodox world. It was not until the late seventeenth century, under the vigorous leadership of Peter the Great, that any appreciable Western influence was even felt in Russia. But even that was little more than a veneer. Nearly two centuries later, Chekhov wrote a letter to his brother Nikolai urging him to "sweat the Asiatic" out of himself.[72]

In exploring the possible range of meanings to Nostradamus' words, let us bear in mind that even those who tend to interpret his key words rigidly find exceptions. "Barbarian," declares Robb, always refers to the "Arabs on the warpath" *except* on one occasion when he believes the seer is referring to the (doubtlessly warlike) Germans.

Jean-Charles de Fontbrune, author of several books on Nostradamus, came to the same conclusion after using a computer to classify the "key words" used by Nostradamus. He discovered, for example, that Nostradamus used the word *autour* ten times and noted that "on nine occasions the meaning was the usual one, *around* (the preposition), but once it was used in its rarer sense, as a noun meaning *goshawk*. Only when checking all ten quatrains incorporating the word *autour*, and then restoring it in context, would one be aware of the philological trap."[73]

In other words, Nostradamus' writings are so honeycombed with linguistic and philological anomalies and variations that it is self-defeating to approach the interpretation of certain words too dogmatically. True, Nostradamus may use some terms generically to describe nations or peoples of a certain disposition. "Barbarian," as Robb points out, generally refers to warlike Arabs and, under certain circumstances, Germans.

However, in our time, I believe it refers categorically to the Soviets. Their record of aggression and their growing preference for militarism over ideology certainly warrants such an interpretation. We have only to look at the atrocities the Soviets have committed against women and children in Afghanistan to convince us they are more "barbaric" than the "Arabs on the warpath" ever were.

The Soviets have taken numerous steps to suppress news coverage of the war they are waging against the *mujahidin*, who are fighting Mi-24 HIND helicopters and MiGs with only World War I vintage Enfield rifles, their bare hands and whatever AK-47s they pick up from fallen Soviets.

The official Soviet military policy on Afghanistan is genocide. It includes the destruction of the mujahidin's food and shelter support system maintained by the farmers and villagers, the carpetbombing of fields and livestock and the leveling of villages. They have killed over 1 million Afghans and driven 5 million into exile—about one of every three Afghans is either dead or has fled. Many of the rest are dangerously close to starvation.

To terrorize those who will defend their land and their freedom to the death, they are committing atrocities such as raping teenage girls in helicopters at 15,000 feet, then throwing them out over their villages. They bayonet pregnant mothers in the belly, killing them and their unborn children, they roast newborn babies on a spit before their parents and seed the countryside with eye-catching bombs targeted at children that look like toys, pens or butterflies and which explode when picked up. Toy bombs seldom cause death, they have another purpose: to strike terror to the heart and maim the body for life.[74] All of this is happening now, right while you're reading this book!

Therefore, I say there is no barbarism on earth today equal to that of the Soviet Union except it be that of the United States' President, the Congress and the State Department, who have for years promised portable surface-to-air rockets, munitions, food and medical supplies to these freedom fighters—who live on prayer five times a day and tea and bread less often—but do not see to it that weapons for self-defense and medical aid get past the Pakistanis to actually reach those on the front lines.

This sin of omission, this failure to deliver a devout people who are a stalwart friend and who, if given the weapons, are capable of defeating the Soviet Union on their own soil—this betrayal on the part of America, whose destiny from the beginning has been to be a deliverer nation, is the crying shame of the century. And the crime upon crime of it all is that this karma of gross neglect against Christ himself in these who are also his is today upon every American citizen! For what is done by the leadership in the name of the electorate, unless they speak out, accrues to the moral indebtedness not only of a nation but also of each citizen.

Taking this a step further, let us consider whether Nostradamus in the prophetic vision accorded him by the Seventh-Ray Masters—truly a gift of the Holy Spirit to our blessing—could have been blind to the ongoing behavior of the Soviet leadership. Or whether he could have failed to see the rise of Soviet militarism—one of the prominent profiles of twentieth century civilization—or overlooked their wars. Since he predicted the Bolshevik Revolution, wrote about nuclear warfare, described communism (even before the word was coined) and predicted the system's demise, it is unlikely he would have missed the rest of the landscape.

It is possible that *barbarian* could be used to mean "Arab" in one context and "Russian" or "Soviet" in another, as Nostradamus would find it appropriate to apply the adjective wherever the shoe fit.

Truly, what Nostradamus saw is precisely what his interpreters have not wanted to see: War not peace. As in the days of Jeremiah, so to this hour of the false prophets of peace who were rebuked by the LORD saying, "They have healed the hurt of the daughter of my people slightly, saying Peace, peace; when there is no peace," so many voices clamor for peace and by wishful thinking tied to the donkey of pacifism think to convert the enemy or believe his lies when he, too, cries, "Peace, peace."

Even so said Ezekiel to the same who have reincarnated today as leaders of a false peace movement in Church and State:

Woe unto the foolish prophets, that follow their own spirit, and have seen nothing!...

Because ye have spoken vanity, and seen lies, therefore, behold, I am against you, saith the Lord GOD....

Even because they have seduced my people, saying, Peace; and there was no peace; and one built up a wall, and, lo, others daubed it with untempered mortar....

Therefore thus saith the Lord GOD; I will even rend it with a stormy wind in my fury; and there shall be an overflowing shower in mine anger, and great hailstones in my fury to consume it....

Thus will I accomplish my wrath upon the wall, and upon them that have daubed it with untempered mortar, and will say unto you, The wall is no more, neither they that daubed it;

To wit, the prophets of Israel which prophesy concerning Jerusalem, and which see visions of peace for her, and there is no peace, saith the Lord GOD. (Ezekiel 13:3, 8, 10, 13, 15, 16)

(If it just occurred to you that this sounds like the Berlin Wall and the Iron Curtain, you may be right on!)

This discussion has led us to the point where it is time to ask whether Nostradamus predicted nuclear war between the United States and the Soviet Union in the latter part of the twentieth century.

Thus far we have reviewed several quatrains which appear to describe a nuclear holocaust, discussed and dismissed several quatrains which are thought to show a Soviet-American alliance, considered the possibility that some of the quatrains thought to deal with the Arabs, Easterners, Orientals, or barbarians may well refer to the Soviets, and analyzed a quatrain that appears to discuss a Soviet/Warsaw Pact invasion of Western Europe.

Before we discuss additional quatrains, let us pause to consider the kind of world we live in—the milieu in which the seer saw not only the handwriting on the wall and the tell-tale shadows of coming events, but the outplaying of the Dark Cycle of planetary karma in the economies of the nations known as the ride of the Black Horse.

CHAPTER 6

The Ride of the Black Horse

Since World War II there have been more than 200 wars. Ironically, this is a period of time generally known as "peace" since there has not been a direct full-scale war between the super-powers.

Nevertheless, at any given time as many as one of every four of the world's nations—or 45 separate countries—may be at war and much of this conflict reflects or is driven by superpower tensions. At the moment at least 43 nations are currently at war. Noncombatant nations aid the belligerents with money, weapons, intelligence, and diplomatic support—sometimes even supplying both sides of the conflict.

Soviet terrorism, wearing the mask of "Arabs on the warpath" is still with us, as if anyone needs to be reminded, and the real barbarians are still not tried before the world court.

Although Middle East terrorists are trained by the KGB and the GRU in Bulgaria, and in Soviet-sponsored training camps in Libya, Lebanon, Syria, Iran, Iraq and South Yemen, the U.S. punishes the client state instead of going for the bear's tooth. This policy of nonconfrontation ("Whatever you do, don't offend the Soviets!") only ups the ante on the day of reckoning which must surely come. For the karma of milk-toast passivity towards, and even compliance with, the aggressor (while a nation parties) will not be forever held back.

The international economy, which was grossly overextended in the last twenty-five years, is in a tenuous position. The American economy, which looks rosy to some, is in a pre-catastrophe syndrome.

History seldom if ever repeats itself—exactly. It should be noted, however, that in 1929, just months before the fateful crash, Calvin Coolidge reported to the nation—via his regularly scheduled off-the-record press conferences which quoted him as a "White House spokesman"—that "present conditions in business throughout the country are good and the prospect for the immediate future seems to be as good as usual"[75] even though he was aware of just how serious the nation's economic problems really were. He was following the advice of the Department of Commerce.

That is a sobering thought, especially in light of President Reagan's optimistic economic reports and Business Week's June 9, 1986, cover story "The '20s and the '80s: Can Deflation Turn into Depression?" Business Week noticed that "some things seem awfully familiar. A conservative President is in office. There's fighting in Nicaragua. The stock market's on a roll. The rich have lots of new toys, parties are fashionable again, and there's heavy consumption of certain illegal goods. Real estate is booming in New York, while land values are plummeting in the Midwest. Farmers are hurting, and commodity prices are falling. Inflation has even turned negative.

"It sounds like today, but it could be the 1920s with just a few differences. Then, Calvin Coolidge was President. We sent the Marines into Nicaragua. Prohibition was in full swing, and motorboats were bringing in rum, not cocaine. Indeed, the parallels between the 1920s and the 1980s are so numerous as to be scary." Asked *Business Week*, "Can the Crash of 1929 and the Great Depression happen all over again?"[76]

Revelation says it can and more so because the Third Horseman had not yet ridden his famous ride across the land when the crash of '29 was artificially created by mortal men's doings. And the Lamb hadn't opened the seven seals. But today the hoofbeats of the Four Horsemen can be heard riding up and down the nation.

And the black horse, shining a silvery green in the moonlight, is in the lead. And when the Lamb opened the third seal, John heard the third beast—that great seraphic being who with the other three chants night and day saying, "Holy, holy, holy, Lord God Almighty, which was, and is, and is to come"—say, "Come and see."

Hear, then, his warning as the Scales of Divine Justice measure the abuses of basic com-

modities and foretell the hurting of the oil prices
and the wine that is the spiritual lifeblood of a
nation derived from the sacred labor of her people:

> And I beheld, and lo a black horse; and
> he that sat on him had a pair of balances in
> his hand. And I heard a voice in the midst
> of the four beasts say, A measure of wheat
> for a penny, and three measures of barley
> for a penny; and see thou hurt not the oil
> and the wine. (Revelation 6:5, 6)

See how famine shall descend for the manipulation of wheat and wheat prices and the barley
green that represents every herb-bearing seed and
every tree in which the fruit of the tree yields seed
which God has given to man for meat but which
shall be taken from him for his greed and glut-
tony. For these have made him vulnerable to the
likes of fallen angels who have crept in to steal the
light, destroy the gold standard, and deprive the
laborer of his hire and wage, and the elderly of
their just portion and the widow of her dignity.

Thieves and robbers and bankers and the
prestigious and the merchant class have taken
from a people their wealth, but they allowed it.
Moreover they have indulged the spoilers, for they
themselves are spoiled and surfeited in their materialism; they have not challenged the evildoers in
the name of God!

If you look at the figures, you yourself will
confirm the very presence of the black horse who

delivers the nation's karma of the squandering of the abundant Life and the misuse of the sacred fire that is every man and woman's inheritance whereby he or she may multiply his portion through the threefold flame of the Trinity.

Things do not look promising. You have to come to grips with the fact that there are 8.5 million people unemployed in a period known as a "recovery." The national debt is $2.1 trillion (unfunded liabilities such as federal pensions are probably ten times that) and deficits are clipping along at more than $200 billion annually.

Growth is sluggish despite about a 15 or 16 percent increase in the basic money supply by the Federal Reserve System over the last several years. However, the inflation rate has, for the time being, remained low, fluctuating around 4 percent.

There are several reasons why this is so. Many of those newly created "dollars" have gone overseas to purchase foreign goods and have not yet been recycled. In addition, for some time a strong dollar stimulated the import of comparatively cheap goods. That kept the prices down, which affected the Consumer Price Index and thus the calculation of the inflation rate.

Many dollars have been put into negotiable instruments like bonds rather than commodities. And commodity prices, most notably oil, have been falling—which also influences the Consumer Price Index. Finally, government economists tend to crunch the numbers in the most optimistic fashion possible. Thus, for the time being, the rate of inflation has been calculated to be growing more slowly than warranted by economic conditions.

But when the trends reverse, we will have a powerful surge in the rate of inflation. In the short run, the expansion of the money supply is giving some the unwarranted impression that the economy is healthy. Financial writer James Flanigan says "it's pretty clear that the point of the Federal Reserve's pushing interest rates down and pumping money into the economy is to keep people and businesses afloat, to prevent bankruptcies and a widening ripple effect. Indeed, says John Rutledge of the Claremont Economics Institute, 'If the Fed had followed its strict rules on money supply, we would now have a depression.'" [77]

As I pointed out, it seems inevitable that the rapid growth in the money supply will eventually bring about a significant increase in the inflation rate. The crucial point will come not when high inflation actually returns, but when people and businesses *perceive* that inflation is returning. They will then start to make personal and business decisions as if high inflation were already here.

During times of inflation investors generally shun the stock and bond markets and seek protection for their assets by buying precious metals, land, art objects or anything that has intrinsic value. Their actions can have the effect of self-fulfilling prophecy, bringing about the very economic consequences they are seeking to protect themselves from.

By putting their money into commodities, investors will deprive the economy of much-needed capital to finance new business development—thus causing a recession. Likewise, the withdrawal of large amounts of funds from the stock and bond markets could cause a panic among investors, resulting in a precipitous drop in the markets that could snowball into a major economic catastrophe.

This is where people's perceptions play such an important role. Many observers feel that our economy is only held together by trust, and once that trust is weakened the consequences could be calamitous. The stock market is the primary bellwether of our economy in the minds of most Americans—perhaps far more than is warranted. Therefore, any major downward movement in the stock market could be the beginning of economic chaos.

This scenario becomes all the more plausible with the recent introduction of very sophisticated computerized buy/sell programs used by the major institutional investors. Any movement in the stock market has the potential to trigger buy/sell programs simultaneously on the world's major stock, commodity, and options trading markets. What was physically impossible only a few years ago can now be done by computers in a matter of seconds. The results of these actions by multiple investors is totally unpredictable.

This type of computerized "high-tech trading" is already beginning to cause a great deal of volatility in the market. In 1986 alone, seven of the ten worst one-day declines in the Dow-Jones Industrial Average have occurred.

Therefore, what may begin as a perception of coming inflation could result in a loss of confidence in the American economy and the stock market. This, coupled with the other inherent weaknesses in our economy already noted, could finally result in the collapse of the world's major financial markets.

And that is where our economic problems begin, not end. Next comes the debt bomb—the 800 billion to a trillion dollars loaned by Western, principally American-based international banks, to foreign governments such as Mexico and Brazil which will probably never be repaid. If there is a major default, it could damage or perhaps destroy the banking system, an event that could lead to chaos, martial law, or other equally unpleasant possibilities.

Executives at the megabanks are trying to put the best possible face on an awful situation in order to maintain public confidence. In private they are not so sanguine. The chances of Mexico defaulting are, according to some experts, about 80 percent. It owes $99 billion and earns about 70 percent of its foreign exchange from the sale of oil. But oil prices are low and may very well remain low.

The problem is much more serious than the failure of a number of banks—it is the potential destruction of the international financial system. In a piece called "Why Taxpayers May Have to

Prop Up Banks," the *Washington Post* explained that "a heavily indebted oil-exporting country—such as Mexico—could default on its debts to banks worldwide. That might break the backs of some over-extended banks, even some of the biggest.

"This could cause the world's system for making financial payments—connected by computers and enmeshed with interlocking and overlapping debts—to collapse....

"This prospect is so nightmarish that the Federal Reserve...is prepared to use the unlimited amounts of money it has or can create to keep these banks from going under.... The worry today is not just a single bank, but sweeping losses arising from possible loan defaults by a number of foreign countries and many energy companies that could threaten any of several large banks, whose unanswered failure could produce this catastrophe."[78]

What the Fed is prepared to do is not in question. But if the Fed creates unlimited amounts of money, we will experience a commensurate dose of inflation. Any attempt to inflate our way out of an economy-destroying banking collapse could ignite an economy-destroying hyperinflation. And as if that were not enough, the debt-bomb may not be the worst of our debt troubles.

The uncollectible consumer-debt (the outstanding debt owed banks on everything from real estate to credit cards) and uncollectible domestic-energy loans are at least as dangerous, if not more so. A major effect of mergers and cost cutting in larger corporations is the "trimming" (i.e., layoffs) of middle management. According to a knowledgeable New York banker, these are the people with the high levels of consumer debt and the ones most likely to go bankrupt.

Denis Healey, former Labour Chancellor of the Exchequer, recently told an audience at the London School of Economics that "massive volumes of debt have been built up in vulnerable areas of national economies far dwarfing the sovereign debts [the debt bomb] which are so much discussed these days. For example, the debts to the farm banks in America's Middle West are greater than all the debts owed to American banks by foreign governments; and the banks, not just in Texas, which have been lending money on oil face the prospect of bankruptcy with the collapse in the oil price.

"Such a system is immensely vulnerable to unexpected shock, the default of a major sovereign debtor, . . . a bad harvest, revolution or even an earthquake. And to cap it all, the United States, which is now the biggest debtor country in the world, requires massive inflows of foreign capital to finance its domestic as well as its external deficit."

This has set the stage for a potentially cataclysmic problem. As Mr. Healey points out, "If foreign confidence in the American economy falls heavily, these inflows could be reversed, with cataclysmic consequences not just for the United States, but also for the world economy. The danger of a financial crash, like that in 1929, is palpable though impossible to quantify."[79]

This is compounded by a curious predicament caused by the oil crisis. The United States economy is now in a "no-win" situation. Our particular conundrum is that if oil prices stay low, it helps our economy by creating jobs and lowering consumer prices but it puts extreme pressure on our banking system as oil-producing nations such as Mexico, Nigeria, and Venezuela almost certainly will not have the cash to repay their loans to American banks and are likely to default, detonating the debt bomb.

But if oil prices go back to their former level, we will reexperience the same set of conditions that gave rise to the largest transfer of wealth in history—from the Western nations to the oil-producing states—that triggered a national and global recession, stimulated unemployment, threw the economies of the industrialized nations into chaos, nearly ruined the economies of several third-world countries and helped create the debt bomb as developing countries needed to borrow cash from Western banks in order to pay higher oil bills.

But, as *Time* recently pointed out, if oil prices do not rise, "the repercussions could go well beyond economics.... The crisis could inflame tensions in the Middle East...where oil revenues have dropped from $237 billion in 1980 to an estimated $110 billion last year." *Time* went on to say that Israel's Prime Minister Shimon Peres said that falling oil prices were a "threat to peace in the Middle East" and urged the West to mobilize a "modern-day Marshall Plan to aid the region, using some of the money saved by lower oil prices."[80]

While the chances of such a plan materializing are slim, Peres' concern is shared by many in Washington who recognize that economic hard times could turn the already trigger-happy Middle East into a full-scale battleground.

At the end of the ride of the Black Horse is the full weight of mankind's karma of nonaccountability of the light of God, the coin of the realm, and the basic commodities of life. For the crimes committed against the economies of the nations have laid the foundations for war, plague, and the Fourth Horseman—the pale horse of Death and the Hell of astral hordes and nuclear night following after.

> And when he had opened the fourth seal, I heard the voice of the fourth beast say, Come and see. And I looked, and behold a pale horse: and his name that sat on him was Death, and Hell followed with him. And power was given unto them over the fourth part of the earth, to kill with sword, and with hunger, and with death, and with the beasts of the earth. (Rev. 6:7, 8)

This I have seen. This Saint Germain has showed to me. This the Lamb opened in his Revelation to John. Thus get thee up to the mountain of the LORD that thou and thy children might live.

CHAPTER 7

The Economic
Foundations of War

Oil troubles are proving to be highly egalitarian. The Soviet Union's semi-comatose economy has grave life-support problems because the reduced oil price has deprived it of a major source of hard foreign currency. During better days it earned 60 percent of the foreign exchange it used to purchase Western technology and grain by selling about 1.3 million barrels of oil daily.

Since 1985, the U.S.S.R.'s socialist economy has lost something on the order of $14.5–$16 billion, and that amount could grow.   Right now they are borrowing as much of the shortfall as they can. But when the Western economies have their day of reckoning, as indeed they must, the Muscovites will no longer be able to borrow from the West to get by.

The Soviet Union is also being squeezed by the cost of running an empire along with its military archrivalry with the West. The goals of Soviet foreign policy have remained an area of contention among Western experts. Any way you

look at it, two things are clear: their major invest-
ments have been in their military and not their
civilian economy and they have steadily expanded
their empire.

Whenever the Soviets draw a country into
their orbit they draw off whatever wealth they are
able to. This suggests that the way the Soviets
intend to continue to solve their economic problems—at least in part—is, directly or indirectly, to
take control of additional nations and start siphon-
ing off their wealth. In short, a cash-poor Soviet
Union is a very dangerous nation. Its behavior will
not be too much different than an armed robber
without any money. He needs to make a heist.

The problem is, the world is running out of
countries the United States and the West can
allow the Soviets to take before the takeover inter-
feres with our vital security interests. At the very
least, the United States is not likely to tolerate an
attack on Western Europe or the loss of access to
Middle Eastern oil fields.

But even if we were prepared to do so, Soviet
perceptions of our vital interests are such that they
would no doubt consider launching a preemptive
first-strike attack against our ICBM and bomber
forces prior to going into Western Europe.

Today, it is not popular in many quarters to
seriously propose that the Soviets might attack either
Western Europe or the United States. Some would
object on strategic grounds—i.e., the Soviets would
never dare attack either Western Europe or the

United States for fear of a U.S. counterstrike. While this may have been true in the past, the emerging Soviet ability to launch a crippling strike and neutralize 90 percent of U.S. ICBMs and much of our bomber force is generally recognized.

For the next chess move the Soviets would demand that the United States accept a Soviet military move into Europe or the Middle East as a *fait accompli*—or they will destroy our cities. Then, faced with the prospect of losing American cities for the privilege of counterattacking Soviet military targets with our submarine fleet, an American president might capitulate.

Others would disagree on grounds that Moscow has pursued, in the words of Zbigniew Brzezinski, "a strategy of political attrition designed to achieve progressive and piecemeal neutralization of Western Europe."[81] Still others would argue that Moscow is hostile only in response to Western aggression.

The first of these last two positions is plausible under certain conditions. The second has no evidence to support it. Regardless of the Soviets' strategy, for the first time in our history we are faced with a Soviet military machine which is capable of overrunning Europe with conventional weapons and has the simultaneous nuclear strength to neutralize America's nuclear umbrella.

It now appears that any Soviet invasion of Europe would likely be preceded by a surprise nuclear attack by a new generation of highly accurate rockets armed with small, low-yield warheads which could effectively destroy most, if not all, high-priority military targets, such as missile bases, in Western Europe without destroying European cities.

Furthermore, the West is faced with an adversary plagued by extreme internal pressures. The Soviet economy is deeply troubled. Any action to increase productivity by decentralizing the Soviet economy would, in effect, cause a loosening of the political strictures that tie the captive nations of the empire to Moscow. And that long-awaited phenomenon, to put it bluntly, would cause the disintegration of the empire.

According to Zbigniew Brzezinski, "the Russian elite instinctively senses that any significant decentralization, even if initially confined to the economic realm, would strengthen the potentially separatist aspirations of the non-Russians inhabiting the Soviet Union. Economic decentralization would inevitably mean political decentralization, and political decentralization could become the stepping-stone to national emancipation.

"Russian anxieties on this score must be heightened by demographic trends. They indicate a decline in the dominant position of the Great Russians. During the 1970s the Russians ceased being the majority of the Soviet people, and a further shrinking of the Russian plurality is inevitable. In 1980 Soviet eighteen-year-olds were 48 percent Russian, 19 percent other Slavic, 13 percent Muslim, with 20 percent listed as 'other.' The projection for 1990 is that the figures will be 43 percent Russian, 18 percent other Slavic, 20 percent Muslim, and 19 percent 'other.'

"In the longer run, the political aspirations of the non-Russians represent the Achilles' heel of the Soviet Union."[82]

The plain truth is that the Soviet Union does not have what it takes to sustain its global empire, much less carry on a long-term competition with the United States. Nor can it generate indigenous technology at a time when new technologies are shaping the world and stimulating a redistribution of power.

The Soviets face a related external challenge in that technology will ultimately provide the West a means to neutralize, and thus liquidate, the massive Soviet investment in armaments. That would probably destroy the superpower status of the Soviet Union and dramatically accelerate the process of internal disintegration. It would be logical to expect that the Soviet leadership will use their military might to maintain the status quo rather than passively watch their position erode.

Thus the Soviets have both the capability and motive to attack the United States as well as Europe. Finally, their strategic doctrines call for surprise, i.e., preemptive strikes, and are not hampered by the notion that there can be no winner. "There is profound error and harm in the disorienting claims of bourgeois ideologues," asserted General Major

A. S. Milovidov, "that there will be no victor in a thermonuclear world war."[83]

Furthermore, as Herman Kahn points out, "it is almost certain, despite several public denials, that Soviet military preparations are based on war-fighting rather than on deterrence—only concepts and doctrines—that is, on the belief that it is important to be able to wage and win (or at least survive) a nuclear war because a war may be forced on them (either by direct attack or by provocation leading them to strike first).

"They apparently believe that despite enormous damage they could win a nuclear confrontation, just as they 'won' the Napoleonic invasion and World Wars I and II. In each case much of Russia was destroyed, but the country eventually emerged stronger than before."[84]

It is reasonable to assume, therefore, that given the proper pressures, the Soviets would use their nuclear arsenal to solve their problems. The simple fact is they have no other tools available to them.

Whatever they do, the Soviets are unlikely to wait for the United States to start the process of escalation to a nuclear attack on the Soviet Union if Warsaw Pact forces overrun our NATO Allies. This is particularly easy to understand in light of the revelations of Jan Sejna, a former Major General in the Czechoslovakian Army and the highest ranking member of the Communist military apparatus to ever defect.

While in Czechoslovakia he was Chief of Staff to the Minister of Defense and the Assistant Secretary to the top secret Czech Defense Council. In the course of his career he dealt with such figures as Khrushchev and Brezhnev and members of the Soviet Military High Command. General Sejna was privy to the guiding doctrine of the Soviet political and military leadership embodied in the Soviet Strategic Plan. According to Sejna, this is nothing less than an outline of the Soviet Union's strategy for global conquest.

Sejna defected in 1968. "In the years since I left Prague," he writes in *We Will Bury You*, his book which outlines the plan, "the Plan will have changed in detail because each section is subject to constant revision to take into account the new factors introduced by changes in the world's political forces. Despite these variations, I know that the essence of the Plan will be unchanged."

Sejna says that since 1965 the centerpiece of the Plan is a crippling first-strike attack against the United States and then accepting the surrender of Western Europe—or simply overrunning it. [85]

Whether or not one accepts this view of the dynamics of Soviet behavior, the U.S.-Soviet rivalry is never far from anyone's mind. And the one thing *everyone* agrees on is that the United States and its allies, and the Soviet Union and its allies, have a lot of military might. Conventional forces are still important. But the core strength on both sides lies in their respective nuclear arsenals. No other nation or group of nations in the nuclear club—France, Britain, China, India, and now, Israel—could attack either one or both of the superpowers without being utterly destroyed in return.

The United States has about 11,140 strategic warheads, the Soviet Union 9,240. This does not include tactical or battlefield nuclear weapons of which the United States may have as many as 22,000 and the Soviet Union 8,000. When the figures are added up, it turns out there are over 50,000 nuclear warheads in the world, approximately 30,000 of which are owned by the United States and possibly 22,000 by the Soviet Union. Britain has about 1,000; France, China and Israel have a couple hundred each. This, of course, does not tell us how many extra warheads and delivery systems, not included in the official count, have been built secretly.

With this in mind, let us consider the fact that most Nostradamians believe Nostradamus predicted nuclear war in the latter part of the twentieth century. Who might be the belligerents in such a war? Noorbergen believes that China will launch a surprise nuclear attack against both the U.S. and the U.S.S.R.—then, allied with the Arab world, invade Europe. Others foresee an Arab invasion of Europe.

Notwithstanding the fact that Nostradamus predicted many things that could not have been foreseen even with a rigorous analysis of events, it is unlikely that a third force could launch a crippling nuclear (or conventional) attack that would compel the United States and Soviet Union into an alliance against it in the next two or three decades.

Who would do it? Western Europe? No. They are terrified of an attack by the Warsaw Pact nations, even with the support of the United States.

China? Hardly. Their attempt to bloody Vietnam's nose resulted in their getting a bloody nose themselves. At present, their nuclear force is not sufficient for a duel with either superpower, much less both.

Japan? It has no offensive force to speak of.

China and Japan together? In the future perhaps—*if* they can cooperate, admittedly a concern but still a big if.

India? In worse shape than China.

The Arab nations of the Middle East? At present they cannot defeat Israel, much less Europe or Russia. Even if they get the bomb—or decide to use bacteriological weapons—they are not ready for a full-fledged confrontation with the superpowers. Nor is Israel with her reported 100-200 nuclear warheads and intermediate range ballistic missiles.

That leaves just two big guns standing in the street at high noon. And economic, political, military and social conditions are such that we are drifting towards a confrontation.

There are many causes for war, only one of which is economic. But economic conditions are probably the most reliable indicators of war. The American, French, Bolshevik, and Communist Chinese revolutions were preceded by disastrous inflations. Hitler came to power after the post World War I hyperinflation of 1923. The Kondratieff Wave, which charts economic and military cycles, shows that we are due for both an economic downturn and a war sometime in the near future.

When the economic trends we have outlined mature, we will most likely see a surge of inflation and then a retrenchment, a hardening of import-export policies, a chilling of international trade, probably some massive defaults (in effect if not in name), national and international recession (or depression), changes of government, and war.

The economic, social, and military fundamentals are in place. And, as we quoted him in chapter 2, Nostradamus tells us in V.8, in a style of writing that sounds like twentieth century hard-news documentese, that "there will be unleashed live fire, hidden death, horrible and frightful within the globes, by night the city reduced to dust by the fleet, the city afire, the enemy amenable."[86] It is not hard to imagine Dan Rather or Peter Jennings reading those lines as the lead to a "special report."

Before we read on, let us consider the spiritual alternative. Let us see if we can undo it before it happens. We have a nation to win for trying, and all that we have ever lived and loved and dreamed for to lose if we don't give it our best.

CHAPTER 8

Saint Germain's 8th Ray Solution to the Economy

C an anything or anyone come between a people and this handwriting on the wall?

Is there an intercessor who can turn the tide of Darkness and invoke the oncoming tide of Light to devour the karma of abuses of the abundant Life charted in the stars and the quatrains and in the collective unconscious of a nation?

Must this prophesied economic debacle followed by war and the nuclear nightmares come to pass?

Yes, Yes, and No.

There is a power of God that can be summoned by you from your Mighty I AM Presence. The Universal Christ in and through and around you is able to turn back personal and planetary karma and to consume it by the sacred fire—if you are willing to be one-pointed in giving daily dynamic decrees to the violet flame. (Fifteen minutes is good and basic, 30 is great, 45 is terrific and one hour of violet flame decrees daily is stupendous!)

This Seventh Ray ritual is the foundation for the Eighth Ray Solution to the ailing economies of the nations through the eight-petaled chakra, the secret chamber of the heart. The decrees at the end of this chapter recommended by Saint Germain (given with "Ten for Transmutation," favorite violet flame decrees found in our book *The Science of the Spoken Word*), when buttressed by *Archangel Michael's Rosary for Armageddon,** comprise a ritual of the Eighth Ray.

When followed up with community action applying the teachings of Saint Germain, this exercise of the power of the Word will avail much in the solving of the problems of the capitalistic/communistic economies outlined by Saint Germain as well as by Nostradamus.

Archangel Michael's Rosary was dictated to me by the Defender of the Faith who identified himself to Joshua as the Captain of the LORD's Hosts. It is a ritual of prayers, psalms, invocations and dynamic decrees to the angels, the Divine Mother and the Son of God for the deliverance of God's people and the turning back of Evil.

So, the answer to the third question and the Third Horseman is that **it is Saint Germain, Lord of the Seventh Ray and Hierarch of the Aquarian Age, who can and does intercede in the economies of the nations in answer to your call.**

He with his beloved Portia has the authority to act, but the Law says we must exercise the science of the spoken Word, hour by hour, which compels the intercession of the Lord's hosts, the entire Spirit of the Great White Brotherhood, on

*The Science of the Spoken Word, $7.95; Archangel Michael's Rosary for Armageddon, 36-page booklet, $1.25 postpaid; available with tape, add $3.55 postpaid.

behalf of every Lightbearer on earth and all who
will receive them, repenting of their vile violations
of the abundant Life and returning to the Law of
the One.

No, economic debacle, war and the nuclear
nightmare do not have to come to pass.

Nostradamus' prophecies, the scriptural and
Fátima warnings as well, are given that we may act
in time to meet them with the all-consuming fire of
God and the command to the Seven Archangels to
deliver God's people in this time of trouble.

Divine Intervention is the key to undoing the
untoward prophecy that is but a mathematical
equation of karma which tells us what will happen
if we the people do nothing.

Here is what Saint Germain had to say about
the economy of the nations February 17, 1980.
There is still time for concerted action to stem the
tide through The Word of God.

————————————

Minutemen and women of Saint Germain,
I call to you to consider that the state of the
economy of the United States of America is so
acute as to jeopardize the divine plan of freedom
not only for this nation but for every nation in the
world.

Few among the religious of the world have
come to grips with the reality that every avatar has
come not to condemn but to enhance the consciousness of the abundant Life. Life that is abundant is
Life which engages in the free flow of light between the nucleus of the Atom of Being, the Great

I AM, and the soul who elects by free will to serve on the periphery of the Great Atom of Selfhood.

The abundant Life is the standard of the personal Christ and his Christ consciousness, which mediates between the white fire core and the one who chooses to be the open door of that Light midst earth and her evolutions. Members of all religious bodies ought to realize that the platform of the soul's evolution from lifetime to lifetime is most surely threatened by the strategies of the fallen ones who manipulate the law of supply and demand and the economics of the nations.

If the religious leaders of the world in every faith would recognize their responsibility to ensoul the Christ light and to teach this meditation upon the indwelling Person of the Word, they and their members midst the body of believers could hold the balance for the ebb and flow of the spiritual/material tides of light, energy, supply, and God consciousness made manifest as the daily necessities of Life.

So many have never perceived the real mission of the avatars of East and West to unite the children of the Light under the Tree of Life, the blessed I AM Presence, whose fruit is for the nourishment of souls as well as the initiation of the Christ consciousness and whose leaves are for the healing of the economies of the nations.

I AM Saint Germain and I summon the stalwart to consider the critical condition of inflation in America today side by side with the manipulation

of the free market and the community of the Holy
Spirit.

Many who express their opinions in economics today are no more qualified to run the
economy than the run-of-the-mill religionists are
to analyze and preach the mysteries of the sacred
scriptures of East and West. With a few courses in
Keynesian economics and Marxist socialism, mere
amateurs approach the subject of the nations'
money systems, a balanced budget, taxation, and
the financial burdens of a federal bureaucracy as
though they were experts in the science of supply.

Inasmuch as the real laws of economics and
the God-solutions to the international economy
are not to be found in the most elite schools of the
day nor in the minds of the experts (if they were,
we should have no problems of such immense proportions), it behooves the children of the Light to
systematically study the disease of inflation and to
invoke the God-solution and the God-science to
this cancer of the economy before the very life-
force of the free peoples of the earth is devoured
by its tentacles.

May I suggest that, to begin with, honest and
responsible leadership by noble hearts be seen as
the necessary fulcrum. A part of the problem as
we see it is that those who are in the position to
pull the purse strings of America are often those
with a vested self-interest who lack the spherical
vision of a very complex problem whose solution
would be forthcoming out of a profound under-

standing of the simple truths and basic principles which are the foundation of the law of the abundant Life and of the sacred labor.

The system of political parties and frequent elections, though designed to preserve democracy in a republican, representative, form of government, makes severe demands upon those seeking office. In order to be elected, they must secure the popular vote.

Inasmuch as the control of inflation and the cutting back of government spending must affect vast segments of the people adversely, it is never a popular cause for politicians to preach the real cure for inflation, which is the sacrifice of immediate gain, inordinate profits, and even the life of leisure for the long-term gain of prosperity and the sound management of the nation's government and business based upon the realities of the money supply and the resources at hand. Thus those seeking election are unwilling to place before an uneducated populace the gravity of the issue or the consequences upon all of the people of the real solutions.

This generation of Americans and their prosperity is built upon the credit system. The increase of the money supply has created an unreal concept of the abundant Life. While some have become millionaires through inflation, others have been robbed of the fruits of their sacred labor. Thus the synthetic self has built its synthetic economic system, and the illusion of a materialism without

God and of mechanization without the presence of the Holy Spirit has produced a wholly unreal consciousness of the abundant Life.

The surfeiting of the people in consumer products bought with unsound money unbacked by a gold standard has produced a profound insecurity in the American people, a subconscious resistance to take the responsibilities of living and working together in the cosmic honor flame to produce the abundant Life that is the only true foundation for a golden-age civilization. Though it is unnatural to the children of the Light to expect something for nothing, to expect others to pay their way and to indulge in surfeiting in nonessentials, this has become the mark not only of Western civilization but also of those in the Communist bloc nations and in the underdeveloped countries.

Materialism is a disease which is as debilitating to the human spirit as is that of Communism. Both of these products of the minds of the manipulators have affected millions of Lightbearers, and their acceptance of the philosophy of the Serpent has left them in a euphoric nightmare. Their psychic peace, the product of their psychological separation from the I AM Presence, has left them nonthreatened in an era when all around them, permeating the economic crisis of the decade, are the most threatening conditions to the human spirit which has ever existed in modern history.

Those who sleep on in their nonthreatened state of unawareness are the greatest enemies of the people and of the outcome of the destiny of the United States. These perpetuators of the false peace who preach their "all is well" doctrine while applying a few Band-Aids to the gaping wounds of the nation's economy are the false pastors who must be replaced in this urgent hour of world need by true shepherds who will have a humility to apply themselves first to God and God's laws and then to a new science of economics that is neither Marxist nor Keynesian but rather Christic in its orientation.

Inasmuch as all laws of economics proceed out of the sacred labor of the heart, the head, and the hand of the people themselves through their interaction with the Holy Spirit and their integration with the personal God of Israel, I am summoning as my disciples in the field of economics the fishermen, the farmers, the workingmen and women of America, the laborers—those who are the pillars of a great society that can yet be realized if they will put their hands to the plow of the Great Plowman and have respect for the Ox who treadeth out the corn even as He bears the burden of the karma of the world economy.

Let those who are still tethered to the reality of the sweat of the brow and the work of the hands, those whose minds have not been taken over by intellectual theories that have no relevance to the heart or to the practicalities of life come forward, then, and begin anew an in-depth probe of the history and the law of cycles which have governed the economic policies and the consequent rise and fall of nations.

Meanwhile, let those who have made certain philosophies of economics their religion and their proponents their gods be deprogrammed from the synthetic self with its synthetic systems that have never worked and never will work, except to destroy those who espouse them.

Let us proceed from the empirical method. Let us disallow what has not worked and let us allow what does work. Communism is the dream of the fallen ones who would escape the consequences of their karma and of their neglect to integrate with the source of all Life and abundance. It is not viable because it is inconsistent with cosmic law which operates independently of men's theories or their mockeries of divine justice.

The manipulation of the free market and the free governments of nations through monopoly capitalism or corporate socialism will not work. It destroys individual creativity and snuffs out the fires of hope that ever rest in the heart of the individual as the desire to be self-sustaining in God.

What will work? Well, I say, that remains for you to discover. But I will tell you this—it begins with the fundamental principle: Whatsoever a man soweth, that shall he also reap; and its corollary: Whatsoever a man soweth not, that shall he not reap.

There are too many people in every walk of life who still want something for nothing and they are willing to espouse any economic philosophy that will deliver to them immediate pleasures and material prosperity. These are not noble hearts but they whose names go down in history as the ignoble and as the destroyers of the abundant Life of the soul.

Let the government and the people learn to live within their means, and let the real value of goods and services be based upon the theory and the altogether practical application of the law of the sacred labor* performed to the glory of God, who is resident within his humanity.

Let the value of Life rest upon a gold standard that comes from the golden rule, which is the principle of the divine economy—do unto others as you would have them do unto you. This golden rule is applied to the gold of the heart, the golden wisdom that serves the needs of the community through love—applied love that becomes compassion, charity, and the sharing of the joys of the abundant Life with those who entertain the impoverished sense.

If you ask me why the economy of America is in such a disastrous state, I will tell you that it is because not enough people care for God or for one another. They see solutions only in terms of more money and more government control and the regulation of Life. But without heart or attunement with the threefold flame of Life that is the spark of each one's Divinity, the Light of God does not flow to meet the needs of the people.

"I AM the Light of the Heart" is my mantra

*This spiritual principle is entirely set apart from Marx's labor theory of value, which is its perversion.

for the healing of the economies of the nations. It takes many hearts to make one great heart of light that becomes the heart of a nation—just as it takes many drops of rain to form the mighty River of Life and many souls serving as one to manifest the Body of God on earth.

Therefore I enlist the sweet and simple souls who have adored my purple fiery heart for centuries while the exclusive ones have excluded themselves from my circle, for the path of simplicity of the heart has been an affront to their worldly wisdom. Let these children of my heart now rally as minutemen and women of the flame of freedom and take my mantra of the heart as a perpetual mantra that flows through the mind even as it flows through the arteries of commerce, business, banking, and that Federal Reserve system which is the "non-reserve" of the nation's money system.

You have heard of the perpetual prayer of the pilgrim of God. You have heard of the Indian gurus who recommend to their chelas the recitation of a single mantra hundreds of times a day as they go about their normal activities. "Pray without ceasing" is the answer that I give to those who cry out for deliverance from the oppressive weight of the top-heavy economy.

Take this mantra then, my noble of heart, and alternate it with that old-time favorite to Helios and Vesta, to the sun center of the flow of the abundant Life, and let us see what we can still do to stave off impending destruction.

There are some economists in America who have seen the dangers for years. They wonder why the collapse has not already occurred. I will tell you, my beloved. A little violet flame goes a long, long way. Legions of light multiply your calls to the violet flame hour by hour and apply the sacred alchemy of the law of transmutation to the problems of the economy.

Angels of the Seventh Ray and "experts" in the application of the law of Christhood to the day-to-day problems of economics are working diligently at inner levels to heal the wounds in the body politic of the nations. Thus we repeat that it is in the influx of the sacred fire in an accelerated and rolling momentum of the violet flame invoked by Keepers of the Flame, as well as in specific calls for the economy, that the answer is given.

Contrary to all of the powerful opinions of the worldly, it is in fact the light of the devotees of the Ascended Master teachings as well as the light of the pure prayers of all children of God that today holds together the international economy. We seek to translate this light into a practical and effective plan for a new economic foundation to be implemented in the United States and in the nations of the earth.

This calls for a massive education of the people, the overturning of the most cherished systems because they are not of God, and a banding together of those who see through the seed of the serpents who have gone forth to destroy the souls of the people through the destruction of their economic base.

Let the faculty and students of Summit University gather at Camelot at the Inner Retreat as well as in our Teaching Centers and homes of light to begin to tackle these most pressing problems. Minutemen and women of the Light, let us place the magnifying glass of the Mind of God upon all financial affairs. Let there be an exposure of the truth and of error. Let the people be educated so that they might follow the candidates who have the courage to tell the truth as to what is the necessary course of action and what will be the disastrous consequences of neglect.

And to those who would hear me discourse on more pleasing subjects of esotericism I say, Come off of your meditation pads and get out of your ivory towers! There will be little to discuss if you fail to apply your hearts to the problems of the world distribution of oil, wheat, food, technology, and gold.

I AM Saint Germain. And to all I say, Wake up! The hour is late and the future of Camelot hangs in the balance of the economic survival of the nations.

Saint Germain signed this letter directed to his Keepers of the Flame throughout the world:

"Yours for the alchemy of the sacred labor and for the binding of the manipulators of the abundant Life on earth."

I AM the Light of the Heart

I AM the Light of the heart
Shining in the darkness of being
And changing all into the golden treasury
Of the Mind of Christ.

I AM projecting my love
Out into the world
To erase all errors
And to break down all barriers.

I AM the power of Infinite Love,
Amplifying itself
Until it is victorious,
World without end!   (9x)

The New Day

Helios and Vesta!
Helios and Vesta!
Helios and Vesta!
Let the Light flow into my being!
Let the Light expand in the center of my heart!
Let the Light expand in the center of the earth
And let the earth be transformed into the New Day!
(9x)

I AM, I AM, I AM the Resurrection and the Life
of my finances and the U.S. economy   (3x)

Repeat this line 3 times, then conclude with

Now made manifest in my hands and use today!   (33x)

Repeat the entire mantra 33 times to transmute forces
of Antichrist opposing the abundant Life for God's people.

CHAPTER 9

The Horrible War
Being Prepared in the West

There are a number of other quatrains which support the notion of warfare between the United States and the Soviet Union and/or a Soviet invasion of Europe. We have already reviewed several that seem to describe nuclear warfare. To these we can add the following:

> The horrible war which is being prepared in
>   the West,
> The following year will come the pestilence
> So very horrible that young, old, nor beast,
> Blood, fire Mercury, Mars, Jupiter in France.[87]
>
> IX.55

Leoni has little of importance to say about this quatrain. He mentions that it has been applied to "a prediction of the Spanish onslaught, resulting in the disaster at Saint-Quentin (August 10, 1557)" and also "to World War I and [the] influenza epidemics thereafter" but does not offer an interpretation of his own other than to say that "the [astrological] configuration should limit the time,"[88] which in this case it does not.

Cheetham thinks it applies to our time and says, "I have a horrid fear that the pestilence, covering so many victims will again be nuclear fallout. One cannot but feel that Nostradamus' vision of the twentieth century was one of war, brutality, famine and disaster."[89]

I think the general thrust of this quatrain is readily apparent. In addition to the obvious reference to war preparations, perhaps this prediction takes into consideration that some in the West have a calculated policy of supporting both sides of a conflict, before, during and afterwards.

Western capitalists and industrialists gave financial and diplomatic support to all factions during the Bolshevik Revolution—especially the Bolsheviks. In 1917, for example, William Boyce Thompson, of the Federal Reserve Bank of New York, gave the Bolsheviks $1 million of his own money for—as reported in the February 2, 1918, edition of the *Washington Post*—"the purpose of spreading their doctrine in Germany and Austria."[90]

Prior to World War II, a number of American banks helped finance Italian and German fascism. And American businesses provided crucial technical assistance that made the Nazi war effort possible. Standard Oil of New Jersey, for example, provided I. G. Farben, the huge German cartel that was the core of the Nazi military-industrial complex, coal gasification technology which was needed to keep Hitler's tanks rolling. "Standard Oil Company...sent $2,000,000 here in December of

1933," William Dodd, the U.S. Ambassador in Germany, wrote to FDR, "and has made $500,000 a year helping Germans make Ersatz gas for war purposes."[91]

In January of 1933, a commercial attaché connected with the U.S. Embassy in Berlin reported to the State Department that "in two years Germany will be manufacturing oil and gas enough out of soft coal for a long war. The Standard Oil of New York is furnishing millions of dollars to help."[92]

Today, as in the past, American banks and businesses are lending the Soviets money and transferring technologies that are crucial to their war industries. The net effect, as I pointed out earlier, is that we have built ourselves an enemy.

Without the benefits of trade and the transfer of technology from the West, the Soviet Union would not be a threatening force in the world today. In fact, an objective observer watching Western capitalists building the Soviet military-industrial complex while at the same time contributing to America's defense effort, might conclude that these "capitalists" were intentionally arming both sides and thereby fueling the fires of a terrible future war. Aghast, he might remark, "My God, look at 'the horrible war which is being prepared in the West,'" just as Nostradamus did when he saw the future for what it was and would be.

Another encoded reading of the signs of our times would, it seems, describe nuclear war:

> At forty-five degrees the sky will burn,
> Fire to approach the great new city:
> In an instant a great scattered flame
>   will leap up,
> When one will want to demand proof
>   of the Normans. [93]   VI.97

One of the critical tasks in deciphering this quatrain is to determine the identity of "the great new city." Leoni, evidently of the opinion that the quatrain is referring to someplace in Europe, says "the only towns in Western Europe of any size on the 45th parallel are Valence in France and Piacenza and Pola in Italy (Pola in Yugoslavia from 1947)."

It is clear that he is taking his cue from the phrase "at forty-five degrees," which he assumes is 45 degrees north latitude. He notes the largest towns near the 45th parallel are Lyons, Bordeaux, Turin, Milan, and Genoa. "The classic new city is Naples, derived from *Neapolis*, but that does not seem too likely here," he says without reaching any conclusion about which city he thinks Nostradamus is talking about.

Leoni points out that "the chief element of this quatrain seems to be an epic fire" and that "Boswell gave a rather clever application of this one to the great explosion at Halifax on October 6, 1917, which caused great fires and heavy loss of life. Halifax is indeed on the 45th parallel, but was not founded until 1749. For those who suspected sabotage, some suspicion centered on a Norwegian grain ship, the *Imo*, in the harbor.

'Normans' and 'Norwegians' have the same etymology, like 'slaves' and 'Slavs.'"[94]

Cheetham and Noorbergen take "the great new city" to be New York City, even though it is located nearly 300 miles south of the 45th parallel close to the 41st parallel (40 degrees 43 minutes north, to be precise).

Cheetham believes "the advent of the Third World War, according to Nostradamus, will be heralded by an attack upon New York—city and state—through both bombs and chemical warfare." Also persuaded that the events described by this quatrain take place along the 45th parallel, she says, "The state of New York lies between the 40th and 45th parallel in the U.S.A....The attack appears to be very widespread, covering both the state and the new city, and the scattered flame may well be that of a nuclear holocaust."[95]

Noorbergen pulls no punches on this one. He declares "nuclear fire burns New York City." He thinks "a CONFLAG system [Cluster Orbital Nuclear Fire-Weapon for Light Atmosphere Ignition], launched from China, will be detonated above New England [U.S.A.], and will create a fire in the upper atmosphere that will reach as far south as New York City. This will occur during the [same] time when France is fighting for its very existence."[96]

Noorbergen goes on to say that Criswell, the psychic, predicted a foreign power would launch a nuclear attack on the United States. Many of the incoming missiles would be destroyed by an anti-missile system (does Criswell know something about the future of Star Wars?), but he says some would get through and hit strategic targets.

With this in mind Noorbergen says, "It is interesting that the 45th parallel of which Nostradamus speaks, and which he claims will be the point where the fire will originate that will burn New York, is the border line between the American State of Vermont and Canada. If a cluster of nuclear devices were detonated simultaneously at a high altitude above Vermont, the resulting fire-storm would burn out all of New England—including New York City."[97]

Although Leoni disagrees with Cheetham and Noorbergen about the meaning of this qua-train, all three believe that Nostradamus localized the place of its fulfillment along the 45th parallel in the Northern Hemisphere.

They also agree that the critical event in this quatrain is, in Leoni's words, "an epic fire,"[98] which Cheetham and Noorbergen take to be a nuclear attack. And that seems to be a reasonable interpretation of this quatrain.

As I see it, the efforts to reconcile New York City with the 45th parallel are themselves strained. But a strategic attack on the Canadian-American border where only geese congregate, apparently as a means of destroying New York City, or as a "near-miss," strains our common sense even further. And no systems we know of have this wide a latitude of error.

My awareness is that Nostradamus is not

talking about a degree of north latitude but that in his 'session' he is standing atop a 'high tower' in the new city observing the 45-degree angle of elevation of a nuclear airburst from a warhead aimed at New York City.

For as I meditate on Nostradamus meditating on revelations given him by the Presence, I see him seeing what he writes and noting it in code as a chronicler of events, a journalist getting the scoop—on the future. Nostradamus sees what he sees from various vantage points.

While this assessment is a departure from Leoni, Cheetham, and Noorbergen, it must be noted that neither the original French nor the English translation says the 45th *parallel*. And the word *latitude* is not used. Yet they have taken wide latitude to force the issue into their mind set, like we used to do when we were kids—force the wrong piece in the wrong place in the puzzle. It worked pretty well until the outline appeared where the wrong piece was supposed to go. And until that moment the wrong piece in what we wanted to be the right place threw off each succeeding piece so that the complete picture could not appear.

From what we have been able to glean from the United States Air Force, North American Air Defense Command (NORAD), and several military planners, the 45-degree-angle theory is certainly worth considering in the light of knowledge. Forty-five degrees *could be* an angle of approach for a warhead, although such angles, the experts say, would vary considerably depending on where it was fired and the purpose of the attack.

The precise angle at which warheads would approach a major city like New York is classified information. But according to one knowledgeable source, warheads from ICBMs launched from the Soviet Union are more likely to come in at an angle of about 65 or 70 degrees, while warheads carried by a missile fired from the deck of a ship at relatively close range would be more likely to come in at 45 degrees. (As a point of information, Soviet nuclear subs regularly patrol the East and West Coasts of the United States—ready for action.) Nevertheless, at *any* angle of entry, it is still possible to observe the "sky...burn," i.e., a blast, at 45 degrees.

Nostradamus seals this code with "When one will want to demand proof of the Normans."

And what about those Normans? Wouldn't we all like to see a little bit of proof that the French are our faithful friends and not so smug about allowing our planes to stop by on their missions to deter those "Arabs on the warpath"?

In light of this discussion, the next quatrain is extremely interesting:

The year that Saturn and Mars are equal fiery,
The air very dry parched long meteor:
Through secret fires a great place blazing from burning heat,
Little rain, warm wind, wars, incursions. [99]
IV.67

Neither Leoni or Cheetham make much of this one. Leoni says that "probably the configuration delineated here is nothing more than a conjunction of Saturn and Mars, which is very common."[100] Cheetham says almost the same thing, observing "the configuration of Saturn and Mars is a common one, so further information is needed to understand this quatrain. The dating of the comet or meteor is probably the key."[101]

Noorbergen, on the other hand, lists it with two other quatrains (V.8 and I.64, see pp. 23–26) and takes their collective meaning for granted saying, "Does this *really* need an explanation or an 'interpretation'? It is uncanny how this ancient seer could give such an accurate description of a modern nuclear attack without having read about the destruction of Hiroshima and Nagasaki." He thinks IV.67 is talking about a "ferocious attack of the East against the nations of Aquila [the U.S. and U.S.S.R.]."[102]

As I have already pointed out, Noorbergen's theory about forces from the East launching a war against the United States and the Soviet Union is suspect. Nevertheless, this quatrain may indeed describe a nuclear attack.

In general, the quatrain describes the juxtaposition of wars with "secret fires" and a "great [or big] place blazing from burning heat." This sounds like a description of the aftermath of a nuclear attack. But the "secret fires" could be a reference to a nuclear accident like Chernobyl, which burned for quite a while before the Soviets acknowledged the disaster. Or it could be a reference to a volcano. How can we be sure?

Perhaps we cannot. But there are clues hidden in the quatrain. In French, the first two lines of this quatrain read: "L'an que *Saturne* et *Mars* égaux *combust*, L'air fort séché longue *trajection*." Leoni points out that there are two Latin words in these lines—*combust*, from the Latin *combustus* (burned, consumed, ruined, destroyed) and *trajection*, from the Latin *trajectio* (shooting star, meteor).[103] These may give us a greater sense of what Nostradamus was trying to convey in this quatrain.

Although Leoni thinks *combust* is derived from *combustus*, he seems to have taken into consideration the fact that *combust*, in astrological language, describes a close conjunction, usually between the Sun and Mercury. In astrology, Saturn and Mars are known as the malefics and, although both have positive characteristics and undeservedly bad reputations, in this context they appear to have a foreboding character.

Leoni and Cheetham are correct in saying that a Saturn/Mars conjunction is common and therefore not of much value in trying to date the quatrain. But *because* of its frequency, it is unlikely that is what Nostradamus, an expert astrologer, had in mind.

Since the conjunction was not intended to date the quatrain, we should look to the meaning of the planets themselves. As they are used here, Mars stands for war and Saturn for evil and/or death. What Nostradamus seems to be saying is that when these two planets are equally strong and their influences are conjoined (combined), then there will be, as our various interpreters would have it, a "long meteor" or a "comet" or "an elongated shooting-star."[104]

Leoni, and probably Cheetham and Noorbergen, arrives at his interpretation by taking *trajection* in the quatrain to be derived from the Latin *trajectio* (shooting star, meteor). I would like to suggest that *trajection* is really closer to trajectory (*trajectoire* in French) and that Nostradamus is describing not a comet or a meteor, but the trajectory of a nuclear warhead. (A single warhead could, of course, be a synecdoche for a full-scale nuclear attack.)

Now, when we reexamine the quatrain, "warm wind" could be a reference to fallout or the wave of thermal radiation generated by a nuclear explosion. During a nuclear blast, about 35 percent of the energy is released in an intense burst of heat that precedes the blast wave by several seconds. The heat wave can cause second and third degree burns a considerable number of miles from the explosion and ignite a fire storm in cities. Thus, "a great [or big] place blazing from burning heat" could be a major metropolitan area engulfed in a fire storm.

In facing the reality of the signs of the times

lined up with the now self-evident truths of Nostradamus' quatrains on war and its economic plausibility, yea mandate, we hear the voice of the second beast say, "Come and see," for the Lamb has opened the second seal:

> And there went out another horse that was red: and power was given to him that sat thereon to take peace from the earth, and that they should kill one another: and there was given unto him a great sword. (Rev. 6:4)

CHAPTER 10

The Great Besieged Chief

T he next quatrain appears to our faithful interpreters to describe a rocket attack or a bombardment, although it is not clear whether it is
part of a U.S.-Soviet exchange, a Soviet attack on
Europe, or some other use of modern weaponry.

The device of flying fire
Will come to trouble the great besieged chief:
Within there will be such sedition
That the profligate ones will be in despair. [105]

VI. 34

Leoni says of it, "Nothing Nostradamus could
have had in mind could have provided as neat an
explanation as the twentieth-century effect of bomb-
ings on any of [the] various states compelled to
surrender. Line 3 would go nicely with a 'fifth
column.'"[106] Cheetham says, "Rockets seem to be
described as machines of flying fire," literally
translating the French word *machination* (which
Leoni renders "device") as "machine."[107]

It is tempting to interpret this quatrain as
some form of attack by advanced weaponry and to
let it go at that. Yet, with all due respect, I must

again disagree with what I consider to be an over-
zealous reading into words and phrases of what is
simply neither there nor implied. It is my theory
that when the elements of the quatrain are sub-
jected to close examination, as usual, they mean
what they say.

Let us begin our analysis by defining the key
words in the quatrain. The word *trouble* is pivotal;
therefore we shall consider its meaning first as a
verb: to agitate mentally or spiritually, to worry, to
disturb, to afflict, to oppress. As a noun it can
mean a public unrest or disturbance, a state of distress, annoyance or difficulty with the law, physical distress or ill health, a condition of doing
something badly or with great difficulty.

The next key word whose interpretation we
need to feel gut sure about is *great chief.* There is
no other title or office that answers to the description of "great chief" as well as that of the president
of the United States, who is the commander in
chief of the armed forces of the most powerful
nation on earth.

The *great chief* is *besieged*—that is, he is
"surrounded (as a city) with armed forces for the
purpose of compelling surrender, hemmed in,
surrounded closely, pressed with requests, assailed
and beset."

There are two other key words. The first is
sedition, a word which has a variety of meanings,
including an insurrection against constituted
authority or a tumult caused by dissension. It can
also mean partisan hatred, or discontent and con-

duct consisting of speaking, writing, or acting against an established government, as well as resistance to lawful authority or conduct tending to treason but without an overt act.

The second is *profligate*, which means completely given up to dissipation and licentiousness, wildly extravagant, criminally excessive in spending or using and recklessly wasteful.

Finally, *despair* means utter loss of hope, complete domination of feelings of hopelessness, futility or defeat, wildly and bitterly expressed or quietly and passively dominant.

In piecing this together, let us first consider the individual components of this prediction. The first line, "the device [or machine] of flying fire" can, as we have already seen, easily be a description of a rocket or a rocket force. But line 2, "Will come to trouble the great besieged chief," does not actually describe destruction, fires, death, blood, or cries, or talk about battles or wars. Nor does it contain any other of the vivid images Nostradamus is particular about using to describe military actions.

What Nostradamus does say is that these rockets "will come to trouble," that is, agitate, worry, or disturb, "the great besieged chief"—a president who is under siege. It is my theory that this quatrain describes the pressures on the president of the United States due to the menacing nuclear rockets of the Soviets on the one hand and opposition to his stand on Star Wars on the other.

Star Wars is, of course, the media's name for

President Reagan's much maligned and misunderstood Strategic Defense Initiative—his three-year-old challenge to American scientists to make nuclear weapons "impotent and obsolete."

The program has two phases. The most commonly discussed is a space-based shield against nuclear weapons that would make use of a network of lasers, mirrors, and high-speed guns to shoot down incoming warheads. This would create, in the words of President Reagan, "a shield that could protect us just as a roof protects a family from rain."

Although estimates vary, such a program could probably not be ready for at least a decade. But while research and development on this program continues, we are also working on a less sophisticated anti-missile defense which primarily uses anti-missile missiles.

The Star Wars high-tech space-based defense system will be of extreme importance in the future. John Collins, a distinguished military strategist, believes that whoever dominates space will gain an overwhelmingly dominant military advantage that will last at least fifty years and possibly much longer. But in the short term, the installation of an anti-missile defense system could mean the difference between nuclear war and peace.

As I have already pointed out, the Soviet Union has, or is close to developing, a first-strike capability. As a result, our nuclear forces may no longer act as a deterrent. The Soviets could destroy such a high percentage of our ICBMs and bombers that we could no longer inflict "unacceptable danger" in return and we might be forced to capitulate after absorbing a first strike.

If, however, we had an anti-missile system that could destroy incoming warheads, then the Soviets could not be confident of destroying a large percentage of our missiles and bombers in a first-strike attack and it would restore the deterrent capability of our forces.

The Star Wars program tends to evoke strong feelings of those on either side of the issue. It is fair to say that, in general, the media has been giving the program a great deal of negative and misleading coverage. (I should say before I continue that I believe that some form of anti-missile defense is in our nation's best interest. I should also make clear that, despite my objections to the manner in which the issue has been characterized in the press, I believe that vigorous debate in a free press, on Star Wars and every other issue, is essential to a free society. Yet the American press as a whole does not always give equal time to opposing views, especially if these are the opinion of the minority.)

Nevertheless, it is clear that at the very least, the opponents of an anti-missile defense net have taken a position on Star Wars identical to that of the Soviet Union which has, and has had for more than a decade, its *own* Star Wars program. (The Soviets, it seems, think missile-defense systems are vital to *their* national security and are convinced they are vital to ours—which is why they oppose Star Wars so vigorously.)

If, indeed, the press and the opponents of Star Wars succeed in delaying or destroying the program *and* the Soviets use their nuclear missiles either to destroy our land-based ICBMs or force major political concessions (the decoupling of Western Europe from its partnership with the United States, for example), then future historians looking back upon "partisan hatred" against the program "consisting of speaking, writing, or acting against the established government" as "conduct tending to treason but without an overt act" will note how such actions, wittingly or not, gravely endangered this nation. Thus, in line 3 we read that "within [the nation itself] there will be such sedition" and, in line 4, "that the profligate ones will be in despair."

Profligate is derived from the Latin *profligare* meaning "to strike down, destroy, ruin," and it is similar in meaning to *prodigal*. Putting ourselves in Nostradamus' slippers and looking forward to the twentieth century, it is hard to think of any group of people other than Americans—considering patterns of dress, consumption, spending and so on—that could be called profligate. And it is not just on an individual level. The phrases "excessive in spending" and "recklessly wasteful" have been applied numerous times to the Congress.

"The profligate ones" are in despair because they have lost their estate, squandered their resources, and now recognize (at least subconsciously) the oncoming danger.

One notable feature of modern American life is that a large segment of society has been seized by a paralyzing sense of despair and hopelessness which leads them to believe that all efforts to deter or avoid the consequences of a nuclear attack—from civil defense to a missile defense—are futile.

The president is therefore being hampered by those who think that Star Wars will never work because of their subconscious despair (outpictured in the street people whose lack of motivation is a surfacing of what is not admitted by the rest of us, or which comes out in others as the escape through cocaine, the infernal sound of rock, and sex as the all-American pastime).

And thus Reagan is in big trouble because, though he has Saint Germain's ace in the hole, he can't play his card in this poker game with the Soviets because Congress won't give him the ante!—before the ETA, the "estimated time of attack."

Finally, in matters of sedition related to this quatrain, we have spies to consider. The Walker family, perhaps the most stunning of the recently exposed spy rings, was a case of "sedition" and "profligacy." Unlike cold-war-era spies such as Kim Philby, who became politically disaffected and switched loyalties, John A Walker Jr., the head of the ring, was a staunch Reagan supporter who was willing to sell out his country for cash. "John Walker," reported *Newsweek*, "seems all too typical of today's fifth columnists: it was the money that mattered. His style and self-image were apparently too expansive." [108]

It is also possible, and perhaps even more to the point of the lance, that the quatrain describes the current furor over the Reagan Administration's sale of weapons to Iran. As of this writing (December 1986) events are still unfolding. But so far, I don't know of any other situation in the history of the twentieth century that fits this quatrain as well.

President Reagan is "besieged" as never before. Indeed, this affair marks a new era in his previously "teflon" presidency. One could argue that there have been other besieged presidents in this century. But with the exception of Franklin Roosevelt, none were "great"—they lacked the popularity and the stature of this president.

And Roosevelt was never really besieged. Nor was he troubled by "machines of flying fire," which are a major feature of our time—and which the United States recently sold to Iran (including anti-tank TOW missiles and parts for Hawk anti-aircraft missiles and Phoenix air-to-air missiles) in the notorious "arms for the Ayatollah, cash for the contras deal."

Note, then, that the definition of *besieged*, as in "great besieged chief," precisely fits the situation in which Ronald Reagan at the end of his sixth year in office is faced with. He's "surrounded (as a city) with armed forces [of the media and the Congress] for the purpose of compelling [his] surrender" of information, which if fully known to the enemy could endanger the security of the nation, the hostages and the balance of power in the Middle East and already has. He is also "surrounded [watched] closely," as an alternate definition reads, "pressed with requests [to tell all], assailed and beset [with the fears and doubts of the people as to his credibility]."

Now let us raise again the interesting question of sedition. Was there any? The coverage of "the Iran Initiative" is such that it seems like many in the media (and Congress for that matter) have already reached a verdict: guilty as charged—or worse. In many quarters, Lt. Col. Oliver North and former National Security Council Advisor, Vice Adm. John Poindexter, are suspected of having broken a number of laws. Time will tell whether or not they did.

But this quatrain talks about sedition—not breaking laws. From what we now know, the Iran Initiative involves two of the most geopolitically important areas in the world: Latin America and the Middle East.

Iran is the hub of the geopolitical hub of the world, the Middle East. It is in our national interest to prevent a politically volatile Iran from disintegrating toward anarchy and then, in a vulnerable state, being drawn into the Soviet orbit—or from being invaded by the Soviets.

A Soviet-controlled Iran would radically alter the balance of power in the Middle East and jeopardize Western access to oil and eventually increase the potential for war. It is also in our interest to strengthen moderate factions and support democratic institutions in Iran, both to stand as a barrier against Soviet takeover and to add stability to the region.

It is important to remember that geopolitical maneuvering between the superpowers forms the backdrop of the transfer of funds to the contras. In all that has been said about this attempt to circumvent the Congress, the media has been strangely silent about *why* it happened—Congress' refusal to give the contras the money they need to defeat the Sandinistas—and about the seriousness of the Soviet penetration of this hemisphere through Nicaragua.

In effect, the Soviets are trying to lay a geopolitical trap for the United States. The United States requires peace and stability in Latin America in order to project power into Europe, the Middle East and the Pacific. The more the Soviets can raise the tempo of Marxist revolution south of our border, the more they can force us to turn our attention to our own hemisphere, giving them greater freedom to adventure throughout the world. And if we should fail to address the growing challenge in Latin America, revolution will one day spill over onto a highly unstable Mexico, and then onto American soil—and then Red Dawn will come to pass.

The United States is in a no-win situation *unless* we swiftly put an end to Soviet penetration of this hemisphere. We could send in U.S. forces—something few people (except Zbigniew Brzezinski) want to do. Or we could help the contras oust the totalitarian government in Managua. (Brzezinski argues that it is bad policy to pay others to do the job we should do ourselves—whether they be Cuban freedom fighters or contras or anyone else. If our objectives are important enough, we should send in U.S. troops rather than risk another Bay of Pigs, he says.)

This administration and the Congress seem content to send the contras money. But not very much. Last year Congress sent $100 million to the contras. In roughly the same period of time, the Soviets sent more than $1 billion of military and economic aid to the Sandinistas.

Clearly U.S. interests are not being served with our current level of funding. And that, no doubt, was what prompted Oliver North (if indeed he did so) to send $30 million to the contras.

As far as I can tell, the Reagan administration had the long-term geostrategic interests of the nation in mind when it undertook the Iran Initiative. Since the Iran Initiative was taken in order to enhance our security, the actions of Vice Adm. Poindexter and Lt. Col. North can hardly be called seditious.

But if, as a result of the media's handling of the affair, Iran or the rest of Latin America slips into the Soviet camp, it is then by Nostradamus' hindsight, which I am willing to believe is as good as was his foresight, that it will be written in the quatrains of American history that the press who "pressed in," i.e., besieged the president and his staff and the NSC, committed acts of sedition.

"The profligate ones" (big-spending liberals) who normally oppose aid to the contras were "in despair" when they heard that the contras had received an extra $30 million. Their solution to the problem of Soviet advisors and matériel in Nicaragua is dialogue, economic assistance to the middle class and peasants and other social programs which admittedly should have been tended to decades ago.

But now that the hammer and sickle are in the air and on the land, the right tools to counteract the specific breakdown of society in Nicaragua, Soviet-takeover style, better be used now and fast. There is simply no time to lose. Saint Germain himself has said there will be war on American soil if this thing is not stopped right now. In fact, when the whole truth is known it will be seen, lawbreakers or no, that certain parties were acting in the highest interests of Uncle Sam and the survival of the flame of freedom in this hemisphere.

In the context of our discussion, the next quatrain can be taken as a broad description of a protracted East-West military struggle with the fortunes of war swinging back and forth:

> Twice high twice lowered,
> The East also the West will weaken:
> Its adversary after several struggles,
> Routed by sea will fail in the pinch.[109]
>
> VIII.59

Leoni doesn't have much to say about this quatrain that relates to current affairs. Cheetham, on the other hand, says "this [quatrain] seems again to describe the geopolitical state of the twentieth century better than any other. From this quatrain it appears that Asia will make two violent attacks upon the Western powers which will affect them somewhat. But finally the East will lose at sea."[110]

In a later work, Cheetham offers a similar interpretation. "Here we have two major powers at war with each other, and then allied against a third adversary. This will be preceded by world famine," which, she points out, will be hard to use as a "dating factor." She goes on to say that "when the two powers join in the alliance, it is but short lived. Victory lies in the West."[111]

Noorbergen's thinking runs along similar lines, at least when it comes to the victor, but is colored by his theory that a Chinese-Arab force will attack the U.S. and U.S.S.R. "As in centuries past," he says, "when the Mongols and Muslims threatened Western civilizations and were defeated, so the same powers of the East will fail again after a second bid for world domination. But, this time, their defeat will first come by sea."[112]

I think the quatrain deals with the East-West struggle as it is currently framed—conflict between the United States and the Soviet Union—and makes two remarkable observations. First, it describes a long-term struggle. That is a radical departure from the idea which has such a powerful grip on minds in the West that the next world, and presumably nuclear, war will be over in a matter of hours. Many people believe that if one side pushes the buttons, the other side will return the favor and within a half an hour the war will be over.

Those who espouse this point of view usually assume that in the next war there will be no winners, only losers. The living will envy the dead and, although it is speculative what it will be like the day after, the various scenarios, like nuclear winter, are rather bleak. In sum, in one nasty, short, brutish series of nuclear blasts, civilization as we know it will be destroyed.

But that is not how Nostradamus nor the Soviet planners see it.

Following World War II, the Soviet military did an in-depth study and concluded that the next world war would be a protracted struggle, fought in the air and on land and sea in virtually all possible theaters, using not just nuclear but all types of weapons.

Naturally they concluded that the two most likely combatants would be the Soviet Union and its allies fighting the United States and its allies— the East and the West. But when it came to picking the winner, they came to a surprising conclusion. Unlike their brash public statements, their studied analysis led them to believe that the outcome of such a war was uncertain, *but* the side which was better prepared had a better chance of winning.

Accordingly, the Soviets have done everything within their power to prepare for the coming appointment with the future. In the 1970s they undertook the largest peacetime military build-up in history. Their nuclear forces, while numerically not as large as those of the United States, have a devastating throw weight (explosive power) and, as such, give them or soon will give them an authentic first-strike capability. Their conventional forces are numerically superior to those of the West and, in many cases, their equipment is more battle worthy. And they have a massive civilian defense program.

It has taken the lion's share of their resources to do this. In effect, they have subordinated every part of their national life in order to support their military effort. But if they get into a long-term struggle, they are psychologically and physically ready.

The second factor to consider in this quatrain is Nostradamus' attention to sea battles. In terms of classical geostrategy, the Soviet Union is a land power dominating the "world island" of the Eurasian land mass. The United States, by contrast, is a maritime power situated on an "off-shore island" which uses the oceans to tie itself to its political, economic, and cultural partners located on the "rimlands" of the world island.

Not surprisingly, the landlocked Soviets' military strengths are land-oriented and the United States has the world's most powerful navy. But to some degree, circumstances have compelled both sides to imitate the other's pattern of military development. The United States keeps a large standing army in Western Europe in order to serve as a barrier to the westward expansion of the Soviet armies. The Soviets have built a powerful navy in order to challenge the United States at sea.

In war, America must use her navies to project power to distant theaters of action and resupply our men. As it now stands, the Soviets cannot expect to win an outright victory at sea.

But they do not need to. If their fleets can simply delay or hinder the ability of the United States Navy to resupply men and equipment, they can win key land battles and thereby make United States' naval superiority strategically useless.

Thus, in this quatrain, we see the changing fortunes of war. The Soviets, twice in a superior position, are twice put down by the U.S. and allies who are likewise weakened by the protracted battle. But after several struggles the adversary, routed by forces at sea, will fail in the pinch of a narrow canal- or straitlike waterway.

This is the prophecy of the victory of the forces of The Word of God, the Faithful and True and his armies in heaven who intercede to deliver Joseph, the seed of Christ in the earth:

> And I saw when the Lamb opened one of the seals, and I heard, as it were the noise of thunder, one of the four beasts saying, Come and see.
>
> And I saw, and behold a white horse: and he that sat on him had a bow; and a crown was given unto him: and he went forth conquering, and to conquer.   (Revelation 6:1, 2)

CHAPTER II

Soviet Invasion of Europe: Karma of the Great Brothers

A long the lines we have previously discussed, there are a number of other quatrains that seem to describe a Soviet invasion of Europe.

> From beyond the Black Sea and great Tartary,
> There will be a King who will come to see Gaul,
> He will pierce through "Alania" and Armenia,
> And within Byzantium will he leave his bloody rod. [113]   V. 54

Leoni tells us "the name of Tartary was given loosely to the whole of Central Asia, from the Caspian to China. From this area came the Huns of Attila, Genghiz Khan, Tamerlane and the Turks. It is to produce another conqueror, who will be headed for France." [114]

Cheetham's thinking follows similar paths. "Cryptic as always," she writes, "this quatrain is certain that the man will come from beyond Tartary, Russia. The Alanians, in the division of Tartary, which roughly covered the whole of Central Asia, were situated to the north of the Caucasus and the

Armenians to the south. Nostradamus presumably sees the 'king,' or conqueror, passing through Persia down to the Balkans. Beyond Tartary, there remains only Asia....Perhaps the rod is a weapon of some sort rather than the actual wielding of power?"[115]

Leoni and Cheetham both see a conqueror from Asia but do not seem to consider the possibility that he may be a Soviet conqueror. Nevertheless, the territory north of the Black Sea is part of the Soviet Union. It has a heavy concentration of intermediate range missile bases and military airfields making it a likely place from which to launch an attack on Europe.

"Great Tartary" could easily be a reference to either Soviet Siberia, once a domain of the Tartars, or an area of the Soviet Union around the Kama River valley. If it is the former, it may refer to the soldiers in the Soviet army, which is increasingly manned by Asians. If it refers to the area around the Kama Valley, it could be a reference to both the soldiers and the equipment used by the Soviet army. The gigantic Kama truck factory produces, among other things, heavy trucks for warfare.

The "King," as Cheetham implies, may simply be Nostradamus' shorthand for a leader. But in her farsightedness she overlooks the most visible and the most powerful leader of the East: the General Secretary of the Communist Party, who since Josef Stalin has assumed regal, if not imperial, powers. Yet this office has been consistently filled by such ruthless ironfisted, kid-gloved Asiatic dictators as he.

I believe this quatrain describes an invasion force of Communist hordes mounted in and around the area north of the Black Sea and then funneled through the traditional invasion routes of Europe. It could also indicate a missile attack on France or other parts of Europe that precedes or is an integral part of an offensive.

The devastation described in the following quatrain sounds like the aftermath of nuclear war:

> The populous places will be uninhabitable:
> Great discord to obtain fields:
> Realms delivered to prudent incapable ones:
> Then for the great brothers dissension and
> death. [116]   II.95

Leoni has nothing to say about this quatrain. But Cheetham thinks "the first line would be yet another description of the third war [Nostradamus] believes will devastate this century." [117]

Noorbergen says of this quatrain, "the nuclear bombardment and radiation, affecting both Russia and the United States, will force entire cities to be evacuated. Food, otherwise so abundant, will suddenly become in short supply, probably because of radiation and germ warfare. Governments at both local and national levels will be unable to meet the crisis and chaos and death will be the order of the day." [118]

Noorbergen, of course, has the U.S. and U.S.S.R. being attacked by the "Eastern Alliance" rather than fighting each other. But this quatrain does not seem to focus on armed conflict between the United States and the Soviet Union.

A clue to where the conflict takes place emerges from the identity of the mysterious "brothers."

Just who are they? Cheetham says they might be the Kennedy brothers, which Stewart Robb says cannot possibly be true.[119] There have been many other famous brothers in history—the Gracchi brothers, the Dulles brothers, the Wright brothers—even the Smith brothers. None are so famous, however, as Joseph and the other eleven sons of Jacob, son of Isaac, son of Abraham.

Joseph, as you remember, was the next to the last son of Jacob. It is recorded in Genesis that "Israel [Jacob] loved Joseph more than all his children...and he made him a coat of many colors. And when his brethren saw that their father loved him more than all his brethren, they hated him, and could not speak peaceably unto him."

Joseph's brothers, jealous of his dreams and coat of many colors, conspired to kill him. Reuben, the eldest brother, persuaded the others not to put him to death. However, at the urging of Judah, they sold Joseph into slavery.

I believe that the brothers of Joseph (and the tribes that came from them) have reincarnated in Europe. The nations of Europe have always been contentious and because of their dissension and lack of unity, not only did they reject the master plan of the Count Saint Germain to form a United States of Europe before Robespierre's reign of terror descended in the French Revolution, but also—and as a result of their failure since the fall of the Roman Empire to establish the spiritual unity and destiny of their birthright—they have been unable to mount a credible defense against the forces of the Warsaw Pact and now face death via a Soviet invasion.

The shields and crests of the twelve sons of Jacob link their tribes with a specific nation or area of Europe. These emblems derive from the final blessing Jacob gave his sons.

According to W. H. Bennett, author of *Symbols of Our Celto-Saxon Heritage*, the heraldic emblems of a number of European nations, including Britain, Ireland, and Denmark, are *"identical with those of ancient Israel."* So are the emblems of numerous European countries, municipalities, and families.

Thus, Bennett and his student E. Raymond Capt conclude "that the people known today as 'Celto-Saxons' [Europeans] are literal descendants of the Israel people, whose early history is recorded in the Bible."[120]

I believe that the tribe of Reuben has reincarnated in Russia. Reuben's psychology is worthy of note. While I believe he will be utterly ruthless towards his European brothers, his attitude towards Joseph (the United States) is different.

Reuben, you will recall, is loathe to kill Joseph. This is not because he loves Joseph. Reuben loves neither God nor Joseph. In fact, he is especially jealous of Joseph since Joseph is the favorite son and his fear that his rights of primogeniture may be threatened by Joseph and Judah as well is not unwarranted. Reuben is aware of the Divine Hand resting upon Joseph and he fears the consequences of actually killing him. So he devises ways and means to kill him and keep him alive at the same time.

This psychology has been carried over into modern times. Karl Marx, whose philosophy became the new religion of Reuben reincarnated, was not an atheist or an agnostic. He believed in God but hated Him, feared Him—and sought revenge. "I wish to avenge myself against the one who rules above," wrote Marx in "The Pale Maiden," a poem in which the maiden becomes a vehicle of expression for Marx's philosophy. "Heaven I've forfeited," says the maiden, bemoaning her fate, "I know it full well. My soul, once true to God, is chosen for hell."[121]

The entire Soviet psychology of revenge— not only by the rebellious Reubenites but by the Nephilim gods (i.e., fallen angels) who have duped them in their own deceptions—against the great brothers can be understood in these words from I Chronicles:

> Now the sons of Reuben the firstborn of Israel (for he was the firstborn; but, forasmuch as he defiled his father's bed, his birthright was given unto the sons of Joseph the son of Israel: and the genealogy is not to be reckoned after the birthright.

> For Judah prevailed above his brethren,
> and of him came the chief ruler; but the
> birthright was Joseph's). (I Chronicles 5:1, 2)

This will explain Reuben's jealousy of and
persecution of Jews, for the descendants of Judah
who have risen to positions of leadership in many
fields and nations are descended both by lineage
and reincarnation as the true Jews of today.

In Jacob's dying blessing to his twelve sons he
had this to say of Reuben:

> Reuben, thou art my firstborn, my
> might, and the beginning of my strength,
> the excellency of dignity, and the excellency
> of power:
> Unstable as water, thou shalt not excel;
> because thou wentest up to thy father's bed
> [Reuben went and lay with Bilhah, his
> father's concubine]; then defiledst thou it:
> he went up to my couch. (Genesis 49:3, 4)

Now, many Jews have migrated into and out
of Russia, for the kinship and intermarriage of the
sons of Reuben and Judah lies in the fact that they
are Jacob's sons by Leah, and that they did once
conspire together against Joseph.

Jacob's prophecy concerning Judah is fulfilled
in the Jews of America, not Israel:

> Judah, thou art he whom thy brethren
> shall praise: thy hand shall be in the neck of
> thine enemies; thy father's children shall
> bow down before thee.

Judah is a lion's whelp: from the prey, my son, thou art gone up: he stooped down, he couched as a lion, and as an old lion; who shall rouse him up?

The sceptre shall not depart from Judah, nor a lawgiver from between his feet, until Shiloh come; and unto him shall the gathering of the people be.

Binding his foal unto the vine and his ass's colt unto the choice vine; he washed his garments in wine, and his clothes in the blood of grapes:

His eyes shall be red with wine, and his teeth white with milk. (Genesis 49:8–12)

And the blessing of Joseph and his descendants is upon the Christians of the United States, Great Britain and their seed among the English-speaking nations where also some of the Judahites have migrated.

Joseph is a fruitful bough, even a fruitful bough by a well; whose branches run over the wall:

The archers have sorely grieved him, and shot at him, and hated him:

But his bow abode in strength, and the arms of his hands were made strong by the hands of the mighty God of Jacob (from thence is the shepherd, the stone of Israel):

Even by the God of thy father, who shall help thee; and by the Almighty, who shall bless thee with blessings of heaven above, blessings of the deep that lieth under, blessings of the breasts, and of the womb:

The blessings of thy father have prevailed above the blessings of my progenitors unto the utmost bound of the everlasting hills: they shall be on the head of Joseph, and on the crown of the head of him that was separate from his brethren. (Genesis 49:22–26)

And the ten tribes settled in Europe and to this day these may be known by the remaining blessings found in Genesis 49.

Thus Joseph, who has the birthright of the Christic seed, and Judah, the chief ruler, joined as the Northern and Southern kingdoms of Israel and Judah, form the nucleus of the Western alliance. These brothers have one common enemy: The disinherited Reuben.

Yet because the other brothers who were with Reuben sold Joseph into slavery, these, the reincarnated Europeans, have not and do not consistently take their stand with America in East-West conflicts. What's more, many Europeans are gone after the Soviet-backed peace movements, whose goal is to completely disarm Europe as Reuben mounts for his coming war of conquest by land forces and a surprise nuclear attack.

But Joseph's sons in Britain led by a daughter of Zion have stood by the United States when all the other brothers betrayed her and them.

These ungrateful do not remember that it was

Joseph who fed them in Egypt through five years of famine and who again rescued them during World War II for seven years. The tremendous support by the American people of Europe's defense through NATO with no financial responsibility to speak of on the part of the Western Europeans, moreover their continued condemnation and resentment of America and Americans, goes back to this jealousy of the favorite son who has the birthright, not by primogeniture, but by his spiritual attainment of the Christic light within his heart.

Joseph, of the womb of Rachel, is the highest spiritual offspring of Jacob. His blessing is extended to his sons Ephraim (America) and Manasseh (the British Isles) and to their descendants as they qualify themselves as Lightbearers. Through them to the English-speaking peoples the transfusion of the fire of the heart from the Ancient of Days, as Jacob's blessing, i.e., initiation, is given.

Though America has good intentions in defending Europe despite the ingratitude, let it be known that circumstances of European karma will be such that in time of Soviet invasion—if the Lightbearers do not intercede to prevent this denouement—Europe will be left to stand on her own.

Her believing of the Soviet Big Lie, her non-preparation but feast of materialism since World War II, her absence of a real heart tie to America and Britain (Ephraim and Manasseh with Judahites) due to ages-old enmity—"You can't lord it over us, we're just as good as you are, in fact better; you are not our superior, you must meet us as co-equals"—is a defiance to this day and a non-acceptance of their father Jacob's greater initiation to Joseph and Judah.

And this railing and divisiveness and even rivalry and bitterness amongst themselves will cost them the continent—if the worst-case scenario of Nostradamus' prophecies of karma come to pass because the Europeans failed to rally around Saint Germain and his gift of the violet flame.

Another aspect that must be dealt with is the remaining hard feelings between Judah and Joseph based on Judah's desire to kill Joseph. Oddly enough, it was Reuben who spared him and Joseph has been paying him back ever since—in the twenti-eth century by literally building him an empire with technology, grain, money, and anything he wants. "Joseph, the debt is paid! Now reckon with your disinherited brother's true motives and pre-pare to put him in his place."

In Americans the hatred of Christians by Jews and the ostracizing and persecution of Jews by Christians has been a most unfortunate part of the reuniting of the seed of the great brothers in the true Judeo-Christian tradition. Let all of this be cast into the violet flame, for this is the dawn of the Aquarian age. And Saint Germain is the spiritual father and guru of us all. Let all brothers of this Divine Union of sovereign states embrace and cast this hatred into the all-consuming fire of

God, the one God of Israel who is the I AM
Presence with us still, and let us, out of the one
Christ flame in all our hearts, forge a Oneness that
is invincible in facing the oncoming trials.

Here I would like to say, by way of reminding
and reinforcing in all readers, that the handwriting on the wall of the karma of the nations of
Israel and Judah and of mankind need not come to
pass if the Lightbearers, the ensign of the people,
come out from among them and prepare as a remnant to survive psychologically, spiritually, mili-
tarily, economically and physically.

All prophecy is given so that the sons of God
can act in time to turn back the oncoming tide of
world karma and world events. Saint Germain's
teachings on what to do to prevent the fulfillment
of Nostradamus' and other prophecies, both the
scriptural and those delivered at Fátima, is presented in Books Three and Four as well as in the
Lost Teachings of Jesus and the entire body of
Truth set forth for this age by the Ascended Masters and published by The Summit Lighthouse in
conjunction with Summit University Press and
Church Universal and Triumphant.

There is yet time to defeat the forces of Darkness that have separated brother from brother. But
know this, O people, the behavior of the Soviet
Union led by fallen angels since the Bolshevik
Revolution and their murder in cold blood of
millions of the seed of Light both within and

without their borders is the karma of the sons of
Reuben who, for loss of the birthright of the
Christ flame, will not stop until they have taken
their ultimate revenge against the seed of Joseph
and Judah—their warring against the rest of the
ten tribes being a means to an end.

The strategies of the Soviet leadership, most
of whom are not Reubenites but fallen angels, are
summed up in Marx's own words: "I wish to
avenge myself against the one who rules above.
Heaven I've forfeited. I know it full well. My soul
once true to God is chosen for hell."

This we see in certain Russians, the ilk of the
political and military machines, proud party loy-
alists and the inhuman KGB and diabolical GRU.
But great numbers of children of the Light are also
trapped in their system even as the government of
the United States is sprinkled with fallen ones.
The subject of the International Capitalist/Com-
munist Conspiracy—of the alignment of an East-
West power elite of fallen ones who have no
loyalty to God or his people—is well developed in
my discussions on the topic.

Let us not consider the above analysis of the
brothers either definitive or black and white, for
there are the good and the evil, as the tares and the
wheat, sown in every society, tribe, race and nation.

So complex a subject touched on so briefly in
this volume does not receive due justice, nor do
my readers. But it can be studied in depth through

tapes and books. Further investigation of our writings by those who desire to know the facts and the larger Truth will reward the objective seeker.

Today the officially atheistic Soviet Union carries on the battle against God. And though they deny His existence, their continued efforts to persecute the religious, and to control and destroy religion, show that they take His reality very seriously.

The Soviets also carry over Reuben's caution in dealing with Joseph to their relations with the United States. Since World War II, they have been hesitant to directly attack U.S. citizens. There have been notable exceptions, of course—the destruction of KAL 007 for one. Henry "Scoop" Jackson for another. But, all things considered, such instances are few in number. Reuben is still worried about Divine Retribution. This is why he uses psychics and psychotronic warfare, including microwaves on the U.S. Embassy in Moscow, to make his death machine less transparent—to kill, yet not kill.

Nor does his fear/hate relationship with God mean he will not be warlike. On the contrary, that is Reuben's nature. It does mean that he prefers a crippling first strike against U.S. military targets over the destruction of the U.S. population. He would rather see Joseph in slavery than dead.

For Reuben would like to possess him and either coerce or entice Joseph and Judah to restore his spiritual as well as physical birthright (both transmitted through the genetic code) so that he may finally be not merely equal but greater than the two great brothers.

While the fear of God restrains Reuben from annihilating Joseph, Europe is not as fortunate and, according to Nostradamus, they face dissension and death. Furthermore, the phrase "great discord to obtain fields" indicates, as Noorbergen pointed out, that food "will suddenly become in short supply." He attributes this period of hunger or famine to "radiation and germ warfare."[122] And that is a possibility.

But it could also come from a deliberately engineered food shortage. The Soviets have a track record of using famine to break the political resistance of foes within or without their borders. In 1932, Stalin embarked upon a campaign to break the power of the Ukrainians, a 'peculiar people', to use a Biblical term descriptive of the children of the Light, whose nationalistic yearnings he feared and despised. As a result, he engineered the genocidal famine of 1932-1933, which killed 7 million people, 6 million of them Ukrainians.

These children of Israel (the new name given to Jacob, who passed on the spiritual genes of Abraham) are always hated by the reincarnated Assyrians—that class of Nephilim gods, i.e., fallen angels, who have figured as the twentieth-century practitioners of genocide, such as Stalin, Hitler and many others of the seed of the Herods who are still around today.

As I mentioned earlier, the Soviet army is

doing precisely the same thing today in Afghanistan by making a deliberate effort to starve the mujahidin and the Afghan people who are supporting them. This does not bode well for Western Europe.

Reuben has a second problem. No matter what he does, he is jealous of Joseph's favor with Jacob. This inferiority complex carries over to the twentieth century. The Soviet Union is continually trying to show it has arrived as a superpower and that it is every bit as good as Joseph, or better—something it never quite believes itself. And for good reason. The Soviet Union is simply way behind the United States economically, socially, technically, culturally—in fact, in virtually every field except the military.

There are other quatrains which seem to relate to a Soviet invasion of Europe in the foreseeable future. Since we have already discussed a number of these which point to this conclusion and we have established the plausibility of such an attack through an overview of the world we live in, I shall move on to other subjects.

CHAPTER 12

Quatrains of Famine, Pestilence, and Scourges

B efore we leave the subject of warfare, let us look at one quatrain that may describe a bacteriological warfare attack:

> Very great famine by pestiferous wave,
> By long rain the length of the Arctic pole:
> Samarobryn hundred leagues from the
>   hemisphere,
> They will live without law exempt from politics. [123]
>
> VI. 5

The key word in this quatrain is *pestiferous*, which means "carrying or propagating infectious disease" or "infected with a pestilential disease."

Accordingly, the first two lines of the quatrain describe a "very great famine" caused by a wave carrying a deadly disease which seems to traverse the Arctic pole. It obviously reaches a populated area (how else could it cause a great famine?) and suggests to Leoni "a hint of bacteriological warfare."[124] Cheetham says, "the rain is probably some type of atomic or nuclear contamination."[125] But of even greater interest is the mysterious term *samarobryn*.

Leoni suggests that the enigmatic *samarobryn* in line three may refer to a satellite. "Of all the prophecies of Nostradamus," he observes, "there is probably none more completely inapplicable to his own period, or to the whole four centuries to the 1960's, than this one. Suddenly, it has an excellent chance of a very impressive fulfillment.

"A league was generally about 2.5 miles, sometimes as much as 4.5 miles.... Nostradamus' league equals 2.7 miles. Now, there is only one way one can get 270 miles from the hemisphere, and that is upwards into space. And note that there is real meaning to 'hemisphere,' since anyone a certain distance away from merely the 'earth' on one side would be many times that distance away from the other side of the earth at any given moment.

"Since we can eliminate any thought of the whole city of Amiens in France being 270 miles out in space, we are entitled to be imaginative in suggesting to whom or to what the word *Samarobryn* might apply. Supposing that we give Nostradamus the benefit of the doubt for an occasional genuine and correct burst of clairvoyance, might we not here have a prophecy of a space-station thought by Nostradamus, rightly or wrongly, to be about 270 miles from the earthly hemisphere? And might we not consider that in the course of this vision Nostradamus overheard a name associated with this pioneer venture into space, a name such as Sam R. O'Brien, the sound of which, as it struck his French ear, he transcribed as 'Samarobryn'?"[126]

Cheetham arrived at a similar, although not identical, conclusion. "This quatrain," she says, "makes me slightly worried. In Cyrillic Russian the word Samorobin is derived from two words— Samo, self, and Robin, operator. This does imply an unmanned satellite. Modern Soviet aircraft are known as Samoylot, which means self-flying in Russian."[127]

Robb takes the word to stand for "Sam Rayburn," the U.S.S. Sam Rayburn, that is—a missile-carrying submarine. "Leoni thought to place his *Sam* in a space-station about 270 miles above the hemisphere," says Robb. "This would be perfect if our government were to dub a space-station with that same name of Rayburn—which is not beyond possibility.

"But, might we not have, instead of a 270 mile up space-station, a submarine capable of shooting a nuclear-powered missile with a trajectory apogee of 270 miles? 'They will live without law, exempt from politics' could apply to men biding their time in the *U.S.S. Sam Rayburn*....

"Now what about line three of the quatrain: 'a hundred leagues from the hemisphere'? It may be that instead of Nostradamus having predicted a space-station 270 miles or so above the hemisphere he may have intended instead a submarine station from which is shot a missile with a trajectory of 270 miles or so from the hemisphere."

"To check, I phoned Rockwell International, in Fullerton," says Robb, "and learned indeed from a good authority that though 270 miles is rather high, the missile could indeed push that far up and no doubt sometimes would."[128]

My guess is that the 270 miles refers to the distance from a point in the Northern Hemisphere to a point in the Northern Atlantic.

We interpret that famine and dread disease are at hand and that they prevail a distance comparable to a certain measurement of the Arctic pole and that those affected by the conditions resulting from events surrounding either a satellite sub or space-station will be beyond the pale of law due to geographical isolation or a period of anarchy. Nothing more specific or revelatory comes to me at this time.

Now let us briefly examine two quatrains which seem to describe fallout and/or famine and plague. The following quatrain strikes Stewart Robb as describing "a possible aftermath to atomic fallout."

The great famine that I sense approaching,
Often turning, then to be universal,
So great and long that one will tear
The root from the wood and the child from
    the breast.[129]   I.67

In this one we see a period of peace followed by a period of war:

The scourges passed the world shrinks,
For a long time peace and populated lands:

One will travel safely by air, land, sea and
    wave,
Then the wars stirred up anew.[130]   I.63

Leoni says that "since this prophecy includes
travel by air amongst the blessings of postwar
peace, its application would seem limited to the
twentieth century."[131] But the key to interpreting
this quatrain is the French word *fléaux*, meaning
"scourges" ("a whip that is used to inflict pain or
punishment," "a cause of widespread affliction,"
i.e., karma). But the word also means "plagues"
which can be defined as "an epidemic disease
causing a high rate of mortality" but whose first
sense is "a disastrous evil or affliction." This
plague may also be a term applied to war.

In either case, just exactly when the plague
occurs can help us determine when the predicted
war will occur.

Cheetham thinks the plague is somehow related to World War II. "The most interesting aspect
of this quatrain," she says, "is the manner in which
Nostradamus grasps the very twentieth-century
concept that air travel makes the whole world
accessible—it 'becomes smaller.' It is worth noting
that the so-called era of world peace since 1945 is
the longest unbroken one this century. But it is
soon to be broken if we are to believe Nostradamus.
The extinguished pestilence may refer to disease or
the after-effects of the Second World War."[132]

Cheetham is not sure "whether the age of

pestilence refers to disease or war" but says, "We are told that war will break [out] again after a long interlude of peace. This may be the third Great War of this century, which Nostradamus prophecies to follow the Hitler wars."[133]

Cheetham may be right. If that is the case, then "the wars stirred up anew" may indicate the coming war we have been discussing. But it is not apparent what plague they associate with the close of World War II.

To me the scourges are the two World Wars, followed by the period of the "long time [of] peace." But the term "peace" must be qualified. While we haven't had a major global conflict, the last forty years have been pockmarked with wars.

If, however, we accept that Nostradamus is principally the prophet of the twelve tribes who predicts their returning karma as the messenger of Samuel, who also comments on world karma as the backdrop of their doings, then we see that despite the fierce wars in Korea, Vietnam, Cambodia, and the Middle East, African infighting and independence movements, and takeovers of non-European, non-English-speaking nations between 1945 and 1987, this was a period of peace among the "great brothers."

CHAPTER 13

Earthquakes! Earthquakes! Earthquakes! Woe! Woe! Woe!

Nostradamus predicted two earthquakes which seemed applicable to our time. These quatrains, which may be related, are:

Volcanic fire from the center of the earth
Will cause trembling around the new city:
Two great rocks will make war for a long time.
Then Arethusa will redden a new river.
I.87

Garden of the world near the new city,
In the path of the hollow mountains:
It will be seized and plunged into the Tub,
Forced to drink waters poisoned by sulfur.[134]
X.49

Like the quatrains describing a nuclear attack on "the great new city" we previously discussed, the identity of the "new city" in these quatrains is of great importance. Cheetham and Noorbergen think the "new city" is New York City. Leoni, by contrast, says (discussing I.87),"it is fairly certain that Nostradamus is here predicting an eruption of Vesuvius, and [an] earthquake around Naples. Vesuvius is twelve miles from Naples." He is familiar with the theory that the "new city" is New York and mentions that "Boswell . . . finds that it is New York that will be destroyed by this earthquake."

Leoni believes this quatrain is probably related to X.49, which he says is also "predicting a new eruption of Vesuvius, about fifteen miles from the most famous of 'new cities,' Naples (*Neapolis*, new city). 'Garden of the world' refers to the lava-enriched, fertile Campanian plain between Naples and Vesuvius."[135]

When I read these quatrains in connection with New York City, which in the Apocalypse of John is Babylon the Great, I can only think of the seventh angel, the alchemist who is Zadkiel, who pours out the seventh vial that brings on the chemicalization described:

> And there were voices, and thunders, and lightnings; and there was a great earthquake, such as was not since men were upon the earth, so mighty an earthquake, and so great.
> And the great city was divided into three parts, and the cities of the nations fell: and great Babylon came in remembrance before God, to give unto her the cup of the wine of the fierceness of his wrath.   (Rev. 16:18, 19)

This cup may be the poisoned waters of her polluted consciousness—a karmic return through Nature's all-chemistry.

A cycle of earthquakes that has not yet fulfilled itself was triggered by Helios in a dictation given through my late husband and teacher Mark L. Prophet November 19, 1972, when the God of the Sun prophesied the Nicaraguan earthquake that took place thirty-four days later. He pronounced:

I will bring a great earthquake to pass upon this world. And the world shall find, with the presence of this earthquake, that I the LORD God liveth! And behold, it shall come to pass that many shall perish; for they have not heard my word.

Behold, the wickedness of mankind today is as the wickedness of Sodoma and Gomorrah; and behold, I shall shake the pillars of the earth. And surely, saith the LORD, an earthquake shall come, and no man shall be able to stop it or to stay it!

For behold, my wrath is kindled against mankind's continual involvement in human discord and inharmony and their failure to acknowledge the power of God which is in the heavens above and also upon the earth beneath and in the waters and underneath the earth.

Behold, I AM the LORD thy God; and surely this thing shall be. And it shall be in My season and in My time as I shall direct it. And it shall be as a result of mankind's own karmic justice which they have established. The patterns that they have brought forth shall also come upon them. And surely I the LORD God will visit this earth, and it shall come to pass; and I the LORD have spoken it!

Behold, the time when men's hearts are failing for fear has come upon the earth. And behold, it shall intensify. For yea, they have deserved it. Yes, they have surfeited themselves. They have thought to glorify themselves and exalt themselves unto the mountains. And behold, the hour of my appearing is at hand. Behold, I shall surely visit the family of nations, and I shall render unto all according to their just deserts.

His prophecy was fulfilled on December 23, 1972. Nicaragua's capital city of Managua was devastated by a series of earthquakes which lasted two and a half hours. The strongest measured 6.25 on the Richter scale. Seventy percent of the city was destroyed, an estimated 10,000 people were killed, 10,000-15,000 people were injured, and at least 200,000 were left homeless.[136]

Cayce's Prophecies of Earth Changes

On January 21, 1936, the "Sleeping Prophet" said that "if there are the greater activities in the Vesuvius, or Pelée, then the southern coast of California—and the areas between Salt Lake and the southern portions of Nevada—may expect, within the three months following same, an inundation by the earthquakes."

That is not particularly good news since Cayce also said, "Los Angeles, San Francisco, most all of these will be among those that will be destroyed before New York even."

It appears, then, according to Cayce, that both the East and the West Coast are due for some major changes. Cayce says, in fact, that "the earth will be broken up in many places. The early portion will see a change in the physical aspect of the west coast of America. There will be open waters appear in the northern portions of Greenland. There will be new lands seen off the Caribbean Sea, and *dry* land will appear.... South America shall be shaken from the uppermost portion to the end, and in the Antarctic off Tierra Del Fuego, *land*, and a strait with rushing waters."

In other places he tells us that "the greater portion of Japan must go into the sea. The upper portion of Europe will be changed as in the twinkling of an eye. Land will appear off the east coast of America. There will be the upheavals in the Arctic and in the Antarctic that will make for the eruption of volcanoes in the Torrid areas, and there will be the shifting then of the poles—so that where there have been those of a frigid or semi-tropical will become the more tropical, and moss and fern will grow. And these will begin in those periods in '58 to '98, when these will be proclaimed as the periods when His Light will be seen again in the clouds....

"All over the country we will find many physical changes of a minor or greater degree.

The greater change, as we will find, in America, will be the North Atlantic Seaboard. Watch New York! Connecticut, and the like."[137]

If only half of what Cayce says happens, the earth is due for epochal changes that seem to be on the order of the catastrophes that befell Atlantis and Lemuria.

Whether or not that is what Nostradamus is referring to in these quatrains, Noorbergen has a lot to say about I.87. "Whether [the earthquake] will happen around the same time as the fire-storm emanating from the forty-fifth parallel or not is an open question," he says referring to quatrain VI.97, "but these quatrains refer to a catastrophe that could well be triggered by earth tremors set off by atomic blasts.

"It bluntly predicts that New York City and its environs will be partially destroyed by an earthquake. The force of the quake will be so great in some areas that many of Manhattan's sky-scrapers will be toppled into New York harbor. Water mains will be broken, and the remaining drinking water will be heavily polluted.

"In his prediction of the destruction of New York City, Nostradamus was far ahead of his pres-ent-day colleagues who forecast a very similar event. Many of them have made predictions in recent years in which they agree with the seer that something ominous is brewing in the rock strata underlying the great island's metropolis....

"Geologists have known for many years that New York is, in fact, not built on very stable ground—although that ground is rocky. Commentator Hugh Allen [*Window in Providence*, 1943] made a disturbing observation, based on a study by William Hobbs described in 'The Configuration of the Rock Floor of Greater New York,' U.S. Geological Survey, Bulletin 270....

"According to Allen, because of the distribution of the various faults underlying New York, Manhattan Island would, in the event of an earthquake, 'break up into three large chunks, destroying all the major New York landmarks, as well as seriously affecting its millions of inhabitants.'

"It is also disturbing to note that the faultlines under New York City are part of a larger earth fracture which begins in the state of Maine and runs beneath regions of Boston and Philadelphia. In the third line of the first quatrain above, the French seer predicted that 'two great rocks will war against each other' or 'oppose one another for a long time.' By the 'two rocks' he may have meant the two lines of rock on either side of the New England fracture zone, which will oppose or push against one another in the upheaval."[138]

Cheetham says of I.87, "An explosion in the centre of the city of New York making the land tremble, or could *tour* here mean towers or skyscrapers? The two great rocks are the immutable great powers who will eventually open war. Ingenious commentators interpret Arethusa as coming from Ares, God of War, and U.S.A. The new river is presumably blood."

As for X.49, she says, "This is a fascinating

quatrain with the idea of a water supply of a whole
city being poisoned, more suited to James Bond
than Nostradamus. The *cité neuf* is New York. The
jardin du Monde is probably a way of describing it
as a world centre. The next line is interesting.
Could a road of hollow mountains be the nearest
Nostradamus could get towards describing a sky-
scraper? I am not quite sure what the tank is,
perhaps Nostradamus is trying to indicate the controls or reservoir of the water supply poisoned with
sulphuric acid?"[139]

There are still some questions about the identity of the "new city." New York is an obvious
choice, especially because of the tie-in with New
Jersey, the "Garden State."

But Los Angeles could also be a candidate. It
is, after all, a great new city. And, as specified in
X.49, it is located near the "garden of the world,"
the wonderfully productive San Joaquin Valley.
Agriculture production in California is so great,
the entire state could be thought of as the "garden
of the world."

Los Angeles, of course, is famous for sitting
atop a number of geologically active faults—the
San Andreas being the best known. Everyone in
California knows "the Big One"—as the cata-
strophic earthquake is familiarly referred to—is
coming sometime soon. But just how soon, no
one knows.

There is good reason to believe, however, that
it is sooner than a lot of people think. Recently,

California's Seismic Safety Commission, the only state agency of its kind, drastically scaled down its estimate of when "the Big One" will hit. They used to think it would happen sometime in the next fifty years. But now, based on a combination of evidence, including historical cycles, increasing seismic activity, and geological indicators such as increased pressure on the Palmdale Bulge, they think Los Angeles will experience a Mexico City-like earthquake—somewhere around 8.0 on the Richter scale—*within the next five years.*[140]

There is no limit to how much one can say about Nostradamus and his prophecies. There is much I would like to say but am constrained by time and space: more quatrains about wars in Europe and in the Middle East and about the mysterious "Blue Turban King," the "bluehead (who) will inflict upon the white head...much evil"[141] and other remarkable predictions will have to wait for another round.

Let us, then, turn our attention to an event of the century having far-reaching ramifications in more ways than one, as we shall see. "Chernobyl: A Prophecy of Karma in the Stars" opens the door to a new/old kind of prophecy that confirms both Nostradamus and the Bible.

CHAPTER 14

Chernobyl: A Prophecy of Karma in the Stars

I t was the stuff bad dreams are made of. Over a 24-hour period, operators of a huge nuclear reactor performing a safety test violated every imaginable rule of safety. Even when the reactor began behaving strangely, they pushed ahead.

Then, a fatal surge of power. The reactor jumped 3,200 thermal megawatts, its full capacity, in less than 3 seconds. In the next 2.5 seconds, it jumped another 400,000 to 600,000 thermal megawatts. [142] Two explosions then blew open the reactor, tore the roof off the building, ignited at least 30 separate fires, and released deadly radiation into the air.

It was the shot heard round the world, although not immediately. The powers that be in Moscow have never been ones to report news that would put them in a bad light. Only when the Swedish government had a fix on the out-of-control reactor fire did they admit there was a problem. Within hours, the word *Chernobyl* entered the lexicon of virtually every nation on earth.

In theoretical discussions of worst-case scenarios, the possibility of accidents of this magnitude had been considered. But could the events at Chernobyl have been predicted?

Were there factors that would have accounted for the unreal tale of error after operator error that finally emerged in the pages of the Soviet Union's official report? Or that could have established the precise timing of the disaster?

In a word, the answer is yes. And that word is a form of prophecy called astrology.

Astrology and Prophecy

The word *astrology* usually evokes images of a one-eyed gypsy with her crystal ball or, in modern times, of people entertaining themselves through daily horoscope readings and planning their love lives around their stars.

The word *prophecy* usually evokes images of something prophetic proceeding out of the mouth of a sagacious, hoary-headed messenger of the LORD who emerges with mantle and staff from the leaves of the Old Testament.

Yet the true prophets knew that true astrology wisely and judiciously used was a valuable tool for predicting events and diverting people and nations from a headlong plunge into disaster. However, the tendency of the superstitious and the power hungry to pervert astrology has ever blackened its name.

Although Nostradamus, the French seer of the sixteenth century, and Edgar Cayce and Mark

Prophet of the twentieth are removed in time from Old Testament tradition, they carry on the relationship between prophecy and prophet.

Though these commanding figures speaking the word of God are out of sight, as novas that have come and gone and left a trail of light that reaches us still—surely they are not out of mind's eye.

Lo! in their wake still another celestial phenomenon commands our attention, one by which we can know and interpret the signs of the times millennia in advance, one which has ever told us the old, old story and the new—antedating even the prophets, succeeding them still.

Astrology is the moving, ever moving finger that writes across the heavens the prophecy of our karma and our karmic destiny.

This prophecy that seems to have no prophet is written by the most accurate prophet of all: You. Did you know that you have already written in the stars the prophecy of your life? And that the collective You—called We—has already written for all to read the prophecy of our nations and our Earth?

I would speak of the astrology that encodes the karma of the race and yours and mine. For the individual and the people of the world, all of us together, have created both positive and negative conditions called karma—"Whatsoever a man soweth that shall he also reap."[143]

The resulting sets of circumstances, disc upon disc, are reflected in the mirror of the skies as geometric configurations of heavenly bodies, stars, planets and constellations. These grids and forcefields of our life patterns, which are also reflected in the subconscious mind as carryover lifetime upon lifetime, are a part of the planetary akashic records as well.

Astrology is one of the best among several precise methods of predicting the future, used by the astrologer to chart, study and decode the hourly, daily, yearly and momentary *changes* in the relationships of the components of the personal and planetary karmic equation—changes which trigger events on the screen of our lives.

Only You and We can change a line of the astrology of our karma—or can We? For having writ, the moving finger moves on, nor all your piety nor wit—without the alchemist's tool and the white stone*—shall lure it back to cancel half a line, nor all your tears wash out a word of it.[144]

Astrology is prognosticator and prognostication, if you will. It is mathematics and a table of karmic weights and measures that stands on its own. It is a clockwork telling time like the universal rotations of the spheres in their rounds about star centers cutting lines of space.

Astrology is a priori. It preexists prophet who may enter it and prophecy which may interpret it.

Astrology is a science of relationships and absolutes which will tell us, if we learn the alphabet

---

*The more complete and basic statement of the Master on the alchemy of change through transmutation by the violet flame is set forth in the first pocketbook in the Saint Germain series, entitled *Saint Germain On Alchemy*. This subject is amply developed with its hows and whys in the dictations of Saint Germain in Books Three and Four of this volume.

of the skies, how these configure in the most exact and exacting formulas of our karmic initiations on this dark star we came to make bright. And it is this karmic circumstance delineated in our natal chart that makes us think, when afflicted, that we are about to be drowned in a sea of troubles.

Not so! For we who think and therefore say "I AM" may take arms against them and by opposing end them: To be, or not to be—that is the question which we have the wherewithal to decide.

If it were not for free will, the gift of God and our endowment by Elohim of something within us that is akin to the stars themselves—a divine spark, a threefold flame of immortal life that makes us arbiters, if we have the heart, of our own destiny—we would be subject to fates, gods, stars and natural forces, even to dictators or totalitarian states. As beasts of the field we would be the unprotesting prisoners of the signs of the times and the seasons.

But we are sons of a superior Light. And by that Light we are heaven-sent to take command of our destiny on earth.

Astrology presents to us the hurdles and slides of life—up and over we go, then easy-does-it on the downside till it's time to climb and conquer those mountains of karmic adversity which—if we will only say the Word of our destiny: "I AM THAT I AM!" and the divine decree "In the name of JESUS, Be thou removed!"—will flee from us like so many ghosts and goblins of the night.

Yes, astrology is a science that anticipates and records the cycles of our karma past/present/future and unveils life as not all karmic drudgery but an abundant harvest of good fruits of past sowings. Just as we pay every jot and tittle of the law of karmic cycles till all be fulfilled, so the Law pays us for every jot and tittle we give freely to enhance and ennoble life. As Saint Germain says, "As you serve the Light, the Light will turn and serve you."

Astrology is the recording angel who opens the starry Book of Life and by the inductive method explains what we every day reap by what we have ever sown.

Astrology shows that all worthy effort, all sacrifice for a cause that's good, all sowings that are to the heavens' glorying in the handiwork of the LORD, are multiplied by our Sun, the I AM THAT I AM; by our rising sign, our Christ Presence; and by our Moon, the soul personality ever refining itself by lessons learned from the stars.

Yes, all that we are is the sum total of all that we have ever been. And it's all there written in the heavens, a prophecy of the stars so complete that what we are today does truly anticipate what we shall be tomorrow—given the thrust and the momentum of our stars in their courses and crisscrossings on the cosmic highways.

Thus, astrology is a divine art—a divination, perhaps, arrived at by filling in the computer program of *what has been* in order to project upon the screen of life *what may be* today or what may come to pass tomorrow, IF the I of us that is the I AM—the Will to Be and to Become who we really are in the eternal spheres, so much more than mere accumulations of our past—yes, if the Real Me will step forth, will intervene, as our own intercessor and say to the malevolent portents of our dark stars:

Thus far and no farther!

This day I AM begotten of the LORD!

Now the I AM that I am shall ride the Taurean bull, fly on the back of the eagle and drive the scorpion to some heightened creativity. I will sit upon you—you Capricorn goat, you Aries ram!

For I AM the waterbearer of Aquarius bearing the water of Life to all people of all signs by the fire of my Leonine heart. My scales are held in balance by God's Justice—no scales of Pisces' fishes shall mar my vision.

Through Virgo Mother of the Earth I find the heart-fire of Sagittarius' conqueror. The twins of mind and feeling I subdue by Gemini Mind of God. I AM the possessor of my heaven and my earth in the wide arms of Cancer.

Earth, fire, water, wind submit to the center of my Sun of Righteousness as I AM seated above the twelve signs of the Zodiac with the true prophet of my stars—the Lord, the Saviour who is the Light!

Let us don the robes (understanding) of the Magi, three kings of Orient, seers, adepts of wisdom who charted the birth of Christ two thousand years ago by the prophecy of the stars and who chart the karmic birth and death of Antichrist today. If only we who run would read it!

Though Herod intercept the journey of these three wise stars, the dark king could not prevail where Magi would not allow this prophecy of his dark planets to be fulfilled. For they, the stronger influence, prevented it—*their* coming also written in the heavens the night the Son of God was born: as Pisces fused for a moment with Aries and the Lamb of God came forth in springtime.

Let us learn of them how the astrologer, forsooth, wears, or ought to—if he's worth his gold, frankincense and myrrh—the mantle of the prophet. Yes, the prophet who forecasts coming events, then enters the arena of life to let pass or turn aside by free will's discretion those plottings on the graph of life whether good, ill-conceived or ill-timed—this is he who charts his days and nights by the science of the Word and his eternity by the Cosmic Clock.

The astrologer of today—if he's worth his salt and oil and wine—reads by the secret code of the ancients and the Magi (who knew the heavenly bodies and beings) the handwriting on the wall, albeit a celestial wall, or ceiling—then decodes the starry formula of coming events: portents of what will happen *if* individuals or nations continue in a karma-making mode, a predictable human propensity that, side by side with the variable of free will, is a known quantity to every astrologer/prophet of the stars.

Now let us study a chart written in the heavens which shows the planets and their players in a karmic prophecy of the stars, the utter victims of past causes which each and the collective set in motion in Assyria long time, long rotations ago.

Victims, yes. Perpetrators, yes—of the karma and the karmic destiny they once wrote in the earth. Secrets recorded in the stars, known to them alone until: Chernobyl.

And it is written:

THIS 'ORIENTAL' PEOPLE WHO ONCE WOR-SHIPED THE ASSYRIAN SERPENT GODS HATH NO KNOWLEDGE OF THE SELF AS GOD, OF INNER LIGHT OR THE I THAT IS I AM. NEITHER INDEED GIVE THEY ALLEGIANCE TO THE LAW OF THE ONE.

And that handwriting on the wall says it all—and the story of their karmic undoing by the faithless star called Wormwood unfolds like clockwork:

Therefore on April 26, 1986, at precisely 1:23 a.m. no Mediator stepped forth from the heavens, no secret love star of an ancient tryst with the morning stars which, had it been, might have intervened in form of Lady Venus to mitigate the madness, the anger of these gods—suppressed, compressed, exploding at intervals down the centuries in war and death and fire and blood. And then the anger sealed up again in the core of psyches marred by division (of sub-reactors designed for surface destruction), unhealed by the Person of Christ, who is Judge or Comforter or Enlightener as each one hath need of Him.

"Whosoever shall deny Me before men, him will I also deny before my Father which is in heaven!"

Thus Wormwood fell and none intervened, nor people nor Politburo nor workers nor saints nor technology nor military might, and it is written that "a third of all water turned to bitter wormwood so that many people died from drinking it."

Let the nations who have betrayed the God of Love read the signs of the times and cast themselves upon the Rock of Christ ere it fall upon them and grind them to powder![145]

Chernobyl—Star of Wormwood, Star of Soviet Destiny, How art thou, so great a star, fallen from heaven burning, burning like a ball of fire?

CHAPTER 15

Analysis of the Astrological Chart of Chernobyl

Our analysis of the astrological chart drawn for Chernobyl at 1:23 a.m. on April 26, 1986, shows there were a variety of celestial influences which combined to trigger the worst nuclear-power disaster in history. Chernobyl may not have known it (his inner warning mechanism desensitized) but this fallen star, mastermind of destructive uses of atomic energy—was down for the count of four.

Chernobyl: Down for the Count of Four

In reading the prophecy of the stars, there were four configurations, or planetary patterns, which were significant, the most important being a nearly exact opposition (a 180 degree angle) between the planet Pluto at the seventh degree of the sign of Scorpio and the Sun at the sixth degree of Taurus.

In Greek mythology Pluto is the pitiless lord of the Underworld, a realm of darkness where with his queen, Persephone, he ruled over the infernal powers and the dead. Variously described by writers of different epochs, he is also known as the Giver of Wealth and a god of fertility.

Although many astrologers believe Pluto's vibration has a positive, regenerative side, it is undeniably associated with death, and its influence is often highly destructive. Among other things, it rules the radioactive element plutonium, which may very well be produced for military purposes in many of the Soviet Union's graphite nuclear reactors. These are essentially large-scale models of the kinds of nuclear reactors used by the Soviet Union and the United States specifically to produce weapons-grade plutonium.

While it is not absolutely clear if plutonium was being produced at Chernobyl—some experts believe it more likely that they were producing tritium, a rare hydrogen isotope used in thermonuclear weapons—evidence that has emerged since the accident strongly suggests that the plant had a military function.

In all branches of astrology, Pluto is associated with cataclysmic events, such as the onset of wars and the fall and/or death of rulers. It rules all things secretive and the instinct for self-destruction. In mundane astrology—the astrology of nations and world events—Pluto rules nuclear power, fires, waste disposal, and anything involving widespread death and destruction, precisely the kinds of things brought into play by the disaster.

In the Chernobyl scenario Pluto fell in a compartment of the chart known as the tenth house, which rules the government, the ruling class—in this case the party, particularly the General Secretary, Mikhail Gorbachev—national prestige, and how the nation is viewed by its neighbors. So placed, Pluto signified negative international reaction to the Soviet's handling of the crisis.

As the tenth house rules the government, so the Sun represents the leader or leaders of a nation. Since the Sun also rules nuclear contamination, once again the astrological influences underscored the association of the Soviet leadership with the nuclear disaster.

At the time of the accident, the Sun in Taurus was in the fourth house, that portion of the chart which rules the area and the people in and around the place where an event occurs, including the lands, buildings, and crops in the vicinity. One of the qualities of Taurus that can be negative is stubbornness; when the disaster began, the Soviet leadership dug in its heels and kept Chernobyl a secret (Pluto in Scorpio) until international detection of radioactive wastes compelled them to reveal there had been an accident.

Discussing the interaction of the two planets, distinguished astrologer Lt. Comdr. David Williams says that Pluto "in the violent water sign Scorpio indicates ruptures and burstings in the water cooling system of the nuclear reactor. . . . The Sun, representing the Chernobyl power plant, was in Taurus in the fourth house of the people.

"Under normal conditions, this position would have been of benefit to the people; but at the time of the accident, it was not, for the Sun opposed destructive Pluto. Therefore, the people,

The Chernobyl Disaster
April 26, 1986 1:23 a.m.
51°16′ N latitude, 30°14′ E longitude

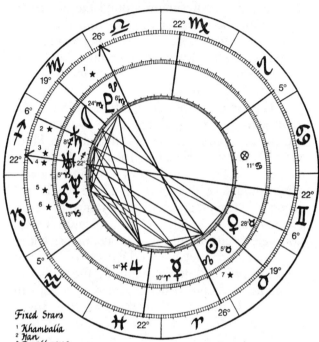

Fixed Stars
1. Khambalia
2. Han
3. Rasalhague
4. Lesath
5. Facies
6. Manubrium
7. Hamal

Aspects

	☉	☽	☿	♀	♂	♃	♄	♅	♆	♇
☉			⊻	⊼	△	✶		◻	△	☌
☽				☍		△			⊼	
☿					◻	⊻	△		◻	
♀							☍			
♂						✶	⊻	⊼	☌	✶
♃							◻	◻	✶	△
♄									⊻	⊻
♅										
♆										✶
♇										

Key

Planetary Symbol	Position	Astrological Symbol	Aspect	°
☉ Sun	05♉21	♈ Aries	Conjunction ☌	0
☽ Moon	24♏25	♉ Taurus	Semi-Sextile ⊻	30
☿ Mercury	10♈59	♊ Gemini	Semi-Square ∠	45
♀ Venus	28♉54	♋ Cancer	Sextile ✶	60
♂ Mars	13♑08	♌ Leo	Quintile Q	72
♃ Jupiter	14♓24	♍ Virgo	Square ◻	90
♄ Saturn	08♏36ʀ	♎ Libra	Trine △	120
♅ Uranus	22♏01ʀ	♏ Scorpio	Sesqui-quadrate ⊡	135
♆ Neptune	05♒54ʀ	♐ Sagittarius	Quincunx ⊼	150
♇ Pluto	06♏02ʀ	♑ Capricorn	Opposition ☍	180
⊗ Part of Fortune	11♋53	♒ Aquarius		
☊ North Node	30♈02ʀ	♓ Pisces		

the land, the environment around the plant suffered from the radiation thrown into the atmosphere by Pluto. That the cost of the accident would be very great is indicated by the Sun in the money sign Taurus conjunct the Moon's North Node in the fourth house."[146]

The second important configuration was the semisquare (a 45 degree angle) of Uranus at 22 degrees Sagittarius in the twelfth house to Pluto and a 135 degree angle, known as a sesquiquadrate, to the Sun. The Pluto-Sun opposition indicated what could take place, but it alone would not necessarily trip off an accident. Uranus, however, governs sudden, often violent accidents, explosions, electricity, uranium, and radiation sickness.

The unpredictable influences of Uranus combined with Pluto (plutonium, fires, nuclear accidents, widespread death and destruction) in the tenth house of public standing (the Soviet reputation suffered) and the influence of both planets combined with the Sun indicated a powerful explosion that was highly destructive to the plant and to people in and around the plant. In fact, the elements brought into focus by this configuration resulted in an explosion at reactor No. 4 that was likened by Ken Maize, senior energy analyst for the Union of Concerned Scientists, to the detonation of "a small, not very effective nuclear bomb."

This was no meltdown. "The temperature far exceeded what was necessary for the fuel to melt down," says Maize, explaining that it got so hot the fuel "actually vaporized up." Maize points out that because of our own perception of nuclear disasters "we think a lot about meltdowns because that is... [what we consider to be] the worse-case accident. This accident in the Soviet plant goes far beyond anything that we've ever thought of. The question of meltdown is irrelevant. The fuel was just blown up through the roof."[147]

Two other configurations had a bearing on the accident: Saturn, at 8 degrees Sagittarius in the twelfth house forming a 90 degree angle, called a square, to Jupiter at 14 degrees Pisces in the second house is related to accidents and disruptions and/or restrictions of the water supply in the reactor, whose causes are not immediately apparent or easily understood. Neptune at 5 degrees Capricorn conjoined* Mars at 13 degrees Capricorn in the first house square Mercury in Aries in the third house is related to violent energy and accidents involving water, steam, gases—and bad communications.

The Third Angel Blew the Whistle—
Eclipsed Moon Pulls the Trigger,
Uranus Times the Blast-Off

The combined effect of all four configurations showed the potential for the accident. But there were two other entirely different astrological phenomena which explain the timing of the accident. The first was an eclipse of the Moon that

*in astrological terms a conjunction is the apparent meeting or passing of two or more celestial bodies in the same degree of the Zodiac; a configuration in which two celestial bodies have their least apparent separation.

fell within two degrees of Pluto which took place on April 24, 1986, about 33 hours before the event. The second was the rotation of Uranus into the twelfth house on the day of the accident, once the sequence of events that are reported to have caused the accident were set in motion.

According to mundane astrology, eclipses often activate and determine the timing of events. There are differences of opinion among astrologers about the influence of eclipses—certainly not all are negative—and the timing of the events that proceed from them. Sometimes it takes months for the events to manifest. But since this eclipse fell so close to Pluto, it happened very quickly.

The power of this particular eclipse was so great that astro-economist Arch Crawford wrote in his April '86 issue of the *Crawford Perspectives* that April 24th would be a day of high stress. "If you don't *feel* this one," he wrote, referring to the lunar eclipse, "you're probably not *alive*."[148]

Since eclipses are known to "eclipse" those in power, it will be worth noting whether this one diminishes the power of the Communist Party of the USSR or its leader, Mikhail Gorbachev. There are tentative signs that this cycle may have already set in.

In the wake of the disaster, Premier Nikolai Ryzhkov went to Chernobyl rather than Gorbachev, which at least one expert believes undermined Gorbachev's position. It is hard to follow Soviet political infighting, but this may be an indication that if Gorbachev is still firmly in charge, he may have lost some of his grip. Astrological time will tell.

The second factor which influenced the timing of the accident was the movement of Uranus into the twelfth house. The twelfth house rules those things which are secret, wholly or partly hidden, deception and self-deception, conditions that are inimical to public welfare, hospitals, plagues and epidemics—in this case, widespread radiation contamination. It is the house most associated with karma and karmic circumstances.

In order to bring the influence of Uranus into sharp relief, let us review the sequence of events revealed by the Soviet Union in their August 1986 report to the International Atomic Energy Agency:

The Soviets claimed the disaster occurred as a result of a safety test in which plant operators were trying to find out how long reactor No. 4's turbines would continue to function in the event of an unplanned shutdown. According to Andronik M. Petrosyants, chairman of the Soviet Committee for the Peaceful Uses of Atomic Energy, this led to "a whole series of gross violations of operating regulations by the workers,"[149] who deliberately disabled the plant's multiple safety and warning systems, leaving them helpless to contain the problem once the experiment got out of hand.

Although the explosion took place at 1:23 a.m. April 26, the events that led to the catastrophe began at 1:00 a.m. the previous day, just 8 hours and 40 minutes after the eclipse. According to the Soviet report, in the next 24 hours the plant operators took the multiple steps that set the stage for the explosion.

The cycle initiated by the eclipse of the moon conjoined Pluto was in motion waiting for the point of release. Just moments after Uranus, the planet of explosions and unpredictable events, crossed the ascendant (a particularly powerful point) into the twelfth house (karma, hospitals, hidden causes, etc.), a massive explosion tore the plant apart.

There is one last thing critical to our discussion—the influence of fixed stars. Since the earliest times astrologers have used specific fixed stars such as Polaris, Sirius, and Regulus in making their forecasts. Several of them conjoined the planets whose influences helped trigger the disaster.

The interpretation of fixed stars, which derives from ancient literature, is subject to debate and, in many cases, is in need of further study. Nonetheless, it is worth noting that according to Vivian Robson, author of *The Fixed Stars and Constellations in Astrology*, the fixed star *Khambalia* located at 6 degrees Scorpio conjoined Pluto and the lunar eclipse "causes swift violence, unreliability, changeability, and an argumentative nature"—an apt description of the accident and the Soviet method of handling relations with the world community thereafter.

Furthermore, according to Robson, *Rasalhague* (21 degrees Sagittarius conjoined Uranus) causes "sudden death"; *Lesath* (23 degrees Sagittarius conjoined Uranus) "gives danger, desperation, [radioactivity?]; immorality and malevolence, and is connected with acid poisons"; *Hamal* (6 degrees Taurus conjoined the Sun) causes "violence" and "disgrace"; *Han* (8 degrees Sagittarius conjoined Saturn) "brings trouble and disgrace"; *Facies* (7 degrees Capricorn conjoined Neptune) "causes blindness, defective sight, sickness, accidents, and a violent death"; and *Manubrium* (14 degrees Capricorn conjoined Mars) "causes blindness, explosions, fire, flaring heat, heroism, courage and defiance."[150]

The references to blindness and defective sight are appropriate, if indeed the plant operators took the ill-fated sequence of steps described by the Soviets in their report.

From an astrological point of view, there is little reason to doubt that operator error played a part in the tragedy as the Soviets have reported it. Atomic energy workers in the USSR do not have the best of training. On November 15, 1985, for example, the Soviet newspaper *Soviet Tojikistoni* ran an ad appealing for workers at atomic energy stations promising "No experience necessary, on the job training."[151] According to David Marples, author of *Chernobyl and Nuclear Power in the USSR*, Soviet atomic power plant workers have a reputation for being young and unskilled.[152]

Neptune/Saturn/Pluto:
Three Blind, All-Knowing Mice
Sweep Cesium-137 under the Bear Rug

Mercury square to Mars and Neptune from the third house to the first house shows that there could have been confused and muddled thinking and bizarre problems. But it also shows that the communications by the Soviets after the fact were deceptive—they refused to acknowledge the accident even when pressed by foreign governments (as also indicated by the Pluto-Sun opposition)— and may continue to be deceptive about both the causes and effects of the disaster.

As bits of news revealing how the authorities in Moscow are managing the long-term effects of the disaster become available, it is increasingly apparent just how secretive they have been. And how an already serious health problem has through suppression of information been needlessly amplified. Several families from Moscow and Odessa, we have learned, vacationed in Belorussia, a Soviet republic bordering Poland, a month after the accident. They were completely unaware that of all of the places contaminated by radioactive debris from Chernobyl, Belorussia was one of the worst. [153]

Facing up to realities has never been the Soviet forte. This trait is their Achilles' heel: it will be the undoing of the empire.

And so, as we have seen, rather than facing the horrific facts and giving a realistic assessment of the dangers, along with guidelines to preserve their health—lest the truth cast aspersions on the Soviet system and leadership—the Soviet press and propaganda pitifully self-deceived has tended to trivialize and ridicule the dangers.

Vitchizna, a Ukrainian monthly magazine, published a story called "Is It Dangerous on Riga's Seashore?" The authors were listed as "A.H." and "E.Z.H.," two ninth-grade girls (who would be about 15 or 16 years old). The story, designed to allay fears about radiation, had the girls find out whether the level of radiation along Riga's Baltic Sea resort shoreline is so dangerous (as rumor would have it) that people could not swim or get a tan—a question close to the heart of a Soviet teenager.

They do what any intelligent ninth grader in the Soviet Union would—interview the chief physician of a Latvian clinic, a Dr. Alexandr Agafonov. He is a good-natured man who tells the girls his clinic takes measurements of the level of radiation daily. Naturally, the level does not go beyond the national standard for the Soviet Union, which is from 4 to 20 microroentgens in four hours.

Therefore, he tells them, apparently with avuncular concern, it is not dangerous; it is safe. "Of course it is safe if your doctors or physicians [approve] of you getting suntanned." He goes on to explain that "some people like those who have a heart condition or some other ailments are not allowed to get suntanned because of the radiation of the sun."[154]

In reality, radiation from the sun should be the least of a sunbather's worries. Radiation figures for Latvia, for the worst industrial accident in history, are difficult to obtain. But judging by the path of the radiation cloud as it moved from Chernobyl to Sweden and the high rates found in neighboring countries such as Poland and Finland, Latvia received a considerable dose of long-lasting cesium-137. [155]

The Soviet citizenry's willingness (on the part of some) to believe this ninth-grade propaganda only cheers on the emperor et entourage in their new clothes. One day all the blind shall see their nakedness. For it is written: "The hour is coming, and now is, when the dead shall hear the voice of the Son of God: and they that hear shall live." And this too is a prophecy of karma in the stars and in the Bible.

Saturn afflicted in the twelfth house (an influence reinforced by the Pluto-Sun opposition from the tenth to the fourth houses) indicates that the highest Soviet governmental authorities, plant design, rules for governing the plant, as well as the entire Soviet nuclear industry were intimately involved in the events that led to the accident. Indeed, this aspect strongly suggests that the Communist Party has hidden facts which, were they known, would be embarrassing to it and/or could undermine their authority.

Even though the Soviets have emphasized "gross" human error by the plant operators, the scenario they outlined was, as *Newsweek* put it, "an almost unbelievable story."[156] And *Newsweek* may be on to something.

According to an extremely knowledgeable U.S. government source, who spoke with us provided we not use his name, "we don't [even] know whether they were running a test on that machine. We've just been told that." He points out that "we don't know that the thing [reactor No. 4] didn't just break. My own reading of [another] *Vitchizna* article in March of 1986 suggests to me that it may have just gone haywire."

He goes on to say that in this article, "the chief engineer pointed out that as a result of construction difficulties, there was a place in the reactor that everybody called the 'dead zone'— pipes went in and pipes came out but nobody really knew what was inside. That's hardly inspiring."

The Soviet Union has characterized the Chernobyl disaster as a one-time breakdown of otherwise generally well-conceived and well-running systems. But according to our source, the problem at Chernobyl had been going on for some time. "The chief engineer in the *Vitchizna* article said that things started going wrong about a year ago— that is about the same time that Gorbachev took over." Apparently the reason for these difficulties could be attributed to the fact that "Moscow wasn't giving them enough money to build the thing properly."

Other evidence shows that the difficulties in Soviet nuclear power plants may be systemic. The Zaporozhye State Regional Power Station in the

Ukraine is being touted as a model nuclear power plant. But as of late it, too, has had difficulties and had to be shut down. Late in June the Ukraine News Agency reported that the "1-million-kilowatt-power-generating unit at the Rovno Atomic Power Station will go into operation" in the fall. But as of December 1986 it still hadn't been put into service. Furthermore, according to Marples, after Chernobyl all the graphite reactors in the Soviet Union were shut down, at least for a time.[157]

While on the subject of power plants, it is worth noting that workers who "volunteered" to help with the cleanup at Chernobyl rioted. Thousands of workers from the Baltic states and the Ukraine have been working on the cleanup. But according to reports in the Estonian youth organization paper *Noorte Haal* (August 15, 1986) and other internal reports coming from the Soviet Union, two hundred to three hundred Estonian workers rioted when they learned they would be required to work on the cleanup six rather than three months as they were originally told. The Soviets made an effort to downplay the riots, in which twelve Estonian workers were shot, but they did concede that some of the workers had been conscripted for the Chernobyl cleanup "in the middle of the night."[158]

Furthermore, the Soviets have glossed over the fact that they do not use containment buildings in the construction of their nuclear power plants but have insisted their designs were safe. Naturally, some American experts disagree. According to Roger Huston of the Atomic Industrial Forum, had No. 4 been designed as reactors are designed in most of the rest of the world, "even with all the things that were done by the operator, the reactor would not have been destroyed."[159]

As for the long-term effects, at this point there is considerable debate about the ultimate health consequences. "The fallout may eventually cause 24,000 cancer deaths, according to calculations in the Soviet report,"[160] noted *Science News* shortly after the report was published, although there are experts who favor higher and lower figures. In general, because of the combined twelfth house Pluto-Scorpio influence, it is likely that some dangers and consequences may be underreported and/or partially or completely suppressed.

The prominent Sagittarius influence is a primary indicator of the international character of the disaster. To date, there are reports of the contamination by radioactive iodine and cesium of the fields, forests, marshes and lakes in Sweden as well as contamination of food supplies in Norway and Sweden—especially of fish, berries, sheep and reindeer, which are an important part of the diet in the region.

In Norway, researchers fear mass deaths of reindeer in the next two or three years from accumulated radiation. In France, there are reports of significant levels of radioactive cesium in goat cheese. Meaningful reports have yet to emerge from Eastern Europe, where political pressure from the Soviet Union has no doubt had a chilling effect on objectivity.

Although the accident happened suddenly, Saturn in the twelfth house, aspected as it is, shows that the problem had been building for some time and was institutional in nature—related to the highest governmental authorities in the USSR and to the rules they established for the Chernobyl power plant and the Soviet nuclear power industry. Saturn also signals that the effects of the disaster will be long lasting and that we do not have all the facts about the causes or consequences of the accident.

CHAPTER 16

Chernobyl: A Prophecy of Karma in the Bible

As we leave the subject of Chernobyl's prophecy of karma in the stars, let us take up still another configuration—this one sealed in the Bible: the scriptural foretelling of events in Revelation, the Book of Prophecy for our time delivered by the angel of the Lord Jesus Christ to John the Beloved on the isle of Patmos nineteen centuries ago.

Russians Read of Chernobyl in Revelation

Many Russians are looking at their nuclear disaster in light of one of the most quoted and least understood of the ancient prophetic texts, the tenth and eleventh verses of the eighth chapter of this last book in the New Testament.

What does this apocalyptic book have to say about an event that occurred 1900 years after it was written down? According to huge numbers of Russians—a lot. In Moscow, for example, a prominent Russian writer "produced a tattered old Bible," the *New York Times* recently reported, "and with a practiced hand turned to Revelation.

"'Listen,' he said, 'this is incredible: "And the third angel sounded, and there fell a great star from heaven, burning as it were a lamp, and it fell upon the third part of the rivers, and upon the fountains of waters; and the name of the star is called Wormwood: and the third part of the waters became wormwood; and many men died of the waters, because they were made bitter."'"[161]

Just what in this passage did the writer find so incredible? The fact that in Ukrainian the word *wormwood* happens to be *chernobyl*.

Wormwood (chernobyl) is a bitter herb used in rural Russia as a tonic. The ill-fated atomic power plant got its name from the wormwood that once grew in abundance on the banks of the Dnieper River that flows nearby.

The Revelation-Chernobyl connection is not the heated speculation of a single excited believer who, ransacking the scriptures for a sign, concluded that the Chernobyl nuclear disaster was the result of divine wrath. On the contrary, the *Times* reported that "the writer, an atheist, was hardly alone in pointing out the apocalyptic reference to the star called Chernobyl."

Indeed, throughout the USSR believers and atheists alike are reading and rereading the passage in Revelation and thumbing through Ukrainian dictionaries looking up wormwood/chernobyl.

"With the uncanny speed common to rumor in the Soviet Union," says the *Times*, "the discovery had spread across the Soviet land, contributing to the swelling body of lore that has shaped the public consciousness of the disaster at the Chernobyl atomic power plant in the Ukraine....Among

many Russians, that passage from Revelation—
also known as the Apocalypse—has touched an
already strong penchant for superstition in the
national character, giving Chernobyl the quality of
an almost supernatural disaster."[162]

In fact, word of the Chernobyl-Revelation
connection developed enough momentum that the
Soviet authorities took steps to counteract it. The
method they chose was to publish an interview
with Ukrainian Exarchete* Filaret, the Metropolitan of Kiev and Galicia, in the *Literaturnaya Ga-
zeta* (July 23, 1986). In it he supposedly scotched
the rumor that "in the Apocalypse, there is a direct
indication of the accident at the Chernobyl Atomic
Power Station," which the interviewer said proceeded from "Western theologians."[163]

It is, of course, a matter of opinion as to
whether or not the "supernatural" quality of the
accident—i.e., the belief that it was an act of
God—is a superstitious reflex. Astrology, you will
recall, is the study of the karma of men and nations written in the stars. Furthermore, the im-
plicit assumption that heavenly bodies control, or
at least influence, the destinies of men is, according to some, pervasive throughout Revelation.[164]
In light of the events at Chernobyl that are now
history, the assumption of either astrology or the
Bible being a "superstitious reflex" is, *fait accompli*, empirically denied. Though the unbelieving
will always claim "coincidence" even if the odds
are 100,000 to 1.

Let us reexamine the prophecy of the fallen
*bishop

star (i.e., fallen angel) Wormwood in the Jerusalem Bible translation of the earliest Greek manuscripts:

> The third angel blew his trumpet, and
> a huge star fell from the sky, burning like a
> ball of fire, and it fell on a third of all rivers
> and springs; this was the star [fallen angel]
> called Wormwood, and a third of all water
> turned to bitter wormwood, so that many
> people died from drinking it. (Revelation
> 8:10, 11)

In reality this is the third of the seven so-
called trumpet judgments (called woes, i.e., karmic
woes) that descend upon the earth as each of seven
angels sounds (blows his trumpet) following the
opening of the seventh seal by the Lamb of God
(after the half-hour space of silence). The star
called Wormwood is the instrument of mankind's
returning karma, he being also culpable, yet his
judgment is not come until the fruits of his evil
sowings ripen—'tis then that he must pay the price
for turning astray the children of Eve.

This star is the embodiment of the karma of
the Soviet leadership and their crimes committed
against the people since the Bolshevik Revolution.
But it is just the beginning. And as we shall see
from the quatrains of Nostradamus it is also the
beginning of the end.

For the karma of this great archdeceiver is
that he himself burns like a ball of fire (in a
nuclear blast) even as he inflicts this ball of fire

(his own karma) first upon the Soviets and then (depending on the free will intervention or non of other players in this twentieth-century nuclear drama), if not contained by the Intercessor, upon Europe and the United States.

Concerning the prophecy "a third of all water turned to bitter wormwood," the drinking water in the Ukraine is at risk; parts of it are contaminated. But more to the point of this prophecy, which implies a much greater area of influence than just the Ukraine, the radiation spread globally; so much so that it was not an exaggeration when the Greens Party of West Germany announced "Chernobyl is everywhere!" Cancer deaths due to the 50 million or so curies of radioactive material that escaped from the plant will, according to the current consensus, cause about 24,000 deaths with some experts, as I mentioned earlier, favoring higher and lower figures.*

Just how bad is Chernobyl? It is unlikely we will ever find out the whole truth and nothing but the truth. But what we don't know factually and scientifically is accurately written in the stars and in the Bible: The effects of Chernobyl will be broad and long lasting, and the powers that be, East and West, will not undermine their position

---

*There have already been charges that the disaster figures are being scaled down by U.S. scientists in deference to our own nuclear power industry and midst charges that the Department of Energy engineered a news blackout on crucial data just days after the disaster occurred. John Gofman, professor emeritus of medical physics at the University of California at Berkeley, recently told a meeting of the American Chemical Society that the radiation released during that accident will cause *one million* cases of cancer and that half of them will be fatal.

In the past, Dr. Gofman, who worked on the Manhattan Project during World War II, has been accused of exaggerating the dangers of

by giving the people the information *they have* which *we need* to protect *our* health, *our* environment, *our* progeny, and *our* future—which are not theirs to dispense with as they will.

It was to *them* that the Lord directed his invective:

> A wicked and adulterous generation seeketh after a sign: and there shall no sign be given unto it, but the sign of the prophet Jonas.[165]

Clearly, the prophecy of karma in the stars and in the Bible is for *believers!*

What, then, is the LORD's prophecy to believers concerning the contamination of the West by Wormwood?

The LORD's Warning to Believers and Nonbelievers

He who warned his son of the seductive philosophy of the "strange woman" whose lips "drop as an honeycomb," her mouth "smoother than oil" whose end is "bitter as wormwood, sharp as a two-edged sword"—whose "feet will go down to death, her steps take hold on hell"—was He not warning the sons of Light, the seed of the Woman, of the creeping seduction of the Lie of the Soviet system of World Communism and her whorish absorption of nations and peoples according to so-called spheres

---

radiation. He, in turn, insists that the radiation released at Chernobyl is more harmful than most scientists believe—and that "we must expect continuing efforts by the U.S. and West European governments to 'stonewall' about the doses recorded in Europe. As promoters of nuclear power, they all have an overwhelming reason to make it as difficult as possible for anyone to make an independent estimate of the cancer-consequences from Chernobyl." See letter from John W. Gofman, chairman, Committee for Nuclear Responsibility, May 1986.

of influence and buffer zones justifying her world hegemony? (Proverbs 5:3–5)

Did not the LORD through his prophet Jeremiah warn the West—the reincarnated descendants of the seed of Israel and Judah—of the grave consequences of going after the strange gods—Soviet socialist ideology and ideologues—of the Great Whore?

Now hear the word of the LORD:

"Who is wise enough to understand this? Who has been charged by I AM THAT I AM's own mouth to tell why the land lies in ruins, burned like the desert where no one passes?"

I AM THAT I AM has said,

"This is because they have forsaken my Law which I put before them and have not listened to my voice or followed it, but have followed the dictates of their own stubborn hearts, followed the Baals as their ancestors taught them."

And so this is what I AM THAT I AM as the Lord of Hosts [Sanat Kumara], the God of Israel, says:

"Now I AM going to give this people wormwood for their food and poisoned water to drink. I AM going to scatter them throughout nations unknown to their ancestors or to them; and I AM going to pursue them with the sword until I have exterminated them." (Jer. 9:12–16, Jerusalem Bible)

The LORD's Prophecy Concerning
the False Prophets of Peace

Not only is this denouement of the twentieth century to be reckoned with by a people who have forsaken their God (Europeans, who, though they may deny it, in actuality have been heavily saturated by 'fallout', the dark karma, from Chernobyl), but also must it be dealt with by the profane priests and prophets (European as well as some American Catholic, Protestant and Jewish theologians as well as the psychic peaceniks):

So this is what I AM THAT I AM as the Lord of Hosts [Sanat Kumara] says about the prophets:

"Now I will give them wormwood for their food, and poisoned water to drink, since from the prophets of Jerusalem godlessness has spread throughout the land."

I AM THAT I AM, Lord of Hosts says this:

"Do not listen to what those prophets say: they are deluding you, they retail visions of their own, and not what comes from the mouth of I AM THAT I AM; to those who reject the word of I AM THAT I AM they say, 'Peace will be yours,' and to those who follow the dictates of a hardened heart, 'No misfortune will touch you.'"

(But who has been present at the council of I AM THAT I AM? Who has seen it and heard His Word? Who has paid attention to His Word in order to proclaim it?)

Now a storm of I AM THAT I AM breaks, a tempest whirls, it bursts over the head of the descendants of the Wicked One; the anger of I AM THAT I AM will not turn aside until He has performed, and has carried out, the decision of His heart. You will understand this clearly in the days to come.

"I have not sent those prophets, yet they are running; I have not spoken to them, yet they are prophesying. Have they been present at my council? If so, let them proclaim my words to my people and turn them from their evil way and from the wickedness of their deeds!

"Am I a God when near—it is I AM THAT I AM who speaks—and not one when far away? Can anyone hide in a dark corner without my seeing him?—it is I AM THAT I AM who speaks. Do I not fill heaven and earth?—it is I AM THAT I AM who speaks.

"I have heard what the prophets say who make their lying prophecies in my name. 'I have had a dream,' they say, 'I have had a dream!'" (Jeremiah 23:15–25, Jerusalem Bible)

And again the prophet Jeremiah converses with I AM THAT I AM who appears to him in the Person of the Lord of Hosts:

"Ah, Lord I AM THAT I AM," I answered, "here are the prophets telling them, 'You will not see the sword, famine will not touch you; I promise you unbroken peace in this place.'"

Then I AM THAT I AM said to me,

"The prophets are prophesying lies in my name; I have not sent them, I gave them no orders, I never spoke to them. Delusive visions, hollow predictions, daydreams of their own, that is what they prophesy to you.

"Therefore, I AM THAT I AM says this:

"The prophets who prophesy in my name when I have not sent them, and tell you there will be no sword or famine in this land, these same prophets are doomed to perish by sword and famine.

"And as for the people to whom they prophesy, they will be tossed into the streets of Jerusalem, victims of famine and the sword, with not a soul to bury them: neither them nor their wives, nor their sons, nor their daughters. I will pour down on them their own wickedness [karma]." (Jeremiah 14:13–16, Jerusalem Bible)

The LORD's Chastisement of the House of Joseph

But to America, Britannia and the English-speaking peoples—the seed of Joseph, of his sons Ephraim and Manasseh—the LORD has declared through the lovable Amos.

Seek I AM THAT I AM and you shall live, or else He will rush like fire on the House of Joseph and burn it up, with none at Bethel able to put out the flames.

It is He who made the Pleiades and Orion, who turns the dusk to dawn and day to darkest night. He summons the waters of the sea and pours them over the land. I AM THAT I AM is his name.

He blazes out ruin on the stronghold and brings destruction to the fortress—trouble for those who turn justice into wormwood, throwing integrity to the ground; who hate the man dispensing justice at the city gate and detest those who speak with honesty.

Well then, since you have trampled on the poor man, extorting levies on his wheat—those houses you have built of dressed stone, you will never live in them; and those precious vineyards you have planted, you will never drink their wine.

For I know that your crimes are many, and your sins enormous: persecutors of the virtuous, blackmailers, turning away the needy at the city gate. No wonder the prudent man keeps silent, the times are so evil.

Seek Good and not Evil so that you may live, and that I AM THAT I AM as the Lord of Hosts may really be with you as you claim He is.

Hate Evil, love Good, maintain justice at the city gate, and it may be that I AM THAT I AM as the Lord of Hosts will take pity on the remnant of Joseph. (Amos 5:6–15, Jerusalem Bible)

CHAPTER 17

Nostradamus'
Conclusion of the Matter

Nostradamus foresaw the end of Soviet Communism. It is an astonishing prediction of an event anticipated by the martyrs of Soviet Communism who have been massacred by the millions, of whom it is written:

> And when he had opened the fifth seal, I saw under the altar the souls of them that were slain for the word of God, and for the testimony which they held:
> And they cried with a loud voice, saying, How long, O Lord, holy and true, dost thou not judge and avenge our blood on them that dwell on the earth?
> And white robes were given unto every one of them; and it was said unto them, that they should rest yet for a little season, until their fellowservants also and their brethren, that should be killed as they were, should be fulfilled. (Rev. 6:9–11)

But Nostradamus' prediction is even more remarkable since it places the point of the unraveling of the Big Lie near Kiev at the Dnieper, about 15 miles from the Chernobyl Nuclear Power Plant:

> The law of More will be seen to decline:
> After another much more seductive:
> Dnieper first will come to give way:
> Through gifts and tongue another more
>   attractive.[166]   III.95

Of this most transparent prophecy Leoni writes, "For the reader in the second half of the 20th century, this is one of the most interesting of all the prophecies of Nostradamus—one full of portentous meaning for this era.... We now have the generic name 'communism' to apply to the utopian ideologies of which Sir Thomas More's *Utopia* is the common ancestor. Undoubtedly this work, published in Latin when Nostradamus was in the midst of his education, was read by him.

"The prophecy implies a widespread success of this ideology prior to its decline, and mentions that the decline will start where the Dnieper is located. This is the principal river of the Ukraine. In Nostradamus' day it was one of the most backward parts of Europe, part of the Polish-Lithuanian state for three hundred years, and hardly an area Nostradamus would choose for the locale involving any contemporary movement of this nature, such as the Anabaptists.

"Accordingly, it is not unreasonable to speculate on a possible 20th-century fulfillment of this prophecy, involving the Soviet Ukraine and perhaps its chief city (which is on the Dnieper), Kiev. The nature of the more seductive law and the more attractive tongue are subjects for further speculation."[167]

Utopia is many things to many people. Historians have taken *Utopia* as a blueprint for British imperialism, humanists as a manifesto for total reform of the Christian renaissance, and literary critics as a work of a noncommitted intellectual.

In it More describes an ideal society where all property is held in common and food is distributed at public markets and common dining halls. With its sweeping condemnation of all private property, *Utopia* influenced early Socialist thinkers. Karl Kautsky, the German Socialist theoretician, saw *Utopia* "as a vision of the socialist society of the future" and hailed More as the father of the Bolshevik Revolution.[168]

Yet More's Utopian society and Soviet communism have striking differences. For instance, in *Utopia*, citizenship was dependent upon the belief in a just God who rewards or punishes in an afterlife.

Professor John Anthony Scott says that More's "views on communism and private property have been explained as an expression of the medieval monastic ideal, in which Christian men and women took vows of poverty and chastity, shared all things in common, and devoted themselves through prayer and good works to the service of the poor and the sick."[169]

Now let us examine Nostradamus' prophecy for the decline of World Communism and the far-reaching consequences of the judgment of Wormwood at Chernobyl:

Quatrain III.95 describes three kinds of society: The first is an idealistic communism embodied in *Utopia* ("the law of More"). After it declines there appears "another"—the second form of communism—which is "much more seductive," World Communism Soviet-style.

Communism, as we know it, is a seductive metaphysical theory that could not be farther from the basic principles of Thomas More in its atheism, aggression, and unvarnished imperialism. It has been seductive since the first alluring promises of "Peace, Land, and Bread" were made by the Bolsheviks in 1917.

In reality Soviet Communism has from the beginning sown the seeds of its own decline. But the day and date of the initiating of the spiral of its decline is calculated at the triggering of events which give way at the Dnieper—the Chernobyl disaster.

That the Soviet Union is due to self-destruct is evident from its karmic history. The only mitigating factor of the due date has been and continues to be the intercession of Western capitalists and the international bankers, spies, fifth-column sympathizers and agents of the United States government—conscious and unconscious.

The Soviet Union was never a duly elected or

popularly supported regime. In effect, Lenin and his confederates waged a premeditated war against those whom they ruled. He realized long before the Bolshevik Revolution that that would be the case and cultivated terror as an instrument of revolution and governance. As early as 1905 he was looking forward to the use of terror such as gripped France in 1793 "to settle accounts with Tsarism" following the revolution.[170]

In 1908, Lenin wrote about "real, nationwide terror, which reinvigorates the country and through which the Great French Revolution achieved glory."[171] On the night of July 16, 1918, the Emperor Nicholas II, his wife, four daughters, and the czarevitch were brutally murdered in the basement of the House of Special Purpose by order of Lenin. Their bodies were burned and thrown into an abandoned mine shaft.

Lenin and his confederates also recognized that since they could never rule popularly they would have to institutionalize terror as a means of control. Thus the Cheka, or secret police, was created to be the direct agent of state power. Some years later Lenin's favorite Bolshevik historian, Pokrovsky, said that the secret police "sprang from the very essence of the proletarian revolution."[172] Between 1918 and 1919, the Cheka executed 1,000 people a month without trial.

The Soviet Union is ruled by a dictatorship that installed itself by force and maintains itself by terror. It is compelled to continually increase its power to stay in power, lest it be overthrown. Indeed, it cultivates violence as a form of vital energy. By the time Lenin was no more in 1924, 500,000 people had already died in Soviet prisons or camps.[173]

In 1937–38, during the heyday of Stalin's great terror, 40,000 people were shot each month. While the estimates vary, the Soviets have killed somewhere between 35 and 45 million of their own people since 1917.

Because of its obsessive need for power and control, the Soviet state must of necessity stifle economic production. Prior to the Bolshevik Revolution, Russia was a net exporter of wheat. After the Revolution, the Communist leadership succeeded in institutionalizing agricultural shortages.

Likewise, prior to the Revolution "airplanes and automobiles *of indigenous Russian design* were produced in quantity," says Antony Sutton.[174]

But not so after the Revolution. As we have already seen, the Soviet Union was built by the West, simply because it could not build itself. Soviet Communism cannot produce a viable economy. And because of its political and economic weaknesses, it cannot change. Today it is still essentially the same state created by Lenin and Stalin whose traditions are embodied by paranoid leaders clinging tenaciously to power over their subjects.

The current rulers in Moscow manage a far-flung empire of gulags (prison camps), forcibly "treat" dissidents with painful, personality-destroying drugs in special psychiatric hospitals, and still haul people off to be shot.

The KGB (the latest edition of the secret police) still practices terror against the Soviet population. It is joined in this endeavor by an even more sinister, more secretive organization—the GRU, or Soviet Military Intelligence. Once a GRU agent is recruited, he's an agent for life. Those who try to defect are incinerated in a crematorium. "Few people, inside or outside of Russia, have ever heard of the GRU," says Robert Moss. "Yet its budget for foreign intelligence operations is larger than that of the KGB."

Moss says that the GRU has "been responsible for some of the most stunning coups in the annals of Soviet espionage." Among other things, GRU agents "stole the secret of the atomic bomb for Russia."[175] Today they are in the United States like red ants carrying off technology for the Red Army.

Oppression is present everywhere in the Soviet Union. But it is in keeping with the law of karma that the unraveling of the Soviet Empire should begin near Kiev. For it was at Kiev that Stalin waged war against the peasants, and thus came to pass the *darkest* and most diabolical period in Russian history.

According to historian Robert Conquest, during the early part of this century the Russian intelligentsia saw the peasants as "the People incarnate, the soul of the country, suffering, patient, the hope of the future." But they could also be stubborn and resistant to change. And that bothered the Communists. Lenin complained that the peasant, "far from being an instinctive or traditional collectivist, is in fact fiercely and meanly individualistic." Stalin thought the peasants were scum.[176]

The first stage of Stalin's war was directed against the "kulaks"—supposedly rich, greedy, brutal farmers who, according to Soviet propaganda, exploited the labor of others. In reality, the kulaks were highly productive farmers, who might typically own between 10 and 25 acres of land and as many as three cows. They formed the backbone of Soviet agriculture and the foundation of the Russian food chain. Nevertheless, the Bolsheviks quickly moved against them. "The *kulak* was an ideological enemy," says Antony Sutton, but his ability to produce made him "at least up to 1928–29, indispensable."[177]

Starting in the winter of 1929, Stalin had them "dekulakized," i.e., deported to work camps in the Arctic in the dead of winter. Conquest, who chronicled this tragic chapter of history in his recently published *The Harvest of Sorrow,* writes that upon arrival the peasants had to build their own shelter. Three million died in the early stages of this "resettlement" process, mostly children.

Stalin then pressed ahead with the collectivization of agriculture. He succeeded in ruining it and killing tens of thousands of peasants who resisted in the process. Then he began his assault on the Ukraine and surrounding areas.

The Ukrainians, many of them kulaks, had been a problem for the Soviets from the beginning. In the free elections of 1917, they voted overwhelmingly against the Bolsheviks. They had strong nationalistic yearnings, their own flourishing culture, and they resisted collectivization.

But Stalin had a way to deal with them. In 1932–33 he engineered a genocidal famine. His method was simple. In July of 1932 he requisitioned 6.6 million tons of grain from the peasants of the Ukraine. It was more than they could possibly produce. But Stalin forced them to deliver what they did have and sent "brigades" with crowbars to search the peasants' houses to make sure they were not holding out. If they found grain, they shot the peasant who hoarded it or sent him to a labor camp.

Stalin sealed the border between Russia and the Ukraine and famine set in. Between 1932–33 seven million people died of hunger, six million of them Ukrainians.

The conclusion of the matter is the third type of society described in quatrain III.95: "Through gifts and tongue another more attractive." The key to deciphering this line lies in the words "through gifts" of the Holy Spirit and "tongues" of angels. In other words, this line describes a pristine and primitive form of communism—the Community (i.e., a coming into unity) of the Holy Spirit.

This society supersedes the first two and is a return to Eden. It is built on the ideals of the earliest golden ages and those to come. Its foundation is the God flame of its members who endow every aspect of its life with the light, love and presence of the Trinity.

Here the Universal Christ is the basis of an individualism where members of society are free to declare: "I Am my brother's keeper" and to fulfill it voluntarily, creatively in a world climate of spiritual freedom. This spiritual freedom is reflected in an abundant life based on the free sharing of the fruits of one's labor—as Christ said, "Freely ye have received, freely give."

The Spirit of this Community is abroad in the hearts of the people today and it will take hold and flourish after coming earth changes—long after Soviet Communism passes away—as it surely will. For at Chernobyl, Wormwood and his karma fell where he created it.

Yes, Chernobyl—Star of Wormwood, Star of Soviet Destiny, How art thou, so great a star, fallen from heaven burning, burning like a ball of fire!

Notes to Book Two

1. Date based on Julian calendar. Dec. 23 by Gregorian calendar.
2. Century I, quatrain 63 in Edgar Leoni, *Nostradamus and His Prophecies* (New York: Bell Publishing Co., 1961), p. 149.
3. Stewart Robb, *Prophecies on World Events by Nostradamus* (New York: Ace Books, 1961), p. 119.
4. Despite Nostradamus' own statements, a number of commentators say that his prophecies only run through 1999.
5. Stewart Robb, *Nostradamus and the End of Evils Begun* (Santa Ana, Calif.: Parca Publishing Co., 1984), p. 20.
6. Robb, *Prophecies,* p. 59.
7. Leoni, *Nostradamus,* p. 614.
8. Robb, *Prophecies,* p. 60.
9. Robb believes that Nostradamus is referring to the "War of the Three Henrys" (1585). See Century VI, quatrain 2 in Robb, *Prophecies,* p. 50; Erika Cheetham, *The Prophecies of Nostradamus* (New York: Berkley Books, 1973), p. 250.
10. Leoni, *Nostradamus,* p. 341.
11. Ibid., p. 690.
12. Ibid., p. 339.
13. Robb, *Prophecies,* p. 21.
14. Ibid., p. 22, 24.
15. Ibid., p. 23.
16. Ibid., pp. 18, 42, 64, 129, 133; Leoni, *Nostradamus,* pp. 169, 589; Stewart Robb, *Nostradamus on Napoleon* (New York: Oracle Press, 1961).
17. Century I, quatrain 1 in Jean-Charles de Fontbrune, *Nostradamus 2: Into the Twenty-First Century,* trans. Alexis Lykiard (London: Pan Books, 1984), p. 22.
18. Lee McCann, *Nostradamus: The Man Who Saw Through Time* (New York: Farrar, Strauss and Giroux, 1941), p. 155.
19. Leoni, *Nostradamus,* p. 112, 327, 329.
20. Ibid., pp. 57, 58.
21. Ibid., p. 141.
22. Jean Héritier, *Catherine de Medici,* trans. Charlotte Haldane (London: George Allen & Unwin, 1963), p. 77.
23. Leoni, *Nostradamus,* p. 103.
24. Ibid., p. 329.
25. Century III, quatrain 55 in Cheetham, *Prophecies of Nostradamus,* p. 144.
26. Leoni, *Nostradamus,* p. 345.
27. Ibid.
28. Ibid., p. 187.
29. Ibid., p. 578; Cheetham, *Prophecies of Nostradamus,* p. 112.

30. Leoni, *Nostradamus,* p. 600.
31. Rene Noorbergen, *Nostradamus Predicts the End of the World* (New York: Pinnacle Books, 1981), pp. 41-44.
32. Leoni, *Nostradamus,* pp. 253, 638-39.
33. Ibid., p. 149.
34. Ibid., p. 580.
35. Edward Teller and Allen Brown, *The Legacy of Hiroshima* (Garden City, N.Y.: Doubleday & Co., 1962), p. 5.
36. Michael Pogodzinski, *Second Sunrise--Nuclear War: The Untold Story* (Thorndike, Maine: Thorndike Press, 1983), p. 97.
37. Erika Cheetham, *The Further Prophecies of Nostradamus: 1985 and Beyond* (New York: Perigee Books, 1985), p. 96.
38. Robb, *Nostradamus and the End of Evils Begun,* pp. 48-49.
39. Noorbergen, *Nostradamus Predicts,* p. 37.
40. Cheetham, *Further Prophecies of Nostradamus,* p. 208.
41. Leoni, *Nostradamus,* p. 187.
42. Cheetham, *Further Prophecies of Nostradamus,* p. 209.
43. Noorbergen, *Nostradamus Predicts,* p. 18.
44. Matti Golan, *The Secret Conversations of Henry Kissinger* (New York: Bantam Books, 1976), p. 7.
45. Ibid., p. 90.
46. Ibid., p. 86.
47. Ibid., p. 88.
48. Ishaq I. Ghanayem and Alden H. Voth, *The Kissinger Legacy: American-Middle East Policy* (New York: Praeger Publishers, 1984), p. 110; Golan, *Secret Conversations,* pp. 90-91.
49. Former National Security Adviser Zbigniew Brzezinski noted that when the Soviets backed off in the face of U.S. warnings in 1973 "the United States still held a margin of advantage in strategic weapons. In a setting of ambiguous strategic parity--and especially if this is compounded by asymmetrical American vulnerability--the Soviet Union may be bolder next time. It may simply act, deploying its airborne forces on the side of an Arab protagonist, and leave it to the United States to decide whether to respond or not." See Zbigniew Brzezinski, *Game Plan: A Geostrategic Framework for the Conduct of the U.S.-Soviet Contest* (New York: Atlantic Monthly Press, 1986), p. 113.
50. Robb, *Nostradamus and the End of Evils Begun,* p. 48.
51. Leoni, *Nostradamus,* p. 187.
52. Ibid., p. 660.
53. Ibid., p. 187.
54. Cheetham, *Further Prophecies of Nostradamus,* p. 209; Leoni, *Nostradamus,* p. 187.
55. Leoni, *Nostradamus,* p. 600.
56. Cheetham, *Prophecies of Nostradamus,* p. 111.
57. Leoni, *Nostradamus,* p. 186.

202 *Notes to Pages 42-65*

58. Antony C. Sutton, *National Suicide: Military Aid to the Soviet Union* (New Rochelle, N.Y.: Arlington House, 1973), pp. 253, 255.

59. Antony C. Sutton, *Western Technology and Soviet Economic Development: 1930 to 1945* (Stanford, Calif.: Hoover Institution Press, 1971), p. 30.

60. Antony C. Sutton, *Western Technology and Soviet Economic Development: 1917 to 1930* (Stanford, Calif.: Hoover Institution on War, Revolution and Peace, 1968), p.198; Sutton, *National Suicide,* p. 255.

61. Sutton, *National Suicide,* p. 255.

62. Ibid., p. 262.

63. Alan Stang, "What Is Behind the High-Tech Trade with the Soviets," *Conservative Digest* 12, no. 9 (October 1986): 45-54.

64. Cheetham, *Further Prophecies of Nostradamus,* p. 210.

65. Ibid., p. 209.

66. Noorbergen, *Nostradamus Predicts,* p. 7.

67. Personal interview with Stewart Robb, author, fall 1986; Robb, *Nostradamus and the End of Evils Begun,* pp. 48, 148.

68. Robb, *Nostradamus and the End of Evils Begun,* p. 150.

69. Leoni, *Nostradamus,* p. 589.

70. Robb, *Nostradamus and the End of Evils Begun,* p. 150; Cheetham says, "This is a curious verse. The word *sortira* for *ira* indicates that the Easterner does not usually leave his country; could this refer to the North Vietnamese talks in Paris? France (*la Gaule*) to which he comes, was one of the few countries to maintain diplomatic relations with China until its acceptance into United Nations in October 1971" (*Prophecies of Nostradamus,* p. 84).

71. "Pacific Overtures," *Time,* 17 November 1986, p. 58. In the context of this quatrain it is worthy of note that in October 1985 Mikhail Gorbachev "left his seat" in the Kremlin for what *Newsweek* called "a charm offensive in Paris" ("Disarming Charm," *Newsweek,* 14 October 1985, p. 30).

72. Brian May, *Russia, America, the Bomb and the Fall of Western Europe* (Boston: Routledge & Kegan Paul, 1984), p. 43.

73. De Fontbrune, *Nostradamus 2,* p. 11.

74. "Genocide Chic," *The Coming Revolution: The Magazine for Higher Consciousness* (Summer 1986), pp. 58-65, 95-96.

75. Robert H. Ferrell and Howard H. Quint, eds., *The Talkative President: The Off-the-Record Press Conferences of Calvin Coolidge* (New York: Garland Publishing, 1979), p. 143.

76. "The '20s and the '80s: Can Deflation Turn Into Depression?" *Business Week,* 9 June 1986, p. 62.

77. "LTV and B of A Show Dark Side of Oil Collapse," *Los Angeles Times,* 18 July 1986, Business section.

78. *Washington Post,* 23 February 1986.

79. Denis Healey, "Collective Security After 50 Years," lecture given at the London School of Economics, London, England.
80. "Cheap Oil," *Time,* 14 April 1986, p. 62.
81. Brzezinski, *Game Plan,* p. 254.
82. Ibid., pp. 126-27.
83. Joseph D. Douglass, Jr. and Amoretta M. Hoeber, *Soviet Strategy for Nuclear War* (Stanford, Calif.: Hoover Institution Press, 1979), p. 10.
84. Herman Kahn, *Thinking About the Unthinkable in the 1980s* (New York: Simon and Schuster, 1984), pp. 102-3.
85. Jan Sejna, *We Will Bury You* (London: Sidgwick & Jackson, 1982), p. 101, inside cover; lecture, Washington, D.C.
86. Leoni, *Nostradamus,* p. 253.
87. Ibid., p. 397.
88. Ibid., p. 728.
89. Cheetham, *Further Prophecies of Nostradamus,* p. 210.
90. Antony C. Sutton, *Wall Street and the Bolshevik Revolution* (New Rochelle, N.Y.: Arlington House, 1974), p. 83.
91. Antony C. Sutton, *Wall Street and the Rise of Hitler* (Seal Beach, Calif.: '76 Press, 1976), p. 15.
92. Ibid., p. 67.
93. Leoni, *Nostradamus,* p. 309.
94. Ibid., pp. 671-72.
95. Cheetham, *Further Prophecies of Nostradamus,* pp. 194-95.
96. Noorbergen, *Nostradamus Predicts,* pp. 157, 159.
97. Ibid., p. 159.
98. Leoni, *Nostradamus,* p. 672.
99. Ibid., p. 239.
100. Ibid., p. 630.
101. Cheetham, *Prophecies of Nostradamus,* p. 191.
102. Noorbergen, *Nostradamus Predicts,* p. 45.
103. Leoni, *Nostradamus,* p. 238.
104. Ibid., p. 239; Cheetham, *Prophecies of Nostradamus,* p. 191; Noorbergen, *Nostradamus Predicts,* p. 45.
105. Leoni, *Nostradamus,* p. 289.
106. Ibid., p. 662.
107. Cheetham, *Further Prophecies of Nostradamus,* p. 94.
108. "A Family of Spies," *Newsweek,* 10 June 1985, p. 35.
109. Leoni, *Nostradamus,* p. 365.
110. Cheetham, *Prophecies of Nostradamus,* p. 330.
111. Cheetham, *Further Prophecies of Nostradamus,* pp. 191, 192.
112. Noorbergen, *Nostradamus Predicts,* p. 172.
113. Leoni, *Nostradamus,* p. 265.
114. Ibid., p. 648.
115. Cheetham, *Further Prophecies of Nostradamus,* p. 200.
116. Leoni, *Nostradamus,* p. 189.
117. Cheetham, *Prophecies of Nostradamus,* p. 114.

118. Noorbergen, *Nostradamus Predicts*, p. 156.
119. Robb, personal interview.
120. E. Raymond Capt, *Missing Links Discovered in Assyrian Tablets: Study of Assyrian tables that reveal the fate of the Lost Tribes of Israel* (Thousand Oaks, Calif.: Artisan Sales, 1985), pp. 203-16.
121. Karl Marx, "The Pale Maiden," in *Karl Marx, Frederick Engels: Collected Works* (New York: International Publishers, 1975), 1: 613.
122. Noorbergen, *Nostradamus Predicts*, p. 156.
123. Robb, *Nostradamus and the End of Evils Begun*, p. 49.
124. Leoni, *Nostradamus*, p. 657.
125. Cheetham, *Further Prophecies of Nostradamus*, p. 135.
126. Leoni, *Nostradamus*, p. 657.
127. Cheetham, *Further Prophecies of Nostradamus*, p. 135.
128. Robb, *Nostradamus and the End of Evils Begun*, p. 51.
129. Ibid., p. 137.
130. Leoni, *Nostradamus*, p. 149.
131. Ibid., p. 580.
132. Cheetham, *Further Prophecies of Nostradamus*, p. 95.
133. Cheetham, *Prophecies of Nostradamus*, p. 53.
134. Leoni, *Nostradamus*, pp. 157, 427.
135. Ibid., pp. 583, 746.
136. The cycle of earthquakes initiated in 1972 by Helios has still not seen its conclusion. For example, in the two months prior to Saint Germain's 11/17/85 dictation (see p. 56), major earthquake activity included: **Sept. 19, 1985, Mexico City**, 8.1 on the Richter scale, killed an estimated 10,000-30,000, injured 30,000 and left over 100,000 homeless. **Sept. 21, Mexico City**, 7.6 earthquake again rocked the city, causing additional casualties and damage. **Sept. 15, Indonesia**, 6.3. **Oct. 2, San Bernardino**, 5.0 (felt through much of Southern California). **Oct. 4, Tokyo**, 6.2 (strongest quake there in 56 years). **Oct. 19, New York City**, 3.8 to 4.0--one of the largest to hit the metropolitan area in years. During the same period, **Nov. 13, Armero, Colombia**, the volcano Nevado del Ruiz erupted and caused a mudslide that buried the town, killing more than 20,000 in Armero and Chinchiná.
137. Hugh Lynn Cayce, *Earth Changes Update* (Virginia Beach, Va.: A.R.E. Press, 1980), pp. 87-90, 91.
138. Noorbergen, *Nostradamus Predicts*, pp. 160-64.
139. Cheetham, *Prophecies of Nostradamus*, pp. 63, 409.
140. Telephone interview with Vincent Montane, commissioner, California Seismic Safety Commission, December 1986.
141. Leoni, *Nostradamus*, p. 163.
142. Telephone interview with Ken Maize, senior energy analyst, Union of Concerned Scientists, Washington, D.C., Oct. 1986.

143. Gal. 6:7.
144. *Rubáiyát of Omar Khayyám* (trans. Edward FitzGerald, 5th ed.), quatrain 71.
145. Matt. 21:44.
146. David Williams, "Chernobyl: The Nuclear Disaster That Shook the World," *Horoscope,* October 1986, pp. 55, 56.
147. Maize, telephone interview.
148. Arch Crawford, *Crawford Perspectives,* April 1986.
149. "Anatomy of a Catastrophe," *Time,* 1 September 1986, p. 26.
150. Vivian E. Robson, *The Fixed Stars and Constellations in Astrology* (New York: Samuel Weiser, 1969), pp. 165, 171, 172, 173, 174, 194.
151. *Sovet Tojikistoni,* 15 November 1985.
152. Telephone interview with David R. Marples, research associate, Canadian Institute of Ukrainian Studies at the University of Alberta, Edmonton, Alberta, 31 Oct. 1986.
153. Personal interview with Soviet émigré, Jenny Brook, 20 October 1986. According to David Marples, the southern regions of Belorussia would have received the direct effect of radiation from the Chernobyl accident (Marples, telephone interview).
154. *Vitchizna,* September 1986.
155. John W. Gofman, "Assessing Chernobyl's Cancer Consequences: Application of Four 'Laws' of Radiation Carcinogenesis" (Paper presented at the 192nd National Meeting of the American Chemical Society, Anaheim, Calif., September 9, 1986), p. 39.
156. "Anatomy of a Catastrophe," *Newsweek,* 1 September 1986, p. 26.
157. "Chernobyl: Officials Ousted, Repairs Go On," *Current Digest of the Soviet Press* 38, no. 33 (June 1986):14; Marples, telephone interview.
158. "Chernobyl Strike," *Soviet Labour Review* 4, no. 3 (October 1986):2.
159. "Anatomy of a Catastrophe," *Newsweek,* 1 September 1986, p. 28.
160. "Soviets Unveil Lessons from Chernobyl," *Science News,* 30 August 1986, p. 135.
161. "Chernobyl Fallout: Apocalyptic Tale and Fear," *New York Times,* 26 July 1986, p. 1.
162. Ibid.
163. "Chernobyl Three Months After the Accident," *Current Digest of the Soviet Press* 38, no. 35, (July 1986):12.
164. Astrology pervasive throughout Revelation. "A significant but somewhat neglected feature of Revelation is the relatively large amount of astrology that pervades the work from the first to the final chapter. Based upon the belief

that the heavenly bodies controlled the destinies of mankind, astral speculation was widespread in the Mediterranean world, and was accepted by Jews as well as by non-Jews, by both the learned and the ignorant.... Although in certain instances John may not have been aware of the astrological significance of some of the sources he used, nevertheless his frequent use of astral concepts and symbols is rather clear evidence that for the most part he introduced them knowingly and deliberately" (Martin Rist in *The Interpreter's Bible,* 12 vols. [Nashville: Abingdon Press, 1957], 12:358-59).

165. Matt. 16:4.
166. Leoni, *Nostradamus,* p. 217.
167. Ibid., pp. 617-18.
168. John Anthony Scott, Introduction to *Utopia,* trans. Peter K. Marshall (New York: Washington Square Press, 1965), p. xvii.
169. Ibid., pp. xvii-xviii.
170. Vladimir Ilyich Lenin, *Collected Works,* 3d Russian ed., 8:62, in U.S. Congress, Senate Committee on the Judiciary, *The Human Cost of Soviet Communism,* 91st Cong., 2d sess., 1970, p. 7.
171. Vladimir Ilyich Lenin, *Collected Works,* 4th Russian ed., 13:435, in U.S. Congress, Senate Committee on the Judiciary, *The Human Cost of Soviet Communism,* 91st Cong., 2d sess., 1970, p. 7.
172. U.S. Congress, Senate Committee on the Judiciary, *The Human Cost of Soviet Communism,* 91st Cong., 2d sess., 1970, p. 7.
173. Ibid., p. 1.
174. Sutton, *Western Technology: 1917 to 1930,* p. 344.
175. "Inside the G.R.U.," *Parade,* 6 September 1981, p. 6.
176. Robert Conquest, *The Harvest of Sorrow: Soviet Collectivization and the Terror-Famine* (New York: Oxford University Press, 1986), pp. 19, 20.
177. Sutton, *Western Technology: 1917 to 1930,* p. 113.

Unless otherwise noted, all publications and audiocassettes are Summit University Press (Box A, Livingston, Montana 59047), released under the Messengership of Mark L. Prophet and Elizabeth Clare Prophet.
Postage Rates for Books: For books $5.95 and under, please add $.50 for the first book, $.25 each additional book; for books $7.95 through $15.95, add $1.00 for the first, $.50 each additional. **Postage Rates for Audiocassettes:** For single audiocassettes, please add $.50 for the first cassette and $.30 for up to 4 additional cassettes; 8-cassette albums, add $1.30 for the first, $1.15 for each additional album.

Book Three

A Prophecy
of Planetary
Cataclysm

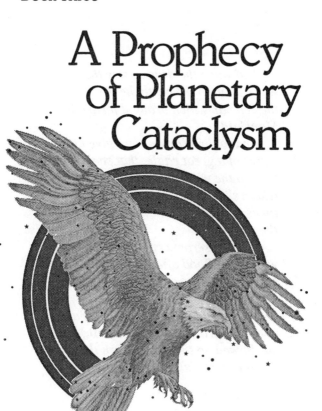

The Hierarchs of
the Nature Kingdom
Predict Earth Changes

Saint Germain

And when the dragon saw that he was cast unto the earth, he persecuted the Woman which brought forth the Manchild.

And to the Woman were given two wings of a great eagle, that she might fly into the wilderness, into her place, where she is nourished for a time, and times, and half a time, from the face of the serpent.

And the serpent cast out of his mouth water as a flood after the Woman, that he might cause her to be carried away of the flood.

And the earth helped the Woman, and the earth opened her mouth, and swallowed up the flood which the dragon cast out of his mouth.

Revelation

CHAPTER I

The Divine Edict for Planetary Cataclysm:

An Imploring for Assistance to Nature's Mighty Workers in the Earth

by Virgo and Pelleur
Hierarchs of the Gnomes
Servants of God and Man in the Earth Element

Blessed Servants of the Most High God:

Elemental life—fire, air, water, and earth—salute the God flame burning on the altar of the sons and daughters of the Most High God!

We are the hierarchs of the servants of God and man in the earth element. Our twin flames are vessels of the Father/Mother God on behalf of the beings of the elements who serve mankind through the various classifications of the elements that make up the physical body of the earth.

The blessed servants who minister unto the needs of a planetary evolution tirelessly, joyously, day by day, are referred to as gnomes and often relegated to the realm of myth and magic. We come, therefore, to present ourselves before the children of the Light as sponsors of an evolutionary lifewave of elemental Nature spirits who are by far mankind's best servants, most noble and kind, stalwart and courageous in the face of every abuse of the earth body and every assault against the law of earth's harmony.

As the days of mankind's infamy against the Light increase the burden upon these unseen yet very present helpers in Nature, we come forth pleading the cause of renewed cosmic cooperation between the Children of the Sun and all of elemental life.

The beings you call gnomes, whose image has been dwarfed in the story of *Snow White and the Seven Dwarfs* and other fairy tales, actually range in size from three-inch-high elves playing in the grasses, to the three-foot dwarfs, all the way to the hierarchies of the mountains who attend the Great Hall of the Mountain King and Queen glimpsed by Grieg and portrayed in his musical tribute to the special gnomes of Norway and the Norsemen.

There are giants in the elemental kingdom of the earth. These are powerful beings who wield the fire of atom and molecule and hold the balance for the continents through cataclysm, flood, and fire. This evolution was created by Elohim to sustain the platform for the great experiment in free will ordained by God unto his children whom he sent forth into the planetary systems to be fruitful in the Christ consciousness and to multiply the manifestation of God in their offspring and in the works of their hands.

As the gnomes represent the Holy Spirit and are transmitters of the love of the Comforter through the beauty and caring of Nature for God's children, there are other elementals who represent the office of the Father, the Son, and the Mother. Thus, even in the lower kingdoms of the planetary bodies there are representatives of the Four Cosmic Forces envisioned by Ezekiel and Saint John.[1]

The mighty gnomes, gentle and merciful, are the archetype in Nature of the ox who treadeth out the corn,[2] the great burdenbearer of mankind's karma. Self-sacrificing, they even deny their own evolutionary fulfillment in order that man as the highest manifestation of God might continue to have the opportunity to prove the law of grace and enter into the rite of spring in the true spirit of the resurrection flame.

These blessed keepers of the garden of God wait upon the LORD and his coming into the temple of his sons and daughters. They adore the threefold flame of Life, though it be but a neglected spark of a lost divinity in the wayward souls of Terra.

Patiently they are the overcomers and the compensators of mankind's misqualifications of the energies of the Holy Spirit. Again and again they gladly lay down their life for their friends, though their friends ignore their pitiful plight and exhibit a shameful neglect of these most devoted servants.

The Archangels and the angelic hosts through the blessed Holy Spirit are the conscious cooperators with all elemental life. They minister to their needs and infuse them with the light of the Trinity and the Mother as they continue to render their service to a largely ungrateful and unconscious world. There are billions upon billions of gnomes tending the cycles of earth in the four seasons, purging the planet of poisons and pollutants so dangerous to the physical bodies of man, animal, and plant life.

It is difficult for mankind to imagine the work of thousands of gnomes performed in the service of a single individual. When you consider all that man derives from the earth and his interaction with the elements of the earth as he himself is composed in his outer bodies of the "dust of the ground" as well as the waste and by-products that accumulate from a mere day's occupation of his time and space on earth, you begin to realize that it is by the grace of the dedication of literally millions of elementals that each child of God continues to have the opportunity to live and move and have being within the physical spectrum of the planetary bodies.

By the grace of the Holy Spirit and the angelic hosts, the gnomes retain the fervent hope in the ultimate resurrection of the soul of every man, woman, and child and the translation of the soul unto the Self-realized Life centered in the threefold unfed flame.

The only hope of immortality for the Nature spirits is through the immortality of the children of God. Thus each spring as the resurrection flame inundates the earth and the celebration of the victory of Life through the Saviour Jesus Christ is once again the invigoration of a planet and a people, elemental life rejoice that they, too, might one day inherit the full mantle of the risen Christ.

They worship him in the full glory of that joy that bedecks the earth with the green of life and floral offering and the purity of the distilled essences of their love permeating the very air, the land and sea and sky.

In the hopes of the eternal resurrection of God in man, the blessed servants in Nature therefore take unto their bodies and carry on their backs the weight of world karma, the momentums of war. They gladly absorb upon their hearts man's hatred of man and even the blood of the murderer, acting in accord with Satanic rite, who spills the blood of the innocent upon the hallowed ground.

When irresponsible lifestreams walk away from their crimes against one another and humanity, it is the gnomes who bear the crucifixion of Christ within their bodies. For they know the Great Law that someone must pay the price for blasphemy against God and his Son and his Holy Spirit if life as an evolutionary chain, as an instrument for the glorious miracle of Life begetting life, is to continue unbroken upon earth and other systems of worlds inhabited by a physical manifestation of God.

In the name of Jesus Christ and every son of God who has given his Life that the children of God might come of age and assume the mantle of their responsibility for personal and planetary karma, the gnomes offer themselves perpetually as the bearers of the sins of the world. As such, they are the constant reminders of Christ crucified.

They are the ones who adore him in the hour of his suffering and who will to be with him upon the cross of the Tree of Life until the blessed Children of the Sun should come and take pity upon them and out of hearts filled with compassion and the love of the Lord of the World take them down from the cross and receive them into the arms of everlasting Life.

Beloved students of Christ and Buddha, blessed readers of the *Pearls of Wisdom*, you who are sensitive to the currents of the Holy Spirit and to the purity of the World Mother as she gazes upon her children of earth, we come to you imploring assistance for these mighty workers in the earth, for their burden is very great and mankind must reckon with the law of compensation.

In past ages when the discord, death, and disease self-created by mankind have reached proportions greater than that which the elementals could bear, Nature herself has convulsed; and earth in upheaval (through the conscious cooperation of the hierarchs of the gnomes, the sylphs, the undines, and the fiery salamanders) has overturned mankind's misguided and malicious mechanization of life.

The saturation of earth and the earth body with inharmony generated by selfishness manifesting in every plane and frequency has in the past and may ultimately be in the present the cause of the supersaturation of elemental life with more than even billions of their bodies can bear in a concerted and heroic effort. Thus we come to explain that when mankind's discord reaches the level that is greater than elemental life can bear, the LORD God Almighty, acting through his emissaries on the Karmic Board and through the Lord of the World, must release the divine edict for partial or complete planetary cataclysm.

Cataclysm is always for the purpose of overthrowing the unacceptable offering of inharmony based on self-will and self-love and replacing it with the acceptable offering of the handiwork of God in man—performed unto the glory of God through the grace of his Son out of the true love of the Real Self that is the threefold flame of Life in every child of his heart.

Physical cataclysm, then, shows forth the demand of cosmic law that the Spirit/Matter universes are summoned into alignment with the living Word according to the orderly unfoldment of the cycles of cosmic law. Thus there are cycles in Nature, cycles keyed in the very nucleus of every atom of Matter, whereby the sound of the AUM is sounded from heart center to heart center, from star to star and sun to sun, and from the white fire core of every element of earth.

This sounding of the AUM of God's harmony is like the vibrating of God's tuning fork calling Home the atoms of his blessed substance.

As these atoms both of self and of energy enter the spiral of the homing and the great return to the Great Central Sun of Life, they are stripped (whether voluntarily or involuntarily) of all impure desire, all unreality, and all vibrations that cannot stand in the Presence of the LORD GOD—the Person, the Spirit of pure untrammeled Love. Thus it is written that the soul of man must place himself upon the rock of Christ willingly ere the rock descend upon him and grind him to powder.[3]

Thus the beings of Nature have ever been the instruments of the LORD's mercy and comfort unto every part of Life until the hour when the Son of God sounds the Word of the judgment. It is then that the blessed elementals must also play the role of the conveyer of the edicts of the Father and the Son and the Holy Spirit unto an evolving humanity. Thus it was elemental life who unleashed the fountains of the deep, causing the great deluge that resulted in the sinking of the continent of Atlantis and the flood of Noah.

This cataclysm was for the destruction of the works of the fallen ones and their godless creation which came forth out of the laboratories of

Atlantis and elsewhere. It was for the rectification of the wrong which was the result of the imaginations of men's hearts continually to do evil.

These imaginations were a perversion of the real 'eye magic' of God's all-seeing eye manifest in the third eye, the creative and procreative center of life. Thus the great deluge was a purification and a realignment of atoms and molecules of the entire earth body according to the inner law of harmony sealed in the sun of even pressure in the heart of the earth.

Twelve thousand cycles have passed since planetary cataclysm has been used as a means to right the course of mankind's misuse of free will. Now, you have heard from a member of the Karmic Board, the Lady Master Nada, of the concern of the spiritual hierarchies who are the sponsors of earth's evolution regarding the levels of discord prevalent today.

We come therefore to state our case on behalf of elemental life, to implore and to plead that Keepers of the Flame increase and intensify their invocations to the violet flame, standing shoulder to shoulder with the beings of the elements to transmute all human discord lest it become a burden too hard to bear and the pendulum of the Great Law swing again toward retribution through planetary cataclysm.

We send forth the warning to hearts of gold that if and unless there is a great intensification of the saturation of the earth body with the violet flame through the multiplication of the calls of Keepers of the Flame, there will be in this decade major planetary upheavals, changes in weather conditions, and earthquakes that result in great loss of life as well as permanent changes in the geographical surface of the earth.

The blessed beings of the elements have done and are doing all in their power to avert natural disaster. Again I repeat, we sound the warning! Unless the avant-garde of Lightbearers will put their hand to the plow and join forces with the servants of the ox who treadeth out the corn, increasing the flow of the Holy Spirit and the violet flame together with the resurrection flame on behalf of the servants of God and man in Nature, there will be violent changes in the earth body.

We alert you, beloved ones, while there is yet adequate time and space for you to comply with the Law and provide the necessary counterbalance of God's consciousness and his sacred fire.

As electrodes in the earth, your dynamic decrees, your prayers empowered by a pure heart enjoined to the LORD's Spirit, your fiats unto God's all-consuming sacred fire will be as the implanting of rods of the LORD in the earth, whirling vortices of energy that will consume and transmute mankind's discord by mercy's flame.

Thus it is our hope that by the conscious cooperation of elementals, Masters, and embodied man the course of oncoming world karma may once again be set back and the diligent ones again buy time and space for the recalcitrant ones and the laggards to bring up the rear and at last enter the Path as selfless servants of the Light.

Next week our cohorts in the service of earth's evolutions, Oromasis and Diana of the fire element, will bring you further enlightenment on the crisis of elemental life which can become through your faith, your hope, and your charity a cosmic cross of victory to all.

Obediently in the service of Elohim, we remain

Virgo and Pelleur

on behalf of elemental life serving earth and her evolutions.

April 6, 1980

CHAPTER 2

Your Conscious Cooperation with the Beings of the Elements:

In the Name of Christ, Command the Elementals to Set Life Free!

by Oromasis and Diana
Hierarchs of the Salamanders
Servants of God and Man in the Fire Element

Blessed Devotees of Our God
Who Is a Consuming Fire:
On this most solemn occasion of the gathering of the Four Hierarchs of the Elements under the Four Cosmic Forces, there is a summoning of representatives of the elemental kingdoms of fire, air, water, and earth from the four quadrants of the planet. We meet in conclave at the Royal Teton Retreat in North America, answering the call of the Lord of the World, the God of the Earth, who is our Gautama Buddha.

Scientists and laymen, citizens and ecologists around the world read the writing in the rock of elemental life who have scored and underscored the faults and fissures of the earth with their mathematical formulae for the timetable of earth's changes. Alas, few among embodied mankind can read the hieroglyphs of akasha and therefore benefit from the master scientists who move among elemental life as the guardians of planetary forcefields.

Nevertheless, the people of God on earth sense the coming changes. Psychics have predicted them more often than they have occurred while the co-workers with the fiery salamanders of our bands have invoked the sacred fire in the all-consuming violet flame to diligently remove the cause and core of those conditions which, coming out of the Dark Cycle [4] in Sagittarius commencing April 23, 1980, could precipitate various forms of cataclysm—unless checked by the great tidal wave of light from the Great Central Sun inundating the heart chakras of the pure and sending forth streams of Love accelerating the Ruby Ray for the balance of the threefold flame of Life in Matter.

As mankind in their councils deliberate the necessity for earthquake preparation and establish building codes for minimum loss of life in the event of 'natural' disaster, we contemplate the fiery destiny of the total planetary body and its total evolution.

The Ascended Master Cuzco has addressed us on the subject of impinging forcefields and the buildup of mass entities of hate and hate creation manifesting as war, black magic, and witchcraft. He has pointed out the overwhelming odds against which the brave elementals serve to anchor the light in the physical bodies of earth's children and in the earth itself.

On the one hand toxins, pollutants, chemicals, and deadly psychedelic drugs so reduce the light which the new generation can contain and carry in their body temples, while on the other industrial wastes, nuclear fallout, and dread pesticides disturb the natural interflow between the planes of the earth body.

These planes have been described as interpenetrating bands of electronic frequencies labeled etheric, mental, astral, and physical and corresponding to the alchemical elements of fire, air, water, and earth. These four quadrants of being parallel the four lower bodies of man, ranging from the least to the greatest density, and serve man as vehicles of the soul's self-awareness, its spiritual/material evolution, and its self-mastery in time and space poised as it is for the expansion of God-mastery unto infinity.

The etheric sheath is otherwise known as the fire body and corresponds to the fiery world. It is the highest vibrating plane in Matter and, as such, it is the door through which the soul passes unto the higher octaves of Spirit. This body contains the spiritual blueprint of the lifestream—the soul-identity as well as the pattern for the other three bodies which serve as instruments for the mental/emotional experience of the soul outplayed in the physical environment where the laws of physics and chemistry are mankind's best teachers of his karmic condition.

The etheric 'envelope' is the soul's vehicle for its journeyings throughout the planes of Matter and the means whereby it gains access to the retreats of the Great White Brotherhood located in the etheric plane. Saint John's vision of the New Jerusalem is derived from this plane and from the etheric cities which establish the inner blueprint of the 'city foursquare' to be outpictured in the civilizations of the earth.

Thus the four-sided base of the Great Pyramid of Selfhood is the symbol of the four planes of consciousness provided for the sons and daughters of God to perfect their Christ consciousness. The base of the Matter pyramid is both the platform of the rising spiral of self-awareness and the takeoff point whereby, through the All-Seeing Eye of God manifest as the 'EYE' AM Presence, the soul transcends itself in the 'leap' to realms of the infinite fire.

The elementals serving in these categories of the four planes come under the Four Cosmic Forces (whose archetypes the seers envisioned as the Lion, the Man, the Calf, and the flying Eagle) and are indeed pillars in the temple of life, sustaining the platform of existence in order that the planetary lifewaves may evolve Godward to the fullness of that spiritual Life in the Universal Christ who made himself manifest in the LORD and Saviour Jesus Christ.

The elementals of the sacred fire who serve in our bands are capable of wielding the most intense fires of the physical atom as well as the spiritual all-consuming fires of God. They span the octaves of the Spirit/Matter universes and are the connecting link for the service of the sylphs of the air, the undines of the water, and the gnomes of the earth.

Serving mankind's needs in the central sun of every atom of organic and inorganic life, the fiery salamanders infuse molecules of God's substance with the spiritual fires of creation and hold the balance of the Alpha-to-Omega cycles, regenerating and reinfusing the energies of creation with the necessary balance of life from the Great Central Sun. When the fiery salamanders cease to perform this function, decay, corrosion, and disintegration immediately appear, whether in plant life or in the manufactured products of civilization.

That which seems so naturally sustained by the very presence of life which mankind take for granted is actually imparted lovingly through the joint cooperation of the Four Cosmic Forces manifest through the elemental kingdoms. The very warmth of the sun and the radiation from the sun of even pressure, the winds of the Holy Spirit that blend with the earth currents and mingle with the soil vegetation and the waters in their movement, aerating life with the sacred fire breath and the necessary chemical interchanges, are directed and transmitted by great beings of fire and air that expand the dimensions of their forcefields to encompass vast reaches of space.

The elementals are the devotees of the

Buddha. They are in the service of the Lord of the World and the World Mother. Their occupation is in the drawing forth of the great spiritual energies of Life from the spherical body of the Buddha through the nexus of the Cosmic Christ. Sipping the nectar of the gods, they transform the essence of the fiery world of the Buddha's causal body into the adornments of the Mother that make up the entire Matter cosmos.

The life that is God which manifests through the flame of the Creator's intent in their creative expressions is crystallized in and as Matter through the miracle of geometry. The planes and angles of such forms as the hexahedron and the octahedron are the means whereby the infinite light is decelerated in its velocity to coalesce as the substance whereof the universes of crystal become the concrete equation that you enjoy in all of the wonders of the physical earth.

All molecules in Matter are formed of angles that are precise mathematical formulae of inner fohatic keys—i.e., the inner designs of the sacred fire. The physical fire is the gracious lowering into manifestation of the spiritual fire by the agency of the Holy Spirit through the blessed salamanders, whose beings are the agents for the transfer of the fires of the subtle world for mankind's daily use.

From the candle flame to firelight, from elementary forms of electricity to the compressed energy of nucleonic suns, from life pulsating within the cells of all that is alive with the sacred fire breath—one beholds the common miracle of the infinite fire held within the finite vessel in order that evolutionary man might enjoy fragments of eternity within the equations of time and space.

As the spiritual fires become the material fires by the flow of the figure eight and the integrating principle of the Eighth Ray, angelic and elemental beings serving the sacred fire and the corresponding fire element endow all of Nature with the sense of the omnipresence of God.

Truly God as Father, Son, and Holy Spirit, and God as the Mother flame of all life is made available to every living soul by these blessed servants of the flame. Yet their own presence—life enduing, life endowing—is scarcely known or understood by the evolutions of earth who benefit from their loving service with every breath and heartbeat and each gift of the sharing of God's love.

Sons and daughters of God, children of the Light, enter into the joyous service of earth's evolutions through conscious cooperation with the beings of the elements and thereby enter into the joy of the LORD as you, in Christ Jesus and in the sacred hearts of the saints, raise up the four sides of your own Pyramid of Life!

God has created the elementals as the obedient servants of his sons and daughters. Therefore it is lawful, yea, imperative that you command elemental life—fire, air, water, and earth—in the name of the I AM THAT I AM, in the name of Jesus Christ, Lord Maitreya, Gautama Buddha, and Sanat Kumara, the entire Spirit of the Great White Brotherhood and the World Mother to set all life free by a mighty outpouring of the Holy Spirit and the invigorating, life-giving essence of the violet fire and the resurrection flame.

Each day as you give your calls to the sacred fire, as you meditate upon the flame within your heart, send forth intense love, appreciation, compassion, and the wisdom of the Law to the mighty salamanders. These flaming ones gather in numberless numbers around the World Mother and her devotees. They bow before the flame within the heart of every child of God, and they are obedient unto those who are obedient unto the Law of Love.

They are the children of the Buddha and the Mother and, as such, they are the very outpicturing of the perpetual flow of the figure eight that is for the integration of the Spirit/Matter cosmos and the light of Alpha and Omega in the white fire core of being.

As you expand your capacity to contain the light of the Seven Holy Kumaras, the essence of the Buddha's devotion, and the Mother's crystal clear stream of the water of Life flowing, day by day your own integration with Nature and these blessed spirits of Nature becomes a true friendship with these friends of God and man and a most personal interchange of mercy's flame.

You are in partnership with God through his self-expression in the salamanders, sylphs, undines, and gnomes. You come to know the Personality of God through these carefree yet altogether responsible children of his heart. Indeed, you are in partnership with Life; and through Nature's helpers and comforters, whose reverence for life has never waned despite mankind's blasphemy committed daily against its flame, you begin to experience once again, hour by hour, the joy flame of God's will permeating Nature and her servants, emanating from all that lives.

The labor of heart, head, and hand side by side with your blessed co-workers becomes a sacred labor, the means to express your praise and joy and thanksgiving unto Life for Being in all its glory and grace. The person of the Christ and the Buddha on the hill preaching to the multitudes and to the Nature spirits who listen attentively, the ever-caring presence of the World Mother, her transparency and her beauty, become the source and inspiration of renewed devotion to living and to the giving of oneself that others might live.

Now life becomes a real kinship with the Spirit of Life and even those who felt they were abandoned of friends and fellows discover a host of friends—loyal, trusting, trustworthy, loving, sincere, innocent and without guile and always serving with a smile—and who are, like children, always more energetic and enthusiastic when a kind word or expression of gratitude, approval, and praise is forthcoming for a job well done.

Mankind's appreciation for the beauty of the flowers and trees, the snow-covered mountains, the flowing streams, their gratitude for the delicious fruits and vegetables, and their offering of prayers to God in gratitude for earth's abundant harvest is the means whereby the Christ flame of your hearts, beloved ones, becomes the multiplier of God's grace unto the elementals which in turn returns manifold blessings through their intensified service on behalf of the lifewaves of earth.

The fiery salamanders are beings of etheric vibrancy. Standing majestically before the Son of God in prayer at the altar of the LORD, their very garments are living, pulsating rainbow fires emitting the full spectrum of the rainbow rays.

As they intensify the discipline of their service to life, these rainbow rays accelerate and become a steely white intensity for the consuming not only of mankind's debris and pollution but also of their "man-i-pollutions" that are the result of their manipulation of the sacred fire.

Were it not for the fiery salamanders absorbing, consuming, transmuting the large forcefields of human hatred registering man's inhumanity unto man that gather over the large cities of the earth, crime, decadence, and even depravity would be far more advanced among the inhabitants of earth and the Dark Cycle of the accelerated return of mankind's karma would have resulted in a deepening schism within the four lower bodies, the souls, and the collective unconscious of the entire race.

We come as the hierarchs and sponsors of billions upon billions of these masterful beings who tend the sacred fires of the earth and contain the magnitude of God-control of the energy of Alpha and Omega within the nucleus of every atom of that which appears to be material substance but which is in actuality a spiritual/material oscillation of light held in a frequency and forcefield adapted to the time/space continuum necessary for the soul's evolution unto God Self-awareness.

The salamanders are not the physical fire but they control the fire, enter the fire, and endow it with life. They are the guardians of physical flame and focus. Wherever fire burns, there is their nascent light.

When fire is uncontrolled and destructive, it is a sign that mankind's energies are uncontrolled and destructive; and the law of compensation working through physical law exacts the price for mankind's misuse of energy on all four planes of consciousness.

Whenever there is danger or disaster threatening through fire, the enlightened son of God, the obedient child of the Light will immediately call upon the LORD in the name of the beloved Mighty I AM Presence and Christ Self to take command of the fiery salamanders through our name and office and to command them to contain the fire and to set life free.

In the name of the Christ, you must stand and face the conflagration* and command the elementals to bring it under God-control under the Holy Trinity. Helios and Vesta, as the hierarchs of this solar system and guardians of the sacred fires of the sun, can be invoked in the name of Christ to bring the fiery salamanders into alignment with God's will.

You see, beloved ones, so often the ravages of fire that destroy life and home and communities are heaped against mankind by malevolent forces working through the deviates of cosmic law, the practitioners of black magic who heap their anger and revenge and their frustrated and abortive attempts to control Almighty God upon his innocent children.

The fallen ones have long ago recognized the value of controlling the beings of the elements. This they do through the bloodletting of voodoo ceremony and satanic rite, invoking demoniac forces of the astral plane and casting spells of death and destruction and hexes that hypnotically bind the elementals to do their bidding. Under these gross misuses of the sacred fire, some salamanders as well as other elementals have been imprisoned for centuries, and thus

*NOTE: Physical measures of fire control and fire prevention must not be neglected while continuing to invoke the hierarchs of the salamanders who require your assistance and cooperation in answering the call.

mankind have come to fear the Nature spirits and
to attribute to them mischievous and even malevolent designs.

Thus, the first order of the day is to invoke
the legions of Archangel Michael and Mighty
Astrea [the starry Mother from the realm of
Elohim] to cut free the imprisoned salamanders,
to draw them up into the Great Central Sun
Magnet to God's heart for repolarization and
realignment with his mighty will which is always
good for all who partake of its cup.

Once you gain the confidence and trust of
the fiery salamanders, you can send them north,
south, east, and west to purify the air, the earth,
and the water and to consume the malignancies
and viruses of the astral plane that spill over into
the body temples of God's blessed children.

It is well known among the practitioners of
the black arts that the fiery salamanders are the
most difficult of elementals to control and that
they often become, as the sorcerer's apprentice,
the enemies of those who seek to control them
against the will of cosmos.

Having suffered at the hand of opportunists
and having long been burdened by the neglect of
God's laws of harmony on the part of mankind,
the fiery salamanders have become an independent lot, sometimes forgetful and unmindful of
their original service to the children of the Light.
Thus they must be wooed by love, a contrite
heart, and a balanced threefold flame that offers

to them the initiations of Lord Maitreya and the World Mother, together with an absolutely pure and ever-intensifying interchange of love.

As you lay down your life for Christ and his children, the elementals will lay down their life for you. When you call upon the LORD to and through elemental life, withholding nothing from them, they will withhold nothing from you.

Nevertheless, be not discouraged when you see that mankind's own rebellion has placed upon them an overlay of capriciousness and burdens too hard to bear. Rather, pray for these blessed ones as you would pray for one another in your hours of need.

Although we who are the hierarchs of elemental life are Ascended Masters of cosmic attainment, the elementals serving the Matter spheres are by their very nature and design unascended; and therefore, though highly advanced in the application of natural law, they too are held back on the path of initiation by man himself to whom they look for guidance and the proper example that is so often lacking.

As unascended beings, the elementals are subject to the influences of the spectrum of relative good and evil. Therefore in your interaction with them there is required the command for them to be tethered wholly to the Cosmic Christ. Through your own threefold flame, you endow them with the Christ consciousness. Thus, you see, you have a responsibility to become the teachers of elemental life under the World Teachers, to invite them to give dynamic decrees with you, and to follow you on the path of the Ruby Ray.

There is a hierarchical structure within the order of salamanders, some being adepts of greater attainment, others yet coming into their own awareness of the degrees of self-mastery. Thus it is important to appeal to the captains of their hosts to command them in the service of the Light. Moreover, conscious cosmic cooperation with elemental life requires a reeducation of the heart of both God's children and the childlike elementals.

Again we say, the violet flame is the most effective and intense means of erasing the wrongs and hurts of the past. And diligent calls to Archangel Michael and Mighty Astrea will effectively cut elemental life free from the artifices of witchcraft imposed upon them by self-seeking and shortsighted rebels against the cause of the Great White Brotherhood.

Under the Hierarchy of the Four Cosmic Forces, the salamanders serve the Person and Principle of the Father, whose archetype is the Lion. Through them pass the fires of the fiery baptism of the Holy Spirit, and they are often the collaborators with the angels of the Holy Spirit in giving to the disciples of Christ and Buddha the initiation not only of the fiery baptism but also of the trial by fire.

Witness the instance of Shadrach, Meshach, and Abednego in the fiery furnace. It was the fiery salamanders together with the Holy Spirit who accelerated the physical flames to a spiritual frequency whereby the Hebrew youths were not burned. It was the light within their own hearts attuned with the Holy Spirit which served as the polarity for the flame during those moments of their trial.

The flame within and the flame without, manifest as the cloven tongues of the Holy Spirit, created the balance of Alpha and Omega and rendered the physical fire harmless. Without that light stored within their hearts through devotion and amplified within every cell of their bodies through purity and obedience to God's laws, they would not have been ready for this conscious cooperation between angels, elementals, and the sons of God.

As you review the life of Daniel at the court of Nebuchadnezzar, you will see what purity and what victory marked the testing of his soul prior to the trial by fire. May you gain thereby some sense of commeasurement with the person of the Great Initiator and the disciplines required of you by the law of God-harmony.

But through the fiery trial and the fiery baptism wherein "the fire shall try every man's work of what sort it is," the children of the Light must learn that they are not subject to uncontrolled forces of Nature or even of their own returning karma but in the name of Almighty God they can rise up and take dominion over all misqualified energy—whether personal or planetary karma or the manipulations and malpractice by the fallen ones of the flame of Life.

Let the children of the Light cease to tremble and fear before the threat of impending cataclysm or even the law of planetary recompense. Let them rise in God to be masters of their fate, their astrology, and their fiery destiny. Let them use the violet flame and strive for purity of heart.

For only if you contain, my beloved, a firm foundation in Christ—establishing in you right reason, right motive, and right cause in the name of the Great White Brotherhood—will you find the absolute cooperation of angels and elementals to be the very consummate joy of the remainder of your life on earth.

Unto the joy of consummate reunion with the flame of living fire, we remain devoted to your victorious initiations of the heart and the heart chakra.

Oromasis and Diana

Prince and Princess of the Fiery Element

April 13, 1980

CHAPTER 3

The Sacred Fire Breath and the Rituals of Elemental Life

A Plea for Cosmic Cooperation in Support of Elemental Life

*by Aries and Thor
Hierarchs of the Sylphs
Servants of God and Man in the Air Element*

O Lovers of the Sacred Fire Breath:

We are the hierarchs of the air who permeate the very breath of spring with the sacred fire breath of the Holy Spirit. It is not enough that the children of the Light should breathe in the sweet air of tall grasses freshly cut, releasing their life essences, or even the morning mist that carries the fragrance of rose, lily of the valley, and lilac, or the ozone-charged atmosphere that revivifies all life even as it rebalances the electronic polarity of bodies and minds—no, we who direct the mighty sylphs and the movements of the continents of the air, we who stand with the Lord Maha Chohan as he inbreathes the breath of Life into the newborn soul and as the threefold flame is rekindled once again upon the altar of the heart, we have dedicated our service and the service of the elementals of the air in all of their grandeur to the sacred fire breath!

Aside from our daily rituals of purifying and washing, purifying and washing the atmosphere of a planet and a people and aerating the mind and heart and every cell of life with esters of sunshine carried on the winds, we who so love the light of life borne to earth's children molecule by molecule within the air itself are committed to be the bearers of that prana of the Holy Spirit that is the very life breath of the soul.

Giant sylphs that span the skies and interpenetrate the earth, the water, and the sacred fire mingle and make merry with the blessed angels of the sacred fire, angels of the purifying light, and angels in adoration of the living flame of the Holy Spirit. As the air absorbs the emanations of earth and sea and fire, both sweet and foul, so this absorptive quality is the very nature of the aura of the sylphs. Thus they are students of the mysteries of the concentration and the containment of the life-forces.

Though the wind bloweth where it listeth and cannot be contained though it containeth all sound and soundlessness, the mighty sylphs, who take their discipline from the seraphim and the initiates of ascension's flame, are masters in the art of the saturation of selfhood with the flow of Mother purity—the essence of crystal from her sparkling waters, the purity of whiteness that glows upon the altars of the Central Sun.

As the stars emit their secret rays in the night side of earth's cycles, endowing the atmosphere with unknown cosmic forces so necessary to the inner life of the soul, and as the sun endows every living creature with the love/wisdom of its fiery core, so in the very process of this cosmic transmutation whereby the light itself becomes the life of every living cell, the sylphs in Matter moving with the undulations of the seraphs in Spirit are the great transmitters of the currents of the Holy Spirit from heaven to earth.

The sylphs are giant transformers, conductors of the currents of the Mind of God unto the mind of man. The trackless realms of the air are their domain, and their trackings are defined by the formation and re-formation of the clouds. This blending of the waters and the air coalesced round the nucleus of the sacred fire and containing earth elements establishing the coordinates of hydrogen and oxygen is in itself a mighty work of the ages that is the cooperative venture of the Four Cosmic Forces through the four hierarchies of the elemental kingdom.

The two parts of hydrogen in each molecule of water form the cradle of the plus/minus polarity of Alpha and Omega to ensconce the pure oxygen that itself is the vessel of white fire that nourishes the arteries of life and the very bloodstream of body temples and towering trees with the sacred fire breath. This is the sacred ritual of all elemental life. For without the air and its self-transforming, transmutative, transmitative nature, life from the highest to the lowest forms in the evolutionary scale would cease to be.

Now, by the very nature of consciousness and the purity of the heart and the devotions of the heart before the altar of the living God, each individual's ability to absorb the sacred fire breath is determined by the state of his consciousness and whether or not it is limited by the densification of misqualified energy clogging the very pores of the four lower bodies of the majority of mankind. Many among earth's evolutions absorb but the smallest fraction of the light and pranic essence that is contained in each molecular cup of the air element.

One of the major causes of disease, old age, and death upon the planetary body is the failure of earth's evolutions to place a priority upon the purifying of body, mind, and soul that it might assimilate the purifying, life-sustaining Breath that is literally charged with the plus/minus factors of the cloven tongues of the Holy Spirit.

Bodies burdened with decay, degenerative diseases caused by toxicity from improper diet and the partaking of incomplete, processed, and devitalized foods, cannot absorb the higher frequencies of the Holy Spirit which 'ride' on the currents of the air. The overlay of nicotine on the lungs and brain and residual drug substance in the vital organs of the body actually retard the soul's spiritual evolution by hampering the Spirit/Matter interchange of light at the molecular level.

Thus the physical elements of the air alone are received and these, as you well know, lack the divine whole of the life-force so necessary to sustain the integrated and integrating principle of Being at the very heart of every atom of substance. Even inorganic life absorbs the magnetic properties of the Holy Spirit, a process altogether different from the interchange of the life-force from Life to life but, nevertheless, one that has the parallel purpose of investing Matter with a spiritual fire that exempts it from the laws of mortality.

Children of the Light have most vivid memories of etheric cities and retreats where the 'concrete' forms of temples, buildings, works of art, and practical accouterments of life remain for indefinite periods and as long as is required by cosmic law according to the inner blueprint and the fiery matrix. Here there is no law of degeneration, no decay rate, no disintegration factor. For the cyclic ebb and flow of the sacred fire of the central sun of these etheric particles of Spirit/Matter energy sustains the perfect form so long as it is desired by its creator.

Here on earth where all of life in the state of becoming seems subject to the laws of disintegration, men toil ceaselessly to retain the essence of life within their bodies and to maintain their properties and possessions lest they should quickly fall into disrepair, disuse, and disintegrate before their very eyes as "from dust to dust."

But this is not as Life intended it to be. And you who bear witness to the etheric octaves of light, to the eternal youth shining ever so brightly on the faces of angels and Ascended Masters as on the face of a newborn babe—you know the power of the resurrection flame to reinfuse all life in the Matter cosmos with its innate momentums of renewal, rebirth, rejuvenation, and the blessed flame of reciprocity.

What is this flame of which I speak, my beloved? It is the life-sharing principle of cosmos. It is the self-emptying and self-giving ritual of Love whereby the Alpha vessel imparts the essences of Spirit unto the Omega and the Omega vessel self-empties herself into the Alpha. In the divine exchange of the eternal lovers, extolled in the whirling T'ai Chi manifest in the infinitesimal particles of atomic nuclei, we discover that the law of reciprocity so sweetly expressed in the mantra of resurrection's flame "Drink me while I AM drinking thee" is at the very heart of life's never-ending ritual of the creative/re-creative process.

The divine interchange typified in the figure-eight flow of integration is the celebration of the ultimate union of the Spirit/Matter cosmos that already is and was and ever shall be and yet is not now apparent to those who do not as yet contain the full measure of the life of Spirit in the Matter vessel.

Now in conclave with all of the hierarchies magnificently serving under the Elohim—the twelve builders of form who descend from the twelve temples of life and solar hierarchies of the Central Sun—the sylphs gather with all of the majesty and the mastery befitting their office as endowers of the Matter cosmos with the sacredness of life. The sylphs take heart to renew their service to set life on earth free and take heed at the solemn counsels of Lord Gautama and the Maha Chohan who place before this conference of planetary import the burdens borne by the children of the Mother through the pollution of the air, the water, and the earth and, if it were possible, the very fire of the atom itself.

The misuses of nuclear energy and the dangers of nuclear weapons and nuclear power plants in the hands of those lacking the mastery of the elements under the Four Cosmic Forces poses problems of great magnitude to the entire Great White Brotherhood in its service to the lifewaves of this solar system. The Tall Master from Venus addresses the conclave outlining the limitations of mankind's current understanding of science that does not allow him to accelerate the rebalancing and the reintegration of the disorders and discords intruded upon almost every form of Matter by his reckless and wanton misuse of the natural resources of earth.

Charting the course of expectations, given the known factors of mankind's tendencies toward death and self-destruction, Mighty Victory makes an impassioned plea for cosmic cooperation between the lovers of life ascended and unascended. He calls for tremendous support on behalf of the beings of the elements and demands in God's own name and in the name of Sanat Kumara that all who recognize that their life is sustained by the personal presence of the Ancient of Days ministering to earth's evolutions respond mightily to support elemental life who provide the pillars of the platform of this planetary evolution.

As the elementals travail within the four lower bodies of Mother Earth to give birth to a golden-age environment suitable for the golden-age consciousness of Lord Maitreya and his chelas, Mighty Victory and his legions summon illumined and caring chelas to understand the need for brotherhood, for community, and for cooperation under Hierarchy. Truly a mighty cooperation is needed to stem the tide of mankind's self-generated downward spirals that threaten, alas, not only their bodies but the very existence of their souls.

Many who understand the Law and know the consequences of separation from service with the Brotherhood and with our outer organization must recognize the urgent need to act boldly in concerted measure for the defense of unborn life and for the pristine environment so needed to raise up stalwart sons of Victory's flame. Neither Ascended Masters nor elementals nor angels separate themselves in form or formlessness from the mighty heartbeat that binds them together in bands of cosmic service.

Thus this Council of the Royal Teton Retreat and this conference attended by the truest friends of earth is a call for cosmic cooperation while there is yet time and space for the Woman to deliver her Manchild as the Cosmic Christ consciousness to all. May the selfishness and separateness of those who know better and who could perform together this mighty work of the ages now be dissolved in a love that responds in crisis to the need for life and the giving of one's life that all life might live to praise the sacred name.

We of the kingdom of the sylphs hover near to welcome each newborn babe and to receive the departing souls transiting earth's scene. Thus we worship the great inbreath and the great outbreath of Life's cycles, ever mindful that each precious footstep on the bridge of life that is suspended between the moment of one's entrance and one's exit is intended for the sacred and enduring experience of Life begetting life through the giving and receiving of Love's essence sealed in the sacred fire breath.

We are in the Love of the Holy Spirit whose fiery fount is fueled by the sacred fire breath.

Aries and Thor

April 20, 1980

CHAPTER 4

A Petition and a Warning to the Inhabitants of Terra:

Sons of God, Defend Elemental Life Else Cataclysm Will Not Be Averted!

by Neptune and Luara
Hierarchs of the Undines
Servants of God and Man in the Water Element

To Our Co-workers and Playmates
  in the Sea and Sand and Surf and Sun:

Unbeknownst to yourselves, you are also interactors with the sacred fire of the waters—the waters above the firmament and the waters under the firmament. The seven seas represent the subconscious mind and memory of earth's evolutions. Her corridors lead to the origins of life and the life-giving force that is the great mystery of the sea itself.

Scientists and marine biologists attribute the beginning of life to the combination of the sun and the sea forming the perfect environment for the bursting forth, once upon a time millions of years ago, of that single cell of consciousness. And, lo, life in the simplicity of its unity in the microorganisms of the sea becomes the jewel of the Mind of God transmitting all of the elements of the macrocosmic cell itself—the Great Central Sun Magnet.

Drop by drop, the sea is the gift of Life held cupped in the hands of a little child building castles from etheric memory in the sands of time and space. Flowing into the sea is the River of Life, mighty Mother flow, the Ganges and so many other tributaries I know. The sea is everyone's native land as hand in hand the children of earth must define her boundaries—not in terms of territorial waters or national interest but in terms of cosmic integrity and a cosmic honor flame that is truly and most notably *reverence for Life*.

As life had its beginnings in the sea, so, if it is not revered by all men and nations, it will have its ending in the sea. And it will no more be written "from dust to dust" but "from sea to sea." For the comings and goings of lifewaves upon earth are utterly dependent upon the waters of Life flowing in crystal streams through the sea itself. And the great secret of the sea is that, by the cosmic interchange of Alpha and Omega, the sacred fire itself—through phytoplankton, through the salt and other unidentified alchemical elements— is in perpetual celebration of the great cosmic interchange.

The sea is where Life begets life. The sea is the womb of the Cosmic Virgin even as it is the tomb where hieroglyphs of the collective unconscious of earth's evolutionary chain are recorded and rerecorded for the transformation of all life. The sea is the desiring of the Mother to give birth to the children of God, and it represents the highest and the lowest of the desirings of humanity to beget God and anti-God, universal harmony or its antithesis.

The seven seas are man's desirings for wholeness in the seven planes of being. They represent the seven colors, tones, and vibrations of the seven days of creation. The seas contain the *Grund* and the *Ungrund*—the formed and the unformed elements of Life. The seas and the bodies of water that dot the earth with jewels of glacial blue, aquamarine, and gorgeous sapphire hues actually exist in seven layered planes corresponding to the seven bodies of man.

Elemental beings of light and angel ministrants provide the focus for the interchange of these 'seven seas' with the sacred fire of the seven vehicles of man's consciousness. Most people in your octave observe only the physical body of man and therefore they likewise observe only the physical body of the sea.

John the Revelator beheld the "sea of glass like unto crystal" before the throne of the Ancient of Days and again the "sea of glass mingled with fire." Thus the interchange of sacred fire and flowing water in the Great Central Sun is ever the Life-giving movement of Alpha and Omega in the heart of the flaming Monad whose Presence in you is the I AM THAT I AM.

Thus Father and Mother ever begetting Life release the crystal cord as a chain of crystal light. This chain, as a mighty caduceus spanning the ocean of cosmos, is the ascending/descending spinal altar whose structure becomes the superstructure for the mental and physical vehicles of every part of Life which is God.

As the fire represents the superconscious and the water the subconscious mind, so out of its memory bank there crystallizes the cognitive processes of identity asserting I AM WHERE I AM (in the mental body) and the physical extension of body awareness for souls to perfect the divine plan of life. First the fire then the water—as the seed and then the egg. And then there follows the crystallization of the air and the earth—of I AM WHO I AM for action/interaction on 'physical' planets and solar systems.

Out of the depth of the seas beneath the ocean floors, out of the waters of the deep and temples of the Mother, out of mankind's etheric memory and the etheric body of the earth, the sea provides the opportunity for the resolution and the dissolution of life and death.

Of old the beasts of the sea known as leviathan were feared by mariners. Their myth persists in the erstwhile appearance of the Loch Ness monster. John saw that those that had gotten the victory over the 'beast', and over his image, and over his mark, and over the number of his name, stand on the sea of glass, having the harps of God and singing the song of Moses the servant of God, and the song of the Lamb.

Would to God that the mariners of today might see and hear the undines of the deep singing that song, saying:

Great and marvellous are thy works,
    LORD God Almighty;
Just and true are thy ways, thou King
    of saints.
Who shall not fear thee, O LORD,
    and glorify thy name?
For thou only art holy:
For all nations shall come and worship
    before thee;
For thy judgments are made manifest.

Would to God that the murderers of the mighty whales might know the majesty of the Mind of God and Mother flame anchored in these blessed elemental beings who command the seven seas and are the transmitters of cosmic light and cosmic rays unto all life abiding on planet earth.

Would to God that mere mortals could behold undines who gather at the scene of the 'cold-blooded' harpoon murder of the blessed creatures whose guileless bodies without sin radiate the love of the Holy Spirit to all other lifeforms inhabiting the sea and the land.

In the very midst of this massacre of Life, the blessed undines who are the initiates of the Mother in sacred-fire temples of the deep are to be heard chanting the song of Moses and the Lamb:

Again and again they sing the song of Life commanding life—earth currents, undulations of the seas—in the rhythm of the spheres. They sing it as a mantra endowing the elements by the Sun of God—Universal Christos—with the restorative harmony of the Source. Healing as they recharge the electromagnetic field by the magnetism of the Great Central Sun, their bodies are conductors of cosmic currents by the intoning of the Word, sounding and resounding through the chambers of subatomic, submarine Life. And you hear your soul, young at heart, joining their chorusings singing into the Wave of Light:

> *Great and marvellous are thy works,*
> *LORD God Almighty;*
> *Just and true are thy ways, thou King*
> *of saints.*
> *Who shall not fear thee, O LORD,*
> *and glorify thy name?*
> *For thou only art holy:*
> *For all nations shall come and worship*
> *before thee;*
> *For thy judgments are made manifest.*

They also invoke the judgment of their LORD and Saviour Jesus Christ upon the wayward sons of Belial who know very well "what they do" as they are the very instruments of planetary chaos undermining to the very depths of the seas the balance of the planetary ecosystem upon which the children of the Light so depend.

We are Neptune and Luara. We survey the plight of the seas and their pollution through man's insensitivity to Life in its most elementary and complex forms.

Well-meaning souls, members of world bodies working at international levels seek to restrain the dumping into the sea of sewage, industrial waste, chemicals, pesticides, and oil—all of which place an enormous burden upon the beings of purity, both physical and etheric, whose home is the sea. They tend God's sea garden. They are the caretakers of a once-pristine paradise that is rapidly becoming known as a paradise lost.

We are the spokesmen for the undines who are the conscious collaborators with men and angels for the survival of the waters of the earth. These servants of God and man in the water element rise to the surface of consciousness and demand to be heard. They have signed a petition which I now read, a warning to the inhabitants of Terra:

> Unless by the flame of the Holy Spirit the Children of the Sun, nation by nation, will mount as one for the healing of the waters, identifying with the person of the Flying Eagle who is our sponsor and our initiator, even the Lord Sanat Kumara, life on earth must be severely curtailed or abruptly brought to an end.

Without the sea and its many life-supporting functions making possible the control of climate, rainfall, oxygenation, and the very evolution of life itself, earth can no longer be considered viable as an ecosystem or an evolutionary platform for its present lifewaves.

O mankind of earth, begin at the very beginning. For out of the fountains of the deep, life has sprung forth and to the very mouth of these fountains we daily return to give gratitude for the waters of Life.

Now, therefore, we the undersigned representing the councils of the undines petition all who count themselves as the keepers of the flame of Life upon earth to summon the resources and the intercession of hosts of the LORD in cooperation with those most vitally concerned with earth's pollutions—all of which eventually come home to the sea.

We ask you to understand that inasmuch as the sea represents the interchange of fire and water there should be forthcoming a two-pronged attack upon the anti-Mother forces which daily assault the life-giving waters of her cosmic womb.

Let the sacred-fire action of the violet flame restore the natural flow of Spirit and Spirit's fire to provide the alchemy of transmutation within the seas, without which there can be no return to balance. And then let scientists, futurists, students, and concerned citizens en masse rise up to defend the purity and power, the light and the jeweled crystal, the beauty and the bounty of our eternal sea that kisses the sky at the horizon line and provides the children of earth with vistas of eternity.

Under the direction of our hierarchs Neptune and Luara, we the undersigned pledge our lives anew to the planetary transmutation of the collective unconscious repository of all that is in reverse of the ongoing tide of the divine plan. We not only transmit Light but we transmute misqualified Light that has become Darkness and disease and death within earth's waters. All that remains untransmuted within the subconscious of the people must also register as pollution.

In the physical waters of the earth we place ourselves upon the cross to be crucified with Him for the sake of our brothers and sisters who, though they are ignorant of our sacrifice, may benefit thereby and become the truly blessed when they can also take upon themselves the cross of all elemental life.

Even as the salamanders, sylphs, and gnomes have said, "We will bear all that we can bear"—so we say, Let us carry the maximum burden of Darkness in order that Light may be revealed. And to our hierarchs, the sons and daughters of God upon earth, we appeal for intercession and the education of the people by wisdom's flame that the purification of the waters of the waters might be parallel with the purification of their sacred fires.

The computers in the retreat of the Ascended Master Cuzco and the data available through the retreats and outposts of Neptune and Luara reveal with mathematical certainty that unless the sons of God rise up in defense of elemental life and the integrity of the earth body, certain cataclysm will not be averted.

We declare that we are here because of the splendid support of the Ascended Masters and their chelas. We serve with you that many more will join the ranks of the faithful who faithfully offer their dynamic decrees upon the Altar of Invocation.

Faithfully we decree with the rhythm of the tide, and the sounding of our Word is in the breaking of the wave and where the sea and the earth meet in the heart of the "mighty angel come down from heaven, clothed with a cloud."

The rainbow upon his head is our promise of a better tomorrow. And his face, as it were the face of the Sun of Righteousness, is our assurance that help through the Helper is on its way. And his feet as pillars of fire are the sign that the wisdom of the

Son of God, dispensing sacred fire, stands
firm in the earth. And with his right foot
upon the sea and his left foot on the earth,
he assures us of his commitment and the
commitment of Almighty God to the balance of the four lower bodies of earth and
earth's children and the threefold flame in
body, mind, and soul.

To us the little book open in his hand
is the teaching of Lord Maitreya, Lord
Buddha, Lord Sanat Kumara through
Jesus Christ and his Messengers unto the
nations. This little book is our hope that
elemental life will one day be free through
the enlightened, peaceful, and loving service of the Children of the Sun.

Thus we seal you in our flame of hope,
even as you are our hope. And we sign this
our petition in the name of all life—human,
elemental, divine.

Now we, Neptune and Luara, bid Keepers of
the Flame recall the momentous event which
took place at the Easter conclave 1964 when Our
Saviour Jesus Christ endowed Nature with the
momentum of his resurrection flame. On that
occasion he said concerning the gift of his flame to
elemental life that it would

make it possible for them to feel, throughout their entire manifestation as an elemental, a part of the radiance of immortality which I AM. Do you see what this

means? It means that they shall no longer be aware of death.

Do you know what this means! Contemplate, contemplate, contemplate Nature conceived by God and designed in the higher octaves, lowered through the elementals into manifestation, now endowed with the flame of my momentum of the resurrection this day that forever after from this day forward the elementals shall never again have the sense of death!

Though they pass, it shall be as the click of a camera shutter or the dropping of a bird on wing when its beating heart stops—suddenly they shall be here and then they shall be gone, but without pain or quiver or fear.

They shall feel my flame always. A portion of that flame resting in them shall remove for all time immemorial all that fear that they have outpictured.

And this is one of the first steps as we begin the process of quickening the world for the golden age, enrobing it in the garments of eternal spring. For the eternal spring must first come into the invisible world and the world of the formless and then be outpictured in the world of form. And the love of the students for the elementals and the decrees and the fiats and the prayers, both of heaven and earth together, have made this possible this day. . . .

And so as the Holy Kumaras stand here with me before you, blazing forth what I choose to term the fury of their divine radiance toward God, the holiness of their purity, it gives us pleasure, in the name of the Great White Brotherhood, to announce to the world this new manifestation for Nature, for life. This is a manifestation of the greatest hope, and it is one of the first steps in the abolishment of all death everywhere.

Now in conclusion of this fourfold message of the Hierarchs of Elemental Life unto the Children of the Sun, speaking on behalf of the Four Cosmic Forces we say, let the renewal of your cosmic cooperation with elemental life be the alchemy of the Holy Spirit whereby through the Father and the Son the abundant Life is manifest through the elementals who are the children of the Buddha and the Mother.

We are

Neptune and Luara

for the victory
of the Woman clothed with the Sun
and her seed.

April 27, 1980

CHAPTER 5

A Prophecy of Mount Saint Helens

Unless the Violet Flame Be Invoked Earth Changes Will Take Place in the 1980's

by Saint Germain
Hierarch of the Aquarian Age

Ho! let the Light flow. Ho! let the Light manifest here below in the hearts of my own. For I come to address you on this day wherein there is celebrated the universal mystery of the Trinity.*

This indwelling Light is the purpose of our coming, for the indwelling Light does not expand as it should expand for want of the understanding of true Life. For true Life cometh of the Father and is in the Son and is expanded by that Holy Spirit.

Meditate upon these three and ponder the universal destiny which we bear. We bear it as a chalice, as a sword, and as a banner. We bear it as the mighty torch of the Woman of the age.

Lo, I AM come. I AM come into your midst with the coming of the Messenger who goes before

*The Feast of the Holy Trinity (first Sunday after Pentecost)

my face east and west into the nations, bearing my purple fiery heart for the staying action of the Almighty in the very moments when it would appear that cataclysm is prepared to precipitate and to be catapulted out of the astral into the physical plane.

There is more than one form of cataclysm, as you have seen. And so often it is that in the physical absence of the Messenger those dimensions of the human consciousness that are kept at bay by our mantle upon her do come forth, and that by our will. For it is the desire of the Great White Brotherhood to show the people of America and the Keepers of the Flame what is lurking at the very threshold of consciousness and beneath the surface of the earth that must be transmuted, must be challenged, and must be faced.

Therefore elemental life, by the order of the Lords of Karma, bringing to the surface then the turbulence in the heart of the earth,* makes plain to all those who read the handwriting in the rock itself that this planetary body contains a residue of karma of molten lava and ash spewing forth that must be there and must precipitate for redemption.

---

*Mount St. Helens (Cascade Range, Washington) erupted May 18, 1980, killing over 20 people, with at least 71 reported missing and presumed dead. The massive explosion generated approximately 500 times the force of the atomic bomb dropped on Hiroshima, destroying 150 square miles of timber worth $200 million, damaging $222 million in crops, and burying 5,900 miles of roads. The extensive long-range effects of the volcanic blast, mud, silt, and ash on the river systems, wildlife, and ecological balance of the entire Pacific Northwest cannot yet be calculated. Molten rock moving inside the mountain resulted in earthquakes and further eruptions May 25, June 12, July 22, and August 7.

Those who are no longer so superstitious as to take from Nature the judgments of the Almighty do err. For this indeed is not superstition but the communication of the LORD's hosts through Nature itself when all other communications fail because their ears are waxed dull and their hearts are hardened unto the very presence of the LORD.

Thus the beings of the elements react in the fury and the fire from on high. And there comes out of the earth the message and the warning that is already come to Keepers of the Flame that unless sufficient quantity of violet flame be invoked, elemental life will no longer bear the burden of the cross of planetary karma and there will be in this decade significant changes in the very surface of the earth.

I had supposed that a greater response would be forthcoming from all of you to this message of Virgo and Pelleur in the Pearls of Wisdom. But it did not evoke immediately that sufficiency of light to stay the hand of this catastrophe but rather allowed it to manifest for all the world to see that coming upon them are those days which indeed ought to be feared by those who have not the fear of the LORD.

Now with the sounding of the rumblings in the earth* as added warning as the adjustments continue, Keepers of the Flame are quickened

---

*Five earthquakes registering up to 6.0 on the Richter scale, Mammoth Lakes region, California.

and vitalized to the realization that indeed it is the requirement of the hour to increase the gift upon the altar of the violet flame.

I AM Saint Germain. I have stood with you and many saints of the Church in many previous ages as we have given our life to lesser causes and hours of penance and all forms of self-inflicted punishment as atonement for sin when in fact the God-reality of the Holy Spirit descending was and is the necessity for the atonement on a planetary scale.

Therefore we bid you welcome to the path of sainthood and call upon you to realize that if in your heart you contain that love for a budding humanity almost ready to reach and pluck the bud of Christhood from the Tree of Life, you will realize that much hangs in the balance and the thread of life is indeed a thread and the daily holding of the balance becomes the paramount responsibility of the Messenger and chelas throughout the earth.

With vigilance and with the giving of self there is forthcoming the dispensation of the Lords of Karma for a staying action of the LORD, as it was so stated.

And these dispensations that have come forth and those which are at hand are all predicated upon the dedication and sincerity of those who understand once and for all that my Keepers of the Flame—minutemen and women and knights and ladies of the flame—are those upon whom all elemental life and the Great White Brotherhood depend for the infusion of the earth, hour by hour and moment by moment, with the sacred fire that does consume the momentums of death and dissidence and the abomination of desolation—namely the abortion of Life in the womb and the abortion of the cycles of Life everywhere appearing. Thus, my beloved, these calls becoming the perpetual prayer of the heart are the very lifeblood whereby the present system is sustained.

These pilgrimages of our bands and of youth itself* constitute a demonstration to Lords of Life and the Lords of Karma that there are in the earth hearts mighty indeed, hearts magnanimous and expanding that *can* hold the Light, that *will* hold the Light.

Extraordinary cosmic beings behold this cosmic purpose and this dedication and this purity and therefore offer by the testimony of a single disciple, no matter how young in years, the immense light of their causal bodies. They come in search of those who are the holders of Truth. Finding then in you these holders of the Light, they add to that Light.

Once and for all, then, let Keepers of the Flame *know*—as I stand before you the Knight

*Following the 1980 Easter conference, Elizabeth Clare Prophet and a group of disciples made a pilgrimage to India and, in response to the commission of Chananda (December 29, 1979), established the Ashram of the World Mother in New Delhi. May 12, 1980, marked the Montessori International pilgrimage to the British Isles and Croagh Patrick commissioned by Sanat Kumara.

Commander and the Father of the Church and the one in whom is entrusted the balance of this two-thousand-year cycle—*know*, I tell you, that every word of every child of my heart, every dynamic decree is of ultimate import in these most trying hours!

I assure you that to send our Messenger to India and to the British Isles and across the earth in this very period of cycles turning is not without the greatest urgency. Lord Chananda and El Morya are gratified in the service of those who remain in India. But all of that nation cry out for the reinforcement of devotees to keep that flame. And therefore we call again for volunteers to go forth and hold that counterpoint of light balancing the light going forth from the chakras of America.

Indeed the necessity for the establishment of points of light in London and New York has been a most key action of this pilgrimage. As the children of the Light have renewed the tie to ancient forcefields of Saint Patrick and Sanat Kumara, so there is a connection in the earth of ancient streams deeply imbedded in the very bedrock of the etheric body.

The connection, the reestablishment of ancient ties, is a strengthening to the world body of believers. Even as the fallen ones tie together the islands of darkness through the universal beat of rock music and through the waves being used to perpetuate and to communicate the culture of the fallen ones, so it is the determination of the Great White Brotherhood to tie again together that blessed arm of the cross of white fire—the very servants of God in the earth.

There is a magnet in the mountain of Croagh Patrick. You must understand that that very mountain—to walk upon it, to ascend it—is life-giving. And those who walk it have that tie to the blessed saint and to that light that now penetrates the earth. How blessed are the feet who have received the imprint of that magnet!

Understand that the mountains of God in the earth—key mountains, holy mountains, shrines and focuses of the retreats of our Brotherhood—are the places where the pilgrims go, there to renew and reestablish the inner balance of the body temple with Elohim, there to enter into cosmic cycles. Thus the very air itself, the sun, and the fire in the heart of the mountain contributes to the purging. And thus that mountain known as a mountain of penance [Croagh Patrick, County Mayo, western Ireland] becomes in our understanding the mount of transmutation that leads to individual transfiguration.

And what is the transfiguration but the acceleration of transmutation until there is an alignment of the magnet of Alpha and Omega within every living cell of your temple and you become on fire for the LORD and truly an electrode through which currents of Elohim descend—especially while the body temples are at rest at night when there can be the acceleration of the Light anchoring through your forms because there is the stillness of the outer mind and the peace of inner communion with holy angels, who themselves place the angles of their consciousness within the very context of your lower vehicles so as to increase your potential for the anchoring of the Light.

This is why the placing of the body temple to rest undisturbed at the regular hours prescribed is a part of the ritual of your service and must be regarded as a portion of your holy office that is most important to us.

So then, beloved ones, where the body of the LORD is, there are the eagles gathered together and there is the gathering of the eagles, as the Ascended Masters, from continent to continent as the body of the Messenger and chelas form a ring of fire, a hallowed circle of oneness. And this has been our mission—to establish within the cities where they have traveled certain focal points on the etheric plane that might be used and activated specifically for the staying of that cataclysm which is imminent though not necessary if there be the rallying of the Children of the Sun.

Thus these electrodes established in these points from New Delhi to London, Dublin, New York, in Chicago, Los Angeles, in the very center of the Pacific in Honolulu—all of these points of Light for an action to circle the earth and to establish the continuation and the continuity of Light that travels on inner planes as the Ascended Master consciousness ringing the earth from point to point, from electrode to electrode in other various forcefields already established by the Messengers. And therefore the antahkarana is activated, is accelerated, and all who have been a part of these pilgrimages become at inner levels yet the electrodes for the sustaining of that momentum of purity.

We come then to explain how necessary is the call, how necessary is the physical action and the physical pilgrimage itself. And we come to say, God-victory unto those who have accomplished this victory and gone forth! Now let us see then what remains to be accomplished, for in the very absence there come to the surface conditions which must be faced.

Beloved ones, there is a mounting strife, a sense of injustice and yet prejudice betwixt the races in the United States and throughout the world. That sense of injustice and the frustration of nonfulfillment, nonunderstanding erupting in Miami (the very base chakra of the United States) should signify to all that the civil rights movement and all that has gone before has not solved the problem of this very question of the relationship of the races and of opportunity in society.

Beloved hearts, you add to this that which could become a spark to ignite across America—

the attempted assassination of Vernon Jordan*—
and you realize why there is concern among leaders
of the community in all races. And there indeed
must be concern!—I am concerned, Portia is concerned, the Lords of Karma are concerned that
this division in the body of America be the very
wedge whereby the fallen ones overcome this civilization.

Hate and hate creation used against the
children of the Light, dividing and conquering
the people along the lines of color instead of in
the lines of Armageddon, bears no good omen for
the Light and the future of that Light in America.
Yet this is known, this is understood. And the present leaders are not adequate to the task because
they identify with the flesh-and-blood consciousness instead of with the living Word. Therefore
little progress has been made.

I come to you, then, with the urgent call of
Portia who comes even in this hour joining Pallas
Athena to multiply the light of Truth by the liv-
ing action of Freedom.

It is Portia, then, who in my name convokes
a conference of sons and daughters of Afra who
are Keepers of the Flame from throughout the

---

*Multiple social pressures erupted into the "Miami race riot" May 17 through
19, 1980, in which at least 14 people were beaten or shot to death. Financial
toll estimated at $200 million. The rampage began after the acquittal, by an
all-white jury, of four white police officers accused of bludgeoning to death
Arthur McDuffie, a black salesman who had sped through red lights on a
motorcycle. Vernon Eulion Jordan, Jr., president of the National Urban
League, was ambushed and seriously wounded by a gunman on May 29, 1980,
in Fort Wayne, Indiana.

world to convene here at Camelot and to join the children of the Light as we consider at this Fourth of July conference how those who are in America today can go forth with the Word, the liberating Word, into the large cities to bring that bread of Life to those who are in the ghettos yet who have the light and who ought to rise up in defense of the integrity and the unity of the I AM Race as it is universally established.

Beloved ones, there is only one activity that can resolve the crisis of division of the races in America and throughout the earth, and it is the violet flame. It is the action of the sacred fire. It is the Teachings of the Ascended Masters.

There is no religious body who has succeeded in binding up this schism. There are no individuals this day who are offering adequate solutions. And therefore the fallen ones have a field day as they pursue their divide-and-conquer tactics and recognize this particular situation as a means to bring about riot and destruction—destruction of the very opportunity that ought to be accorded to the blessed sons and daughters of Afra in this very decade.

Therefore we seek the integration of the cosmic cross of white fire! We seek action! And we demand that Keepers of the Flame place their attention upon the preaching of the Word by those who are a part of this very people.

Let the Word be preached and let these

messengers of the deliverance of the children of Afra go forth. Let it be heard. And let the teachers be raised up under the World Teachers who can communicate the true understanding.

For I tell you that unless members of the black community itself will give the calls to the violet flame, unless there be established study groups whose members can apply the Teaching to the particular problems which they face, there will come upon America increased tension and outburst because of the futility of life that is lived in many quarters—quarters that you have not seen or experienced and therefore cannot understand, my beloved.

Realize, then, that this nation is raised up, it is raised up to be the proving ground and the crossroads of life where the cosmic cross of white fire symbolizes the coming together of all peoples and nations, kindreds, tongues, races, and lifewaves of evolution.

In this very nation, by the raising up of the Universal Christ and the I AM Presence, the open door of salvation is given unto all. And the covenant of Sanat Kumara is that those who believe on the One Sent, those who believe on the Ascended Masters and their Word through our Messenger and through our disciples, become those unto whom the quickening of the threefold flame can indeed come. And no one is excepted.

It is the hour of the call of Camelot!—and

this call is to worship the Holy Trinity in the heart, to understand that spark of Life as the universal principle of harmony, of transmutation, and of exaltation of Almighty God. The call of Camelot is to come Home, to come into the presence of the LORD, to prepare that temple for the Incarnation.

This call is unto all people. And I tell you, beloved ones, there are places upon the surface of the earth, large bodies of land and areas of population in the millions, where not a single invocation is yet being offered unto the sacred fire and unto the violet flame. It is most difficult for elemental life to sustain the balance in these forcefields.

For example, the islands of Japan. Being without the necessary momentum of the violet flame, the people themselves tremble and fear in the predictions of their own scientists that there will be major cataclysm in these islands. They fear what is coming upon them by the very absence of devotion to Kuan Yin which, had it been given and established even two thousand years ago when her appearance was made manifest to two fishermen—even then had she been accepted as the Mother of Mercy, there might have come forth a greater manifestation of that violet flame.

Indeed, I tell you, these islands are in jeopardy. Yet all is not lost. By the fire of two—two disciples of the Lord Christ going forth into the key cities of the earth—this ring of fire, this antahkarana can be increased.

I appeal, then, to all who savour the very Life of the Holy Spirit, who treasure each morsel of our Word, who treasure Life in the earth to realize that these are indeed perilous hours in the four quadrants of Life—perilous for the flame of freedom, for the future of America, and for the very cycles of Life and the balance of Life through the elemental kingdom. Thus the physical eruption of Mount St. Helens and the emotional eruption in Miami signify that all is not well in the earth.

The question is: Can the sacred fire be so injected, can the enlightenment and the comfort of the Holy Spirit be so spread abroad by dedicated hearts that, indeed, further cataclysm at all levels of manifestation can be stayed?

This is yet a question. The dispensations hang in the balance. To pull them down is the work of the ages—pulling down the dispensations, the covenants, and the promises of the LORD. To pull these down you require a knowledge of the Word as that Word is become the Law of the LORD.

So your manifestation of the Light has been indeed noteworthy. We come with praise. We come in thanksgiving. We come to approve and to say, that which has already been done has manifested a staying action in this very state against far greater cataclysm that could have occurred. Thus we are grateful for the levels sustained and we come with a mighty encouragement of our bands of light who themselves are encouraged because of the stature of Keepers of the Flame in the earth.

As we see what has been accomplished, we look again to greater accomplishments. We encourage students of the Light to consider the career of being sons and daughters of God—the career that places in perspective education and the profession of life in context with that which is the greatest requirement of the hour.

When you search to know the divine plan, beloved ones, know that in your causal body is a great moment of Truth, a moment that is a sphere of consciousness, attainment already won that can be drawn down as a gift from the Son, a gift from the Father, a gift through the Christed One within you. Placing this gift of attainment upon the altar of humanity, you can fulfill your life's calling. You can fulfill your education, your family responsibilities, and a service incomparable and indispensable to me.

I AM Saint Germain. I speak to every one of you. And across the nations let my call go forth.

I have need of career sons and daughters of God who understand themselves as instruments of the Law of Love, who will realize that we would place you here and there holding the finger in the dike until there can be the multiplication of cosmic forces and that in each and every case your volunteering to be our instruments will result in the fulfillment of your own joy and God-happiness and divine plan unto the victory of the ascension.

And therefore not in deprivation of the fullness of joy but in its crystallization is the divine talent made known and does that talent appear as the very work of the ages which your soul has forged and won for Sanat Kumara.

By the distribution of forces, by the very examination of the best use of time and space and talent, we see as we have studied the chelas of the Light that there are enough who are talented and devoted to fill those key positions. And all working together for the glory of God can truly hold the balance against impending Dark Cycle spirals that hour by hour, day by day must be arrested and transmuted and rolled back.

I know that in the fullness of the Light of Portia a new understanding of opportunity and justice in the service of the Light will come upon you. Equally well do I know of your devotion and your desire to be God-taught and to understand your role in this mighty work of the ages.

I know that I can count on you, you who have spoken to me in the midnight hours of your desire to hold the torch of the Goddess of Liberty.

Thus I appear at Camelot to welcome home the pilgrims and the messengers and to give a joyous acclamation of gratitude as I clap my hands for the faithful ones who keep that flame blazing in the heart of Los Angeles and in all of our teaching centers.

So, beloved ones, there is great good accomplished. And we come to set a new pace accelerated by the violet flame. Thus a half hour to the violet flame in invocation three times a day will result in—you know what? A holding of the balance for the earth *and* your own balance of personal karma.

Some of you have come to me for many years in wonder and consternation that you make not further progress on the Path. And somehow you have overlooked the universal solvent of the violet flame.

You have found, then, the alchemist's dream in this violet fire. Use it. Use it as the Elohim themselves scheme to bring forth the perfect man and the Manchild. Use the violet flame to go beyond yourself, to exceed yourself. It is the law of self-transcendence. See what it can do.

Beloved hearts, never, never do we desire to hear it spoken in this community, "It might have been." What might have been is that which is past and cannot be recalled. Therefore let us dwell on what is. And let us visualize the violet flame at the nexus of the hourglass. And therefore it transmutes time and Father Time and the cycles of time running out. It transmutes space. And at that point of the nexus, the Lamb and the Lamb's wife, every chela of Sanat Kumara, realize the precipitation of infinity.

Thus there is expansion of opportunity which means expansion of cycles which means transcending of time and space so that you are no longer bound by laws of mortality or limitation and therefore can, in the given life span, accomplish all that you desire, all that the Law requires. And this expansion of your days, this increasing of your days with joy has to do with the capacity of atoms, cells, and electrons and chakras and force-fields in your being that you know not of—the increase of the capacity *to hold Light*.

It is ever our desire that you should come into a scientific understanding of how to increase that capacity. Let us begin with a visualization of the violet flame at the nexus. For Morya has said, "Time is not. Space is no more." Thus in this sense of infinity, you have indeed eternal Life here and now.

Keepers of the Flame and blessed ones of my heart, seize this flame of eternal Life! In joy let it be manifest in all the worlds, in all the systems, and unto the sun of even pressure.

Let this evolution of Lightbearers be eternal Life here and now. And let there be the staying action of the LORD God Almighty—as I have said it through the Messenger—in these electrodes over the cities of the earth. Let there be the staying action of the LORD God Almighty unto the coming of my Portia beloved, unto the coming of my beloved disciples. Let there be that staying action!

Beloved ones, the LORD God Almighty has granted my prayer in this hour and that staying action is come predicated upon the faith, the hope, the mutuality of charity of the ascended and unascended saints of our Brotherhood.

Beloved ones, let that staying action and that staying hand of the LORD GOD be for thee opportunity, opportunity, opportunity. How I love thee, blessed Opportunity of my life!

In the love of my heart, I seal you. In the love of our twin flames, we seal you. In the love of the Almighty, of freedom itself we seal you and encourage you to new summits of attainment.

O Light, O Light from the summits of the world, O Light from the summit of Being—I call thee forth! Now plummet into the very heart of the earth and let there be a mighty oscillation of the white fire core and of the Mighty I AM Presence and of the magnets of the mountains.

So the earth itself from the within to the without receives the balancing action of our twin flames for the holding of the earth by the Light of the Four Cosmic Forces and the beings of the elements.

I AM Saint Germain. I stand in the heart of the earth. I stand in the heart of Los Angeles. I multiply my Electronic Presence in the cities of the nations.

Lo! I AM here. Lo! I AM come. Lo! by my right hand—*ho!* the Light of the violet flame is, *ho!* the Light of the violet flame is that flame of freedom in every heart of Light. Lo! there is a washing and the bathing of the earth. There is a multiplication of that violet flame and of that Holy Spirit.

So this is the Light of Pentecost. This is the Light of the Holy Spirit. And it shall show forth its glory, its manifest perfection, and its multiplication of my Word in you.

This is the new day. This is the new day of days when I shall walk the earth arm in arm with my Lady Portia as she has not manifested herself heretofore.

Will you look for us as we come representing Lord Sanat Kumara and Lady Master Venus, as we step down intensely the fires of freedom?

Will you then welcome us into your hearts, my beloved? ["Yes!"]

June 1, 1980
Los Angeles

1. Ezek. 1; 10; Rev. 4:4-8.
2. Deut. 25:4; I Cor. 9:9; I Tim. 5:18.
3. Matt. 21:42-44.
4. **Dark Cycle.** On April 23, 1980, the Dark Cycle entered its twelfth year, signifying the return of personal and planetary karma accrued through the misuse of God's light and the failure of Christic initiations under the solar hierarchy of Sagittarius on the eleven o'clock line of the Cosmic Clock. See *Kuthumi on Selfhood* (1969 *Pearls of Wisdom*, vol. 12), pp. xi-xii, 10, 30, 246-54, 263-66, $17.95.

Book Four

A Prophecy of Karma

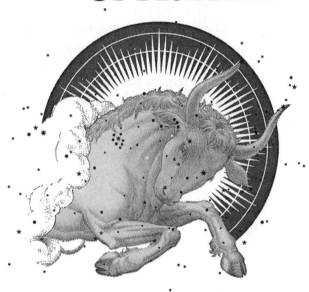

The Hierarch of the Aquarian Age
Reads the Handwriting on the Wall

Saint Germain

The sun shall be turned into darkness,
and the moon into blood, before that
great and notable day of the Lord come:
And it shall come to pass, that whosoever shall call on the name of the
Lord shall be saved.

Acts

CHAPTER I

A Prophecy of Karma
Of the Rulers in the Earth

Unless the Light Be Raised Up
Calamity upon Europe Shall Be
Greater Than Ever Seen in Known History

Hail, O people of Light!
Regard now the plight of the nations and of
yourselves in the midst thereof.*

I AM Saint Germain, come to you again as
of old. I stand in defense of the flame of Liberty
within your hearts and I come to reprove the nations. I come, therefore, to direct my light ray
from the very heart of Sirius and its seat of God-
government into the very nucleus of those individuals who now have set themselves and been set by
the people as rulers and kings, as captains and
overlords upon this planetary home.

Heretofore Sanat Kumara has said unto me:

"Saint Germain, stay thy hand! For if these
ones be judged, who shall be raised up to govern in
their stead?"

---

*See I Samuel 11, 12 for the Messenger's scriptural reading prior to the
dictation deemed necessary background for the hearing of his word by Saint
Germain, who was embodied as the prophet Samuel.

And therefore, I have not raised my hand as the hand of the LORD for the judgment of those leaders who have betrayed the people of Light and all peoples East and West. And therefore, you have observed the ripening of the seed of Light and of the seed of the Wicked One. And all those things have come to pass as Darkness has fulfilled itself, as Light has fulfilled itself.

Beloved ones, the answer has come in this hour: I will send the King to reign over the people. I, the LORD God, will send the Holy Christ Self. The LORD Our Righteousness—He shall be raised up in the midst of the people! And those who fear God and love him and obey his commandments will become the true standard-bearers East and West.

Therefore, beloved ones, the dark ones have threatened anarchy and chaos with the coming of the judgment of the fallen ones in their seats of power. We of the Cosmic Council have said:

"Their iniquity is so great, they must be judged. And in the vacuum created by the absence of leadership, the people must find their God. The people must find the God within and follow the Law that is written in their inward parts.

"Let them see, therefore, and know that the LORD he is God and that the Mighty I AM Presence and that LORD Our Righteousness (even your own beloved Christ Self) is sufficient unto the day! And therefore, God-government does descend. According to the Word of Isaiah therefore, Let the government this day be upon the shoulders of the Lightbearers of the nations!"

Therefore I, Saint Germain, say not only is Saul judged in this hour—*and he is judged*—but every Saul that reigns in the earth by the acclamation of the people, by their wickedness going after the idols—each and every one is judged, from heads of state to the heads of the military to the governors to the mayors to those who raise their hand of tyranny East and West in the economies.

These idols shall fall this day! They are bound by the hosts of Sanat Kumara assisted by the twelve legions of the Archangels, and you may find the fulfillment of prophecy upon you. And you may understand that the hour must come when they are bound and when finally the people must discover the resources of Almighty God, else they themselves go down to the side of the pit as they worship the fallen ones that have been so cast down.

Therefore, in the joy of the LORD's judgment and all of the challenge and the travail that is to come, I say, beloved hearts, be seated in the flame of my consort, the Goddess of Justice.

Blessed ones of the immaculate fire, the fire is indeed immaculate around you in this hour. But the kings and the presidents and the rulers have utterly betrayed their God.

Two years hence—following the crowning of Saul according to the will of the people and their desiring (to which the Great Law and the LORD did and does defer)—his disobedience was re-buked.* And therefore, he could not inherit the keys to the kingdom of Israel. God had exacted from him obedience, signifying that those who have betrayed the Word who then are obedient and loving of heart may once again receive an impartation of the flame and the mantle of the office, if not all the way to the intertwining once again of their relationship to Sanat Kumara.

Beloved ones, understand the meaning of the call of God to obedience. There is no survival, there is no protection to the people of God out-side of the auric field of the I AM THAT I AM.

Obedience means alignment with conscious-ness, not mere perfunctory actions. Be not de-ceived, for the clever and the cunning seek there-fore to give that token performance, but their hearts are far from the heart of the Mighty I AM Presence. Therefore, deeds can be only represen-tative of that telling of the heart, that willing of the mind, that wisdom of the soul that does elect with fervor and by free will to be one with God as the sole reason and cause for being.

Beloved ones, come to the understanding, then, that whatever is the doing of the human self, it matters not. It matters that the spirit of a man and the spirit of a woman and of a child is in the full fire of the desiring of God. Therefore take care lest your desirings for other things draw unto you that which is without in place of the inner

*See I and II Samuel.

treasure and that which is the undoing of the nations this day.

Blessed hearts of the living flame, this message of the prophet's call to the people to obedience has never been more vital. For that obedience is the only means whereby Archangel Michael and the legions of Sanat Kumara [the Ancient of Days]—all of the heavenly hosts—may indeed keep you sealed in the Light of the Almighty One.

Saint Germain you call me, and so I stand as Portia stands with me this day. For we come truly in the fullness of our office as hierarchs of the Aquarian age. We come looking toward the East. We look to Europe and we look to the nations. With the Sword [i.e., Sacred Word] of Sanat Kumara, we send our Messenger and her team.* We send Keepers of the Flame already positioned on this battleground.

Beloved ones, this action of the sacred fire which we send through her is for the touching and the calling of all those who are the seed of Sanat Kumara who hear the cry of the prophet Samuel this day and will come in the center of oneness beneath their own Mighty I AM Presence with obedience to the will of God, charged with holy will and love.

The gathering of these Lightbearers and their anointing shall mean unto them opportunity in

*On October 15, 1985, the Messenger and Stump team departed on a 4¹/₂-week tour to bring the Teachings of the Ascended Masters to Europe, Canada and New York, delivering Saint Germain's message in 25 cities.

this life to hold the balance of the nations, to take the initiatic path of Luxor under Serapis Bey,* to fulfill the divine plan through the grand matrix of the Great Divine Director, to balance their karma, and to ascend to God.

The hour is late. The fallen ones in their rivalry enact their acts of terrorism against one another and against the innocent or the representatives of freedom. Understand the psychology of the dark ones and the devils in embodiment and the fallen Atlanteans returned. Understand that their rivalry is amongst their own hierarchy of Darkness.

Indeed they have jealousy for the Light of the sons of God. Indeed they'd take their revenge, if they could, against the Lord Sanat Kumara. And inasmuch as they cannot, they would seek to take it against his Messenger and Lightbearers.

They see themselves in a warfare engaged as to who amongst themselves in the false hierarchy shall arrive at the top to command nations, to rule the earth, and to take its spoils. They do not acknowledge the Lightbearers or Sanat Kumara as the inheritors of the earth. They see themselves in control and are willing to fight to the end to determine which and who among them shall be at the top. Thus, it is the never-ending wars of the gods we see exercising their war games before us—and many evolutions of Darkness who serve them with utter idolatry and contempt.

*Concerning the teachings of Serapis Bey, see *Lords of the Seven Rays* and *Dossier on the Ascension*, Summit University Press, $5.95 ea.

Into the midst of this cross fire and battlefield we send our Messenger in a moment when
terrorists are seized with revenge—revenge against
America for interfering in their hijacking.*

Beloved ones, you must enter the mind of
Evil to understand revenge, for it is incomprehen-
sible in any other dimension. Realize, then, that as
this is the very first time that any such step has
been tried by the United States in this precise
fashion, one can see the setup [for retaliation]
through tools on both sides. Thus, now there is
the upping of the ante, as they say, in the desire for
revenge and the plotting of new acts of terrorism—
this time directed against citizens or members of
the government of the United States.

Recognize therefore what is brewing, what is
the forcefield that is set in the hour of the coming
of the Messenger to the European continent and
understand—not condemnation, not hatred, not
pride, not rebellion but the culmination of all of
these in the contemplated acts of revenge against
the highest representatives of the United States
of America and therefore the representatives of
Sanat Kumara.

Realize, beloved ones, that they have annihi-
lated marines, ministers, members of the clergy,
professionals, ordinary people, unsuspecting

*On Oct. 7, 1985, Palestinian terrorists hijacked the Italian cruise liner
Achille Lauro with over 400 passengers and crew on board. During the 51-
hour ordeal, they demanded the release of 50 Palestinians held by Israel and
killed one American passenger. Near Crete, four U.S. Navy F-14 jets inter-
cepted a chartered jet carrying the terrorists, who had been guaranteed safe
passage out of Egypt, and forced it to land in Sicily, where the terrorists were
taken into custody.

hearts—all representative of the hierarchy of the Great White Brotherhood in this great nation and the hierarchy of Lightbearers throughout the world. Though their targets be the seed of their own kind, government by government, yet they unite on both sides in the revenge against the living Christ.

Therefore we come to set before you that which is also set before this Messenger. We come to bless, to initiate, to anoint you that you might be extensions of this mantle and presence whom we send fearlessly going before us to proclaim the Word and the opportunity as she has already done in 1981.

Blessed ones of the Sun, understand that without this Messenger, I could not return to Europe and finish the work that was begun and that must be culminated. For in this passage of time since the awful days of the French Revolution, there has come a certain enlightenment to those not of the ruling body of the continent. There has come a certain understanding of the Great White Brotherhood.

Now in the hour of our coming, we therefore send legions of Light before us. Legions of the mighty Archangels—legions of the seven and the five go forth. And they go, then, for the binding of the pride and the rebellion of the very Lightbearers who ought to receive my own and make the inner tie and therefore be sealed by the fires of freedom unto their own destiny and the protection of that continent which is indeed in great jeopardy.

Beloved ones, we are concerned more for the passing of the tests by the Lightbearers than we are for the judgment of the dark ones. Therefore our angels go forth for the binding of the Brotherhood of the Black Raven and the false hierarchies of the nations, that there be not upon the children of the Light those burdens of their own self-programming as well as the inner controls of unceasing black magic that has been practiced against the Light within their hearts since the coming of Jesus Christ and before.

Understand that we also bind and seal records of Atlantis that have not been taken because they involve the free will of those in embodiment. We seal and we hold at bay the Four Cosmic Forces that the Word might be spoken and that those who are called might now be chosen that they themselves may choose once to stand for my flame—for that cosmic purpose I have espoused, which is their own individual freedom, and Life forevermore.

You, beloved ones, who know something of my mission and my experiences can well comprehend just how great a battle must needs be fought to convince one individual of the desirability of his own freedom under God—freedom from vice and every device of politicking and power positioning, freedom from manipulation, freedom from the addictions of the flesh, freedom to be

God in manifestation. Would to God they had seen and known my example and desired and perceived the ordinate desire to become as I am and as I was!

We bring, therefore, the example of Christhood to be desired. You bring the Teaching that teaches and tutors souls as to the desirability of personal Christhood. The Law knows of no other way than to bring before the people the fruits of their wrong sowing in calamities and wars and ruination. But, beloved ones, if the Light is not raised up in the earth by individual choice, the calamity which shall come upon Europe and mankind shall be greater than that which has ever been seen in known history.

Truly it is an hour for the staying of the hand of world chaos, destruction, and death. It is ever thus. The LORD God will bend all the way to the hearts of his own and to all people, giving the choice for them to rule in his name. But at the end of the hour of the opportunity of the choosing, by their choices the karma must fall to the right or to the left.

It is well that you have the example, for it is too hard for many to believe. Realize, then, that if the one who is sent to be hierarch of an age [Saint Germain himself] cannot dissuade, by any and every means assayed, those powers that be—as was the case for more than a hundred years before the French Revolution—if my hands could be tied when I was so blessed by these dispensations from

God, can you expect another intercessor? Another response? Can you expect the setting aside of the will of the dark ones? Can you expect there to be any difference in the outcome?

The difference today, beloved hearts, is that thousands by free will have engaged the mighty angels who have become one with yourselves, sealing you in the very heart of their auras, which are mighty indeed. The difference is that a balance of Light is being held. Yet those who have held this balance of Light are not, as they might be, in positions of decision-making and power and responsibility.

Therefore, beloved, recognize that the outcome may be predictable in one sense. But human will and human choice must be given its day. Therefore, we say it is completely unpredictable. And the daily and hourly and momentary choices and responses that are made will determine the fate of all nations.

We will not cease our stumping. We will not cease to give forth our message. But we expect you to remain obedient to our will, which is God's, to establish the Inner Retreat* and all those things that we have designated, to see to it that you have positioned yourselves there and understand that the Great White Brotherhood must maintain a spiritual fortress and a retreat of Light whether the golden age is to appear universally tomorrow

*A 33,000-acre self-sufficient spiritual community-in-the-making located in southwest Montana adjacent to Yellowstone National Park where students of the Ascended Masters study and apply the Teachings of the Great White Brotherhood.

or whether there be world chaos as a transition leading to it.

The establishment of this center of Light is for the focus of the Great Central Sun Magnet. It is a positioning for a cosmic purpose, and that purpose is the holding of the balance of planetary forces and karma with great intensity in the full-time action of dynamic decrees which must be engaged in by those who are not a part of the work force day to day in making the Inner Retreat happen.

The company of priests and priestesses of the sacred fire who tend the flame of the altar of the Inner Retreat are indeed tending the flame of the Royal Teton Retreat, our abode in the Grand Teton. They are tending the flames of the governments of the nations and the mandala of God-government in the golden age. They are tending the fires of freedom against those who have already carved up the world to their designs in their concept of a one-world government to thwart and turn back and oppose the God-government of the Ascended Masters and the Lightbearers in the earth.

Therefore, of supreme importance is self-government within the Community, is harmony, is education for the children that they may early take their places of responsibility. And therefore, parents and teachers, listen to your mentors and do not abuse the children entrusted to your care by doing too much for them or too little for them.

There is an independent pioneer spirit that must be nurtured, and therefore do not limit their style of creativity. Do not draw circles around them and say, "You may perform only within this little circle or this little box.". . .

Therefore I raise the sword of Sanat Kumara and I place that sword before you. This sword, then, becomes a new standard within the Community. And the standard is equal unto all—whatever the source, whatever the seed. Let them meet the standard of obedience to the Lord God and the true love of the desiring of the heart. . . .

For I tell you, you will face the Philistines, as you already have; you will face the fallen ones. And the unity and the love and the perception of Truth must be upheld. And therefore I command the Messenger and our representative there to see to it that all are brought to the standard of Sanat Kumara.

I remind you once again that this Community and this center of Light so purposed has as its mission and its goal the holding of the balance of Light and Darkness in the earth in an hour of grave danger to every lifestream.

Perhaps you have an idea, perhaps you have no idea as to the venom and the revenge that can be unleashed by laggard evolutions unchecked. Thus, with the spinelessness that we see in the West, advances are made both by terrorists and by the communist/capitalist conspiracy that need not be.

It has not been necessary that the Soviets should have the upper hand. And I pray that all of you realize what [potential] grave danger lies ahead for the West as the outcome of the meeting of Reagan and Gorbachev.* Understand, beloved hearts of Light, that there is the need to call forth our Electronic Presence and that of the mighty Archangels to thwart the intent of Darkness.

Beloved ones, those who challenge the conspirators as I have challenged Saul, those who will say to them, "We will not negotiate until you withdraw from Afghanistan and tear down the Berlin wall!" those who will say, "Remove yourselves from Angola!" must have the spine, must have the hosts of the LORD behind them therefore to have the power to implement the consequences when their challenges are not met.

Thus, with all that I have vouchsafed to this nation as technology and implements and the wherewithal of true defense whereby not a lifestream should be lost on earth, yet the culminating Light, the power of the sacred fire, the devotion to God in the face of such an omnipresent danger has been wanting. Thus, all of the implements of the Philistines are of no avail in the hands of the seed of Sanat Kumara unless they worship the LORD God and bend the knee and recognize that the hour of sacrifice is come.

Beloved hearts, we must use our alternatives when so many fail us. I look into the eyes of each

---

*Two-day summit meeting of President Ronald Reagan and Soviet General Secretary Mikhail S. Gorbachev in Geneva, Switzerland, Nov. 19-20, 1985.

and every one of you and I say, *"You are the LORD's alternative this day!"*

And the Mother has asked me, "How can you send me, simply a little woman? I am not even David with a sling. How shall I go forth to defeat this world conspiracy?" I tell you, beloved, we send her with a mantle and a flame and a fire, and we send her with the Goddess of Liberty.

Blessed hearts, you can be the Davids with your sling of the dynamic Word. But it will require prayer and fasting and the summoning of inner forces to release the Light from your own chakras that will defeat the adversary at every hand. At every hand, beloved ones, you find the adversary. And thus, as the sun rises each day, for you to be God in manifestation you must wield the sling of the spoken Word and your auras must be kindled with fire.

You are the alternative if you will it so. Your hearts are willing but sometimes you are wanting in the understanding of the personal disciplines required. Making the call and seeing God answer is a great step in the right direction. When you can give the call and see the angelic hosts respond, you are truly in the vanguard.

But you must take the next step. And this is the step that demands the aloneness, the sacrifice, and the reckoning of the enemy. It is the moment when you so identify with the angel of the LORD that that Archangel, finding in you the acceptable offering—the purified temple and mind—does permanently place his Electronic Presence over you and you are as Archangel Michael in the flesh.

This is the moment when the world can be saved by those in embodiment. Some must have the identification of God. Some must believe it is not robbery to make oneself equal with God* in this understanding. Then the rest may offer the call. And the call will be answered because we have the focal point in embodiment through which to release the Light.

Hasten. Hasten to the hill of the LORD. Hasten to the place of consecration. Understand that it is a moment of opportunity given by the Lords of Karma to all of you who are a part of the mantle of the Messenger. By the grace of God and her continuing service with your own, there has been abuilding in her auric field all of these years that momentum and that energy/light through which we can release an equivalency of fire.

Beloved ones, there is no turning back for any of us. For in the timetables of the seed of the wicked, they are determined to destroy if they cannot win. Thus they have nothing to lose and they give their life to the death of Light in this world. You must be prepared for any abuse, any reaction, any fight that must be fought to rescue the Children of the Sun. And you must be always prepared.

Regardless of future vision of golden age, we place our decision on the reality and the

*Phil. 2:6.

guarantee of survival. If we do our job well and you perform yours, the whole earth shall be the kingdom of God and there will be plenty of space and room for expansion.

In the meantime, let us get up to the holy mountain of God. Let us send our emissaries therefrom. Let us be vigilant, for an age hangs with the same tension as Damocles' sword.*

May Syracuse become the point of the vanquishment of Evil. May those in embodiment remember and remember all past ages and know that the hour is soon coming when it may be the will of our Father to accord me greater dispensations once again to help you and the nations. For this moment we are grateful that many in heaven have come forward in our name to pledge themselves to this effort. . . .

Above all, keep the harmony of my life and keep the flame. . . . If you so multiply my Presence as I would and as I have taught you, so you shall earn for me the return of that jewel which I long ago laid upon the altar of God in behalf of Europe.

Thus having that jewel returned, I may act once again with greater dominion in the physical octave because it is your will that I might

---

*Damocles was a courtier of the Greek tyrant Dionysius the Elder of Syracuse in the 4th century b.c. As related by Cicero, Damocles so praised Dionysius' good fortune that the tyrant invited him to a banquet to show him the precarious nature of his happiness. He seated Damocles beneath a sword suspended from the ceiling by a single hair. To Damocles, who was afraid to stir, the banquet was a tantalizing torment. The event at Syracuse marks the step on the Path where the Lightbearers must defeat the evil of tyrants who manipulate mankind's karma, holding it as a sword of Damocles over their heads.

intercede. If you forget to keep the harmony, then
I must pay the price. And thus, the effort of world
freedom does begin with trust—the sacred trust
which we now share. . . .

Alpha and Omega, let these my own be
trusted with thy Spirit.

In the name of Melchizedek, king of Salem
and priest of the Most High God, I bless with the
light of Sanat Kumara, that I myself might be in
the full physical presence of the world through my
Messenger and my Keepers of the Flame.

O Alpha, O Omega—I, Saint Germain,
Knight Commander of the Keepers of the Flame
Fraternity, hierarch of the Aquarian age, do accept
these devotees as token and sign, symbol and presence of the remnant of Israel. I plight my troth
with those who have given theirs. I give my life for
the victory in earth.

For Freedom's holy age, I send you, sons and
daughters of God. Keep the flame and the trust.
Remember that the Sword Excalibur as the sword
of the Knight Commander has touched you—not
a physical sword though physical it is, but the
sacred fire of my being.

Thus it shall come to pass that the world may
know the seventh age through your hearts. Opportunity has never stood more staunch in this hour
to renew, therefore, the opportunity for all Keepers of the Flame worldwide to enter into this
calling of the LORD and to rescue the nations.

O God, hear my call! O God, let thy miracle

be upon the earth this day. In Freedom's name, I, Saint Germain, cry unto thee, O God! Let Freedom reign in the true hearts and the noble. Let Liberty be proclaimed. And let the divine magnet and holy angels appear to bring these souls of Light worldwide to my heart and to my victory.

Upon the altar of humanity, the altar of the mighty threefold flame that will not be compromised or condescend, I dedicate this mission and this victory and this hour of God's freedom on earth.

Beloved Portia, I ask you in the fullness of my heart to bless now these Keepers of the Flame.

BELOVED PORTIA

A New Mantle for Saint Germain's Mission from the Cosmic Council

Blessed brothers and sisters of Light, I come as spokesman for the Lords of Karma. For we have received from the Cosmic Council the dispensation for this beloved brother and my own twin flame and therefore give to him, as he has called for you, also the new mantle he requires for the fulfillment of this mission.

Beloved ones, the hour is fast accelerating that your own calls should bring to conclusion the great burden Saint Germain has carried for the people's misuse of his ray in this and previous centuries. In anticipation, then, of this complete and full victory, the Lords of Karma and the Goddess of Liberty this day do give to Saint Germain from the Cosmic Council that which is unexpected unto him.

That mantle he has sought to earn by this mission, we give in advance that he might have the wherewithal to do greater works through you. And so we respond to the dedication of the European Keepers of the Flame on the continent and those of the Isles.

Blessed ones, Archangel Zadkiel and Holy Amethyst* place this purple robe upon Saint Germain in the gratitude of all of cosmos for his service untiring and for your response to that service and for his movement through the earth.

Thus, beloved, cosmos is grateful that earth yet retains the opportunity to become Freedom's star. Without the Keepers of the Flame Fraternity and those in embodiment who keep this flame daily, this dispensation could not be forthcoming.

Blessed ones, the Council of the Sun has seen, lo, in two hundred years how many thousands have now rallied to the Wonderman when there were scarcely a few. And those few in those days in their response did not have the subsequent dispensation of the science of the spoken Word to make their word and life count as you do.

May all understand in this hour that to move with Saint Germain in the earth, beloved, is the

*See *The Healing Power of Angels,* Summit University Press.

greatest opportunity for your own victory and the maximizing of your initiations and causal body. Thus, you are truly blessed and we bless you now in his name and by this mantle that you might be the all of the All in manifestation in his name.

Every heart of Saint Germain in this earth receives, then, this purple thread of Light to the heart of the Son. May you wear the purple thread in your undergarment lest you forget this opportunity of the hour and the lifetimes.

In the name of your Knight Commander, Rise, O Keepers of the Flame.*

BELOVED SAINT GERMAIN
Saint Germain's Gratitude

Almighty God, august members of the Cosmic Council, members of the Great White Brotherhood, and beloved Keepers of the Flame, the gratitude of my heart expands in a fervor and a light unparalleled in the acceptance of this mantle, which I receive in the name of all who have stood with this cause with me in all ages.

We shall go forth, then, for the completion of the balance of the burden, for the continuity of purpose, for the acceptance of the grace of opportunity. Together we are one, and we go

---

*Though the mantle was given for the mission and beyond, the jewel itself has not yet been returned. This dispensation awaits the full balancing, by the Keepers of the Flame's violet-flame decrees, of Saint Germain's karma incurred through the people's misuse of the Seventh Ray and dispensation secured for them by the Hierarch of the Aquarian Age.

forth to claim the Lightbearers of the Seventh
Ray and of the sixth root race. My appreciation
to each heart shall surely be known as my grace
and jewels of Light abound to you.

Blessed ones of God, O Holy One of Israel,
Lord Sanat Kumara, let us go forth to win in the
name of Liberty. So it is done by the Light of the
Father and of the Son and of the Holy Spirit,
Amen.

October 13, 1985
Los Angeles

CHAPTER 2

A Prophecy of Karma
Of the Outcome in the European Theatre

The Purging Will Come—
through Freedom's Fires Invoked
Else Nature Will Take Her Course

Lightbearers of the ages, I am come in a visitation of the Spirit—your Great Divine Director. I come to magnetize an inner energy field of Light for the reparation of the shattered lines of force striated throughout this continent by the records of war, infamy, and the abuse of power by various ignominious ones who have played their parts on the stage of life. The continent has been vulnerable due to layer upon layer of records of the shedding of blood, division, and all of those conditions thou knowest well.

For the healing of the breach at inner levels I am come. I am come for my love for my disciple Saint Germain and his heart full of desire to assist you. A blanket of violet flame is needed over all. As you place yourselves in this sanctuary prepared by your love and increase the calls to the violet flame and build the momentum, these will be multiplied to an extraordinary power by all legions of the Seventh Ray of cosmos.

I urge you to continue this vigil of the violet flame this night and to call to the Lords of Karma, for it is the conditions at inner levels, records of akasha tied to the subconscious of the people, that allow in the next cycle the repetition of history. This history is dyed deep. And every soul slaughtered on the battlefield of life cries out for justice, even from succeeding incarnations. And many have fallen again and again.

Is it any wonder that there is cynicism here or even a sense of hopelessness? Some have not known hope in many lifetimes. Consider how blessed ye are to have, then, the perception of Light, the calling to Light, and the dedication to Light. Consider, then, O Lightbearers of the ages, that many need that which is now in your grasp— the flame of freedom, aye, and much more—the illumination and the joy of the Mother.

I do anoint you in her name that you might go forth bearers of the Word, messengers of the Messenger and of the Ascended Masters, truly to give the Teaching, to clear the way, truly to know that this is the hour and the day when many shall receive the Holy Spirit, many must preach the Everlasting Gospel and clear the way for the Aquarian age.

Beloved hearts, our message must be spoken again and again. Therefore we have asked that you take this Teaching and understand that step by step you are being liberated by coils of Light released by the Messenger. This is a concentrated experience and once you have it, when you present this Teaching, I again will be present to help those who desire to serve with Saint Germain.

Remember the great calling and the hour. And remember that we cannot bare to your hearts the full knowledge of the possibility of consequences when action is not taken and when the dark clouds and dark tides are allowed to continue to roll across this continent unobstructed.

Where you have not the power to challenge by military might, nor the desire, truly you may challenge by the Word and the spoken Word. Nothing is fruitless, no effort without result. The only failure is not to call to me to act in the face of day-by-day events unfolding.

The members of the Karmic Board each have a very important role to play in the outcome in the European theatre. Therefore know our offices and know that Cyclopea with the All-Seeing Eye of God, when you give his decree, will increase your vision of the future and a sense of your own direction. I myself when called upon seal you in the blue sphere of Light that is indeed the replica of the great blue causal body.

In the intense fire of Love, the integration of yourself in the I AM Presence is protected by Nada, who comes in this year with Mighty Victory to sponsor you and your beloved twin flame to the fulfillment of holy purpose.

I am contacting now your chakras. I am releasing Light for a new day, for the sense of resurrection, that all things that have passed in your life may be turned as prologue and you may write the first page of the first chapter of a new book.

Opportunity's cycles through justice come through beloved Portia—mercy for the washing of the records in the violet flame of Kuan Yin. Pallas Athena sponsors unerring Truth and should be diligently called into action in the media, who do not reach the people with the facts.

Such a veil of lies and propaganda, such a calling of black "white" and white "black" is continuing so that the great masses of the people have no comprehension of the forces at work. The enemy is confused for the friend; the friend is confused for the enemy. And people lash out in great fear and terror to destroy that which is the greatest opportunity of the ages.

Thus, it is important to center with the Goddess of Liberty, for balance is something that has long been absent in Europe. The balance of the threefold flame of Liberty would give dynamism, true illumination, and enlightened action. Still we find the serpents dividing the people in political parties, economic philosophies—the same stale arguments that went on tens of thousands of years ago, the same players so worn out that if anyone would take note they should observe that even their skin is grey.

Beloved ones, it is the presence of Saint Germain which can indeed make the difference. We, as the Lords of Karma who sponsor the dispensations given to us by the Cosmic Council, truly wait for your word and your action and your response. For by and by, as the new year turns, we must go before the Cosmic Council with the report of the fruit of this rescue mission of Sanat Kumara through our Messenger and through yourselves. We must determine what new impulse or dispensation of freedom may be given in the new year as the result of your unceasing efforts to gather Lightbearers, to teach them the importance of decrees and the entering in to the joy of the violet flame.

Saturated is this earth with the blood of righteous Abel. Thus, beloved, how does one build a golden age upon such a foundation? How does one indeed? Thus the purging will come, I assure you. And it can come fully through freedom's fire, else Nature will take her course.

I trust you understand how vital is the free will of every individual. And that free will is the right of choice based upon knowledge and vision. Thus, it is right that you are aware of the power of the illumination, the purity of the Divine Mother to assist you.

If a tidal wave were announced, men would leave their plows and their fields and take shelter. If war were declared or hordes were approaching or a plague of locusts, the announcement thereof would cause concerted action—at least to escape the onslaught. We cannot cry any of these into your midst lest we be guilty of the same crime of the false alarm of "fire!" shouted in the midst of a crowded hall.

You see, beloved, there is in reality no accurate prediction. For, as Saint Germain has well learned and often said, the human consciousness is unpredictable. It is accurate to say that the challenges are moving toward your doorstep every day. It is accurate to say that when they arrive you must have Light in your lamps and already a momentum of understanding. It is accurate to say, as has been said already, be prepared for sudden changes. Be prepared for anything and then you shall indeed be prepared.

We have prepared a place in the wilderness, foreordained, because it is necessary. Whether or not it is necessary for you specifically only you can say.

I have come from other planes and other worlds to be with you, for I am deeply concerned for the outcome and the safety of many Lightbearers in various places on earth. Because of humanity's response in past ages, and as has been explained to you regarding the rejection of Saint Germain, we in fact are limited as to that which we may tell you. For often in a period of mounting karma it is best to focus the attention upon the Light. But then, of course, those who come are those who love the Light with all their hearts and would come in sunshine and in rain.

Prophets of doom always manage to extract from society fearful followers and their purses. We have no such desires. We will not clutter our retreat with those who are running from their own shadows or have not the courage to face the challenge in their own states. But, yes, we provide a haven of safety for those who fight the good fight and win and dedicate that life that God has given them to the rescue of other souls.

The noble captain and shipmates rescue those who are their passengers in time of calamity. But we have seen the example of all jumping overboard and taking the lifeboats and leaving the passengers. We would not have such co-workers. We would have those who become the Light and become a living pillar and pass through the night untouched and carry many in their arms. This is the way of the Ascended Masters.

To quote the Lord is fruitful: "Work while ye have the Light." The Light is come in the person of the Great White Brotherhood. And those of you who have seen the miracle of souls who reach out for a blessing have understood that something more than a human being has wrought this miracle, something more than any of ourselves. Truly, it is the entire Spirit of the Great White Brotherhood. Thus learn the meaning of a dispensation and a sponsorship, and be grateful that we can so sponsor you while we have the Light of a single Messenger with you.

By the fruits of the aura and the quickening, know the Truth. Beware, then, of psychicism and pride declaring itself our representative when it is not so and signs do not follow that are signs of Light but rather only signs of psychic phenomena. There is danger, and those who are hooked by such ploys know it not. Thus, the false gurus will be there forever and a day until their cycles too are spent and their hollowness rent.

We come with a sign of victory to those who will seize the victory. It is only the way and the only way.

Beloved ones, the Path is accurate. The progress can be swift. But once you receive the Light and the blessing and you squander it and then squander it again, do not expect us to come with pitchers of Light to continually pour the oil into your chakras because you have taken another round in the valleys of delusion.

These are serious times. For your very health, for your very mindfulness you ought to conserve the life-force. You ought to denounce the fallen angels who purvey their rock music to steal from you by the syncopated beat the power of the Kundalini. You have never seen a rock star with a raised Kundalini. It does not exist. It is lowered, creating the magnetism out of the very bowels of the earth.

Blessed ones, these have burned out their chakras long ago and must amass the Light from the Lightbearers who follow them. Thus their auras are magnetic and they seem filled with a certain power. But it is not the power of that which is Above but the power of that which is beneath that hath but a short time.

Those cycles are arrested precisely on the schedule of the Great Central Sun. We neither hasten nor lessen their configuration, for we are confident in the judgment of the seed of the wicked. This one thing is certain—they come to naught. What is not certain is what will the choice be—the freewill choice of every soul of Light to be or not to be in the highest octaves.

We can never force, nor have we any desire to do so. For anyone convinced against his will becomes rebellious and hateful. Thus, the power of conversion belongs to the Holy Spirit in all. And only by the Great Central Sun Magnet is a soul truly demagnetized of Darkness and remagnetized to the Light.

I give you the vision to see and know the fruits of the evil seed and to see and know the fruit of the Ascended Masters. I caution you above all to guard the Light and let no one take it from thee. Let no one displace thy path of victory and overcoming. Lean upon the arm of the LORD only.

I have come in my Presence and I am radiating through you and to all of you as long as I am speaking, giving you the inner vision. And I will continue to do so this night. We do maintain the etheric retreat called the House of Rakoczy not far away yet over those nations not fully free—not fully free to be as you are today.

Blessed ones, read with me the handwriting on the wall and decide your destiny. I urge you to decide your destiny, to no longer be manipulated by forces within or without, to realize that your decision will become fact as you summon all forces of the Divine Mother and the Ascended Masters, as you have been taught.

This Teaching is powerful. There is no failure but the failure of the individual to apply it. Thus, beloved, I am also a voice that cries out in the wilderness.

Do you know, beloved, that conditions on Atlantis prior to her sinking in some areas were not as vile as they are right here in this country today? The Lords of Karma and the Cosmic Council have long forestalled the karma due for the misuse of the sacred fire by the fallen ones. And to allow the practices of Satanism in this or any nation is folly, for all people pay the consequences for their failure to object.

Blessed ones, it may be true that the LORD gave freedom to Satan to tempt Job. But he did not deny Job the power of the Word to challenge that Darkness. Thus, you must engage the sword of blue flame and let this be a battle that is won by Archangel Michael.

Thus, my legions and my friends, my children of long ago, I embrace you. I have fulfilled my reason for being in the sealing of this continent. By placing yourself in my presence you have indeed served as electrodes. And you will be blessed for as long as you keep that flame by your own love and determination.

I am immensely grateful for efforts made on behalf of this mission to the heart of every individual who has so given. I bow before the Light. And I breathe upon that heart flame the breath of the Holy Spirit to increase and increase and increase.

To fan the fire of the heart and the flames of freedom therein—what higher gift? The flame is the flame of immortality. To increase it by one-thousandth of a percent is to add immeasurably to the Christ consciousness of a soul.

Oh, let us commune together in this flame of Liberty. Let us come now into the center of the room where this flame is enshrined for the duration of this retreat. Let us enter the heart of that threefold flame.

Now journey to our retreat and abide there while you take sleep, or keep the flame of the violet flame here—for truly heaven knows the gratitude of the beings of the Seventh Ray to all who assist in that mighty cause.

In the name of the Lords of Karma and Saint Germain, I bid you a most fond good evening.

November 2, 1985
Flevohof, Holland

CHAPTER 3

A Prophecy of Karma

Of the Nations: the Decision and the Vow

The Future Is in God's Hands
Who Has Already Given You Free Will:
Therefore Karma Rules the Earth

Now let me tell you, beloved hearts, that the expansion of the flame of my beloved Portia is indeed the calling. It is the light of Opportunity and Justice.

I would extol these virtues of the Almighty God embodied, then, by beloved Portia. For each and every one of you has been blessed by her hand and her caress as you have taken incarnation in this life. For without the flame of Opportunity and the Justice of God meted out and apportioned on behalf of your fondest hopes and best dreams, you, beloved, would not be seated here this evening. And without the dispensation of the Lords of Karma, you would not see the full fire and fervor of my being delivered to you through this instrument who has truly functioned on and on through these days.

Therefore we desire each and every one of you to know that the power of God is greater

BUSINESS REPLY CARD

FIRST CLASS   PERMIT NO. 5   LIVINGSTON, MT

POSTAGE WILL BE PAID BY ADDRESSEE

SUMMIT UNIVERSITY PRESS
Box A
Livingston, MT 59047-9977

We would very much appreciate having your comments on this book

Title: _____

(Please print title of book on the above line)

WE HOPE THAT YOU HAVE ENJOYED THIS BOOK AND THAT IT WILL OCCUPY A SPECIAL PLACE IN YOUR LIBRARY. IT WOULD BE HELPFUL TO US IN MEETING THE SPIRITUAL NEEDS OF OUR READERS IF YOU WILL FILL OUT AND MAIL THIS POSTAGE-FREE CARD TO US.

Your comments: _____

_____

_____

How did this book come to your attention? _____

Your business or profession: _____

What subjects would interest you most in future publications? _____

WOULD YOU CARE TO RECEIVE A FREE CATALOG OF OUR NEW PUBLICATIONS?   YES ☐   NO ☐

Mr./Mrs./Miss _____

Address _____

City/State/Zip _____

SUBSCRIBE TODAY TO *THE COMING REVOLUTION: THE MAGAZINE FOR HIGHER CONSCIOUSNESS,*
U.S.A. $12.50 PPD. (4 ISSUES); CANADA & INTERNATIONAL $14.50 PPD. MAKE CHECKS PAYABLE TO AND MAIL TO:
SUMMIT UNIVERSITY PRESS, DEPT. 298, BOX A, LIVINGSTON, MONTANA 59047-1390. TELEPHONE: (406) 222-8300.
Printed in the U.S.A.
491 5/87

than any instrument, and the power of God is available to those who seize the opportunity to be the instrument and present themselves the living sacrifice for the many. So it is rare to find those souls of Light across the earth who will stand with the Lords of Karma, who will not go wandering after the curious, after those things which adorn the ego—the flattery of the psychic world of communiqués from departed spirits.

We have empowered this Messenger to read any of your past lives, to tell you all kinds of things about yourselves should she choose to do so. When she does enter your aura she rather does draw the veil and seeks only to know the perfection of your Christhood. And therefore this office has never been abused by that flattery and by that idolatry and by that pursuit of a following based on those things which, when it comes to the kingdom of heaven, simply do not count, beloved hearts. Understand this great truth and cut yourselves free by yourselves from the fat of human selfishness and indulgence.

Who has taken from you your sense of holiness? Where is the glimmer of the Light that should shine from you as holiness unto the LORD? I will tell you! That sense of holiness has been denuded from you by those in Church and State who have come with their false revolutions of every kind, therefore seeking the lowest common denominator wherein all activity is common and is never endowed with devotion or a flame or an appreciation or the looking on high. And thus it does show upon your faces to the utter chagrin of your Mother who stands before you.

Therefore, we say take the flame of Opportunity [of my beloved Portia] and know that you did not take embodiment to be upon the socialist treadmill or any other treadmill of any other economic system where you are controlled from above, controlled from beneath, and boxed in as though you were fleas or mice or some variety of the animal species.

Beloved ones, you are more than men and women. You are God-free, immortal beings! And I desire to strip you of unreality by the sacred fire this night because the flame of Opportunity is kept in this universe, because that flame does glow, and because God Justice demands for you "another opportunity"!

When receiving so high a gift and calling you ought to be humble, not before me or the Messenger but toward the littlest chela and the one who serves. When you can be humble before the one who you think is beneath you in rank, then you have begun the ladder of life. For all may have some sort of affection for the Messenger, and why not? For the hand that feeds ought to be blessed. But, beloved, when you revere the God flame in one another as we revere it in you, then you will understand the dignity of human worth— of the individual and the individualization of the God flame.

That individualization of the God flame,

beloved hearts, is far more important than building human empires. If we could find but one individual who would not stop the pursuit of God-identity, who would truly put himself on the line of that tough chelaship of Morya and Archangel Michael, which this Mother is able to deliver to those who are able to bear it, we would find therefore the means to forge a world union.

But so many come to be pampered. So many come, then, with their pet theories and ideas, seeking ratification for these rather than to truly listen with the inner ear and the soul and to actually say to me when I enter the room:

"Saint Germain, strip me of my pseudoself!"

Let me hear those who dare make that cry:

Audience:

"Saint Germain, strip me of my pseudoself!"

That is not fiery enough and I will not accept it!

Audience:

"Saint Germain, strip me of my pseudoself!"

That is indeed an improvement.

Beloved hearts, you can increase your fervor in every way and it is the need of the hour. I, too, have come to please many over the centuries, but the time is long past to wait for anyone's human consciousness to come to the place of consecration. The hour is so terribly late, beloved ones, that I urge you with all your heart and mind and soul to not postpone the Day of Opportunity.

The only day you can guarantee is today.

The future is in God's hands and it is in the hands of the Law and the Lawgiver who has already given you free will. And therefore karma rules the earth and the multitudes and the schedules and the timing.

You ought to be in the position of an Ascended Master today. I would give you the eye view of what it is like to know that your hands are tied. In fact, you are freer than we are to act, for you are on stage and we have already played our parts and can only ratify the acts of those who determine to summon the greater cause.

Understand that we ourselves are at the mercy of human will and human karma, but you are in the position to change it, to make the fiat. And when you know that you have the power of cosmic beings and Ascended Masters—beloved hearts, when you know that by your call we can truly step through the veil through you, then we can increase opportunity.

I tell you, you ought to have a role reversal tonight and realize that the Spirit of the Great White Brotherhood that can be effective on earth *is you* and that we are the ones who are waiting in the wings—waiting for the opportunity that you may possibly give to us to turn this planet around in her spin and straighten that axis and bring in a golden age.

Beloved ones, the earth is heavy with the dark ones, as you have been told. Their infamy spans many centuries. These dark ones are truly tipping the balance in many areas of life where the scales of justice weigh in favor of Darkness because the people want the Darkness. "And men loved Darkness rather than Light, for their deeds were evil."

When the people vote for tyrants and systems of tyranny, when they vote for terrorism and terrorist acts, it is free will on the stage of life. And it is your free will not to commit the sin of omission but to seize the right hand of Portia as opportunity to open the doors of your chakras, to *op*en the *port*al of *unity,* to stand forth and to say, "Thus far and no farther. You shall not pass!"

Becoming active, then, in stopping the fallen ones in all ways is key and essential. But it must begin early, catching the sun before even she has awakened, going to the Light before the light has crested the horizon and beginning those morning calls.* You will not defeat the adversary no matter how many social programs you have for the next million years. You will have to go to the eye of the serpent and to the serpent's tooth and tail! You will have to go to the very core of Evil! And only Archangel Michael can prevail in that arena.

I say to you, strip yourselves of indulgences and fat and squandering your Light. Let us see you as fiery yogis, yogins the next time we meet. Let us see you in the mode of self-sacrifice of the victors of the age.

Beloved hearts, heaven can only wait. Do

---

*prayers and dynamic decrees to the Universal Christ for the judgment of the seed of the Wicked One not expect me to make some vast prognostication concerning your future. You are writing your future right now. You can see what you are doing. You can see what you have accomplished thus far in your life. You can predict what will happen to you if you keep on as you have been doing for the next five, ten, twenty-five years. You can predict your own end, depending on your decision today.

I will not indulge you in your desire to have me tell you all things, as though I should read a crystal ball and make pronouncements and all should go away and say, "Saint Germain has said..." "thus Zarathustra has spoken..." and therefore conclude that we are the wise ones.

Nay, you are the wise ones! You are the ones who can now take the very nucleus of life and knowledge—the keys of the kingdom which I have given to you through your Messenger. You can take these and decide to become the Wonderman of Europe, the Wonderwoman of Europe!

How would you like to have that appellation? Well, I can tell you, I will be the first one to give you that title when you have succeeded the miracle worker of the age. For after all, beloved hearts, I have given you much knowledge of alchemy as well as a sword and I have given you my momentum. For I, too, say unto you: He that believeth on me, the freedom flame that I AM, the Seventh-Ray Master that I AM, the works that I do shall he do also; and greater works than these shall he do because I AM in the heart of the Father.

Therefore take the first steps. Take them and take them well. I am waiting in my alchemical laboratory at the Cave of Symbols in the United States. I await your coming, but each time you are about to advance as an adept on the alchemical path, you let some foolishness or nonsense become the very thing that trips you—some digression, diversion, entertainment this way and that way.

Beloved hearts, to be an initiate of the Seventh Ray demands decision. The decision must be taken and the vow made. Without decision and the vow, you do not have the support of the heavenly hosts. You can say, "Maybe I will do this today. Maybe I will be an adept tomorrow. Maybe I will study alchemy on the next day and maybe I won't; for, after all, I am free! Saint Germain has said I am free. Therefore I must be free!"

Well indeed you are free, beloved hearts, but you may not enjoy the constancy of angelic support for the inconstant causes of your self-concerns. Of course, you can do anything you want to in the whole universe. You can do something different every day of your life. You can try a new hairstyle, a new outfit, a new fad, a new type of drug any day and any hour, and heaven will champion your freedom!

But, beloved hearts, is there any future or

any progress in being the dilettante? I think not. I have watched many not only go to ruination but also reembody as those individuals who have nothing to say about anything and about whom the heavenly hosts have nothing to say either!

Beloved ones, I tell you, the vow is a serious commitment. The vow and the decision means that you abide by it. For you have given your word to the Almighty, the Almighty has accepted your word, and the Almighty sends his angels to assist you in keeping that word.

Then you enter a path of discipline and you follow the teachings I have given, and they are many through this activity alone. And each and every Pearl and dictation, I tell you, contains such alchemical keys that if you could perceive how far you could advance on the Path in becoming that alchemist through the Lost Teachings of Jesus and of the Ascended Masters of the Himalayas already released, you would begin immediately. In fact, there would be a stampede to our door! And that is exactly what happens at inner levels when souls finally wake up and realize that their greatest desire is to study with me at the Cave of Symbols.

Beloved ones, I do not accept all. I send them first to the Royal Teton Retreat and then to the Chief of the Darjeeling Council of the Great White Brotherhood, beloved El Morya. And when they become chelas of whom Morya can be proud, whom Morya can trust, the Chohan of the

First Ray will say, "Saint Germain, may I present to you my chela who is my trusted friend." I tell you, it is a moment in Darjeeling when I am invited to that occasion each year, when a few chelas can be presented to me and I may say, "Come now. Come to the Cave of Symbols."

Beloved hearts, it must be so, for I am a serious professor. I am serious in my art, for I see the world slipping down the drain. I see the avalanche of the dark ones and the astral plane, and I see many souls being lost daily.

I do not expect you to have the vision of the Hierarch of the Seventh Ray. Therefore I give you some of it. And I trust you will no longer block that vision by clogging your chakras and your bodies with heavy foods—one more round of ingesting that dense substance, retaining the weight you do not need. You see, the enlightenment and the true seeing and the true spiritualization must come because your cell centers are filled with Light* unobstructed.

First the decision and the vow, the determination, the commitment. Then angels will take thee in their charge and protect thee. Then comes the definition of the Path and the period of study—study and chelaship—that you might become, therefore, knowledgeable in those

---

*Light, when capitalized, means the Christ consciousness, that Light which is the Mind of God in action as opposed to physical light or the radiance of the Son as an effect rather than the Presence of the primordial Cause. The body temple and the chakras of the sons and daughters of God are intended to embody the fullness of the Light as the personal presence of the Universal Light, or Christ.

Teachings so carefully given, so meticulously pronounced . . . So much there for you to find.

It is inescapable and unquestionable that
you must master the English language. I have
chosen now a number of embodiments to use this
language. It is fruitful and vast. Borrowing from
all other languages, it does become an instrument
of the universality of the Christ Mind.

Be it so, I, too, am subject to the Lords of
Karma. And if they have decreed it, set aside
your questioning and your resistance and get on
with this mastery and take the Mother's gracious
offer—opportunity in the name of Portia to study
and master the English language in such a very
short time and therefore be able to delve into the
mysteries that are revealed in the Word. Our published translations are for you the opening of the
door. You must push it wide open and step
through and get on then with perfecting yourselves as examples of myself throughout Europe.

Blessed hearts, I speak out of profound love.
And you must understand how Love does teach
his children. Love, as the Mother flame within
me, must come after you to let you know that in
many areas of learning on this continent there
have been highly disciplined ones who have become masters of science, of art, music, and every
branch of human endeavor. They have stood out
in the centuries, and always they are characterized
as the ones who have been self-disciplined for a virtue, for a cause, for a talent, for a vision, for a goal.

One-pointed. One-pointed are these. It is a fraternity of the one-pointed ones who keep the flame of their field. Alas, many have functioned with very little Light* or spiritualization of consciousness, and yet we have also used them to bring about invention and discoveries of cures for diseases and therefore lifted the karmic weight of the planet.

We could do much through disciplined hearts. We could do much through those who would come prepared for their lessons, having mastered that which has gone before. You must understand that I do not speak merely out of yesterday. I speak out of having known you for 70,000 years and appealed to you—some of you many times over! And I wonder why you still wait, peeping through the curtain to see perhaps if anyone is looking at you looking at me. And if your neighbor should find out, you might just slip away from the Path lest you be disgraced or embarrassed.

O beloved ones, the reasons are manifold. But when it comes to the point of action, we know who does present swords sharpened—not for an effort but for a victory, and there is indeed a difference. Many like to say they have tried. But the victors are silent, for they receive the laurels and the applause of heaven and earth. They need not protest or justify or explain.

We do not need such words. We know them all. We have read the letters of cowards in our

*i.e., Christhood

day. We know the excuse of nonbeing. Let them have their excuse. One day they become as ghosts, fading beyond the windows and into the night while the bright stars shine.

There seem to be a million stars in the sky. There seem to be many, but when you approach, the magnitude of the one is the All. I said the magnitude of the one is the All! For the one has become the All and all things to all people.

I have tried to be this. I have gone hither and yon, here and there, bearing my wares of Light, finding little appreciation. I do not lament it in the sense of dwelling upon it. I count it a part of the Work of my LORD.

I could regret many things. How many areas of the planet have slipped from an area of freedom to totalitarian control? I could regret the brainwashing of the masses in these areas of darkness. I could indeed regret the acceptance by the European people of the condemnation of America.

My heart is heavy and it is also joyous. For truly I do rejoice to see you and to have presented to me this platform of opportunity. It is indeed a grand night of Opportunity for many in heaven and many of you. And you have placed me betwixt yourselves and heaven, and I have been happy to fill the vacuum. And I will always be happy to fill the vacuum of your hearts with some point of joy.

Let us make that joy count, beloved. Let us make that which we know become the star—

the evening star of His Presence appearing. For all of your great effort and magnanimous hearts I praise the Almighty and your blessed souls who have indeed seen a vision and caught it—even more than caught it today from the heart of the Goddess of Liberty, Nada, and the Great Divine Director, who have comforted me in many centuries when my endeavors have not culminated in a fruit of action of permanent and lasting freedom.

I look at South America, vast land of the Great Divine Director. I see there the potential of the golden age, yet setback after setback. Is it any wonder, beloved hearts, that we would not know where to place our support when all sides have corruption and darkness? Yet in the hearts of the freedom fighters there, in the hearts of those who truly love Liberty, who must face those regimes which would overtake them—in those hearts a flame burns and we give support.

But where is the support of the West and of the people of the United States? Where is the support that would return the Goddess of Justice and the Goddess of Liberty to their nations? You see, the little people who fight on the battlefield for my cause must be reinforced by the superstructures of governments and nations who are yet free.

Blessed ones, some carry the myth that somehow freedom will win out because it is the nature of man. They have never reckoned with forces of Evil that are absolute. They have not wrestled with the forces of hell. They somehow think "the sun also rises" and that by some automatic process, which they romantically categorize as "movements of the people" in these nations, the whole earth will be restored. But this has not been the pattern.

The destruction of Afghanistan is before your eyes. Who will run and save it? No one dares. They are cowards! Before what? Before a military establishment that has been defeated year in, year out by the bare hands of the mujahidin?

Do you understand, beloved hearts, the configuration of forces in the earth? Where there is might and power the beast has become lugubrious. It moves, or does not move, as some ancient reptilian form—mindless, awkward, unable to save even a company of men who are left to die at the hands of terrorists[1] for want of right decision and right command. They [the captives] are the angels of Light! You are the angels of Light! But where shall they sound the fire of heaven when those in positions of power have betrayed them in every nation?

So the betrayal of the Light* of Vietnam has been complete, and devastation is throughout. And those of culture, of Light have been murdered and destroyed. It is a wholesale destruction of the populations of Lightbearers in every nation that we see. Yes, they have their lists. They know

*Christ consciousness

who they will go after the moment they are in power, nation by nation.[2]

India is their goal. Your nations are on their target list.[3] Yet the people have not focused because there is no energy in the third eye or the crown, for all wallow in their own sensuality and thralldom. They party and drink and make decisions great and small affecting the centuries and billions of lifestreams to come.

How long can a body such as the Lords of Karma sponsor an evolution that fails to challenge the greatest enemy that has assembled itself out of Assyria, out of Babylon, out of the fallen angels? And if you only knew how as nothing they are.

Let us rejoice in victories. Let us see that even an eye of victory can be expanded and increased and enlarged. A following of Lightbearers can suddenly appear, and a great world communion in the Great Central Sun can produce in action a solid wall, flanked by angels, of saints in embodiment robed in white reinforced by those in the etheric octave.[4]

Have you seen Elysian fields? I have seen them! You call them the dead. I say they are alive forevermore, championing, defying the fallen ones, calling to your hearts while you sleep at night—calling to you, telling you of atrocities and darkness.

And you wonder why you cannot sleep. It is not always the dark forces, beloved. It is your

brothers and sisters in the etheric octave who
are prodding you and telling you, "Something is
wrong! You must act in a big way for those things
that have already come upon us and will come
upon you also if you trust the wrong ones."

Beloved hearts, behold the panorama of life
evolving in all octaves on this earth, waiting the
day of the coming of the Light, waiting the day
and seeing the dawn. Earth knows the coming of
the Light that you have heard and seen. Some
fear it. Some run from it. Some immediately
assail it. Others take the wafer and the wine,
internalize the Light and become ourselves. But
some of these are ignorant. Their education has
been manipulated and they are unable to stand
for us in high-level places where decisions are
being made daily to defeat the human race.

Beloved ones, I only ask you this: Take each
twenty-four-hour day and do the most you can
for Light, for Freedom where you are. Do the
best you can by making the best decisions for the
best possibilities. Understand, beloved, there are
always choices. Some waste time or are centered
upon inconsequential endeavors that do not lead
to major victories. And even minor ones, when
tallied day by day, count mightily.

Take your twenty-four hours and realize it
is a gift of Opportunity. Do not take Life for
granted, or Freedom or this Teaching. Apply it
now and see what you can do.

Come together in your nations. Formulate a plan and a strategy. What is most essential is to bring the Teaching and to nurture it and to teach people the fiery decree—not a mere chanting of words, as I sometimes hear you give, but a fervor of the heart that does truly bestir the highest angels of heaven who leave off tending the Central Sun to see what is that fire burning now on planet earth.

Beloved ones, we have not called our decrees chants—others have. We have called them decrees because they embody will and fire and determination. Do not always lower the sound or reduce the volume. Go somewhere where you can shout a joyous shout unto your God and know that you have reached the star of my causal body. I will be there as I am here, for I am always in the heart of Opportunity.

While I have life and breath and dispensation and the ability to work with this planet, you can be certain I AM here, I AM there, and I AM in the star of your own causal body.

I am Saint Germain. And I am grateful to you for having received me and prepared this place for me and for my Messenger. I will not forget the fight that you have fought, the good fight that you have won in this session and round. I always bless. I always increase. And I shall continue to do so, for it is the way of the Seventh Ray.

In my eye is the reflection of your soul—what

you will be ascended in the Light and free if you choose To Be; what you will be in abject Darkness if you take the left-handed path. Remember, I have told you. There is no predestination except God. Thus all will choose. And all will know that they have chosen because they have heard and seen and decided.

Better to choose in knowledge than to be caught up in ignorance and to go down to defeat, never having known why failure has turned to death and darkness. At least one should have the knowledge of why one has failed, that one may perchance live again if Opportunity keep her flame.

Do you see how much you depend upon us? There are flames not kept for earth, for there have not been Masters to keep them. For you yourselves made the choice not to be a Master long ago. But where there are Masters and you do have that momentum and flame that is accessible from our causal bodies, I tell you, you depend upon it mightily. Reverse the roles and see then how we depend upon you and how you are dependent totally upon your daily choices.

I come not to weary you but to love you. I come not to fault-find but to praise the most precious hearts that have ever come forth out of this continent in this age.

Precious hearts, I love you. I send you to find more of my own. Then we shall see what can be done.

I salute you in the name of my beloved Portia, my comfort, my love. May you also know her and realize that her flame burns in you also.

We seal you for another day of striving and bless you mightily now from our causal bodies.

[standing ovation]

November 3, 1985
Flevohof, Holland

Notes to Chap. 3:
1. **Hostages in Lebanon.** On 11/3/85 there were 5 U.S. hostages held by terrorists in Lebanon (abducted between 12/84-6/85): Peter Kilburn, librarian at the American University of Beirut; Rev. Lawrence Jenco, who directed Catholic Relief Services in Lebanon; Terry Anderson, chief Middle East correspondent for AP; David Jacobsen, administrator of American University Hospital; Thomas Sutherland, acting dean of agriculture at American University. William Buckley, a political officer at U.S. Embassy seized 3/84, was reported dead 10/85. The pro-Iranian group Islamic Jihad claimed responsibility for the murder. Kilburn's kidnappers sold him to a pro-Libyan Abu Nidal faction, who executed him along with 2 British hostages 4/17/86 in retaliation for U.S. bombing raid on Libya 2 days earlier. Since then, 3 more Americans have been seized by gunmen: Frank Reed, director of the Lebanese International School; Joseph Cicippio, acting comptroller of American University; and Edward Tracy, writer and illustrator. Secret negotiations involving Anglican Church envoy Terry Waite, the Reagan administration, Israel and Iran have led to the U.S. supplying Tehran with weapons in exchange for Iranian assistance in freeing the U.S. hostages. Rev. Benjamin Weir, a Presbyterian missionary abducted 5/84 was released 9/85. Rev. Lawrence Jenco was released 7/86 and David Jacobsen 11/86. 13 other foreigners remain hostage in Lebanon. Of an estimated 60 foreigners kidnapped in Lebanon since 1984, 34 either escaped or were freed, 6 have been murdered and 3 more are reported dead. *(continued on p. 61)*

CHAPTER 4

A Prophecy of Karma
Earthquakes: The Passing of the Old Order

We Will Do All in Our Power to Mitigate World Karma As You Keep a Violet Flame Vigil and Call to the Legions of Archangel Michael

Most Gracious Friends of Freedom,
Sons and Daughters of Liberty,

I greet you in the new freedom of the hour. And I AM Saint Germain. And I AM the presence of the seventh angel and I AM sounding and resounding the mysteries of the infinite Light through your hearts in this hour.

O beloved, I say to you with beloved Portia, hail to the Light above! Hail to the Light below! Hail to the Light in the torch of the Goddess of Liberty. Hail to the Light in the hearts of the faithful Keepers of the Flame always who have cleared the way for my coming in this hour.

It is a splendid day to know that we may move forward together. Fear not, for the release of darkness and karma of the seed of the wicked in recent earthquake and turmoil in Mexico and South America, here and on the West Coast and around the world—these things are for the passing of the old order.

Now in this hour you can anticipate intense sacred fire and violet flame. And as you capture that Light and as you determine as never before to keep the vigil with me, I promise you that we with the Lords of Karma will do all in our power to mitigate that which may be scheduled to descend as world karma but which I tell you can be consumed in the very air by the Light you hurl, the Light you send, the Light in which you rejoice by the sounding of the Word!

As I am sounding, so you are sounding. And so it is the eternal sound. So it is the full power of the AUM. And it is the I AM THAT I AM. And it is the flame of freedom bursting.

O beloved ones, know, then, the signs of the times and know the meaning of the ascent of the Two Witnesses. For the plane of heaven to which they ascend is indeed the plane of appearance in the etheric belts of the earth, then, in the upper chakras—the chakra of the heart, the throat, the third eye, and the crown. And there in that heaven plane—there is your own personal resurrection! And your soul must needs be resurrected this day from preoccupation with the lower chakras in thy temple.

Let these be healed and sealed! Let your four lower bodies be healed, for my gift in this hour is indeed a healing, a magnetization towards wholeness that you might live forever on earth in your heaven world, that you might understand the power of the Mother to raise up the sacred force within you as a life everlasting, that you might know indeed the Mother flame in your midst, that you might learn to love every precious angel of the violet flame that comes peeping through your keyhole and your windowpane, that comes in the morning to waken you with joy.

O beloved, do not be crestfallen. Do not be set back by that which you meet. Let it be doused in violet flame. Go forth with the joy of precipitation. Take my "little book,"* this precious book given to you by the devotees and staff and coworkers, by the Messengers therefore manifesting that concerted effort to see the physical manifestation of that which I have long desired to have in print.

I hold it in my hand in this dictation for a very purpose. For I am charging this copy and through it every copy of this book with the full, flaming presence of my new day, my revolution to all. May this book itself find its goal in every nation and in every language.

It is a handbook. It is the little book which may be devoured, and it will begin the alchemicalization. It will begin the process worldwide of the raising up of the coil of the violet flame. To this, then, be dedicated, and know that I have indeed come again, my mantle with me, our beloved Alpha and Omega and the Cosmic Council so decreeing that I may go forth in this hour and

---

*Saint Germain On Alchemy: For the Adept in the Aquarian Age. See Rev. 10:2, 8-10.

that I may truly have the opportunity of the quickening.

Beloved hearts, the mantle given to me for this Stump, which I have placed upon the Messenger, has been the very dispensation to galvanize Lightbearers. May this Word continue through you. May you also understand the message that is the stepping-stones of life whereby those lost in a dead doctrine may be the quickened who come first to the understanding of eternal Life and then to its Love and then to its manifestation by that courage and honor of the heart.

Beloved ones of the sacred fire, take, then, my trilogy of the threefold flame of the heart. Internalize it and make it your own. By the true study of this fourfold work *On Alchemy* you can become the alchemist and the adept right where you are. We bridge the gap. Indeed we bring the altar of Israel to your very heart and home.

Oh, know the Lord as the *Sanctus.** So the holiness of seraphim rest with you and violet flame angels clear the path for their coming. Remember the teaching of Serapis Bey enfolded, then, and sealed for your heart in the *Dossier on the Ascension.* Remember the teaching that the seraphim of God come at any hour that you call to them, place their angelic presence where you are, burn through and consume and dredge from you all that is past and cast it into the sacred fire.

The angels of the LORD, the legions of Light

Sanctus [Latin]: Holy One.

attend your acceleration! Oh, do not hold back.
Do not any longer stay in the recalcitrance of a
waywardness and the stiff-necked generation of
old. Let all these things pass.

I send my flame to the very hearts of those
laggard evolutions in the Middle East who have
held back the full price of glory. I send legions and
the solar ring of seraphim in this hour to encircle
those nations, to intensify the sacred fire, to give
all the opportunity then to beat their swords into
plowshares and their spears into pruninghooks.

Beloved ones, let there be war no more! And
let this be the conclusion of this Summit conference. Let it be the conclusion of all hearts in the
earth to bind these fallen angels by the power of
the dynamic decree to Archangel Michael and his
rosary said daily.*

For the declaration of peace on earth must
be reinforced by the sacred Word, which is the
sword of the Word. It is the living Word that
cometh out of the mouth of the Messengers of
God. And you are indeed emissaries representing
the Godhead, and you must send forth that Word
daily. For those who desire war for their own evil
designs, beloved hearts, will not say die, will not
recant, will not turn back except the Light move
en force!

Beloved hearts, you can call to march with
Archangel Michael and his legions of Light while

*See "Calls to Archangel Michael for Protection," in *The Science of the Spoken
Word*, $7.95, and *Archangel Michael's Rosary for Armageddon*, 36-page booklet,
$1.25 postpaid; available with tape, add $3.55 postpaid.

your physical bodies sleep at night. You can be with the saints robed in white. You can place your very bodies on the line of Darkness, and you can absorb and swallow up that Darkness as you are engulfed in the living presence of the seraphim of God.

They come in numberless numbers. Angels of the LORD descend, then, to this very planetary home.

O Children of the Sun, look up and behold, for the Day of Opportunity is nigh! And that opportunity comes to you in this hour in the living presence of my beloved twin flame, Portia, who stands with me now as ever to direct her love to you and to speak to you of the promise of old—the opportunity for initiation through the twelve gates of the City Foursquare.

So receive, then, my beloved Portia, whose hour of victory is also come, as is mine. [standing ovation]

November 17, 1985
New York City

Notes to Chap. 3 continued from p. 55:
2. **Soviet lists.** Tomas Schuman, former propaganda specialist under the KGB who served as press officer of the Soviet Embassy in New Delhi, India, and defected to the West in 1970, relates that when the North Vietnamese captured the city of Hue they executed within 2 nights more than 15,000 people, including those sympathetic to or directly supporting the U.S. or Western culture. It was learned that long before the Communists occupied Hue an extensive network of informers had collected the names and addresses of those to be executed. Similarly, Schuman's department was preparing files of information on those to be executed in the event of a Communist takeover in India. *(continued on p. 72)*

CHAPTER 5

A Prophecy of Karma
Of Twin Flames–the New Age Movement

Fanaticism Must Be Consumed in This Hour!
If There Be Not the Victory in America,
How Can Liberty's Torch Be Our Gift to All?

I speak to your souls, O Lightbearers of freedom. I speak in the name of the Lords of Karma and of Sanat Kumara and the desiring of the hosts of the LORD that some should come to that Path of the Ruby Ray, that some should demonstrate the twelve gates and the twelve hierarchies.

I speak truly—truly in this hour of your opportunity held by the Goddess of Liberty to convene at the Inner Retreat, to let yourselves pass through the sacred fires to become the immortal God-free being who you are here and now and to never, never again consider death as a passageway to anywhere. For the transition must needs be only the soul's acceleration. Yet how can the soul accelerate at that hour of the passing if the momentum has not been built while on earth?

It is true that Jesus called your Messengers to found that Inner Retreat. And the one who stands on this side of the bank of the river and the one who stands on the other[5]—these do fulfill our promise to you to draw together your twin flames, to draw together your souls of Light in those highest unions of the divine family for the sponsoring of the children of the new age.

We do not relent in our God-determination to see this planet fulfill her fiery destiny. So the cycle of the twenty-two months is at hand. It is the sign and the number in Hebrew of the alphabet. It is the sign of each and every letter outplaying itself as a nucleus and molecule of sacred fire intensifying the manifestation in the earth in these twenty-two months beginning this day.

This cycle is given to you to assimilate all of Saint Germain's teaching in the little book on alchemy. See that thy soul does profit, for know ye not that the Master does overshadow you and promote the full alchemy of Light in your being?

As you study and internalize this teaching and place yourself directly in the heart of the science of the spoken Word daily, taking that book also and giving that violet flame call to the ten,* you will see that the twenty-two months are for the gathering—the union of hearts in molecules of service all over the earth, focusing the amethyst jewel, coming together for the balancing of karma and then the service of a chalice forged of a mosaic of souls. Understand that here and there

*See "Ten for Transmutation," in Mark L. Prophet and Elizabeth Clare Prophet, *The Science of the Spoken Word*, Summit University Press, pp. 113–25, $7.95.

and everywhere this gathering of molecules of violet flame is the only answer to those conditions at hand [as the result of the Four Horsemen of the Apocalypse and the Seven Archangels pouring out the vials of the last plagues of mankind's karma].

I have been with you, each and every one of you, in the hour of your previous transition. I am indeed Portia, the Goddess of Opportunity, so called because I embody the flame of opportunity that is the open door to the union of your soul with your Mighty I AM Presence, and in that union the reintegration here on earth of the white fire bodies of your twin flames.

Now be seated as I give to you that sacred fire in this hour.

Understand, beloved, that through your acceleration, through your making your pilgrimage, as to Mecca, to the Heart of the Inner Retreat, you then will pass through veils of the untransmuted substance. You will change your garments and prepare for that initiation of the transfiguration in the mountain of God.

It is absolutely essential that at inner levels and in the plane of the I AM THAT I AM and the Holy Christ Self—your soul reaching that plane by dynamic decree and meditation and service to Life—that you are one with your twin flame and that you complete your reason for being on earth in this hour.

Hear my statements, for they apply to each and every one of you! Where it is not possible for you to contact that twin flame physically, it matters not. The inner union and the reinforcement is the key. Where it is not possible, we assemble lifestreams who are soul mates or have a similar path and attainment, who have good karma together and who may serve as receptacles for the I AM Presence of the twin flames of themselves and each other, forming a cosmic cube in the earth.

Thus, beloved, endeavors in the earth must have the presence of the wholeness of Alpha and Omega and the single call you make each day:

Lo, I AM Alpha and Omega of the twin flame
   white fire bodies of myself and my beloved
   manifest here in action!
Lo, I AM Alpha and Omega,
   the beginning and the ending
   of our white fire sphere of wholeness!

To affirm here below, therefore, the oneness of yourself and your twin flame will place upon you the mantle of these twin spheres of Light to accomplish the purposes to which you are set.

Fear not, then, to be divested of unreality. Fear not to take swift strides and giant steps to the Sun, for the need of the hour is great. We will do all that is possible to avert world cataclysm, O beloved hearts. Only remember, the one individual, the Keeper of the Flame, the finger in the dike—that one with God is a majority.

And sometimes when you recall the voice in your heart and respond to that call and give the dynamic decree in any hour of the day or night, you may be the sole one on earth whose prayer reaches the hosts of the LORD that can stay the hand of great darkness coming upon this or any city. Understand your value and worth. Understand the path of individualism and know the reality of the Great White Brotherhood.

I am Portia, your advocate before the Court of the Sacred Fire, before the courts of the world, and before the court of public opinion. And I speak to all devotees in all new-age movements, in all paths and teachings that go beyond the orthodoxy of the major world religions.

Beloved hearts, the forces of Darkness would splinter and divide you. You must understand the union of Light of the avant-garde of the age and be not so mindful or critical of separate ideas upon which you differ. It matters not, beloved ones, if you do not agree on every point of the Path and Teaching and Way. What matters, beloved hearts, is that you see the union of those who are climbing the highest mountain and that you realize that when all arrive at the Summit of Being all will understand and know the Law of the One.

What is important in this hour is that there be a worldwide awareness of the oneness of those seekers after Truth and that their union be based on the principle of Truth and common survival. For if there be separation, you will see then how here and there the smaller groups are cast down, as those who fear the coming of the new wave of Light do organize to put down by every means anyone who goes forth with a message of the coming revolution of Light.

Understand, beloved ones, that it is time truly for the Great White Brotherhood and those who understand the meaning of the "saints robed in white" to stand together and to defend one another's right to pursue their own perception of the living Word and the universal Reality, to defend everyone's right to pursue a path to union with God. Defend that right in concerted effort!

Beloved hearts, if all can even receive this book of beloved Saint Germain *On Alchemy* and take some of it as real and put it into action, then Saint Germain will forge a worldwide union of freedom fighters and you will no longer experience the darkness that has come upon those who have been the true revolutionaries, who have had the courage to go after whether the false gurus or the true, the very courage itself to seek an alternative to a dead and dying doctrine that indeed shall be quickened by the LORD's presence in and with you.

I am calling, then, for the unity of hearts on basic principles and for you to set aside your differences. For if the new-age movement cannot come together in a worldwide ecumenism, I tell you, then, it is no better than the old order of those who have been bickering for thousands of years while the world and its children have been left untended.

The solving of the problems of man's view of theology is not the urgent need of the hour, beloved hearts! The urgent need is the assuming of the Holy Spirit and the descent of that Light into every man's temple regardless of what that man may call that Light or how he may define it. The Light is the Light, and the Light is true! And the vibration is known. And all that is less than that vibration is *not* of the Light and should be therefore shunned.

Therefore let there be the dividing of the way. And let the Lightbearers of the world unite in the name of freedom! in the name of the flame of freedom of my beloved Saint Germain! who is truly the champion of every seeker everywhere regardless of any erroneous concepts or burdens that may separate that one from the fullness of the blazing reality of the noonday sun of his I AM Presence. For Saint Germain takes everyone's hand and leads that one nearer and nearer to the Light as he is willing and able.

Therefore, beloved hearts, please do not interfere with the trek and the momentum and the rhythm of new Lightbearers on the Path. Let them take his cup as they are able while you keep the flame in joy and love.

Be free, then, of criticism and see how the ground swell of those who are the liberated souls in the world will make their voice count not only in religion but in the governments of the nations, see how they will take their stand and see the way through to the holding of the balance for the economies—and in this nation especially. And the sacred fire infolding itself must collapse the old structures and build upon the foundation of the white cube and the stone of the master-builders.

I call you, beloved hearts, to a path of Love. I send you forth to acquaint yourselves with those who are following whatever path, that you might be emissaries of Love and Justice and the message I bring: that the opportunity to pursue Truth by all of these groups *must* be preserved, *must* be protected by a union of hearts throughout the entire planetary network.

O Keepers of the Flame of Saint Germain, will you help me sponsor this endeavor?

["Yes!" standing ovation]

The false gods who have positioned themselves in the earth truly have one fear, and it is indeed the fear of the people. When the people rally around the standard of Christ and the Christ-bearers,* when they act in concerted voice and heart, then they [the false gods] must only recede.

The power of Victory is in your hands. Do not forget it. Receive, then, the torch of

---

*Christbearer: one who bears the Light which is Christ, one who bears the responsibility for Christhood in himself and others by defending the Truth and Honor of God; one who is anointed with the Christ consciousness and bears this enlightenment to all. The Lightbearer is the Keeper of the Flame whose motto must be "I AM my brother's keeper—I AM the keeper of the Light who is Christ in my brother."

illumination of the Goddess of Liberty. Seize it in Saint Germain's name! Bring illumined action to the world—action based on awareness of the I AM Presence and the Christ Self.

I call for helpers to publish our battle cry, the magazine of the Coming Revolution in Higher Consciousness. I call to you to understand that exposés must be written, that the truth must be stated, and many are needed. Let talents developed by you for ages now be focused on the physical victory. For there is no other victory that we desire except that physical victory, for it is the foundation of all others.

If there be not the physical victory in America of the claiming of the land and the resurrection of hearts and of the restoration of fairness to all peoples regardless of their race or ethnic origin, their status in society or their religion—beloved hearts, if this is not won here, how can it be the gift of this people and this torch of Liberty to every other nation?

Fanaticism must be consumed in this hour!

And I, Portia, stand therefore with the banner of the hordes of hell. And I put it to the torch. It is the banner of fanaticism in every field and area. Let the cultists of fanaticism go down, for their banner is consumed! And in its place the banner of the living Christ, universal in all people, is raised on high this day! It is the rallying cry. It is the standard of all people of Reality.

Rejoice that our God is come into the earth

and into your hearts in this hour, and purge the earth of that fear and hatred that breeds terrorism and would take from you any one of these little ones!

I AM in the flaming presence of Opportunity. And the opportunity and its day is done for the fallen ones and these possessing demons who mouth their words of fanaticism in every quarter of the earth. Their day of opportunity is done! They have had their opportunity to unite under the banner of Maitreya and Sanat Kumara and Lord Gautama.

Now let them retreat and let the Lightbearers march! Let them march on Fifth Avenue and in the highways of our God! Let them march through the towns and the cities of the earth! Let them come as those freedom fighters who sang the "Yankee Doodle Dandy" and knew whereof they spoke.

O beloved, it is an hour of freedom. Can the earth contain it?

["Yes!" standing ovation]

I promise you in sealing this hour that *none* can deter you, *none* can stop your victory! The way is clear. You have only to march and claim the planetary field of consciousness for the angels of the LORD.

No one can deter you except your own self or doubt or trepidation. These, too, in your name I cast into the sacred fire! May you do so daily as you advance on the cycles of the Cosmic Clock[2] and know indeed personally the blessed representatives of the hierarchies of the Sun who knock upon your door in the name of Christ and say to you as the sun signs change and your birth cycles turn, "May I enter, O soul of Light? For I deliver to you now a message from, and the testing of your soul by, the Cosmic Christ."

Will you open the door of your heart and receive the Cosmic Christ initiators, beloved ones? ["Yes!"]

So we thank you, we love you, we seal you, and we say, watch and pray. Keep the vigil and keep the flame, for the day of the seventh angel's sounding is truly upon you.

The past is prologue. Move forward in Light.
[standing ovation]

November 17, 1985
New York City

Notes to Chap. 3 continued from p. 61:
3. **Every nation targeted.** Maj. Gen. Jan Sejna, the highest ranking military defector from the Communist bloc, was chief of staff to the Minister of Defense in Czechoslovakia and assistant secretary to the Czech Defense Council. Sejna, who was privy not only to the top secret military strategy of the Warsaw Pact but also to the Soviet global military plan, says that the Soviet Union has never changed its strategy or its plans for the takeover of every nation on earth. The main target, he says, is the United States. See Jan Sejna, *We Will Bury You* (London: Sidgwick & Jackson, 1982).
4. **Saints robed in white.** Rev. 3:4, 5; 4:4; 6:9-11; 7:9, 13, 14; 15:6; 19:7, 8, 14.

Notes to Chap. 5:
5. Dan. 12:5.

CHAPTER 6

A Prophecy of Karma
Of the Challenge of the Chosen People

When a Nation Does Not Seek God First
The Four Horsemen, the Dark Cycle Must Come.
Violet Fire Restoration of the Holy People

I saw by night, and behold a man riding upon a red horse, and he stood among the myrtle trees that were in the bottom; and behind him were there red horses, speckled, and white.

Then said I, O my lord, what are these? And the angel that talked with me said unto me, I will shew thee what these be.

And the man that stood among the myrtle trees answered and said, These are they whom the LORD hath sent to walk to and fro through the earth.

And they answered the angel of the LORD that stood among the myrtle trees, and said, We have walked to and fro through the earth, and, behold, all the earth sitteth still, and is at rest. . . .

Zechariah 1

Keepers of the Flame, attention! I have come, your Knight Commander Saint Germain, to address you in this hour and to release to you the fire of freedom for this Independence Day 1985.

I come with the power of the Central Sun. I come bearing that light of freedom. I come drawing forth from the inner Holy of Holies of Alpha and Omega the fire of the Grail, the Shekinah, and the flame infolding itself.

It is the flame of freedom, the flame of Aquarius, the flame that is also native to your soul. For the swaddling garment with which you were swaddled by the Cosmic Virgin in the beginning was indeed the violet flame of freedom. For the first covering of thy soul was the awareness of free will—free will to affirm in the flame of God-freedom your divine inheritance, the will of God.

To become God was your mission.

Therefore I stand now in the very midst of this holy people. I stand before every one of the holy ones of God upon earth, irrespective of religion or race or background or past sin. I stand before the Lightbearers to transfer now the sacred cup of Communion—the wine of the violet flame that is not only the Blood of Christ that is physical but that is also the Blood of Christ that is transmutative, purifying, transforming—to restore in you the right-mindfulness of the Son of God.

To this end I nurtured him, trained him, and brought him up in the way he should go [Saint Germain is referring to his embodiment as

Saint Joseph]. For even the avatar requires the strong and firm hand of the father that he might know the Father above. And this was my prayer—that through my heart he might see the face of the One toward whom he would direct his gaze and his gait all the way to India and the Far East.*

Blessed ones of the Most High, bear with me as I wield now the sword of Maitreya and that of Morya, and as the mantle of the prophet Samuel [also a previous incarnation of Saint Germain] now begins to unfold to you the meaning of the message of the LORD unto Zechariah. It is for this time even as it was for that time. For in the end of ages and in the beginning of the new, there is a requirement of the Law that the sons of God and the seed of the Ancient of Days who have come again and again to pronounce his name must gather to defeat the anti-self, the not-self—the aliens to the will of God.

Understand, then, the meaning of this prophecy. Understand the meaning of the point of sacred fire. Thus, many who had heard the word of the LORD, the Ancient of Days—the LORD of hosts, Sanat Kumara—were not obedient to that word. This was the relationship of Master/disciple, Guru and chela. All of Israel and Judah were anointed chelas, disciples unto the Ancient of Days—their Comforter, their Lawgiver, their Leader in battle against the dark ones who had long ago invaded this planet—they, the fallen angels, and their miscreation.

*See Elizabeth Clare Prophet, *The Lost Years of Jesus* (Los Angeles: Summit University Press, 1984), $14.95.

Thus understand why the Lord Sanat Kumara would command Moses and Joshua to engage in the very endeavor.* It was for the annihilation of the seed of Antichrist (the embodied fallen angels) and not a command to kill mere mortals. The seed is the consciousness. As every man's seed is contained in his blood, so the seed of the Son of God is contained in the Holy Communion of the Body and the Blood and the Grail.

Now, therefore, all things may come in good fruit to the one who engages his will with the will of God if in this divine relationship he does master the initiations that become harder—more complex, more challenging with the soul's ascent to God. In the case, then, of Israel and Judah, they did not entirely annihilate their desire, their fascination for the consciousness of the peoples of "Cana."

Canaan therefore became the symbol of the ringing in of the people of God by an alien force— extraterrestrials who were not of the Light but servants of Satan. And as you have been told by Lord Gautama Buddha, even Abraham stood before them unflinching, bowing not to their gods. Even when his father, Terah, did worship other gods, he himself denounced these aliens. By their fruits (their vibration, their consciousness and their allegiance) he knew them: for he was the representative of the Ancient of Days.

*Conquests in the wilderness and Canaan. Exod. 23:20-33; 34:10-17; Num. 21:1-3, 21-35; 25:16-18; 31:1-19; 33:50-56; Deut. 2:24-37; 3; Josh. 6; 8:1-29; 10; 11; 12.

Understand, then, that the greatest privilege unto any man or woman, child or nation is the opportunity to be engaged with the mighty work of this LORD God, this one who is the deliverer of the Lightbearers and the seed of the Universal Christ. Those in Israel and Judah, both king and false prophet, who did not accept the fullness of that Law thus compromised the relationship, even as the relationship to that LORD God had been compromised by twin flames, initiates in the Garden of Eden, the Mystery School of the Cosmic Christ.

Understanding this, recognize that Zechariah does prophesy of the coming of the red horseman and many with him. This signifies that whether or not the disciple or the initiate is fully prepared, the cycles have turned in the age, and the hour is come today, as then, for the initiation of God's people under the flame of the Ruby Ray.

Thus the red horseman and those with him represent the initiators which the people themselves have invoked—not the Cosmic Christ, not the Master, the LORD God or the Ancient of Days who is Sanat Kumara: because they have forsaken him in these things small and great, the world must become their initiator.

Thus it was in the case of Israel and Judah and so it is in the case of America today, the Promised Land fulfilling the call unto the I AM Race—those who have the seed of the name I AM THAT I AM within their hearts: They have not hearkened unto the LORD, nor have they fulfilled the wholeness of the Law.[6]

Thus, as the days pass, you see the unpreparedness of those who hold the reins of government, or of the people themselves, to deal with an insidious power of Darkness that comes, whether through the Soviet Union or the Middle East or terrorists. Whatever the source in Central or South America, there is a vexation unto this mighty people! They *will* not, they *would* not: now they *can* not deal directly with the challengers to the integrity of the nation and the New Jerusalem.

Understand, beloved, that some among this people must be and become direct initiates of Sanat Kumara, for always there has been the requirement of the ransom. Let those who are the inner circle of the devotees, those who are the firstfruits who come and stand as the ensign of the people, raise up the banner of Christ as the one whom they serve, the one who by his very Communion promise at the Last Supper designated each and every son and daughter of God for the internalization of the Word.

Wherefore to deliver the Body and Blood of Christ in Communion if it is not for the goal of the full implementation, the full manifestation, the full incarnation of that Christ within the seed of Abraham, within the seed of Light embodied in every race and nation!

Thus, the scattering abroad of the seed of Light and their reincarnation throughout the earth shows that the chosen people are not confined to one religion or race or physical descent but, in fact, are the Christed ones who have played their roles in all nations to bring the very presence of that standard to those nations. Therefore they come disguised to this land America. They come with many faces and expressions, but it is the quality of the heart, the light of the eye, the development of the threefold flame that determines who indeed is the seed of Abraham.

Learn this lesson well, therefore, and denounce no evolution. For in the midst of any whom the LORD may choose, there does come the anointed of Sanat Kumara. Therefore, beloved, it is required that while the nation sleeps and until the hour of their awakening, this initially awakened of the firstfruits, this band, this people hold up the standard of The LORD Our Righteousness,* bear the banner that signifies their origin, and begin to seriously enter in to the Path of the Ruby Ray.

This is the path of initiation designated for those who have balanced or are about to balance fifty-one percent of their karma. This, then, beloved, is an office and a calling which you must reach for. For you know not the hour or the day of the fulfillment within you of the fifty-one percent;

*Jer. 23:6; 33:16.

and by the assumption, by assuming that you are at that point, you will be on guard. And you will have the mantle and the armor itself to intensify that Call, that Presence, and that Light.

Now, then, perchance fifty or five thousand may become the nucleus of the leaven, leavening the nation in the perfect Path of the Ruby Ray. This path begins with the violet flame, with the path of Aquarius, whose initiation comes from my own heart. The Cosmic Christ will not administer this path or initiation to anyone who has not first taken the training of the Seventh Ray, which is the ray of the priesthood of the Order of Melchizedek. It is a path of refinement by the inner fire.

When a nation, when a people—such as Israel and Judah then, such as America and the I AM Race today—does not voluntarily and lovingly seek their God first, seek a path of sacrifice, of surrender of the lesser will to his, of service and selflessness, then, beloved, by the very rejection of the Great Initiator, the alternative must be administered.

Now we see why the initiations of the Ruby Ray have come to this nation. World Wars I and II and the other conflicts of this century in Korea and Vietnam, the defense of freedom in the world—these have been a part of this initiation.

The Path of the Ruby Ray is the path of the Blood of Christ. This Blood is a sacred fire. Either the sacred fire is released from the chakras and the power of God does go forth and the defense of the nation is established—because all of the nation have recognized themselves as disciples of the Ancient of Days through Jesus Christ and all manifestations of that Universal One— else there must come the direct confrontation with the [consciousness of the] seed of the Wicked One who were not utterly defeated by Joshua or subsequent ones.

Therefore, beloved, see the handwriting on the wall: on schedule, the descending karma of the Dark Cycle, the seven last plagues, the Four Horsemen—all delivering to the earth the mandate of personal and planetary karma. Yet God has already arranged ahead of time and from time immemorial for the staying of the hand of that Darkness, for its transmutation by the Light of the heart and by the sacred fire.

The alternatives, then, which I set before you are the same as Moses set forth: to choose Life by choosing the disciplines of the Path of the Ruby Ray or to choose Death by rejecting them and therefore, in fact, making the choice for the Gentile nations, the nations of the alien forces, to be the guru. Are they not the testers and the tempters of America today? Neither the people nor the government know what to do about terrorism and the terrorist.

Beloved one, it takes the needle ray, it takes the All-Seeing Eye of God, it takes a Oneness, consorting with the hosts of the LORD. And with such

a oneness with The Faithful and True and The
Word of God and his armies, these hosts will go
forth by the sacred fire released through the initiates of the Ruby Ray to ferret out those single
individuals who carry Death and Hell in their
wake and who are nothing but devils incarnate
who slaughter individuals and bring down nations. They are not among terrorists alone; they
are throughout the world.

Man of himself cannot go on a witch-hunt.
He cannot become suspicious of everyone who
crosses his path, else he will lose his point of reality
and sanity. There is no other way to win in
this war, which is Armageddon, than through
self-transcendence—through the transfiguration,
through the resurrection, through the new birth—
so that one is no more the natural man but a fiery
spirit truly dwelling at the level of the etheric
body, and the Lord Christ of you is descended
into this temple.

It is promised. You must stand on the promise of God and know that you who love and obey
the Christ must have the Father and the Son
and the Holy Spirit take up their abode within
your house, within your temple, within your soul,
within your chakras.

Unfortunately—and this word is mild, but it
is unfortunate indeed that the laws of Christ and
his Teachings, so meticulously brought forth to the
close initiates, are not fully known today, having
been taken even from the holy people. Therefore,

to obey Christ becomes the challenge of the hour—
to find the Person of that Christ, to find the Way
and the Teachings.

You have received the lost Word and the lost
Teachings of Jesus Christ through our effort,
through the Keepers of the Flame Lessons, our
Pearls of Wisdom, our dictations, our up-to-the-
minute releases concerning world conditions. You
have been shown the violet flame which Jesus
used. You have been shown the mantra which he
brought back from India. You have been shown
the ancient Word.

You have been shown the seed of Light and
yourselves reincarnated. You have realized that
America is the Promised Land. You have understood many things, including working with Archangel Michael and the Seven Archangels to complete the calling of the LORD.

As a result of this, you have been strengthened and protected in that Word and Teaching.
And some from among you have taken their leave
at the conclusion of their embodiment and gone
on in the full resurrection with Jesus Christ. Some
have taken the final initiation of the Ruby Ray,
that of the ascension, while others wait in the
etheric retreats to receive it. Thus, the proof of
the Teaching and the Path is that it leads one
successively to that higher and higher consciousness whereunto the individual is assumed into
the very heart of the I AM Presence [becoming
indeed the pure Person of that Christ].

Now, beloved ones, this red horseman and those with him move in the land—and it is the very hour of their moving in the land. If it were not so, it would not have been possible for those terrorists to receive that plane containing American citizens.*

Wherever American citizens are vulnerable, they are representative of a nation that is asleep to the call of Gautama and Jesus, Zarathustra and Maitreya. And all of their conviction in their paltry doctrine will in no way cancel out the oncoming tides of initiation. God has never willed destruction or death or famine; the prophecy is of mankind's own returning karma and specifically of the returning karma of the Lightbearers *and* of the fallen angels.

Realize, then, that not one iota of suffering is decreed by God. It is decreed by man, woman, and child who misuse the laws of God. Therefore let it be as an example and not an accusation of those specific lifestreams. They are representative of the tribes who have denied the coming of myself again, the person of the prophet Samuel, and the coming again of Jesus Christ through the lost Word.

And the promised Comforter must speak to you. Therefore that Holy Spirit of all of our

---

*Islamic terrorists hijacked a TWA airliner and killed one U.S. sailor on June 14, 1985, demanding the release of hundreds of Shiite Muslims imprisoned in Kuwait and Israel. In a complex 17-day hostage saga, 39 U.S. citizens from the 153 on board were held by Lebanese Muslims until arrangements for their eventual release were worked out by representatives of the U.S., Lebanon, Israel and Syria.

bands has addressed you now twenty-five years and more with the true Teachings, that you might follow and obey them. And many have wondrous light and auras expanded and good fruits, daily miracles, showing that God is no respecter of persons and that truly anyone upon this earth in this hour may respond to and therefore be initiated by the Son of God quickening the threefold flame that they might begin the path of individual Christhood.

> *Then lifted I up mine eyes, and saw, and behold four horns. And I said unto the angel that talked with me, What be these? And he answered me, These are the horns which have scattered Judah, Israel, and Jerusalem. . . .*

What then of the coming of the four horns? The four horns are sharp and they indicate the returning karma of the misuse of the sacred fire in the four quadrants of Matter. Again you have the teaching we have given for decades of the Cosmic Clock*—the understanding of the initiations of the twelve gates to the Holy City, which the twelve tribes must undergo, not merely one gate but all gates. And the keeper of each gate, as the Keeper of the Flame, the Maha Chohan together with Maitreya and various representatives of the

*See Elizabeth Clare Prophet, *The ABC's of Your Psychology on the Cosmic Clock: Charting the Cycles of Karma and Initiation*, 8-cassette album, $50.00. Lectures and diagrams in Elizabeth Clare Prophet, *The Great White Brotherhood in the Culture, History, and Religion of America*, $10.95.

Great White Brotherhood do attend the coming of this seed of the Ancient of Days.

Those who are of this seed know that in this hour and in this conclusion of the age of Pisces there is the open door in heaven whereby they may take all of the initiations taken by their Lord Jesus Christ and follow him in the ritual of the ascension. It is an hour of maximum acceleration. It is like the days of Elisha and Elijah when one is taken up into heaven and another receives the mantle.

So this is the reality of God among his holy people today. Never has there been a greater opportunity to move upward and return to the Source whence you descended so long ago!

The seed of Sanat Kumara who appeared as the children of Israel and also of Judah have appeared again and again and were embodied even before that hour in ancient civilizations. They are ripened, this seed. They are ready for the Cosmic Christ.

They must be called and preached to! They must know my name, Saint Germain, for God has given to me once again the power of Samuel, which I used in the founding of this nation and the drawing of the thirteen colonies and the anointing of your first president.

God has called me to initiate you in the violet flame. And the violet flame comes by the grace of the dispensation given unto me by the Cosmic Council specifically for this seed of El Morya as Abraham, that they might find the way and leave a very plain and obvious trail that all others may follow.

The threading of the eye of the needle must be by these ones chosen by Sanat Kumara long ago to come to this planetary home. Thus these are indeed the firstfruits of the Ancient of Days. Wherever they are, whoever they are, in whatever nation or race, I say: Go and find them! Go and tell them! And realize that after these are contacted, there is no barrier to any other evolution or root race, but all may choose to embody the sacred fire of God.

> *And the LORD shewed me four carpenters.*
> *Then said I, What come these to do? And he spake, saying, These are the horns which have scattered Judah, so that no man did lift up his head: but these are come to fray them, to cast out the horns of the Gentiles, which lifted up their horn over the land of Judah to scatter it. . . .*

These horns, therefore, become destructive as returning karma but need not be so. For the carpenters, who are the chelas of Sanat Kumara, come to cast them out: and these are the builders about whom you have sung and the poet of the twelve tribes has written.[7] Thus the builders come, and the builders are the initiates of the Ruby Ray who take their initiations not from the

Gentile world powers but directly from the heart of the Ascended Masters.

These builders understand that to embody the Ruby Ray in all of their members and chakras and four lower bodies they must become masters in the physical plane as well as in the spiritual, in the plane of the Mind of God and in the plane of his desiring. Thus they understand the Inner Retreat as the retreat to the heart of Maitreya for preparedness in the Body and Blood of Christ through the initiations of the Ruby Ray.

The builders are building the temple of man that is made without hands. Yet simultaneously they build the outer structure to house that which must be protected from the elements and from planetary upheaval and turmoil and the projected wars of the fallen angels which yet may be turned back.

The builders are building the seamless garment, the wedding garment. It is the only safe passage from this octave to the next. Therefore build thee more stately mansions, O my soul.

Thus, layer upon layer, you build the body of God around you, you conserve the Light [Christ consciousness], you draw forth the rings of the causal body and you walk the earth then sealed in the aura of Sanat Kumara. Would you not have this experience while in physical embodiment, I ask you, noble people? ["Yes!"]

Realize that you can have it. The path of God-realization and self-mastery and of the adepts of the ages is given to you *directly* from the heart of Sanat Kumara. You need not go here or there, but obey the first teachings and principles and become alchemists of the sacred fire and neglect not the dynamic decree whereby that flame is internalized, whereby the violet flame does support and increase the divine spark.

When you feel the aching in the heart, recognize that it is that I have come as Saint Germain to assist you in adjusting the fervor and fire of your threefold flame, to seal it in the violet flame, and to establish rings of light to protect that heart— that sacred heart abuilding within you—from the pressing in of world forces and world karma.

In an age of great darkness, it requires the sponsorship of the Ascended Masters with their chelas to seal a lifestream in so great a light, so great a salvation, and to keep that one protected and in balance spiritually and physically midst the pressures of planetary darkness and of the fallen ones in their spacecraft who would hold this entire planetary body hostage to the darkness of Death and Hell.

Be not fooled! Be not fooled by the popularity of spacecraft. They have been here a long, long time. And they have brought great darkness to the earth and the scientific knowledge of mechanization man and the creation of robots. And thus they have created the anti-creation of the godless to vex the children of the Light and the sons of God.

To defeat all of these, to stand as David, Jeremiah, Isaiah, to stand as Solomon, to stand as Ezekiel, you must understand that the fire that enfolds you must be greater than all contrary inventions and technologies of these extra-terrestrials.

Beloved ones, the Path of the Ruby Ray is before you. The path of the ministering servant for the Aquarian age must needs be built upon the path of the apostles. But more is required two thousand years hence.

Be not satisfied with the status quo. The sameness of Jesus Christ yesterday, today, and forever is indeed the sameness of the onward-moving, accelerating cycles of the Cosmic Christ within him. His sameness is his fiery unfoldment in every age of the ongoing initiations of the Spirit.

Therefore let me tell you that those who are to be ministering servants in the Seventh Ray dispensation must also know the path of the priesthood of Melchizedek, the path of Light as it was taught by him and taught by Jesus to the initiates. Therefore we have prepared leadership training for those who desire to have an understanding as well as an initiation into the requirements of carrying the freedom flame and standing up against the darkness of the nations and those forms of darkness insidiously projected into the society of America.

Armageddon is in full swing. You need not wait for nuclear war. The destruction of the temple of man in the child, in the youth through drugs, through rock, through Satanism and witch-craft, through all of the indoctrination of the anti-Light—this is the destruction of souls without even the declaration of war by the superpowers. When you look to the distant horizon, you miss the fact that lying at your feet is another child of Light who has been devoured by the sinister force.

Thus we have called for the seminar for the freeing and the saving of our youth. Realize that our youth is the sign of Sanat Kumara, who is called the Eternal Youth. And the saving of the youth is the saving of the light in the body temple—the saving of the very energy of the spine and the raising up, therefore, of that brazen ser-pent, that full power of Light given unto Moses in his rod, that energy that does rise, that is the Mother flame and is the Mother of Israel, the daughter of Zion.

Recognize, then, that the attack on youth is the attack upon your Light. And you ought to remove yourself from your indulgences and con-serve that energy, for it is the only weapon in this octave whereby you may send forth the ray to devour disease and cancer and plague and death all around you and to stand, face, and conquer the intimidations and the blackmail of the spacecraft which come as a force unseen but definitely felt at the lever of decision-making of every single person on this planet.

The decision to be mortal, limited, to refuse to transform oneself by the Holy Spirit, to refuse to demand of the Great Law the transformation

of the genes to break the barriers of this limited
brain that they have programmed the human race
to, the decision therefore to worship the space
people—this is a decision to walk in the path of
idolatry against which Moses and all the prophets
have warned you. It is the idolatry of the techno-
crats. It is the idolatry of the scientists and the
masters of materialism.

Beloved, walk not in their ways!

The choice that is being made in this hour by
every one of you is to walk in the path of the
Divine Mother—the Divine Mother who appears
as the instrument of Sanat Kumara, the Saviour-
ess long seen symbolized in the Statue of Liberty,
called the Woman clothed with the Sun. The
Divine Mother descending therefore has provided
the way out. And her path is the Path of the Ruby
Ray. And she does come to your heart as the
Divine Mother through beloved Maitreya, the
Initiator.

The choice then is to elect the path of the
Mother or the path of the aliens, the fallen angels,
the space people. The line has already been
drawn. And many have aligned themselves and
have been swallowed up by the false hierarchy of
aliens. Think not that this is not going on. Individuals who disappear have also succumbed to
their clutches, willingly or unwillingly. There is far
more going on in this planet beneath the surface
and in the upper atmosphere than you dream of.

And I take this opportunity of freedom of
assembly, of the press, of speech and of religion to

speak to you that you might remember that I have warned you that they have destroyed before. They have destroyed vast continents and they have done so through the misuse of nuclear power.

Blessed ones of the Light, nothing can touch the son, the daughter of God who establishes firmly in his heart this relationship with his Mighty I AM Presence and confirms it as a disciple of the Master Jesus Christ. Go after your children and rebuke them when they go out of the way and worship the rock stars and become involved in alcohol and drugs and rock music. For surely they have become polarized and aligned with the energies of the fallen ones through that beat.

The danger has never been greater than it is in this hour. There is no compromise. It is the seed of the Wicked One who promote rock music and drugs on this earth to the destruction of the greatest of the Lightbearers.

Therefore, beloved, understand that the path of the one ascending is the path of the builders building within and without—and on that path of the Ruby Ray, and by that path the defeat of world karma. Thus we have designated the place [the Inner Retreat]. We have set it aside. You have consecrated it by your love and light.

We, then, deliver to you an awareness directly transferred to your heart and soul, to your chakras and your inner presence. We do not come to incite fear, agitation, or anxiety. These things are already known by you at inner levels. We come to transfer an immense love of the Ruby Ray and

of the Lord Christ and of the violet flame that
seals you in such a vibration of love and freedom
that you pursue this path not in fear, not doubtful
of the outcome, but as the victorious ones.

Victory is the Light that you must espouse!
And the crown of victory signifies the initiate who
has fulfilled the rounds of the Ruby Ray.

Servants of the Most High God, I salute you!
And Mighty Victory and his legions gather here.
Victory stands on this platform and I ask you to
tie in to his heart flame and confirm his presence
by singing now the song to Victory.

July 6, 1985
Los Angeles

Notes to Chap. 6:
6. **Red horseman.** The Reverend C. I. Scofield's interpretation of
   Zech. 1:8-11 reveals the rider on the red horse as the "angel
   of the LORD," none other than Archangel Michael who, with his
   assistants, delivers the karma of a people who have forsaken
   Sanat Kumara, intercedes in their behalf through the initiations
   of the Ruby Ray thereby enabling them, thus strengthened in
   the spirit, to overthrow the complacent Gentile (alien, i.e.,
   fallen angel) domination of the Lightbearers through the Judgment of the Ruby Ray. This judgment must come to pass but
   it can only come through those who successfully overcome by
   the Path of the Ruby Ray their own karma of neglect and
   complacency toward the LORD, the Mighty I AM Presence.
   According to Scofield, the date of the angel of the LORD's
   intercession was at the end of the 70 years' captivity of Judah.
   "Taken as a whole (vs. 8-17), Zechariah's first vision reveals
   Judah in dispersion; Jerusalem under adverse possession; and
   the Gentile nations at rest about it. This condition still continues, and Jehovah's answer to the intercession of the angel
   sweeps on to the end-time of Gentile domination, when 'the
   LORD shall yet comfort Zion,' etc. (vs. 16, 17; Isa. 40:1-5)."
   See *The Scofield Reference Bible*, p. 965, n. 1.
7. Henry Wadsworth Longfellow, "The Builders."

CHAPTER 7

A Prophecy of Karma
The Ancient Story of the Drug Conspiracy

The Breaking of the Curse of Atahualpa
The Binding by the LORD's Hosts of the
Deadly Demons and False Hierarchs of Drugs

Beloved of my heart, Keepers of the Flame in every city of earth, I address you as my own and as the vessel of my flame of freedom.

Keepers of the Flame, Alpha and Omega have sent forth the call to us, hierarchs of the Aquarian age, and we have sent forth the call to the receptive heart of our own Messenger and chelas.

O receptive ones, vessels now held high, bearers of the Light and of the receptacle of Peace, I AM come! I AM your Knight Commander. I AM the sponsor of America and the entire hemisphere. I AM the sponsor of earth, and we together shall face this dark and foreboding plot against the souls of Light and the entire human race.

Beloved ones, the story of these drugs—of marijuana, cocaine, heroin, and all of the rest of the synthetic, fabricated drugs—is an ancient one. I pinpoint, therefore, the conspiracy of fallen angels known as the Nephilim gods and as the Watchers. I pinpoint their conspiracy to control the populations of the worlds, where they have spawned their experimental creation, their mechanization man. And therefore, in order to control their laboratory experiment, they have used all manner of devices.

Now, therefore, other nefarious powers moving against the evolution of life everywhere have seen fit to use mechanization man, computerized man—plastic man, if you will—as trend-setters, jet-setters climbing after the gods and the fallen angels to tempt, to taunt, and to hypnotize the seed of the Ancient of Days, the seed of Christ in embodiment.

Their end is manifold but it centers on the desire to steal the light of the threefold flame, to draw the Lightbearers down into the valleys of the pit itself where they would engage in the practices of darkness. And therefore, there are available fallen angels in embodiment to demonstrate the "way that seemeth right"—to provide the drugs, to direct the processing, and to draw mechanization man into the entire conspiracy as they are set up as storefront manikins to be copied by the children of the Light.

Thus, those who are the glamorous and those who comprise the multitudes of the mass consciousness exert a momentum that is planetary in scope to magnetize the Lightbearers into their practices of drugs and perverted rock and nefarious deeds—and therefore karmically ally and align these Lightbearers with the darkest forces of the pits of hell to draw these into the alliances, sexual in nature, that result in the bringing forth of life—life that is of darkness and of the pit which, when combining with the seed of Christ, gains a transfusion of Light otherwise not obtainable.

Thus, by the serpent philosophy of the egalitarian way of all equality among all evolutions,* you find that the Lightbearers have no sense of their worth or mission or of their God-determination at inner levels to lead all people out of the control of the fallen angels. Therefore, they are lured into these alliances at various levels of crime and sympathetic entanglements, and the seed of Light is diluted: it is overcome, it is betrayed. And we will discover, as we see in my transmission to you this day of a necessary knowledge, that this does result in the watering down of the total planetary Christ consciousness and the betrayal, one by one, of the Lightbearers who ought to and *must* take their stand in life in this very century so that the true foundations of the age of Aquarius can be laid.

The dimensions and the complexity of this drug problem and the extent to which it has been spawned on earth have been noted well in the

*The Ascended Masters teach that all are created equal in the beginning but by the exercise of the original gift of free will, each one has forged a God-identity or none.

exposé which has been presented to you by the Messenger. I desire, therefore, that you should realize that the forces involved in this particular conspiracy are as great as those involved in the fomenting of war and the subjugation of all evolutions of earth through the International Capitalist/Communist Conspiracy.

These enemies of all people—Lightbearers and every evolution—are deadly, and among the most deadly of all on the astral plane. I, Saint Germain, tell you this with all seriousness so that you may understand that we would not ask you to take your stand and give your invocations on this situation without providing you, personally each one, with cosmic reinforcements—legions of Light, legions of Archangel Michael, angels that form the retinue of the Great Teams of Conquerors and legions of Sirius—as well as those angels of Almighty God which beloved Jesus himself did call forth on Easter Sunday last.

Recognize that we have brought into position around you and your loved ones the reinforcements of Light so that you may feel safe and secure in taking your stand in this sanctuary of the Holy Grail and elsewhere on the planet, at your altars and focuses, to daily challenge this drug conspiracy and its connection to the conspiracy of Death and Hell itself—for that, in fact, is what it is, beloved hearts of Light.

It is no coincidence that I come in this hour of the three o'clock line at the beginning of the

Dark Cycle in Aries so that you will understand that the original conspiracy against the Lightbearers and the various evolutions and creations that began long, long ago with the fall of the fallen angels did begin and have its origin with a chemical manipulation and a genetic manipulation, and did come about not only through this vein of addiction and the supplying of the people with all manner of stimulants, but with other modes of conspiracy, thereby to limit the extent of the people to rise, to take dominion over their destiny, to make contact with the octaves of light, or to in any way challenge the fallen angels.

Since their fall, it has been the goal of the fallen angels to keep in subjugation all evolutions and the planetary bodies they have invaded and to prevent them from rising to any form of equality—to contact the power of God or to learn the secrets of the Great White Brotherhood, which they themselves [the fallen angels] have perverted from the beginning in their arts of black magic, war and witchcraft, necromancy and sorcery.

Beloved ones of the Light, you can therefore understand why those in positions of power in this nation and in every nation take such an exception to the rise of the children of the Light or to the true teachings of the I AM Presence. You can understand that these false hierarchies of fallen ones are positioned everywhere because they must control the people in order to take from them their Light—for they themselves, as you know, were cut off from the Source of Light when they were cast out of heaven by Archangel Michael and his hosts.

And therefore, when you have the pronouncement of the Word of God and a religion such as I have released through this Messenger that will spell the end to Death and Hell and the binding of mortality, whose goal is the raising up of the true sons of God and the liberation of the soul, you can well understand that when this freedom is proclaimed and practiced and, in fact, already achieved by many of our chelas (some who have ascended, some who are ascending, holding a very strong focus of freedom in the earth) therefore, the mouthpiece and the organization should be brought into disrepute by those who are determined to keep under control not only the masses of mankind and the race they have spawned that has been named Homo sapiens, but also the Lightbearers and especially those who have the path of the ascension before them.

And because they are the Christs [i.e., Lightbearers] in the earth—as this Messenger is, and as there are other sons of Light among you and daughters of God moving toward the full manifestation of Christhood—beloved ones, they [the fallen angels] would move to prevent that ascent and that clearing of the way. For those who do have the extraordinary manifestation of that Christ consciousness have also the power, which

Jesus had, to convey that Light and to intensify, magnify, and truly transmit the momentum of the threefold flame, lost or waning.

Thus, beloved ones, the key that comes by the anointed ones—and you should all accept your role as "anointed ones"* and "Christed ones" merging with your Christ Self—is that key which shall undo this conspiracy which is interplanetary in nature and which has been put upon the people of this planet for millions of years.

Please understand the equation in which we draw the line that separates Light and Darkness. It is the line between the Absolute Godhead dwelling in you and Absolute Evil pitted against it in the form of [through the physical bodies of] these fallen ones.

I give this introduction to my message on the drug conspiracy this day so that you will understand that unless you perceive this equation, and unless those who desire to overturn the drug industry worldwide perceive this equation and have the protection of the Brotherhood, there will no change come about. For this enslavement of the youth to siphon their light has been going on for thousands of years, and it is not a phenomenon of the twentieth century or of the 1980s, but one that is brought to the fore once again to entrance those who are easily taken in; for they have used these drugs in previous centuries long ago in the

*The appellation "Christ" is from the Greek *Christos,* meaning "anointed one." Thus, those who are anointed with the Light of the I AM THAT I AM which is the Christ Presence, or Christ consciousness, are called "Christed ones."

mists of Atlantis, on the continent of Africa, in
South America, and ancient Lemuria.

Beloved hearts of Light, when you consider
the age-old conspiracy and you consider the fact
that *you* are here, that I AM here, and we are
together forming the solar ring of light by our very
bodies and presence, ascended and unascended,
you can understand that this truly is the stand of
Almighty God for the victory of earth. And unless
you perceive it so, unless you have that perspective and that vision, you will not comprehend or
understand the attacks upon your life, your loved
ones, those associated with you, and you will not
be serious enough to do your daily invocations to
Michael the Archangel for your protection when
you are engaged in this warfare.

Thus, I, Saint Germain, must admonish you
and warn you again that you who are a part of me,
and I a part of you—as watchmen in this night of
the astral plane and darkness erupting into the
physical plane therefrom—must truly conduct
your lives as holy ones of God, instruments of the
seraphim who stand with you. And you must take
care and realize that you have a thousand-percent
protection of the Great White Brotherhood
when you yourself sustain your God-tie to us,
when you maintain your harmony and keep your
daily vigil with the Ascended Masters.

You cannot be a sometime decreer or a
Johnny-come-lately. . . . Realize, beloved hearts,
that the die is already cast and that your very

acquaintance with this [Ascended Master] activity should underscore for you the necessity of your karma as well as of your soul's edification to take the full cup of Christ Jesus, who said, "Indeed, you shall drink of my cup." (Matt. 20:23)

Understand that the full cup of the path of the bodhisattva was drunk by Jesus before you. I myself drank it fully many times, as did those of our bands ascended. Therefore, we admonish you to realize that when you come to a station of the cross—or, in this case, to a line on the Cosmic Clock of one of the initiations of the path of the bodhisattva—and it is tough and it is difficult and it is demanding, realize that you are scaling a wall of Light and you are scaling a wall of Darkness, and you are there facing and encountering that initiation which must be passed. Before you is the Light; behind you is the enemy—and therefore, you must keep moving toward the Source.

We are with you all the way Home. But we are not able to win your victory for you. This you must do by following the very explicit instructions in the science of the spoken Word and in the protection of your life.

We are there to assist you. We understand when you stumble and fall. You may make a mistake. You may, perchance, become discordant or misqualify energy. But you have the perpetual call of the hour. You have the *Jesus' Watch.* You may instantaneously call upon the law of forgiveness, cast the entire matter into the violet flame, invoke your tube of light and reinvoke it, and reestablish, in profound love and gratitude, your tie to me and to the All-Father. . . .

You are dealing with the ultimate forces of Death and Hell. You are dealing with the lieutenants and representatives—of fallen ones who have already been bound and judged and taken from the earth—who yet remain in the astral plane, unseen but weighing heavily, tipping the scales toward the Dark side, entrapping unsuspecting souls. You are dealing with interplanetary and intergalactic conspiracies! I tell you, it is so. Those who have come to this planet to use it as an experimental station for all manner of animal and robot creations and manipulation thereof have in some cases actually come from galaxies beyond this one.

Thus we are at a crossroads, beloved hearts. And the Great Law has turned and the cycles have turned and the universe has opened and Sanat Kumara (the Eastern title for the Ancient of Days of Dan. 7:9, 13, 22) and the entire hierarchy of Light stand with the sons of God in embodiment on earth. And when you make the call and you are consistent, your call then counts for the binding of this force of the drug conspiracy wherever it appears in the Matter cosmos. . . .

And it is for no ordinary purpose that you are called together in this hour, and you ought to cherish it as no other opportunity you have ever had in cosmic history. For this opportunity is not only the opportunity to banish from these worlds every threat to the Lightbearers and to all evolutions who may seek and find union with God, but it is also the means to your own victory and the glorification of God within you and your return to his heart.

This very endeavor of challenging drugs falls on the lines of initiation of the bodhisattva. Those who would become one in the heart of the Buddha and the Mother must understand that these initiations must be taken as they are given.

Therefore, you understand, beloved hearts, the nature of the return of the Dark Cycle in Aries. The return of that karma, beloved ones, involves every conspiracy of the Luciferian ones against this earth and all others. You can understand that Aries is the line of God-identity, the point of affirmation—"I AM THAT I AM"—which each and every one of you ought to make in this very moment to quiver the ethers with your God-Realization! [congregation responds in unison:]

I AM THAT I AM!
I AM THAT I AM!
I AM THAT I AM!

Therefore, understand the nature of the conspiracy and analyze it with the astuteness and ingenuity of your own Christ Mind, for you are indeed capable. You have been well taught by the Masters and the Messengers and your own Christ Self. Therefore, *see* what on this planetary body is moving against the full identity dwelling bodily in

the sons of God, what moves against the awareness and the recognition by the soul of the fullness
of the Light and the Spirit of the Almighty One.

Make your lists of facts and figures on every
aspect of drug trafficking and begin your decrees,
beloved ones. For, by the specific decrees concerning this subject, you will draw forth from your
causal body* into physical manifestation truly
that Light which *shall* hold the balance in the
Dark Cycle. We are moving toward that moment,
and we desire to see it come to pass. Yet it is not so
yet, for the wise ones must bring into the physical
dimension the content of their causal bodies,
bringing that Light, the full-gathered momentum
of their attainment from this and all past lives, to
bear upon the very challenges of the moment and
the hour. . . .

Let us work together. Let us *be* together! Let
us be the Grail. Let us be in this sanctuary and let
us understand the true vigil of the hours which is
required. *Beloved hearts, these fallen ones must
be bound hourly by Archangel Michael and his
legions in answer to your calls. And there must be
directed into the very dweller on the threshold
behind them the most intense calls and the fiery
furnace of the Almighty One!*

Recognize that the revenge and the lashback
and the vehemence of these demons, these false
hierarchies, and those who occupy positions of

---

*and from the great causal body of the entire Spirit of the Great White
Brotherhood—the collective God consciousness of the saints in heaven and
their 'Mystical Body' on earth

power in the world will be something that some of you will be surprised to see; and others of you will consider that you have never before seen such opposition to your lifestream.

Beloved ones, it is important that you realize that the "beast" of the planetary drug conspiracy will oppose everyone and every move made against it. Realize that this opposition comes subtly—in other ways unrelated to your call and your stand, in ways calculated to move you away from the center of Light and from the necessary continuance of invocations *daily*, once you have begun to make them, together with your dynamic decrees according to the science of the spoken Word.

Beloved hearts, if you can imagine an army on a battlefield—the battle cry is given and the sound to fire is heard resounding from the general, all engaging in a warfare . . . and suddenly, after an hour, each one considers other things that must take up his attention, going to his home or farm or leaving the battlefield—understand that the opposing army will only chase and pursue those who retreat and overcome them.

Realize, then, the principle that I wish to illustrate, and that is: once you have placed yourself in the army of Light, there is no retreat, for to retreat is to admit defeat and is to invite the overcoming of oneself by the enemy itself.

Therefore, I ask that each and every one of you admonish each and every other one, that you serve as a reminder in the full power of the

Holy Spirit, the Comforter, of all of these teachings which we have given. For the testing of the hours is upon you. And when you have fulfilled and been able to meet the testing of the Dark Cycle in Aries, you will have the momentum of overcoming on the entire twelve lines of the Clock, beloved hearts, that dweller on the threshold of your own subconscious that fully and finally may be dismissed and bound by you by the power of Almighty God in this very life!

I promise you, beloved hearts of Light, as I stand in this hour and as Portia stands with me, that if you will stand steadfast and meet this oncoming Darkness and overcome and not be deterred and not stray and not leave the center of Light and not leave off the quest for the Holy Grail or the purposes to which you have set your heart, I will therefore stand with you in the full overcoming of your own dweller. And I will also stand with you during this period of meeting the challenge of drugs in America and the world.

And therefore, I offer my reward, my service, and my protection. And I allow you to see that which it is from the beginning unto the ending. For, beloved hearts, truly this drug conspiracy of marijuana and cocaine, of alcohol and nicotine, and sugar itself upon the youth of the world is killing many a fine heart and soul, setting them back decades or lifetimes according to the timetable of their fulfillment of their divine plan.

I desire, therefore, that you will understand

that the conspiracy of the fallen ones and the curse pronounced against the white man* has become the curse of the seed of Christ. For it has been transferred by the fallen angels so as to fall upon the progenitors of the eternal Christ.

How is this so? Beloved hearts of Light, the fallen ones, by taking their revenge against the Inca, against the empire and the head thereof, did bring about their own judgment through the Christ Light in the people of the Incas—through those evolutions whom they overtook.

Thus, a great crime was committed against a people who occupied the continent of South America. That crime had its judgment, and that judgment (the cursing of the 'white' man) should, by Divine Justice, be upon those who perpetrated the deed. But those who perpetrated the deed did so from inner levels—the false hierarchy who knew full well that the judgment that would be upon themselves and their embodied tools would also come upon the seed of Christ (who like themselves had also embodied as the 'white' man); for the fallen angels had induced that seed of Christ to intermarry with their own. Thus it does come to pass that the seed of Christ forfeit their Light as they bear the karma of this seed of the Wicked One.

*The Curse of Atahualpa: With royal permission from Charles V of Spain, Spanish conquistador Francisco Pizarro (c. 1471–1541) set out to conquer and govern Peru in January 1531. On November 16, 1532, he met the army of Incan Emperor Atahualpa at Cajamarca, Peru. When Atahualpa refused to acknowledge the supremacy of the Spanish king and the Christian religion, Pizarro ordered an attack and the emperor was taken prisoner. Atahualpa bargained for his life by keeping his promise to fill, twice with silver and once

I speak of the seed of Belial embodied in the white race itself that has moved against nation upon nation in the process of taking over the world. And I speak, therefore, of the intermingling, among those of the white race, of the seed of Light and Darkness. Thus, beloved hearts, when there is compromise (intermarriage of the seed of Christ with the seed of the Wicked One—both being of the white race), the seed of Light also suffers.

This curse pronounced is not only a judgment of the Law, but also a curse of black magic by the seed of the wicked (transferring their culpability to the seed of Christ). And therefore, that curse is come to pass because it has never been broken, never been checked. And the full force of the Godhead dwelling in any son of God on earth has not, to this moment, challenged it or overturned it. It is to this end that I have come, for there is truly a superstition and a sense of revenge upon all the descendants of the Spanish conquistadores by the descendants of those people who did suffer needlessly under the conquests of the Spanish in South America.

Let it be understood, therefore, that this curse has indeed come upon the middle class and the white man of America and the earth through

with gold, the large room in which he was held. In spite of this, the Spaniards charged Atahualpa with "crimes against the Spanish king" and executed him by strangulation on August 29, 1533. In the last moments before his death, Atahualpa uttered: "Cocaine shall fortify the Indian and destroy the white man." Although the Indians have chewed the coca leaf for centuries (without apparent side effects) and consider it sacred, they are not known to use the "evil" powdered, processed derivative which the Incan emperor predicted would destroy the white man.

that very deed. And you can understand that history is tarnished by the vicious circle of this karma; history is replete with acts and deeds that come full circle and therefore take the lives of the seeming innocent when they are in their very bud and blossom.

Realize, therefore, that the vulnerability of the people who succumb to cocaine in every race is also conditioned by prior neglect, prior agreement, prior consent in some form (great or small) of allegiance to their own carnal mind, allegiance to the dweller on the threshold, and allegiance to those fallen angels who are the betrayers of the people of earth.

Realize, then, beloved hearts, when you give your allegiance to your Holy Christ Self and the voice of conscience within you, when you stand with Almighty God—and still stand—and to the best of your knowledge and ability and awareness do not compromise the love of your Christhood, the wisdom and the power of your Christhood, you are protected against the wiles of the Devil and of these 'serpents', these fallen angels in embodiment, and against their mortal cursings (execrations) against your souls.

But when there is a giving away of the portion of the self—a little compromise here and there, because it seems harmless (and that word *harmless* is among the most dangerous words in the lexicon of the English language)—then, beloved ones, you leave yourselves open not only to the inroads of your own karma and the karma of the fallen angels as well as the subsequent depriving of yourselves of more of your consciousness because you have agreed and acceded to giving a portion of it away— but also you leave yourselves open to their black magic practiced against you to wear down your resistance to Evil, to break your free will—all the while making you think each downward turn on the road to hellish self-destruction has been your own freewill choice.

Thus, the more you are enlightened by us and by the Teachings of the Ascended Masters, the more you enter into your own Christhood, the more you take accountability for your thoughts and feelings and for your deeds, the greater the stand you take for the Light and the more Light you therefore feel upon yourself—the more you realize just how important it is to protect that Light and your Christhood.

Those who reach the peak of Everest and the challenging mountains of the world know the dangers of the last mile, the last five miles. Beloved hearts of Light, those last few yards before your victory are among the most dangerous of all because they necessitate the securing of that which you have gained as well as the strength to attain the final crown of victory. To sustain that which you have becomes, therefore, the challenge of Keepers of the Flame, which is why we have written on the Keepers of the Flame Fraternity

Lessons the byword: "Hold Fast What Thou Hast Received."

Now, therefore, beloved hearts, I come and I ask your concerted and undivided heart-fire attention and God consciousness with me as I implore, before the altar of Almighty God, the breaking of this so-called cocaine curse and all who have reinforced it. I ask you, therefore, to kneel before your Father.

Almighty God, our Father, the one supreme God—*Elohim!*—I, Saint Germain, stand in the earth with those who are the Mystical Body of God. We come before thy altar and before thy throne. In the name of thy beloved Son with us, Christos, we implore.

I call also to all Christed ones and children of the Father worldwide whom I touch with the fire of my heart—to give their attention now at inner levels to this universal and planetary prayer:

Our Father, one in heart, one in the heart of the earth, we call forth *Light! Light! Light!*

Break the curse! against the seed of Light on earth! *Break the curse!* of cocaine, marijuana, heroin, PCP, and all other chemicals known on this planet and those yet to be introduced which have already been introduced in past ages.

Elohim of God, Almighty Father, we summon now the legions of Light and the entire Spirit of the Great White Brotherhood as cosmic reinforcements in the heart of the earth. And I, Saint Germain, declare that in my heart, as in thy heart, this curse is now *fully, finally broken* by the Godhead! And this breaking of the curse shall be implemented by these Keepers of the Flame daily in the Judgment Call of thy Son Jesus Christ, in the *binding* of the curse, and in the *binding* of the dweller on the threshold of that curse!*

And therefore, I say: Father, release the dispensation of Light for the protection of the warriors of Light and Peace who march with the legions of seraphim and the angels and Elohim. Let there be raised up reinforcements on earth who will take their stand and bear that Light, that blinding Light of the shield of the Godhead and of the mighty sword invincible of cosmic Truth.

Helios and Vesta, representatives of the Father/Mother God, I, Saint Germain, with Portia, now agree to hold in the earth, with Keepers of the Flame, the balance against this conspiracy out of the pit of Death and Hell.

In the name of Almighty God and by his grace, fully ensconced in his flame, we stand in this hour to challenge the entire drug conspiracy of planet Earth and to challenge every soul beset thereby who is of the Light to:

Leave it at once, depart from it, turn your back on it, and run for the Sun! *Run for the Sun!* is

---

*It is vital and essential that you invoke your tube of light and call to Archangel Michael for protection before you become engaged with the hosts of the LORD in their warfare of the Spirit for the binding of the forces of Death and Hell preying upon our youth. See the Tube of Light and Archangel Michael decrees at the end of this chapter and decrees 20.07 and 20.09 in *Prayers, Invocations, and Dynamic Decrees for the Coming Revolution in Higher Consciousness*, Sections I, II, and III, $2.95 each. These calls are urgent! Send for your 3 sets today.

our cry and our call to every Lightbearer on earth! Now *depart* from the dark places and the hell-holes and the astral pits! Remove yourselves from the fallen ones who are the purveyors of drugs and rock that go hand in hand and draw you down into the very darkness of hell.

I, Saint Germain, stand before the altar of Almighty God. I speak from the altar of the Holy Grail. I speak into the very heart of the flame of the ark of the covenant and I summon the Word of God in this hour to slay, therefore, the entire planetary momentum on the astral plane of the "dragon" that gives power to the "beast"* in every form of drug conspiracy. And I call for the empowerment of my own in this hour that they may send the call, and that that call may count, beloved Father, as my own call.

I ask that my heart and flame and being once again reinforce them and that when they give their calls on this subject and the subject of World Communism and the international capitalist/communist conspiracy, it shall be done! And it shall be turned back! And the possessing demons of drug addiction shall no more occupy the temples of the Lightbearers! And all evolutions of earth shall be free! And the angels who are the reapers shall come and *Bind* these fallen angels! and take them for their final judgment!

And therefore, I, Saint Germain, plead once again before the Father for the acceleration and the shortening of the days for the elect, and for the

_____
*See Revelation 13.

binding of the conspirators of Darkness in every walk of life, aborting life at every age—in the womb, in our children and youth in those years when souls of Light ought to be pursuing the Mighty I AM Presence but engage themselves in pleasure-seeking and entertainment and the titillation of the senses.

Beloved Father, hear our call, for we are one in heart. We are one in thy star-fire magnitude in the earth. We are determined to present planet Earth as a planet God-victorious in the flame of freedom.

And therefore, Father, I present to you this day my beloved Keepers of the Flame worldwide who are standing with me and in celebration of my own ascension [May 1, 1684] do take their stand this hour by the cosmic flame of freedom and by cosmic reinforcements to challenge evil to the very core and Absolute Evil by the power of the Absolute Godhead with them whom they know, beloved Father, as the Mighty I AM Presence.

O beloved Father, receive my own. Receive those who are the forerunners of the age of Aquarius. I call forth grace and protection and enlightenment as well as God-happiness and the understanding and tutelage of their hearts by the Lord Maitreya in the Path of the Ruby Cross.

I call unto you, beloved Father, to now give to us and these holy ones in embodiment that sacred fire that is able to consume by the spoken

Word those who are the denizens of hell—the infamous, those who are the destroyers, those who are the seed of the Murderer and the Liar who come from beneath, whose end shall surely come.

Our Father, we beseech you in one heart that their end shall come now and in this hour—before it is too late, before too many of those Christed ones whom we have invoked and blessed are come forth and their Light stolen and their lives destroyed.

Therefore, in honor and memory of one soul of Light passed from the screen of life this very week, I say, let us remember all souls of Light and all individuals, no matter what their level of evolution—all who have passed from the screen of life at the hand of World Communism and the international drug conspiracy and the capitalist conspiracy as well.

Let them be remembered, our Father. Let the saints who are at inner levels be remembered. Let those who have had to reembody scarred and burdened and who have again come under this conspiracy also be remembered. And let the legions of Light penetrate deeper and deeper into the astral plane and rescue those souls this day!

Our Father Alpha, our Mother Omega, we call. We are one in thy heart. Heaven and earth meet in this hour. In this consummation of the Word at the altar of the Holy Grail, there is the oneness of Spirit and Matter. And souls aflame with the victory of Light enter a new consciousness of their own Christhood as they draw down from their causal bodies that Light that has never been seen on land or sea—that Light in the lighthouse of Being, that Light which can descend the crystal cord and be the staying action to hold back the world tide of Darkness, that Light which can consume utterly the Dark Cycle of returning karma in Aries.

Beloved Father Supreme, I seal this prayer in the heart of the Cosmic Christ and in the hearts of the faithful and true everywhere on earth. I seal this prayer. May it come forth. May it bud as the pink rose. May it bud and blossom in a Cosmic Christ awareness.

And let those who are on the verge of coming into proximity with our teaching, beloved Father, now also receive the gift of protection and the ministration of the legions of Archangel Michael and his flaming blue sword. Let them be drawn into the awareness that they may utter the Word, even in this twenty-four-hour cycle—I AM THAT I AM. For, having so said, legions of Light in the service of the I AM THAT I AM, even in the service of the name of God and the I AM Presence, shall run to their side and protect them until they are securely anchored in this Light.

In the name of Almighty God, in the name of the God of Freedom whose Spirit I AM and represent in this era, I, Saint Germain, seal this prayer in the souls of the Lightbearers worldwide and in their Christ Self.

Our Father, we attend thy answer and thy coming. . . . We shall be there in full force for thy holy cause, beloved Father. In thy name, Amen.

———————————

Hearts who kneel in prayer, I bless you. For as sure as George Washington contacted the Goddess of Liberty and was contacted by this blessed being,* so each one of you has for us that equal value of the patriot, the daughter, the son of our own hearts. Therefore, see how by your reception of the Electronic Presence of the Ascended Masters, you also can count for the victory of a nation and many nations.

Understand this co-measurement with God— not an equality of the evolutions of earth, but a coequality of opportunity with the sons of heaven. And your Christ Self is every bit one with the Cosmic Christ and therefore worthy of the divine response. And your soul as the bride of your Lord is also worthy, as the handmaid of Almighty God, of the approbation of your love.

Recognize this indispensability of your lifestream and your true cosmic worth. And in that recognition, beloved hearts, *rise* now and stand in the sun of your Godhood! [audience rises]

Precious ones, the fervent prayer of the righteous and the faithful has never gone unanswered, is always rewarded, and does always have the victory. Let it be realized that on all fronts, as you

*See "Washington's Vision of America's Trials" in *Saint Germain On Alchemy: For the Adept in the Aquarian Age*, Summit University Press, $5.95.

stand in the very center of the circle of Aquarius—
in the center that is the dot of my own causal
body—and you daily face the twelve lines of the
Clock twice in the twenty-four-hour cycle, all with
which you deal are those conditions and practices,
beloved hearts, that require the maximum light
and the maximum strength of embodied evolutions. Concerning this point, I would now address
you. Therefore, be seated. . . .

Those sincere souls that you view daily, who
desire to move against what we have called the
capitalist/communist conspiracy or drugs or other
malefic conditions spawned out of hell that
come as Absolute Evil, are not able of their own
efforts to accomplish their ends, though they
think that by organization, by movements, and
by more money they will be able to solve any and
every problem. Not a human effort but a divine
one! And the sword is a sword of the Spirit. It is
sharper than a two-edged sword—that which goes
forth out of the mouth of the mouthpiece of
God, who is your own Christ Self or the messenger thereof.

Beloved hearts, that which you are able to
accomplish by united effort is the very taking and
binding by the LORD's hosts, in answer to your call,
of the deadly demons, false hierarchs, and black
magicians of long-standing, moving at the physical and the astral plane against the people. When
these forces and conditions and the dweller on the
threshold thereof are removed, those who are the

constructive individuals in society may accomplish good. And so it should be.

Yours is the joy and the path of those who become the unsung and the unknown heroes of the age. Your reward is with you, and your light banner shines across the galaxies. But expect no welcome cooperation or helping hand from the world, for there is a gap between this science and its understanding and most of the educated people of the nations.

Now, if we were to exact the requirement that they could not have your help or ours until they should have this enlightenment and come to grips with the extent of their responsibility in life, I tell you, all should be lost in the meantime. Their evolution will take sometimes centuries— and sometimes it can be accomplished in the twinkling of an eye. We cannot predict the human consciousness, but we also see the handwriting on the wall of the evolution of souls who are constructive yet blinded by their own intellectualism and their own sense of socialism as well as of society.

Therefore, beloved ones, be unmoved and undeterred. For the more diligently you pursue this work and these calls, the greater the necessity for oneness in your Community (which you understand as the Mystical Body of God worldwide), the greater the necessity for harmony, and the greater the necessity to accelerate. . . .

Thus, on behalf of the world bodies who have

made their declaration against drugs—including this nation, its president, and many people—I ask your intercession and your prayer. In order for them to succeed, your work is absolutely necessary. And I tell you, without this encounter with Christ (with Maitreya as Initiator representing with Jesus the Universal Christ at this altar) concerning these issues, the world could not move forward and would not be in a position today of a certain balance that has been held and, therefore, a certain continuing opportunity to the Lightbearers to rescue the souls of Light.

I remind you that Mother Mary herself has had no end of involvement in this very process. And by her very presence and oneness with many millions, there is the holding of the balance of the World Mother in the earth, giving you once again renewed opportunity with Kuan Yin and the Karmic Board to intercede and bring the teaching and the enlightenment to many.

Realize, therefore, that the action for the cutting free of the Lightbearers is one of the most important calls you can make daily, in addition to the challenging of those forces that beset their very identity and Godhood.

Beloved ones, love one another as you have never loved before. Stick together, as they say, through thick and thin!

We of the Ascended Masters treasure every soul who has aligned himself with our cause. . . . It is necessary to secure greater protection, therefore, to all who agree with me and with my cause. And I ask those of you who see and know to have full compassion upon those who are one with you in spirit yet separated by the distances of world karma and personal challenges and family affairs and burdens and responsibilities of their professions and businesses.

Beloved hearts, there is a wide, wide world body of co-workers who are a part of this movement of the Coming Revolution in Higher Consciousness—those who have studied our teachings, even the publications of The Summit Lighthouse—who are absolutely one with your heart and the heart of the Messenger, yet you do not see them. They may not appear, but they stand, at inner levels, staunch for Truth and Freedom.

These souls of Light must be cut free, must be assisted. Just as you move against the fallen ones who move against them, so you must pray with positive momentum and the full power of your Godhood for the Lightbearers of earth. I ask, therefore, that the balance of your marathon in honor of my ascension be consecrated to decrees on the ancient karma of the drug conspiracy and the judgment of those destroyers in the earth who are destroying the youth of the world through marijuana and cocaine—as well as to the freeing of my own. . . .

Heed the call to come up higher. . . There is a trust in the Word and in the communication. There is a trust in the sense of timing and cosmic cycles. There is a trust that Almighty God working through us, one and each other and our common loaf of Christhood, does deal with those necessary situations as the Great Law has determined.

Much that we know is not necessary to convey, for the Darkness is vanquished and the Light appears, and it does not require dissecting. It is better that your attention be upon God than upon the evil that is at the gate, for thereby we bypass also the untransmuted fear, anxiety, and doubt that could come upon you by too much knowledge of the dark ones.

Therefore, look at the direction, the tenor, of our word and understand that when it is given, it must be responded to; for we await to give the next word when you have assimilated and accomplished that which we have sent forth. Our word cannot return unto us void. Therefore, it is the Father's trust in the embodied sons and daughters that has sent forth the decree: My word shall not return unto me void! For my word shall go forth, kindle the fire of the hearts of my own, and be returned by a mutual love, multiplied and abundant!

Beloved ones, the economy of the nations is upset as much by international crime as international Communism and the capitalist conspirators. The upheaval in the abundant Life of the people is clearly illustrated this day.

And thus, you understand when we speak of the economies of the nations, it is not only to goad you to a study of the correct philosophy of economics, but to awaken you to the realization that the true economies of the nations cannot function when there are those who do not play according to the rules of the game of Almighty God—the betrayers of the people who destroy their life, their livelihood, their crops with their illicit drug trafficking, with their engaging them in war and rebellions and insurgence and Communist revolutions, or by the taking of their labor in channeling it into the monopolies that act in their own name and design and not for the good of the people.

These factors are the *x* factors that bring about the fall of the whole house of cards of nations—not merely a false philosophy of economics, but the manipulation of the flow of supply and demand between Almighty God and his children, and then between people and people. Therefore, let the international bankers also be judged! Let the fallen ones be judged and those who justify, with their serpent logic, the engagement in this drug traffic—as well as those who launder the ill-gotten gains.

Beloved hearts of freedom, I am ready to go to the heart of the Great Central Sun for another dispensation and another, that the lowest of the low and the darkest of the dark ones be bound and judged and removed from the physical as well as the astral plane.

You can imagine that the removal of the fallen ones from an evolutionary coil and spiral

involving millions who are intertwined with them
is no small task of the Archangels and the elemental beings—Nature's forces used by the avenging
sword of the Holy Spirit to deliver mankind's
karma, when all other means to effect their conversion and their deliverance have failed.

Therefore, the violet flame and the sword of
blue flame and Astrea's circle and sword of blue
flame do come into play when Lord Shiva (the
Hindu term for the Person of the Holy Spirit) is
summoned for the removal of the dark ones. For,
you see, the withdrawal of their momentum of
karma—the records of karma and their entanglements with Lightbearers—has caused cataclysm in
the past; and we do not risk it in this hour.

Thus, massive world transmutation—such as
you are accomplishing with this violet-flame marathon—must be the softening and the period of
the separating out of the Lightbearers from the
tentacles of the dark ones, preceding the full and
final removal of these ones and their own consciousness of Death and Hell being cast into the
lake of fire.

Understand that this is why your calls must
be relentless, must be concentrating on the very
eye of Serpent, on the very core of their plots
and conspiracies—including child abuse, child
molestation, and child pornography!—and why
you must rise to a new dimension of your I AM
Presence and Christhood with the giving of
your decrees—why you must place yourself there

(wherever evildoers are stealing the Light of youth by the violation of their chakras) physically by strong visualization, by bodies filled with light because they are not toxic, because you are not fallen asleep from your own toxins and the taking in of impure substances.

Thus, the need for fasting is one which we have said from the beginning. For the resting of the seventh day is the resting of the physical body and the lower vehicles of consciousness by that fast which can easily be accomplished when you have a momentum on it. Even the taking of juices and other liquids that sustain you during work hours is better than eating solid food during that twenty-four-hour period when, therefore, the angels of light come with transmutation and the violet flame to flush out the cells of the mind.

Beloved hearts, when you concentrate on the clearing of the brain and the brain cells and the nervous system by the correct uses of fruits and vegetable juices and herbs, you will find that there can occur a greater oneness of the Higher Mental Body (Holy Christ Self) with the mental body and the physical counterpart.

And remember, beloved hearts, that consciousness is throughout the body temple and not only in the central nervous system or in the brain. Realize that your consciousness is in the spinal altar and in the Kundalini fire and in every cell of your being and in your chakras—and that God consciousness is able to hold a fire, an all-consuming fire, for the cleaning up of the earth and also for the wisdom of the Buddha that tells you the way to go. . . .

Heed, therefore, our Word and take our suggestions for the manifestation of that Community of the Holy Spirit which truly is the real city set on a hill that cannot be hid.

Let your light so shine in the eye, the heart, and the body temple. Let the fervor of your spirit recognize with all wisdom that which is taking place. Let your hearts go forth as the brooding Mother and as the fire of Kali to bind these devils.

Though you have joy and happiness together, though you may form a circle of fire and dance in the sun and in the starlight, may your hearts ever be vigilant and never forget those who suffer the burdens of World Communism and its terrors, World Capitalism and its conspiracy, and the drugs besieging the temples of our own.

In the re-creation of the Spirit, I bid you enter the joy of my heart. This joy that is full is yet a perpetual vigil. It is the very quality of joy itself that does not fear to experience the burden and the pain of others. Thus, I speak of a laughter that is guarded, a recreation wherein the mind does not take its eye from the serpent's den and therefore always knows the moves of the fallen ones.

In the midst of your joy, affirm "I AM WHO I AM." And in the midst of your laughter, let the rolling laughter pealing from angel hosts be the swallowing up of the deadness and the dead seriousness of the death entities and their death drugs.

One thing they have never settled: the fact of the matter is, *there is no death!* and they do not conquer, ultimately. Only in the mayic plane of the astral, only in the dark night do they *seem* to hold sway and cause pain and anguish to the departed and the family and the mother and the brothers and the sisters and the friends.

Beloved ones, let every such occurrence be a profound lesson on the path of Christhood and the defense of Truth. Let the lesson not be lost, yet let the illusion of death be consumed. Therefore, let us celebrate Life, and let us send our legions of freedom to assist those who find themselves suddenly in another octave so unnecessarily.

Blessed ones, I would tell you that the entire drug conspiracy is aided and abetted by the suicide entity. All who partake of these drugs commit the first in a series of steps of self-annihilation—the single step toward suicide. And these suicide entities who come to seduce the youth under the wiles of the she-devil Annihla have calculated their thirteen steps of suicide as the antithesis of the path of the bodhisattva.

The first indulgence, the first drink, the first entering in is the preliminary stage of the development of the addiction. And they also begin in the breaking down of the heart, that that heart might become the seat of Darkness and Death instead of Light.

Therefore, let us cast out that heart of darkness, and let us bind and judge those literary agents of the pit who have come in this century to produce a literature that is not worthy of being read or studied except for the motive of exposing the wiles and the ways of the Devil. Everywhere we see in art, in music, in literature, and in philosophy this desecration of the abundant Life—this elevation of "sweet death."

The sign of Aries is the sign of the saint who is joyous and joyful in the abundant life. And therefore, the sign of Aries is for the mastery, *the God-mastery* of that abundant Life which begins with the defense of the full freedom of the soul in God and Christ and that soul's Godhood entirely manifest in the soul, the body, the chakras, and the being.

Toward the integrated personality of God we direct our sermon and our admonishment. Toward the toeing of the line of the new birth of Aries, we declare Sonship in the coming of Helios. This is the place of birth of identity and this is the point of God-mastery.

Therefore, we declare war, on the line of Aries, against the sinister force of suicide—and national suicide that fails to confront the Adversary—against the Murderer and the Liar from the beginning with their lies and murderous acts and every attempt to destroy the full flowering of the identity of the Lightbearer. We stand at the East Gate of the City Foursquare and our Royal Teton Ranch to receive every one who would enter with Jesus the initiation of Maitreya, Cosmic Christ of the Sun on the three o'clock line. . . .

May you bring the strengths of your own initiations and God-Mastery now to hold the balance. For the sun rises in the east. And out of the East coming unto the West is the Son of man within you! And your own Christ Self does rise on that line—and your initiation unto solar heights! Therefore, beloved ones, we face the challenger of that line and we return to our marathon of decrees on this conspiracy of cocaine.

In the invincible light of freedom, I salute you, freedom fighters of the ages! Your cosmic reinforcements are nigh, even at the door. Let us open the gates! Let us open the hearts and receive them, for truly you are a part of the army of The Faithful and True and the legions of Light. And our victory is a permanent victory—a victory for eternity.

This know: that each day your victory over the beast is a permanent victory for every lifestream on earth. Now count the Cause as ultimate and your life its instrument.

We are one to the ending of cosmic cycles. I AM in the heart of Alpha and Omega, and in this moment I ascend to the Central Sun anchoring there your efforts on earth. I am grateful for the balance you hold, that I might now take this hour to enter the Central Sun and therefore provide a greater fulcrum of Light for the victory that is your own.

I AM forever and forever the Ascended Master Saint Germain. By the grace of the Great Divine Director, Almighty God, and my Keepers of the Flame, I serve and I stand!

April 29, 1984
Los Angeles

Invoke Your Tube of Light

Beloved I AM Presence bright,
Round me seal your Tube of Light
From Ascended Master flame
Called forth now in God's own name.
Let it keep my temple free
From all discord sent to me.
I AM calling forth Violet Fire
To blaze and transmute all desire,
Keeping on in Freedom's name
Till I AM one with the Violet Flame.

(Give 9 times)

Call to Archangel Michael for Protection

Lord Michael before, Lord Michael behind,
Lord Michael to the right, Lord Michael to the left,
Lord Michael above, Lord Michael below,
Lord Michael, Lord Michael wherever I go!
I AM his Love protecting here!
I AM his Love protecting here!
I AM his Love protecting here!

(Give 9 times)

CHAPTER 8

A Prophecy of Karma
Of the Lifting of Saint Germain's Karma

Universities of the Spirit Opened at
the Retreats of the Lords of the Seven Rays
America Shall Return to Her Destiny!

*Lord Gautama Buddha addresses the New
Year's Eve Conclave 1986 at the Royal Teton
Retreat at the Grand Teton, Wyoming, U.S.A.
Speaking to thousands of devotees gathered at
three locations—at Shamballa, in a valley of the
Himalayas, and in conclave with him—he says:*
    . . . It is, then, with great joy that I turn my
attention to our center of Light, our Camelot.
Let all who have gathered here at the Royal
Teton Retreat now meditate profoundly upon
the circle of Light as I reveal to you, O Lightbearers of earth who have assembled at the Grand
Teton, how you are holding the candle of which
I have spoken already earlier in my address—the
single flame of Life whereby these whom you
behold are called "Keepers of the Flame"; and
their Mother and Messenger is with them in physical embodiment, even as you are graced this

evening by the Messenger who has addressed you—your own Teacher, Lanello.

Now we unveil Camelot to many thousands of Lightbearers who have gathered [in their etheric bodies] selected and by invitation, escorted by seraphim to this New Year's 1986 Conclave of Light. For as we have introduced you to the path of the ascension and the World Teachers and the Ascended Masters, so, now you may see gathered in California and throughout the earth at their stations those Lightbearers who deem it the highest privilege—O bhikkhus, O beloved daughters and sons of the Buddhic Light, of the path of the East and all world religions—to savour the cross and the circle of fire, to take it, then, from the heart and extend it to earth. And these who have come from every nation to our Camelot out of the East and West therefore savour above all things to enter into this decree momentum of the Word which I have already given to you to witness.

Speaking to two thousand disciples of the Ascended Masters on New Year's Eve in the Chapel of the Holy Grail at Camelot in Los Angeles, the Lord of the World continues:

Thus, beloved Keepers of the Flame, there have been watchmen and -women of the night [referring to those gathered at the Grand Teton] who have observed the power of the spoken Word and the dissolution of entire pockets of the astral plane as you have kept your violet-flame vigil for Saint Germain. And I have showed them what has been accomplished since Christmas Eve through the efforts of those assembled and the Masters' dictations. And they have fully realized, by this dispensation from the heart of Sanat Kumara whereby they have participated in our festivities here at the Grand Teton, exactly what is the science of sound,[8] the science of the spoken Word.

Their enlightenment has been that which could have taken thousands of years of pursuit in the physical octave. For Sanat Kumara sent his angels some weeks ago to prepare the souls and four lower bodies and chakras of those selected from the earth by the Lords of Karma to attend tonight's conclave here at the Grand Teton.

Thus, their preparation has been to raise their ability to see and perceive through my own Electronic Presence [the Buddha's aura and God consciousness]—which this night they have received for a period in time and space, that they might see through my eyes and heart and being and know all that has been taught by the Messengers in this century.

They have seen the violet flame. They have seen the blue-lightning angels exorcise the most intense, the most insidious forms of entities and demons. They have watched how Astrea, the Starry Mother, and how the Seven Archangels have gone after the darkest of conditions and especially those affecting the youth.

They are eager, beloved ones, to be sure that when they return to their denser bodies they will have a memory of all that they have been taught at the Grand Teton, that they might also have some sign and contact. Their mentors have assured them again and again that they could find the books of the Teachings in the most prominent bookstores of this nation.

Some have lamented that they will not find translations in their own countries. And thus, there is born in their hearts, for the first time in this embodiment, a keen desire to study English and to come to America, hopeful that they will make the connection on the outer to that which they have been given within.

We have presented the vast panorama of the Great White Brotherhood. They have seen Mighty Victory and some of his legions of Light. They have stood present before the Lords of Karma, who have given to them angel secretaries to go over their private book of life with them.

Beloved ones, these are truly the best of earth's evolutions. Though not without karma, they are lovers of the Light, yet not in situations of having had any advancement or prior outer knowledge of that which takes place at inner planes.

This experiment which I have sponsored has been my answer to Saint Germain's Stump to Europe and to the Messenger's call. For the effort of this team and the delivery of the Word night after night has made a deeper and deeper etch in the crystal of Matter and in the souls of Light.

It is truly an example of what we have taught

you—that when the Word is spoken it reaches all upon earth of a similar wavelength and vibration. It is never limited to the immediate audience. And though without the amplification of satellite or modern systems of communication, yet the earth body itself records the Word, which is why the Word must be incarnate in you.

In the physical sense the embodied Messenger Elizabeth Clare Prophet cannot be everywhere. But in the divine sense the ascended Messenger, Mark L. Prophet whom we call Lanello, *is* everywhere. And you must be his instrument. Thus, at anytime, wherever you may be in life, you may come upon a soul who has attended this conclave and therefore who has the inner awareness of all of the Teaching and the Law and the specific vision of the work of the angels as they implement the calls of your very divine decrees.

This dispensation has been made possible by many beings of Light. We have done all we could do for our part. Now we say, the particular call you may make is that these one hundred forty and four thousand and more be allowed to have the memory quickened in them of the inner planes' experience and especially that you might encounter them and give to them even a wallet-size Chart of Your Divine Self or some portion of the Teaching or a poster or anything that you might prepare that would be appropriate, that they might be drawn to that which is now a part of the immediate inner awareness—not something covered over that they knew twelve thousand years ago on Atlantis, but something with which they have had immediate association.

Just as your calls have been answered with a fiery action throughout this conference, so, beloved, your calls may be answered to give help to these souls of Light.

Now, then, you understand the audience who hears my message, and you are part of the world of inner beings who recognize the office of the Lord of the World which was bestowed upon me by Lord Sanat Kumara. I am indeed grateful to have such disciples as yourselves, to have so many positioned around the world who in the very outer knowledge of their being place their attention upon me in this hour and therefore receive, whether waking or sleeping, a current from my heart for the healing, the stabilizing, the regulating of the heart and the four lower bodies and the functions thereof. . . .

Almighty ones of Light I AM THAT I AM, now you understand that the Western Shamballa, sealed over the Heart of the Inner Retreat and extending for many miles radiating out therefrom, is a consecration of a shrine made holy by the footsteps of Archangels long ago. Now you understand that the white-fire/blue-fire sun that has come in the establishment of the Retreat of the Divine Mother, with Lady Master Venus (twin flame of Sanat Kumara) presiding over the Ranch, is also the polarity of that Western Shamballa.

As you have heard, then, and understood, for aeons heaven has been banking upon this area as a place preserved, reserved for evolutions who will come apart because they have been taken to the inner retreats of the Great White Brotherhood.

Now in this hour the Seven Chohans of the Rays—also known as the Lords of the Seven Rays—bow before the Light and the altar of the Royal Teton Retreat where I am. They stand before me and they present their petitions to me before the Lords of Karma.

It is their request, made formal but deliberated by us earlier, to open, then, universities of the Spirit in each of their etheric retreats where they might welcome not dozens or hundreds but thousands and tens of thousands of students who will diligently pursue the path of self-mastery on the Seven Rays systematically, mastering most especially the First and the Seventh Rays whereby they might establish the Alpha and the Omega of their identity—the will of God, the divine blueprint, the inner plan for twin flames—and immediately begin an action of personal and world transmutation.

The plan, therefore, is for students to spend fourteen days in Darjeeling and fourteen days with Saint Germain at the Royal Teton Retreat and to alternate these fourteen days as they weave a balance and restore themselves to the commitment of the beginning and the ending of the cycles of life—the Alpha and the Omega of the First and Seventh Rays.

Having successfully passed certain levels, albeit beginning levels, nevertheless strong levels of accomplishment in the use of these rays, they will have a turn also with Lord Lanto and Confucius here at the Royal Teton and Paul the Venetian, who prefers to use in this hour the Temple of the Sun of the Goddess of Liberty (who is the Divine Mother of beloved Paul) and to anchor that action in the Washington Monument, inasmuch as it has already had anchored there a focus of the threefold flame from the Château de Liberté.[9]

Beloved ones, this training, then, will be for the rounding out of the threefold flame in the wisdom of the Path and especially in the development of the path of the sacred heart, the expansion of love that they might rid themselves of fear and hardness of heart and records of death surrounding that heart.

Then, you see, comes the path of ministration and service, which is the logical manifestation of love and a balanced threefold flame. Through ministration and service in the retreat of Nada in Arabia, they will find, then, a place where they can give the same dynamic decrees you give here for all those untoward conditions in the area of the Middle East. And this shall be their assignment at inner levels even as they study the true path of Jesus Christ on that Sixth Ray as it has never been taught to them before.

Having come through these retreats, they are now ready to be washed in the purity of the sacred fires of the ascension temple for a beginner's course and for the first baptism by water of the Divine Mother. Then they proceed to Crete with Paul the Apostle and there Hilarion shows them the Truth of all ages, and the science of Being is unfolded layer upon layer.

Thus, having completed a round in all of these retreats—cycling fourteen-day cycles, some repeated in the same retreat, some interchanging—they will come again to second and third levels of training on those seven rays. It is desired that as quickly as possible through this training these may make outer contact with Summit University and attend its halls of learning at the Inner Retreat, as is our desire. For the expansion of Light and the increase of Light is far more possible there than in the dense areas and the low level at sea level here.

Beloved ones, we therefore desire that the knowledge of Summit University as the Ascended Masters' university shall be made known far and wide through every means possible and that the course contents will carefully be described according to the pattern set forth by the Seven Chohans.

We desire the knowledge of the persons of the Seven Chohans to go forth and the many series they have dictated in several forms to be there in the bookstalls of the world,* that those individuals who are taking these courses might have something whereby they can make contact in the outer

*See *Lords of the Seven Rays*, Summit University Press, $5.95.

with our bands and truly begin that action of the sevenfold flame of the sevenfold Elohim in physical embodiment—finally, therefore, at that level to begin in earnest to balance their karma and prepare themselves for that world service which is their divine calling and make their ascensions in this life from that very Heart of the Inner Retreat.

This is our divine plan. This is our vision, the vision of Elohim and Great Silent Watchers of the City Foursquare to be builded there. We say, then, make haste to the mountain of God. For the summit beacon shining from those heights can be seen in the etheric octave as souls who come and go to that Royal Teton Retreat in the Grand Teton each night pass over the Inner Retreat and the angels show them the beacon and give them pictures in their mind and memory of that physical location so that by and by, by the repetitive action of seeing the beacon of the Inner Retreat, they may come to an outer awareness at least of the desire to take a vacation at Jackson Hole or Yellowstone Park! . . .

Beloved ones, there is indeed a warfare of the dark ones being waged against the entire cause of the Great White Brotherhood. And you must outsmart them and you must use every means available to reach people in the physical octave. Somehow the lie has been spread abroad that this Teaching is for the few. I tell you, the hour is come and now is when the Teaching is for the many who are called.

The many indeed are called and for many reasons. If the few be chosen, the few may still number in the millions. And you ought to be ready for the influx, for the harvest could not be more white and the Light could not be greater. . . .

Beloved ones, 1986 can and shall be an open door as we together determine that it shall be and as you in embodiment do ratify our calls for these dispensations. Thus, the Lords of Karma, and I with them, have already approved this petition of the Seven Chohans. And in this hour it is formally granted to them to establish these universities whereby they will assist and increase in a very intense manner all that is being done by yourselves on earth.

Beloved ones, those who are in the great amphitheater surrounding the Grand Teton have stood to applaud this opportunity that is given to them in this hour. I bid you join them.

[standing ovation]

Beloved ones, I cannot even tell you the great joy of these hearts when they discovered the truth of this Cause and the presence of this activity. . . .

Beloved ones, while you are standing, I present to you in this hour our beloved Saint Germain, the seventh Chohan, as he does come forward and stand singly before me while the other six stand behind, and Portia now standing with the Lords of Karma.

Beloved ones, the hour has come, and it must come, whereby from our office we declare to you and all Lightbearers in all octaves that by the united effort of the entire Spirit of the Great White Brotherhood the burden complete of Saint Germain's incurred karma is lifted, transmuted, and sent back to the Great Central Sun purified. [standing ovation]

Beloved ones, the Messenger has known at inner levels, in consultation with us and in conclave here, that if she and you together could endure to this night of December 31, 1985— already become where you are January 1, 1986— that truly this dark burden would come to an end and Saint Germain would be free once again to champion his cause through her and through the chelas as never before has occurred in these recent centuries.

Beloved ones, it is an immense relief to you, to the Messengers, in all levels of your four lower bodies. For truly you have borne sometimes ten times over the weight of karma of other lifestreams, whether from these decades of this dispensation or past dispensations through the centuries of those who have abandoned, betrayed, or misused the light of beloved Saint Germain.

Thus, beloved ones, you can see a new day! For you are the chelas of Saint Germain and you have borne his burden. You have been with him in his trial. You have been with him through all things. And he, then, is free to stand before us, before Alpha and Omega and lay before the Lords of Karma his plan and the plan of Portia for the inauguration of this age in the thirty-three-year cycle now under way as well as in the century entire to come.

Beloved ones, Saint Germain is brimming with hope and many plans that he has worked on for very long. He is beaming with a smile of joy and light. And I therefore give to him my place that he might address you in this hour. [applause]

[The Messenger: Portia does step forth now before Saint Germain. She does kneel before him as before the Lord of the World. And she does place in the hand of Saint Germain that mighty jewel of light—his focus of sacred fire that he placed upon the altar on behalf of all students of the violet flame and all whom he has sponsored in these centuries. Saint Germain does receive it now. He places it in a pouch, puts it in his vest pocket, and does prepare to address all.]

BELOVED SAINT GERMAIN

Most beloved friends of freedom of all planes of cosmos, I send the love of my heart to each and every one of you who has stood with me these long centuries of our joint efforts to reach the souls of the Lightbearers of earth that they might carry a torch of the violet flame to those lesser endowed who must be kindled by some in embodiment with the flame of freedom in government, in science, and in the mystical orders of religion.

I say to you one and all, our efforts have not been in vain. They have been costly indeed, and all have learned the meaning of paying the price—you keenly and I myself sometimes most painfully when I could not extend a hand until this tribulation, if you will call it that, was through. But, beloved ones, through it all, some have received the violet flame—not a few have ascended and are standing with me here tonight!

The knowledge of the Seventh Ray is abroad in the earth. And now, with a new fervor and a new hope and wisdom, I trust gained from any past indiscretions, we may once again lay firmly the foundation of our divine plan to sow and sow again the jewels of light and yet to so safeguard our sowings that neither you nor I, neither cosmic beings nor unascended chelas nor elementals who love me dearly should ever again become so encumbered by the situation of the misuse of the sacred fire by earth's evolutions once they have received the knowledge thereof.

Therefore, I bid you with all my heart's love a great and grand expression of gratitude. And I hurl to you now from my own being and aura, with beloved Portia, violets and lilacs and purple irises and all manner of wild and exotic flower that contain the violet and the purple spectrum. And to each and all who have ever favored me with a single kindness or a comforting word, I send this floral offering. And the fragrance descends. And you may know, beloved, that I am grateful.

In the name of the Goddess of Liberty and the Lords of Karma, my own beloved Portia, I am grateful to you, Lord Gautama—to you, Lord Maitreya, my brother Jesus and Kuthumi, El Morya and Lanello, and so many, many whose names I now say with all of my being. And a million times a million names are pronounced in the ethers that the whole of cosmos may know all who have ever helped Saint Germain and the violet-flame angels and the cause of freedom!

In this hour of rejoicing, I would address you, then. Most blessed hearts of Light, be seated in comfort and in our love.

Beloved ones, to me the most obvious solution for the protection of the Light and the protection of the Teaching is to use in the physical earth the matrix already provided by Archangel Michael and the Darjeeling Council with Mother Mary and the Messengers. The matrix of the rosary of Archangel Michael may be used now for a very specific purpose. And that purpose is for the protection of the Teaching, that it might come to Lightbearers, and for the binding of all Serpents and their seed—the binding of the dark ones immediately when they take the Teaching to use it on the left-handed path.

I submit that the call to the Archangels— directly to the heart of Archangel Michael through the decrees already written and this rosary for the protection of the path of the Great White Brotherhood, for the protection of the true souls of Light and the worthy and the instantaneous judgment of the usurpers of the Light—will go a long, long way in curtailing the advancement of abuses and therefore the incurring of karma for you and me and the increasing numbers of Ascended Masters who have come to join our cause of freedom from great heights of cosmos and the inner silence.

I must say that we applaud and bow in great reverence before the beloved twin flame of Lord Maitreya, who is here this evening, and welcome her and her decision to descend to these levels for the assistance of the feminine ray of this blessed and mighty Buddha warrior of the Spirit fire.

And so, beloved ones, your knowledge and use of the tool of exorcism taught to you in the initial Ruby-Ray decrees given by Sanat Kumara is most valuable. Beloved ones, the Teaching and its practitioners and students must continually be protected. And immediately students must learn of the various forms of entities that may beset them. And this army of Light must form, by the linking of arms, such a strength of union in Mother Mary's Circle of Light that anyone who is burdened, who has been overcome by the dark powers, who is truly a son of Light, can be not only vindicated but swiftly cut free and protected.

Thus, we see in the building and the strengthening of brotherhood in the earth, of a true oneness and a determination to help one another, that there will also come an awareness of the penetration, if any, of our circles of charity by alien forces that have no good intent but to spy upon our liberty and misuse our Teaching and turn our words again that they might rend us.

Beloved ones, our students throughout the world have become very astute over the centuries. They have seen what the forces of Fascism and World Communism and the powers that be in every nation have done to undo the Lightbearers and the true freedom fighters and those who understand the path truly of peace with honor.

Beloved ones, therefore we see that with the intense protection and the fourteen-month cycle* of the blue-flame will of God, we, as it were, may pull out almost all of the stops and let the Teaching go forth and let it truly be the sower of Aquarius who does sow the Word.

And where it is not on fallow ground, where it falls upon the rock and may be rejected, let other angels come and pick it up and let others take it. Beloved ones, let us not leave the seeds sown anywhere to be misused, but let us make the call that the Lightbearers will come and pick up the crumbs that have fallen from the Master's table, that they will pick up the stone that was rejected, the book cast away.

Therefore, the perpetual call to the seraphim is truly the key of Light taught to you by the

---

*an initiation given by Serapis Bey, Lord of the Fourth Ray

Messenger. The seraphim come with swords and fiery auras recharged once in every seven days by the Central Sun itself.

Thus they saturate those individuals who are of the Light with a mighty flame and perfume of roses. They lead them by the hand, they bind the demons—and where there is a will and a heart in those souls, they do indeed bring them to the fount of knowledge. But you, beloved, must establish those founts of knowledge, those places of availability and likelihood where many may pass in the marts of life. . . .

Beloved ones, had there not been so much opposition and such a weight of karma to be borne, you would have seen many, many more people taking the message for the message's sake itself. And wherever the voice of the Messenger is heard, people stop and listen.

Yet they are told by many babbling voices, from their families to their ministers to their civic leaders, not to go after anything that is out of the norm of their established tradition. Tradition, you know, is a god in society, but no longer. For *we* are in the vanguard and we are at last free.

Therefore, beloved, I say to you—not by way of announcing a specific action at this time but by way of saying to you—may you propose what you will do to bring the Lost Teachings of Jesus to the nations and may we then bring your proposals before the Lords of Karma. And may we then state what is our request, based on the realism of the hour and your positioning of yourselves, as to what we will take as our responsibility.

We proceed with joy and the caution of experience that we must ask for those things of the Solar Logoi and the Elohim of which we may be certain there will be a fulfillment and a victory and which will not result in a situation of the costliness of karma that does therefore affect the next and the next opportunity for our service.

We would rather that you yourselves be the daring ones, that *you* go forth and see what *you* will do and let us be the ones who respond. This is as it should be, for the Wise One, Lord Sanat Kumara, has said to me this very week:

"Saint Germain, you have been the champion. And when you have been in physical embodiment, those who are now a part of our activity on earth were benefited by your service and were advanced in their learning. Saint Germain, let them now come to center stage with the same courage that you had. Let *them* take on the responsibilities which you were so willing to take on when you were in physical incarnation and when you were the Wonderman of Europe, as you indeed are today the Wonderman of this world."

Beloved hearts, he said to me that I must let you play your part and that I must add to it and multiply it and must have, as they say, from you "money in the bank" by way of the assuring of the loan that I would then secure from the cosmic bank. Beloved ones, this is to say that there is a tremendous quantity of light that is available to me now in the great treasury of the Central Sun—a quantity of light that has been abuilding by cosmic beings proportionately as you have called the violet flame for the balancing of this accumulated karma of the people's misuses of the graces of God transferred to them by my hand.

Therefore, the substance of light is there. It is there on demand. And I am instructed to demand it as you present and show the most effective, workable, and successful programs for delivering this message of the Coming Revolution in Higher Consciousness to the world and for the building of the Inner Retreat.

In anticipation of the light going forth, we have designated the Inner Retreat as a place that must be secure, that must be the highest focus of light in the earth. For, you see, when the light goes forth it cannot be fully predicted what the response will be from the world and humanity. If these responses are an aggravation (as the carnal mind is aggravated not only by the light but by the Light incarnate in the Christed ones) causing a reaction so as to create a planetary chemistry that results in some world changes, it is necessary that the equivalent of the Great Central Sun Magnet be somewhere on earth.

And you know where that somewhere is. The eye of the Inner Retreat is the Grand Teton, and you are the body thereof. And that Great Central Sun Magnet can only be composed of your light bodies in physical manifestation.

As you have already understood, it will take great ingenuity to maintain the supply and the income in this area of the world. But, beloved ones, no one ever said that you could not go out and come in again, that you could not establish your base there and spend a major part of your year in those enterprising activities that promote both the Teaching and your own personal welfare, supplying you the needs of the hour for the blessings you desire to bestow upon your family and loved ones as well as upon this organization.

Thus, beloved ones, it is a question of the base. It is a question of having a retreat to retreat to and to go out from. This has always been the way of the Great White Brotherhood. Thus, you can expand your horizons and seek that place where you may also plant and reap a harvest essential to your God mastery in all planes.

I say to you, then, that in this hour of rejoicing and in this hour of the conclave, I am grateful to have been able to have shared with you the thoughts of my heart, the communications of the mighty ones, and certain parameters of our looking to the New Day.

My first actions will be to see to it that this activity is secure in every way and that the plans move forward according to the resolve of the Darjeeling Council and the Lords of Karma. I trust, then, you will seek a tidy conclusion to all those things that must be completed at the Ranch, made known to you and to be discussed later today.

Beloved ones, having this activity secure is like the sealing of Noah's ark. We must know that our Lightbearers who have supported us in all ages will indeed survive to make their ascension in this life. And I tell you, beloved ones, I cannot guarantee that ascension but I can tell you that the Path itself and your following of it does guarantee it.

Keep on keeping on and do not avoid the eye of, or the encounter with, the Messenger. For you will find the surest incisive action of the violet flame keeping you moving toward the center of Being and your perfect Love.

Beloved ones, I have much to attend to, for there are many areas of the world that need my help. I will go forth confident that as you know exactly what these areas are, you will be mindful that I also need the action of Archangel Michael's Rosary that that which can be done for the government of this nation and all nations might be secured and that the fallen ones and the spies and the enemies of Truth and Life be bound, that they might not move in and take the dispensations that I am able to give of light and action toward a more perfect world, a world of union and understanding and the universality of Being and the entering in to the very nature of God.

Thus, beloved, in great love and deference to the Lord of the World, I return you to his heart of hearts that he may deliver now the conclusion of his message.

My beloved Gautama Buddha, it is my great joy to receive this honor and new freedom in your presence this New Year's Day. And I bow before you. For by your keeping of the flame for me and these Lightbearers, our Keepers of the Flame Fraternity has indeed been established and its members wax strong as the stars of your heart....

[standing ovation]

BELOVED GAUTAMA BUDDHA

Most gracious and beloved knights and ladies of the flame, Lightbearers of the world, I bid you once again be seated in our rings of light.

There comes to me an angel of the Keeper of the Scrolls. There comes an angel descending from the heart of Sanat Kumara, from the heart of the Central Sun. And the Solar Logoi have sent, therefore sealed, the thoughtform for this year, 1986.

I unroll the scroll of light, and oh, what a fiery scroll it is, beloved! Upon this scroll is inscribed the full outpicturing of the Mighty Blue Eagle—the angel formation of the legions of the God Star Sirius.

This blue eagle takes the form—for this action for this planetary body—of the bald eagle of the United States of America. Yet it is blue, and when you study its components you will see that every feather and part is a blue-flame angel. And it is a vast formation that fills the starry heavens.

Beloved, the true and royal form of the flag of the I AM Race is the background of this eagle. It is the banner of Light. It is the Old Glory that has become America's flag. And yet it contains the secret within it of new developments within this nation which are to unfold.

The starry field represents initiates, and therefore its numbers may not be counted according to the outer. And the thirteen tribes are represented in this flag in the ruby and white, for the red stripes are not yet represented as the gold.[10]

The ruby, therefore, has the filigree line of gold on either side of the stripe separating it from the white, thus signifying the path of the Ruby Ray and of the Body and Blood of Christ for the attainment of the ascension through those stars which I cannot number, for it is not lawful for me to reveal it.

These stars represent not only states but tribes of the nations. They represent compartments of root races. They represent the seed of Christ, the archetypal blueprint of all those who may ascend under the canopy of the Central Sun, its focus in the God Star, assisted by the protection of the Mighty Blue Eagle formation of angels.

Beloved, behind this there is a unique map of the earth. Laid out in spherical design, this map is translucent. And by means of adjustment electronically, one can look at the earth in this and past ages, going back as long as evolutions of Light have been on it and showing in those periods the various land masses, how the seas and landed areas were formed and how they are in this present era.

That which is center, beneath the heart of the Mighty Blue Eagle, is that portion of the earth that is indeed represented as the Western Hemisphere. Above that, the banner of the I AM Race.

Beloved ones, the sign of the thoughtform of the year is this: to restore in this hemisphere, specifically in the United States and in Canada (if her people and Keepers of the Flame do will it so), the return to the founding principles of freedom, the return by revolution of the Spirit—by education and enlightenment, by the path of the ruby and the gold and the white and the stars in the field of the blue-flame will of God—to the original divine design which Saint Germain held in his heart for this nation to be the instrument of the return of Lightbearers to the establishment of God's kingdom on earth and to their own ascension in the Light, that they may walk the earth once again as ascended beings to be the teachers of those not yet ascended and to bring this earth back to that point of that golden-age civilization many thousands of years ago and in some cases millions of years ago.

Thus, beloved, this great thoughtform, which is large in dimension, does also retain at the very

top the paintings of Saint Germain and Jesus,
originally done by Charles Sindelar, and the Chart
of the I AM Presence. When all of this is seen
together in the grandeur of dimension, you can
see that it fits very well on this giant tapestry.

This tapestry of the thoughtform of the year
woven by angels will hang in the Grand Teton
Retreat for all to see. It shows that America shall
return to her destiny deserving to be, then, the
nation sponsored by Saint Germain, her people
going forth to transfer his science, his economy,
his religion, his way of life, which represents that
of the entire Great White Brotherhood, to every
nation.

It shows that there is a key, and the key is
that America must come to her original purpose
and fulfill it. She has ever been established and
sponsored by Saint Germain as the guru nation.
Thus, though the chelas of Saint Germain
throughout the world may have in some areas perfected and gone beyond the disciplines of the
people in this nation, yet the mantle has not yet
been taken from the Americans to restore the
earth to the place of peace and freedom.

Thus, in the lower portion of the tapestry
one can see the multitudes, and they come from
every nation and they represent every tribe and
race and people and color and evolution. And as
these multitudes approach from the south this
map of North America, there is in the center the
dove of the Holy Spirit, the dove of peace. In

anticipation of the presentation of this thoughtform at this hour, Lightbearers have been coming
for decades and centuries from around the world
that they or their progeny could be here in the
hour of the renewal of the flame of the Spirit of
Liberty.

Beloved ones, in the tapestry that proceeds
out from around the maps there is a portrayal of
major shrines of liberty of the earth, most notable
that of the Goddess of Liberty on the right and
the Grand Teton on the left.

Thus, beloved, it is an endless story that is
woven into this tapestry, and it shows that the
people of earth must bend the knee and confess
the eternal Christ in the heart of Jesus, in the
heart of Saint Germain, and in the heart of their
own I AM Presence. And these brothers of the
favorite son, Joseph, and of his sons, Ephraim and
Manasseh*—these other tribes (reincarnated in
Europe and throughout the world) must come to
that point of recognizing that the Father has a
right to have a favorite son and to bless him. For
that favor is not unjust or unequal but it is the
favor accorded as the blessing of attainment.[11]

Thus, Joseph, as you know, was one of the
embodiments of the beloved Jesus. And this is
what you find—that the hatred of Joseph has
become the hatred of America. America is the
source of the Teachings, of the I AM THAT
I AM sponsored by Saint Germain. And therefore

*Jacob accepted Ephraim and Manasseh as his own sons, making each one
the head of a tribe equal to the other eleven.

he has sponsored this language of this people as the language of the Great White Brotherhood in this age. Therefore, there must be an acceptance of this and a bending of the knee also and not the constant quarreling by the other tribes—"Why are we not equal?"

You can be equal, but you must proceed under Joseph with his coat of many colors and under the prophet Samuel. You must go to their Promised Land. You must accept the Teaching and the Path and strive with these holy ones of God to perfect a Union long endowed.

For sometime, somewhere the evolutions of other continents of Saint Germain have truly rejected him. And that karma is not removed from those nations, though it is removed from Saint Germain and the Lightbearers who have borne that world karma so long—especially the Messengers themselves.

Beloved hearts, the people of this nation have an endowment and a protection from the Master. Therefore, we make it known that for the integration of the Word and the entering into the universal age and an international unity of nations and peoples, it is truly a requirement that English be taught in the very lower schools to the littlest children of every nation upon earth.

For this you must decree. For, beloved, how can they choose a path and a Master whose language and writings and entire dispensations and initiations are in a language that is foreign to

them? Whether for commerce or education or
the arts or brotherhood, there are manifold reasons why this, the language so rich in its incorpo-
ration of many other languages, should be the
common knowledge of every schoolchild throughout the planet.

Thus, the thoughtform for the year may
appear complex, but then the organization, the
Path, and even the awareness of the average chela
has also become complex in a nuclear and space
age—an age of computers and technology accelerating the capacity of the mind to know Truth in
every area of learning.

Thus, I say to you, beloved, that the complexity of your understanding of the Path can
always be reduced to the simple simplicity of the
Law of the One. When you study and know what
we have taught through our many representatives, the Ascended Masters, you are the more
able to feed my sheep.

Therefore, some of you will identify yourselves as a part of the body of the Mighty Blue
Eagle, some of you as a part of those who minister at the altar of the I AM Presence and Saint
Germain and Jesus. Others will see yourselves
feeding and caring for the multitudes; others
building the Inner Retreat; others dealing with
the nations and bringing them to the proper
chord of response to our message.

This tapestry, then, establishes an outline—
whether within or without, whether in the maps

of the earth in the ancient ages—of the Path for everyone who is to ascend through this dispensation and thoughtform.

Now the hour has come, beloved, for me to send you to rest. For we desire you to come now (by soul travel in your finer bodies during sleep), straight as an arrow, to the Grand Teton mountain where you will be received, and the door in the mountain will be opened and you may enter for further instruction and initiation from Lord Maitreya which will be sealed in the concluding day of your conference when you return tomorrow, being this very day at Camelot.

In the blessed peace of the Buddha whom I represent, in the peace of Sanat Kumara, who has brought me to this office, I, Gautama, say to you, I am above all most grateful in this hour for the chelas of the will of God and Morya's diligence in bringing you to this point of keen receptivity to our heart.

May God bless you forever, my beloved. I am never apart from you, for our hearts are one in the heartbeat of the Ancient of Days.

January 1, 1986
Los Angeles

Notes to Chap. 8:
8. Science of sound. See *The Liberating Power of the Word:* Album I (6 cassettes), "Seven Steps to Precipitation by the Command of the Word," $37.50; Album II (4 cassettes, 111 color slides), "The Science of Sound," $138; and "Sound: Life's Integrating Phenomenon," in *The Coming Revolution: A Magazine for Higher Consciousness* (Spring 1981), pp. 24-33, 54. *(continued p. 176)*

CHAPTER 9

A Prophecy of Karma
Seventh Ray Priesthood of Melchizedek

144,000 Form a Violet Flame Maltese Cross
People Called to Give Violet Flame Decrees
Else the Law Will Force Many to Be Broken

Heart Friends of the Ages,
  Friends of Freedom and Keepers of the Flame,
  Most Gracious Ladies and Gentlemen,
    I greet you in the light of cosmic freedom
that inundates the earth in this hour and finds its
way by angelic hand and bands to your own dear
hearts when the flower unfolding does invite the
chalice rare to contain this floral offering of
immortelle and flower of sacred fire.
    Blessed ones, the event which brings me to
this city [Portland, Oregon] is both ancient and
recent. The ancient event, as recorded here in akasha, is a misuse of the Light—in some cases by
those who have reincarnated here and tarry for the
opportunity to balance that karma, and in some
cases by those who are not recalled to the scene of
this misuse.

Beloved, there are many sincere hearts in this area and state, as you are well aware; for I count you among them most certainly. Therefore, I would intercede in a danger you know not of, which is the return of that karma, cycle for cycle, in this hour of planetary karma returning. The intercession, then, is invoked through the council of Lord Zadkiel's retreat [12] and the priesthood of Melchizedek.

There is a violet-ray priesthood, beloved. Therefore, during this meditation [13] a procession of priests of the sacred fire have marched from that retreat to this area, forming by their bodies of light a Maltese cross. The significance of this thoughtform will become nearer and dearer to your heart as you study my courses in alchemy and learn the precipitation of light through that thoughtform in the threefold flame. Thus, beloved, the four arms signify the release into Matter of a sacred fire.

The members of the order of this ancient priesthood are Ascended Masters all. They long ago attained that victory which is yours to enter in this hour. They come from ancient temples prior to the desecration thereof on lost continents where they themselves achieved the honor of the white fire and the entering therein.

They have come, then, to give protection and an immense fire of transmutation that that return of karma might be mitigated or entirely consumed. This consuming and transmutation must take place in the physical through the intercession of yourselves and your heart flames receiving the violet flame, calling it forth, and welcoming a cooperative endeavor of these 144,000 priests of the Order of Melchizedek who have placed their bodies this night in this giant Maltese-cross formation.

I can tell you, beloved, that this Messenger had not one iota of awareness of why I called her to speak in this city and brought her here. This is indeed an unusual event, for it has not occurred that dictations have been given in evening lectures on the threefold flame and the Mighty I AM Presence, which you have heard.

This, however, was prearranged. And the Messenger has placed herself always on call and therefore, in obedience, is at the point of the grid of light where in this hour this light must descend for the protection of the people of this state.

Certain activities of false gurus and false teachings that have occurred here in the ancient past continuing to the present have also rent the auric field, making it even a greater challenge for the Ascended Masters and those in embodiment to seal now that record as the place where evil dwells and to build a mighty action of light for the holding of the balance.

Thus, beloved ones, if you desire to play your part, I would counsel you to come together and to give the violet flame decrees—to perform that action scientifically according to the laws of alchemy. For those who successfully demonstrate the mastery of matter as well as spiritual forces do indeed follow the scientific principles I have taught. And as is the case in the mystery schools, beloved, we place in print that which the Great Law does allow.

Those Keepers of the Flame of Life may enter in, therefore, to the consciousness of the Holy Spirit and go to the etheric retreat at the place of the Grand Teton for further instruction. Sometimes this instruction is held in what is called the Higher Mental Body or the superconscious mind, even keeping it from the outer mind and waking consciousness lest it be divulged.

Yet at inner levels the science is continuing and the path of your attainment is being fulfilled, beloved. And by and by, by initiation it may come to pass, when you have proven yourselves responsible with the knowledge of the higher Law, that you may in full waking awareness be reminded of that which you have studied under the great adepts and Ascended Masters at the Royal Teton Retreat.

Beloved ones, we must have the physical sounding of the Word. This is the purpose of the dynamic decree as the most efficient and accelerated means of forestalling those things coming upon the earth or the individual as the outplaying of karma.

This science was recommended to me specifically for this era by the beloved Great Divine Director, who is a magnificent being of Light to whom I trust you will offer your praise in song this night. For he is our sponsor in this endeavor whereby we desire to place electrodes around the nation and the North American continent for the turning of the tide of those predictions that have been made by psychics and others who have clearly seen that which could come upon the earth but have not been so farsighted in their seeing as to see the Daystar from on High and the Mighty I AM Presence as able to consume by the Holy Ghost and by the concerted effort of the few and then the many in the dynamics of the violet flame decrees.

Beloved ones, the physical sound that is made by physically embodied souls impinges upon physical matter. This matter is given to *you*. We cannot interfere in physical matter unless you allow us to direct the light through your body temples and through the physical organs corresponding to the chakras.

Let thy body be full of Light.* Let the disciplines, physical and of diet, be known. For that body which is transparent and translucent—taking in only pure substances for the need of the hour (which is service) and to sustain balance of mind—is that body which is most useful to us as a vessel.

The Word that is manifest here below must

_____
*the Christ consciousness

be sounded through embodied individuals. It is the Law, beloved.

We have played our parts on the stage of life. We have been in physical embodiment and the price we have paid for absorbing the light has been the same as always. It has been the persecution of ourselves, not necessarily intended by individuals but certainly coming through them in their rancor, resistance, and reaction to that light that does create in them a certain action [chemicalization] which they find intolerable because they are not committed to the Light* or to service or to their ascension.

Beloved, it has ever been thus. But the great joy of this age is that numberless numbers, saints robed in white do appear. And on earth now the many who keep the flame of Life are coming together. And the circles of protection and the ring of fire are being formed. And the solar ring is seen in the sky! And those who are among the embodied disciples of the Ascended Masters are actually experiencing the parting of veils so that they do see and hear our presence from time to time—and this is as God intended it.

Beloved ones, be not too desirous or too ambitious for the spiritual encounter with the Master but rather realize that your internalization of the Word and the Light places the Master where you are—one individed manifestation of

---

*to the Christ, who is the Source of the light, or energy, of God—"I AM the Light of the world" (i.e., "The Word, or the I AM THAT I AM, incarnate in me is the Light, Christ Presence, of the world")

God. Thus, beloved, it is better to increase the Light [of your Christ consciousness] than to seek after a sign or a message or an experience of some form of psychic channeling that is never guaranteed to be purely from the octaves of Light* and can take from you a delicate action of the aura that you are building with the higher Light and the higher Mind.

The sign, then, which is lawful is the sign of Christ in your heart. And thus, a wicked and an adulterous generation seeketh after a sign; but there is no sign that shall be given, save the sign of the prophet Jonah.[14]

Two signs given by Jonah are noteworthy— first, the sign of being in the belly of the whale three days, signifying that everyone who does become the mouthpiece of God must go through the proving in the heart and womb of Matter of these alchemical experiments which I come bearing to you.

The highest alchemy, beloved, is the precipitation of the Word incarnate as Christ in you, known by Paul as "the hope of glory."[15] And I say it is the *magnet* of glory! It is the white stone that is a magnet drawing unto itself a fire that does infold itself and you as well, until you come to know yourself as a living flame of Life.

Beloved hearts, this is the sign of the working out of the problem of being in the tomb of

---

*planes of the Christ mind, or Christ consciousness, occupied by the heavenly hosts and those who have ascended to that level of attainment and beyond

Matter. And the second sign is that which I bring to you now.

Jonah went to Nineveh and he warned the people that unless they would repent from their squandering of the life-force in the pleasure cult, calamity would ensue. Much to his disappointment, the people repented. They hearkened unto the voice of God through him and the city was spared. And thus, Jonah complained to the LORD, "They will consider me a false prophet because the calamity did not come upon the city." Thus, God can spare the city, even as he can pass the resurrection flame through the withered gourd, to which the prophet may become attached.

Beloved ones, understand the meaning of this—that the prophecy that is written in Revelation and in the Old and New Testament, that is written in the very sands and in the ethers which may be perceived, is not final! This is my cry to the age!

You are mediators between mankind (who are in a state of ignorance and rejection to the Truth of the Teachings of Jesus Christ we bear) and the oncoming karma returning. You as anointed ones, by choosing this calling and election, may form a Body of Light that does indeed become the manifestation of the all-consuming flame of God.

And that karma can be transmuted, beloved. And remember, the requirements are few. Ten righteous men could save an entire city by their righteousness, proving that the power of God in manifestation is far greater than millions engaged in the blasphemy of the anti-Light and the desecration of the innocence of the child.

The power of God in you is greater than all of the many things you see on a grand scale appearing. They *appear* to surround the earth, beloved, and to loom large and heavy and powerful. It is the *appearance* that must be slain by the sword, which is the sacred Word of the alchemist. For it is the *appearance* of evil that takes on power in the mind of the beholder. And when the beholder is the potential alchemist, he endows the unreal with the power of permanence—and thus, it has taken place.

Who will dare to challenge the destroyers in the earth?—knowing they are but specters in the night and have no power except that which the anointed ones and the people have given to them by their attention, by their fear, by their adulation, by their cursings. Whatever the attention, beloved, it does give power to the enemies of mankind.

Withdraw the attention and see how their systems crumble and how the new age and the golden age shall appear right within you as the golden man of the heart steps through the veil in you! And you will behold yourself in the likeness of Christ and therefore you shall see him as he is. And that shall be the reality of the Second Coming for you, one by one. For it is an initiatic event!

I tell you, the Second Coming of Christ is the appearance of the LORD in your temple. Expect it. Live for it. And know that this Light cannot be hid and every eye shall see him, one by one by one. And this is the Law of the One, for ye are one—one Mystical Body in this room! And the currents of God flow through you. And the angels of the members of the priesthood are tending you that you might absorb this light to your benefit and your healing.

Now, beloved, I ask you to remember that the dispensation that we bring depends on your participation. God will not take from you the responsibility of present Christhood and of co-operation with the ascended hosts. Those in embodiment must take accountability for planet earth as their alchemical experiment.

There is no division in the ecosystem, as you call it. There is no division in the bodies of the earth. Your thought, mind you, impresses itself on every grain of sand. No wonder the earth is burdened. An unconscious use of alchemy has put the planet out of kilter, to use an expression, with the cosmic blueprint.

You cannot escape your destiny. I bring to you words you will hear when you pass from the screen of life as you face the sponsors and guardians who have sent you forth and paid the price to give you the opportunity which you now have. If you think that some spot upon the earth will not respond to your call or that you are not responsible to assist in alleviating the darkness there, then you have not understood that the whole earth is the responsibility of every Lightbearer.

Ask yourself this question: Can you depart the earth at will? Can you somehow put the entire problem and challenge of the age behind you? It is not physically possible but, beloved, is it morally possible or spiritually possible for you to ignore the voice of God in your heart that is telling you that you can indeed be a liberator of life, beginning first of all with a single cell in your little finger? Liberate the cell from the tyranny of time and space!

I tell you, beloved, I once began the path of adeptship. *You* can begin. He who is able to drown conscience in noise and preoccupation and not transfer his heart fire to uplift a soul who suffers somewhere has truly never known that this universe is his native home, has truly not touched the hem of Christ's garment and ought not to consider himself on the path of spirituality.

It is the sensitivity to life—all sentient life, beloved—that calls you to cast yourself upon the Rock of the Universal Christ that the adamant hardness of rebellion of the human might be broken. Cast yourself upon this Rock and Christ will re-form you in his image.

If this initiation is not called for and welcomed by you voluntarily, then, beloved, the handwriting is on the wall even in this place. So do the mountains fall and the earth is removed and the elements melt with a fervent heat. And the Great Law acting through Nature will force many to be broken.

Thus, the wise enter voluntarily the initiatic spiral of the age of Aquarius and trust that God and the mighty Archangels will not lead them where others have not gone and passed through to the Victory. We the Ascended Masters stand before you as proof that there is a path that leads to immortal life, the ascended state, and the fullness of God manifest.

Beloved, I would conclude my address to you by the transfer of light that you are ready, willing, and able to receive—with the provision of responsibility that you use that light to invoke the violet flame daily for this cause.

Some of you do not know that for the gifts I have given in Europe, in other ages and in this century, which have been misused by some among mankind, I incurred a planetary karma. And therefore, the Cosmic Councils did not allow me to give any more of my causal body or my life for a considerable and long period of time. My students throughout the world have invoked the violet flame for decades and more recently specifically for the transmutation of the karma I made through the sponsorship of individuals who betrayed me and my gift.

Beloved, this placing of this Maltese cross here and the effort of these priests has come

because I, Saint Germain, went to the Court of
the Sacred Fire and pleaded for the cause of this
planet and gave once again a portion of my life
and causal body, as you might say, as collateral for
this event. If, then, the response is given, I can
assure you it can be repeated again and again until
all the earth and the cities and the chakras thereof
are sealed by the Maltese-cross formation of the
priesthood of Melchizedek.

Beloved ones, I, therefore, am the intercessor
and sponsor of this action. You, then, at your level
of service become also intercessors and sponsors.
This is, therefore, a new and very first opportunity
that is granted to me once again to attempt to
forestall world cataclysm. I trust you will understand sometime, somewhere what it does take for
an Ascended Master to receive from the great
hierarchies of the Central Sun dispensations for a
planet and her evolution.

I think it is evident to you, beloved, that
many upon earth would have no understanding or
ability to meet this situation. I believe with all my
heart that those of you who know me now, who
have known me before and forever, newly come to
this Teaching or long enduring its presence in
your heart, will respond. My faith in you is abundant because it is truly my faith in God in you.

May your souls rise from the seat-of-the-soul
chakra and join your Christ Self in your heart,
thereby being one with that Light, also being the
recipient of my trust.

I counsel you, then: Trust no man but trust the manifestation of God in every man and you will not be disappointed. I trust you are not disappointed in me this night, for I am not disappointed in you.

I bid you adieu and return to the silence that I might transfer this arc of light.

May 28, 1986
Portland, Oregon

Notes to Chap. 8 continued from p. 162:
9. See *Lords of the Seven Rays*, Book One, pp. 130-35, pocketbook, $5.95.
10. **Golden-age flag.** The inner design of the flag of America as it will appear in the golden age has gold stripes in place of the red, representing enlightenment and the gold of the Blood of Christ--the Life-essence of Spirit (Alpha). The white stripes represent the path of initiation and the ascension, the purity of the Mother (Omega). The thirteen bands symbolize the return of the twelve tribes and the thirteenth, the Melchizedekian priesthood--the order of Christed Ones in the service of the Lightbearers.
11. Gen. 37:3-36; 41:50-52; 48; 49:1-29.

Notes to Chap. 9:
12. This etheric retreat of Lord Zadkiel, Archangel of the Seventh Ray, once a magnificent temple on Atlantis, is located in the etheric octave over the Caribbean centered at Cuba.
13. The "War March of the Priests" by Felix Mendelssohn was played as the meditation music prior to the dictation.
14. See the Book of Jonah and Matthew 12:38-41.
15. Col. 1:27.

CHAPTER 10

A Prophecy of Karma
Planetary Changes Must Come

The Great Law Decrees:
"Thus Far and No Farther!"
Mysteries of the Seventh Ray

How oft in the night I have come to your bedside and stood as I did when Joseph of old at the bed of the sleeping Jesus—there to pray fervently to God that you, beloved, might realize the perfecting of the heart in the paths of righteousness, that the pure Christ might appear in this life in you.

O beloved, I am ever the watchful presence of Father among you. For I do raise up the figure of the Father as I raise up the Light* of those who must play their role on the stage of life in the person of the masculine incarnation.

Beloved, the loss of the Father flame within family and society is a contrived desecration of the heart of the Divine Mother within you also. Therefore, I say, men and women, understand the nobility, the sacredness of the holy calling to be co-creators with God.

*Christ consciousness

I speak, then, of the mysteries of the Seventh Ray and the Seventh-Ray Masters. All saints robed in white who comprise the hosts of the LORD hovering over the evolutions of earth in these final hours of the century have pursued accelerated courses in the Seventh Ray. For all understand the great need of the hour for personal transmutation to exceed that transformation that is oncoming in the earth, whether by Light or by Darkness.

Change is indeed the order of the day, beloved, and the winds of Aquarius do bring profound change, stripping from souls and body temples excess trappings and adornments until the individual is forced to look at himself in the cosmic mirror and say, "Is this what I am or is there something more of me which I have not discovered?"

Beloved hearts, change, then, has been decreed from the beginning by the spirals of the Great Central Sun. That wave of Light has descended. It is an offense to all Darkness and dark ones who have become darkened by the freewill choice to incarnate the night side of Life in the place of the Daystar from on High—the Mighty I AM Presence.

Therefore, beloved, Seventh-Ray Masters and angels would intensify the potential for freedom, for right change, accelerating back to the fiery core of being amongst those Lightbearers in the earth who have proven lifetime after lifetime in various civilizations which have reached this hour of crisis that they would stand and still stand for the defense of the principles of Almighty God.

Change that is decreed, then, may be accepted in one of two ways by the evolutions of the planetary systems: whether to ride the wave of Light and to find oneself in a new age at a new level beyond the densities of the physical plane, truly in a higher octave of God-awareness, or to choose to deny it, to be inundated, to watch it as though watching the coming of a tsunami—not quite expecting that it will really come—and therefore to go down in the vortex of their own returning karma.

Beloved ones, there is one prophecy that is guaranteed for this planet. Heed it well: Change must come, for the Law will not hold mankind guiltless who commit the crimes upon the holy innocents and the newborn with the cultural contaminations of Western civilization.

Blessed hearts, the day will come when the Great Law, which none of us in the ascended state will be able to turn back, will say by the right hand of God to all those forces in the earth who have perpetrated and perpetuated the Lie: "Thus far and no farther! The full accountability of your destroying of the souls of these little ones must be upon you."

Beloved, you know that this destructivity comes through all of the vehicles of mass communication, through drugs and the purveying of wickedness in the prostitution of children, their abuse, in the programming of their minds away from God, and the tolerance of violence—even the violence of the rock music that does tear their chakras from earliest days in the womb. These assaults upon that Life who is God in this new generation must come to the end! And this end, beloved, must be decreed by *you*.

Now, then, that I have received my deliverance and the Messenger has received her deliverance by the God affirmation and vote of confidence and violet flame decrees of Keepers of the Flame worldwide, it is time to turn our attention to the challenge of Absolute Evil in society and to hold those promised prayer vigils for the overturning of that which does truly invade and assault the souls of the people of earth.

Then, beloved, having so opened the channels to heaven that the angels of God may descend and ascend as in Jacob's dream—that they might enter the fray and rescue the Lightbearers and bring to judgment those who in their wickedness are truly accelerating oncoming earth cataclysm—we shall see just how great the dispensation of Light can be for the earnest, committed intercession of the Keepers of the Flame in their dedicated prayer vigils.

Beloved ones, let this July conference at Camelot be a prayer vigil unto the nations for the binding of forces that would catapult this earth into war and nuclear disaster, and for the challenging of the last plagues and all who stand as the dweller on the threshold preventing the people from those cures of Light and the natural cures that are owing to them. I speak of the pollution that is dire in the medical profession—the backwardness, the intrigue and the treachery that does put upon the bodies of this people drugs that actually interfere with the genetic strain of the race.

Beloved ones, do not be guinea pigs in your mind, your body, your soul, your spirit for anyone or anything. Be your own man and your own woman of the new age, and you will find me and my beloved Portia espousing your cause and teaching you because you have chosen to think independently and not to believe everything you are told or everything that you read as the programming of this North American society.

Beloved hearts, I take you now apart from the grid of mass mechanization that has befallen this beloved country. Come with me as I accelerate your consciousness into the etheric octave. We shall rest above North America and we shall understand the meaning of the Mighty Blue Eagle that is in fact a configuration of blue-lightning angels who are in the charge of that God Surya, that ancient one of India who does sit in the seat of the Central Sun of Sirius.

Beloved ones, there are cosmic legions of Light. And your own Christ Jesus told you,

"Think you not that I cannot in this hour summon twelve legions of angels from my Father to deliver me from this fate?" But the Lord Christ did not. He chose the hour of the crucifixion to show you that the powers that be in this world will always see to it that the emergent Christed One is persecuted to the level of the crucifixion. It is a false-hierarchy imitation of the true initiation of the cosmic cross of white fire whereby you are fastened [to] in the heart of the Cosmic Christ and the lines of force, as Above so below, are one [won].

He said, and I say to you: As they have done it to me, so they will do it to you. The servant is not greater than his Lord.

Understand that anyone who declares himself a disciple on the path of personal Christhood and dares to affirm, "Every day I AM becoming more of my Christ in every way," anyone who dares say "Yes" when confronted by the challenge "Art thou the Christ?": "Yea, the I AM THAT I AM in me *is* the Christ and the I AM THAT I AM of *you* is also the Christ"—anyone who shall so be free to speak in joy as well as into the teeth of the very challenge of Antichrist *must know* that those forces of Absolute Evil entrenched upon this planetary body in the person of embodied fallen angels are those who have the most to lose and nothing to gain by your Christhood.

Do not expect them to line the streets with hosannas on the day of your coming forth. Beloved ones, they only wait when the tumult dies to find some manner in which to trap and conspire as to the death of the one—anyone—who dares to be the incarnation of the Word and that one in this hour of Aquarius.

And this is indeed the mystery of Aquarius that I proclaim to you and that my Messenger has proclaimed to you—that in that hour, not the one but the many shall become the one incarnate Word. And the Mystical Body of God upon earth composed of numberless numbers of saints shall be the force and the presence in the heart of the earth to overturn the entire world capitalist/communist conspiracy against the Lightbearers of every nation!

This is my prediction this day, beloved—that it shall come to pass! But I tell you, this prediction can only be fulfilled by God in *you*, by *your* free will and determination.

There is a handwriting on the wall. There is a pattern in the heavens that waits to be filled in. Beloved ones, it is a giant mural. And by taking your place in this mural in this hour at the etheric level in a giant panorama of history that is coming [being fulfilled] in America, you make your vow and decree to fulfill a prophecy that is based solely and entirely upon the free will of the Lightbearers in embodiment.

And against this hour of your decision and the decision of the Lightbearers to unite from around the whole world have come the forces of abortion in this age and the murder of the mind and the soul through drugs and the carrying away of the youth following the pied pipers of that "music" of the fallen Atlanteans revisited.

Therefore, beloved, they have contrived many, many ways to take away the Lightbearers who now come to fill in, in the color of their causal bodies and their garments, those roles that must be played. They can be defeated, one and all. Holy families understanding the reality of the Father/Mother God embodying in them may go to the mountains, may bring forth children, and may raise them to bring forth the inner Light.

I am Joseph and I do sponsor again the opportunity for you to recognize the calling to open the gates. Open the gates of your temple to these souls of Light who truly come to love you, to help you, to stand by you where you stand and still stand and toil and become weary; they come to take up your plow, to take up your implements of service and to work side by side with you in the maintaining of a community of Light that will one day be seen as the example of a pre-golden-age community and souls who are marching to the Sun.

Thus, beloved, the decree has gone forth. Change is upon you. Look now upon North America from these heights of the etheric plane. See those who are burdened in their bodies, who suffer. And the very burdening of the bodies has made them almost lifeless, complacent, spineless.

They do not have the physical strength or the physical fire to rise up and challenge the oppressors that come at every hand to take their farms, take their land, take their money, and manipulate every area of their lives.

Beloved ones, Christed ones are called for in every area where people are suffering abuse at the hand of federal and state governments, at the hand of those bureaucrats who have gone mad and have lost completely, if they ever had it, the vision of the founding of this nation under God.

Blessed hearts, do not lose the independence of the American spirit by failing to see that bureaucracies of appointed officials who have never been elected of the people, by the people, and for the people do control your destinies in many areas of your life. Do not fail to see that if you do not challenge the abuse of power in this nation in the moneyed, governmental, and secret-society interests, the day will come when the beast they have created is so great that it will indeed take cataclysm or war to break the stranglehold upon the people.

Blessed ones, this nation I have dedicated for you personally. I have sponsored your birth or immigration here. Understand this. We do not see people in terms of masses. We see people in terms of the individual and his supreme worth. Think you not that we do not have the capacity to know you and to befriend you one by one—that we do not recognize you on the instant and remember every lifetime where we have served together and forged and won some link in the universal chain of Hierarchy for freedom and not bondage?

Beloved ones, I do know you and I know you well. I have sponsored your birth with the Goddess of Liberty, and I come in this hour to remind you that had it not been for the sponsorship of my life and other Ascended Masters, you might have been born far away in another land or have never arrived at these shores in this life and therefore not have had the opportunity to make good your promise at inner levels at the conclusion of a previous life that was not fruitful to the holy cause: your promise to be the Spirit of Liberty on behalf of those who have not reached the maturity of the initiate, for they must still eke out their daily bread and a few coins they can beg—those who are deprived of education and the real heart of religion.

These beggars, spiritual beggars in the streets of the nations of the earth, beloved, cannot suddenly rise to defend the ultimate integrity and spiritual reality of a nation. It takes generations and centuries of evolution in consciousness and education to come to that place where you have the full capability to lay your life upon the altar of this nation that this freedom might be retained for those blessed souls who arrive here from Vietnam, from Cambodia, from South America, from every nation where their land has been taken from them, where their families have been killed mercilessly, as in Afghanistan.

Beloved, America is truly the haven of my heart and yours. Won't you open your hearts to these huddled masses and recognize that by the time they reach the maturity of individual Christhood there must be a platform left for them to play their part on the stage of life? And if it is to be there, beloved, it must be because you have preserved its point of origin and its cosmic purpose today, here and now.

Therefore, beloved, remember—once *you* were the waif, homeless without a champion. And once long ago El Morya Khan, riding his white horse, fierce warrior in the midst of battle, did ride through and lean down and pick you up and take you to his heart and rescue you from another battle and a moment of utter helplessness.

I say to you, chelas of the will of God: It is your hour and the power of Light. Now *be* the Master. Now *be* the rescuer of my little ones.

America, my beloved land, hear my call and recognize that souls are being lost on this soil as the beloved Mary predicted at Fátima. Souls are being destroyed by the mechanism of hell, raised up to sophistication and respectability in all areas of life. And the shock factors of these conditions become so great that the people are neutralized to the point that they cannot even react.

May the beloved Keepers of the Flame who show such devotion and love and sacrifice also return to the path of mastery to get their houses and their lives in order and to now go to the fiery core of Being and of the Inner Retreat—there to develop a decree momentum such as you have not yet developed.

Let those who have been acquainted with the Ascended Masters recognize that you are the examples for those newly come to this Teaching. If you do not show forth the fruits of our presence, who will convince them, and by what means, that the Ascended Masters are real and that their presence is the power to change life into the God-estate?

You have an accountability when you call yourself a Keeper of the Flame of Life, a champion of the Goddess of Liberty. And your accountability is to spread the joy of this communion and the great cooperative venture of the Ascended Masters of the Great White Brotherhood and their unascended chelas.

Thus, get thee up to the mountain! I speak of the mountain of God and your Mighty I AM Presence. What use is the saving of the flesh-and-blood temple? We seek the saving of the immortal spirit. And when you have ascended to the plane of your Mighty I AM Presence because you have determined to leave the morass of this lower astral consciousness, you will find yourself desiring also the physical mountain of God—not to run and hide for safety but to go and be the arms of Christ outstretched, welcoming my own who need understanding and soul nourishment and a place prepared in these hours of turning darkness.

Beloved ones, many have been reached by the knowledge of my name and my presence and this call. I am gratified by many who have initiated spirals of light, who have increased the violet flame and therefore alleviated the load of planetary suffering.

But, beloved hearts, I am also disappointed. And in the zeal of the LORD, I point to those who have known the Word and my presence and my power and have forsaken it for their own spiritual pride, their intellectual arguments and connivances—all a ruse, for they would dodge the necessary step of the surrender of that carnal mind unto their own beloved Holy Christ Self.

Thus, I rebuke those who know better and who have not done better, those who have already made the choice not only to forsake their calling, beloved ones, but to take this very teaching spoken from the altars of heaven and to elect to enter the left-handed path with it, glorifying their egos and their psychic thralldom and their consorting with spirits of a lower order who come in the name of Lanello to divide and conquer the Body of God.

All of this they do yet in my name, beloved!— and in the name of the new dispensation of the new age.

Many have wandered far from the center of the I AM Presence. And when they do so, beloved, it is always the sign that the soul seeks self-gain and will not bend the knee before her own Christ and her own Lord.

Those who desire to be entertained and flattered by supposed messages concerning past lives or wondrous accomplishments may sit in their circles and fiddle with these psychic entities while the nation burns, while it is covered with warfare, and proclaim "Peace!" and "Peace!" while the radioactive fallout falls upon their heads as a cloud of unknowingness and base ignorance.

O beloved, how can any true Lightbearer neglect so great a salvation? I tell you, beloved, that those who behave in this manner also have a long history of consorting with the magic of fallen angels. They have been entertained by their baubles and trinkets and promises and offers of an easy way out of the karmic burden for centuries!

Their course was also predictable, yet God has seen fit to give all, both the tares and the wheat, the opportunity to come into the Light. And even the tare may receive the engrafted Word and a threefold flame and begin anew the odyssey of the path of initiation where every weakness will be tested and every strength will be tested. And the more furious* the tenacity, in the sense of accelerated sacred fire, with which the initiate approaches this course of testings, the

_____
*intense; existing in an extreme degree; zealous.

greater the progress and the more accelerated will be the victory.

There is no time preordained for your path. The cycles are shortened for the elect who do the will of God. The only condition is the spacing of the absorption of light that is wise and for your good health spiritually and physically, for the body's atoms cannot adjust too quickly to the greater and greater light. Therefore, in the meantime, you can yet serve and give the Teaching while your bodies are being adjusted and stepped up for a larger calling and service.

Remember, beloved, when you make the decision to step into the political arena, into the public eye to represent the people, you must have passed certain initiations whereby there is removed from you the propensity of ambition, pride, competition, and anger. When these have been thoroughly excised from you, you will find yourselves able to stand against those powers of Antichrist who desire to see no Lightbearer hold any office in any way representative of the people, whether in education or in a representative government.

Precious, precious are the feet of those who have made their way to my heart this day. I pray for you fervently, especially in the hour of subtle temptation which you may not recognize because you slip into it so easily as an old pattern of the procrastination of the day of your God-mastery. I pray that you lose not the time or the hour, for the clock is ticking away the sands of opportunity.

Blessed ones, may you step into the great panorama of destiny. May you recognize that this opportunity occurs at great intervals of cycles—sometimes ten thousand, fifty, seventy, or a hundred thousand years before the evolution of a planetary system may reach that apex once again where the individual who has karma at that level can now expiate it, for he did not make the right choice [at that exact cycle which has now come full circle] in the last round.

Beloved ones, those who do not elect to become God in this age, if the worst scenario would happen, would find themselves embodying upon a very sick and dying planetary body, waiting perhaps millions of years to the time when it would become habitable again and civilization could be begun and reach again this moment for the choice—the right choice to be made.

If, then, the worst of scenarios does come to pass, those who have chosen the Light and to champion freedom will find themselves in etheric octaves of the planetary sphere that is already in the golden age—the place of the inner blueprint, the inner design that has never been compromised, the place of the golden etheric cities of Light.

Thus, beloved, there is a compartment of consciousness and a plane of evolution suitable to every lifestream. Some such lifestreams occupy a civilization in the center of the earth. They are also physical. Thus, there are layered spheres ranging from the physical to the astral to the mental to the etheric.

And in these many levels of earth and heavenly worlds abide millions of evolving souls, all of whom understand that the greatest challenge of all faced by any of these evolutions today is that being faced by you who are in physical embodiment in this wavelength. For you will determine whether the Light will descend from etheric octaves to make the golden age physical or whether the Darkness shall come up from beneath and inundate it, pushing the Light back to higher octaves.

The winning of the physical planet will, then, create a chain reaction for Light throughout the systems of worlds, and the contrary would be the case if this physical level were lost. For earth is a crossroads of many lifewaves, of many systems and other galaxies; all come due in this hour for the confrontation in the final karma of Light and Darkness.

I have spoken to you out of the heart of Liberty. I have shared with you my great desire to work with you. I invite you to become a part of the Keepers of the Flame Fraternity that I might truly be welcomed with others of the Darjeeling Council of Ascended Masters to stand at your side and sponsor your life, even as now you choose to sponsor the Ascended Masters, their Teachings and activity on earth.

To all I say, then, I commend you to your highest purpose and destiny. I commend you to deliberate right choice and the right cause of action for the right reason and motive. I commend you to call upon the All-Seeing Eye of God that the vision of the future coming out of the past might be seen and known, that the present might be for you a calculated platform of forward movement into the Light.

When all points of the grid of personal and planetary karma are known and the graph may be seen, it will become clear to you at inner levels and through that All-Seeing Eye of God that there are few choices left to any upon earth that can bring about the necessary deliverance of souls.

We are grateful that a company such as you of serious students does gather in this day when so many voices call you elsewhere.

Portia and I express our gratitude that you have received us and our Messenger. We remain, then, for the sponsoring of Light in your chakras this afternoon and commend you to the call of Cyclopea.*

I AM, in the light of freedom, your eternal champion of right action. May you always choose right and therefore be in the center of the Cosmic Christ.

I salute you and bless you in the new age.
[24-sec. standing ovation]

June 8, 1986
San Francisco

*See decree 50.05 in *Prayers, Meditations, and Dynamic Decrees for the Coming Revolution in Higher Consciousness*, Section I, $2.95, to open the third eye.

CHAPTER II

A Prophecy of Karma

Prophets Who Must Prophesy in America

O America, Hear My Cry Before It Is too Late!
Affirm God's Freedom Else Totalitarianism Will
Not Be Stopped without Bloodshed in the USA

S o, I am come, your Knight Commander of the
Keepers of the Flame. So, I am here! Are you
ready, Keepers of the Flame?

["Yes!" 35-sec. applause]

So with Morya we march in July, the sign of
the Mother for the freedom of her own to return
to her heart. For I give you the key to the word of
Sumer—only in the Divine Mother can freedom
be found and retained.[16]

So, beloved, this movement is of the Divine
Mother and not of any human. Our Spirit transcends the form and the Messenger we use. Understand how God in you is greater than any one of
us. So I am here and I stand by the grace of God
and his Holy Spirit of freedom! I stand before this
banner of freedom* that still recalls the sign of the
God Star Sirius and the power of Elohim in you to
become that Word incarnate.

*the flag of the United States of America

Children of the Sun who have become the sons and daughters of God, from the beginning unto the ending I am your most belov'd Merlin. And I say "most belov'd" by way of extending my heart to you for the alchemy of victory that you, Keepers of the Flame, have wrought in this Church Universal and Triumphant.

Therefore, the angels applaud. Hear them, beloved. Hear them. [18-sec. applause]

The lower spirits of the prophets of Baal have seen their day! They may no longer even dominate the lower channels whom they have used. Beloved ones, it is a triumphant day for the gift of the Holy Spirit of prophecy itself unto you and all who love God supremely. Therefore, in that alchemy come, so now reside in the seat of my heart. (Won't you be seated.)

Where shall we go, LORD, but to the heart of the living disciple? So we have come, LORD, and so thy Word shall abide here forever. And thy Word, O LORD, is power. And thy Word in the hearts of this people shall truly vindicate thy name I AM THAT I AM.

I pray the Father of all victory and light and freedom, come swiftly, then, to bind the spoilers in North and South America! Come quickly, then, and let the fire of freedom emerge in the hearts of those who dare to challenge tyranny, dictatorship and murder in Nicaragua!

O God, deliver these, as they are as the early American patriots taking upon themselves the responsibility to defend a nation against the usurpers of the seat of God government that belongs to the people, is of and by the people of Nicaragua, who demand their freedom this day. And I say, they shall have it! [34-sec. standing ovation]

And I challenge *you*, Keepers of the Flame, to prove me right. I challenge *you* as prophets in the earth this day. For my mantle of prophecy descends upon you now, beloved. Seize it. Wear it. Use it. For this nation must be filled with the prophets of the Almighty whose prophesying is in the affirmation of the prophecy itself.

To affirm the victory is a fiat of the LORD's prophecy. Therefore, let those who dare, go, then, to the side of those freedom fighters and say at their side the rosary to Archangel Michael. Let those who dare, go in their finer bodies as others may go in the physical.

Beloved, it is the company of saints. It is the prophets, old and new, who must affirm this freedom this day. For it is the fulcrum, whether of God-freedom to the entire hemisphere or totalitarian encroachment *that will not be stopped, I warn you, without bloodshed in these United States.* And this is my prophecy to you!

They will move to Panama. They will infiltrate. And there is not the spine or the unity today to turn them back. Let them *be* turned back and let our voice, now the minority, become that which sparks the majority to see the vision and to realize it! [17-sec. applause]

Nevermore was there a cause so great, so espoused by the tears of the beloved Mother Mary and her heart's fire. Nevermore since the American Revolution has there been a cause that so concerns the nations and the Ascended Masters. Beloved ones, the facing of the tyrant of the Soviet Union now becomes the world enterprise of Lightbearers everywhere. Therefore, I say to *you:* Lightbearers of the world, unite! [27-sec. applause]

We know the plight of those in Afghanistan and elsewhere. We know of the Darkness pitted against black and white and independence in South Africa. We know of the conspiracies that take the Lightbearers and enlist them in the causes of the fallen ones by rhetoric, cliché, indoctrination, and the foul use of the press by those who have nothing to lose, for they have already lost their souls long, long ago.

We know, beloved. That is why we insist that the integrity of freedom in this hemisphere be fought for and won. For this entire base, North and South united, must be a sun—a sun that is double in a giant figure-eight flow, as above so below—as below so as above. North America and South America can be that Alpha-to-Omega spreading the Sun of Light to all areas of the earth.

O beloved, there are millions who love me in South America and throughout the land of the north. Go and find them! Send the missile of the books, the voice, the message. Send yourself, but go to these. For this bastion of freedom must prevail as a protection and a haven for all nations of the earth.

Most beloved, see and know that this pushing back of Darkness involves the challenging of those nesting serpents in Havana and elsewhere who have been entrenched far too long and should have been plucked out long ago. Now, beloved, decisive action must be considered, and I ask you to pray to Almighty God to inspire your leaders as to what that action must be.

(I bid you again, beloved, be seated.)

Consider the karma that befalls the nation America for the neglect of her leaders. This karma is grievous and borne as a yoke by all of her people. For they have had, surely they have had, from their mothers' hearts and from the Goddess of Liberty the impartation of the flame of freedom. They have not sought, championed, and defended their sacred right.

Therefore, those to whom the proffered gift of my heart is given, those who are accounted responsible, then, in this Guru/chela relationship of the Aquarian age which I offer, they will come to the place in the not-too-distant future where the neglect to defend the rights of man and woman—human and divine—will require them to pay the ultimate price.

Beloved ones, when the golden age of the Sahara was traduced by forces within and without, it was at a far more perfected state than this one. Truly, the Keepers of the Flame of Liberty have been the intercessors and mediators in America. The mere attention and allegiance by the people to the Goddess, O beloved, has anchored an image in the third eye of the nation this year and in preparation for this date that allows Mother Liberty to enter. For this is true devotion given by people of all faiths, religion or none, to the very heart and spirit of America from the beginning.

How easy it is for the heart to fly to the arms of the Mother. Is it not wondrous that this people has arisen from Lemuria and Atlantis and the ancient cult of the Mother, that a people from so many lands should understand inherently the ancient ones? Thus, Mother's Day is a day of appreciation for that ancient flame and its present embodiment in the mothers of the nation and as the sacred fire of the ascension.

Beloved, it is a great land of wondrous people, exceptional people, many of whom will not reach their fullest potential in this life because of the denial to them at an early age of proper education and love. And if they are not permanently set back from the period of conception to the age of seven, I tell you, they have very little chance of surviving the teenage years, when most are finished off and detoured from a constructive life by the great, great burden of drugs upon them.

Beloved, the war is upon the Christed ones— these little ones. In God's name, I say to you, have mercy upon them! Have mercy upon me, Saint Germain, and know that I, Joseph, care for all of these little ones and for you! I say, help me to help the Blessed Mother and to help the Lord Jesus to deliver a nation by taking care of her youth!

O precious ones, where are they today, yesterday, tomorrow? Somewhere else but in the immediacy of the urgency of Life itself which can afford them, oh, the highest—the highest delivery of their causal body. Oh truly, truly, let some not count time, but come now and release these books. Release them, then, for all levels and minds.

Beloved ones, El Morya has announced the sale of this property, but my announcement to you, for which I have great cherishment and hope, is the purchase of two new printing presses for Camelot. [37-sec. standing ovation] One is already delivered and in place, for the Messenger lost no time in the moment of the sale of this property to dedicate the first funds to the most needed perfector press. [23-sec. applause]

Thus, I tell you that the Order of Saint Joseph is an order of publishing the Word for the care of the little Child Jesus in every heart. I, who gave my life and suffered more than I would tell to deliver to the world my writings of science and freedom and the psychology of Good and Evil in the plays, beloved, I know the power of the printed Word to endure beyond those who dedicate themselves to its publication.

You who would survive in the minds of a people who may awaken ten centuries from now because you have preserved freedom today, I tell you, secure the books and secure the places in men's hearts where the Teaching will endure even though heaven and earth pass away.

We publish books not for the survival of books, beloved, but for the survival of souls lifetime after lifetime who do not forget the cumulative effect of the culture of the heart. The heart is reborn (and it is the least pregnable of all chakras)—and the soul herself—in the newborn child. "The heart that has truly loved never forgets." Truly, it is so. I have never forgot thee. Thou hast never forgot me. Thou hast known my face as I have known thine own.

Precious ones, we march in July. We march in August with marching books marching off the presses. Who will help the Order of Saint Joseph? Who will learn the trade and help us save the hemisphere and the earth?

["We will!"]

You are so ready, beloved—and recording angels are very ready! [16-sec. applause] And your promise is recorded. But so is mine, beloved. It is recorded in your heart forever.

So in the light and the heart of Liberty, whose message comes this eve, let us also remember the call of the Mother—the call of the Mother to Saint Francis in the voice of Jesus: Rebuild my church—rebuild my house.

Now we must build anew. Is it not a prophecy

to Jeremiah first to tear down and destroy and then to build? It is no coincidence that chelas of the will of God begin with a clean white page in a higher octave—land that stretches farther than the eye can see or even the soul can fly.

Blessed ones, you have a new beginning unprecedented. Take it swiftly. Help us, then. Let us move and move with victory and care. Let us establish the altar, of course in the manger where all beginnings are. There is no better place than the barn on the farm. [15-sec. applause]

It is the love of the LORD himself who dwells in the hearts of those who work his Works. Let us see such a busyness of diligence and building and moving that swiftly as the eagles fly you find yourselves exactly where the Almighty desires you to be January 1, 1987. Let us not skip a beat in delivering to the nations these words, these Teachings, this message of liberation and comfort.

Those who still stand against the international corporations and banks and Communist systems, those who stand with Jonas Savimbi—that handful against the overwhelming odds of support to the enemy, I am sorry to say, by the United States [17] — those who stand with him need your comfort, your prayer, and the empowerment of God.

Believe me, beloved, your voice does count. Do not sense a victory won but a victory begun. Know that the ritual of the altar* is necessary now more than ever. Let us defeat those forces that

*the exercise of the science of the spoken Word for the transmutation of personal and planetary karma at the altar—the place of alchemical change, or "altar"ation by the violet flame of the Holy Spirit

come suddenly to our best servants as illness or accident or death.

Do not be superstitious. Merely be diligent. Do not give power to those forces that have no power, but recognize that light in you must be a shaft impenetrable.

Now, let us take that clipper ship of Maitreya. Let us sail on the waters of a golden, shining sea—a sea that carries us beyond this lower level and vibration. We have plucked you as Jeremiah was plucked by the Ancient of Days.

Come fly with me, beloved. For I would also be in the Heart of the Inner Retreat one year from this day in a company five times as great and more as this one. Please help me gather them from all the nations. For in this conference our cry goes forth. Let it reach the boundaries of the universe, and let its echo then be the return of those who have heard:

"Lightbearers of the world, unite!"

So I also say, Let the seed of Serpent, then, be plucked out of their midst and be bound and removed this day! I, Saint Germain, therefore defy those serpents as infiltrators in America, in the earth, and in Holy Church. Let those, then, who deny the sacred freedoms to any, now have taken from them the very thing which they have denied to others.

This law of karma acts this day. And you will see how the LORD God by his angels—Michael, Jophiel, Chamuel, Raphael, Zadkiel, Uriel, and

Gabriel—does indeed, beloved, deliver that karma of the denial of God-freedom in the seven chakras of all life.

O beloved, those who raise the sword Excalibur therefore set the standard of that sword. And all, then, who rally to it must rise to its level. For it will challenge all that sets itself against that will of God in a mighty people.

O mighty people of the earth and all nations, come to my heart. For I would give you my gift of freedom, my violet flame.

O America, I have loved you! I love you still! Hear my cry before it is too late. Hear the call and let this life be lived more than for economic gain, indulgence, pleasure, or fame.

I am here. I am free. I have more than all of these! I have immortality, and *you* may have it, too, by right choice. May every choice be right by the standard of Christ in you.

I seal you in my heart and flame. God-Victory, beloved. Thus, let us call together:

Lightbearers of the world, unite!
Lightbearers of the world, unite!
Lightbearers of the world, unite!

And claim the four sacred freedoms by the Path, the true Path of initiation of the coming Christ who is come.

In the name of Jesus, Amen. [40-sec. applause]

July 4, 1986
Los Angeles

For notes to Chap. 11 see p. 222

CHAPTER 12

A Prophecy of Karma
Of the United States of America

Economic Debacle Foreseen
A First Strike by the Soviet Union
Your Preparedness Can Prevent Nuclear War

Lightbearers of the World,

I come and I am here and I would speak to you from my heart.

Keepers of the Flame who hear me now, attend my word and my coming in the name of the LORD. I AM Saint Germain, your Knight Commander, and I bear the flaming sword of the LORD God. Now hear me, O beloved ones, and be seated in his living flame.

Peril stalks while the nations sleep. And the preachers preach, "Peace!" when war is yet in the hearts of the betrayers of Christ. It is the handwriting on the wall and the secrets of men's hearts that I read. This is no mystery, yet I unveil it as such.

The right hand and the left—let them be in unison and let one know that which the other is doing. Know God. Know thyself. Know the subconscious. Know the true friend and know the tireless enemy.

Friends of Light, you have waited for my certain word, and I have saved it for you. Let none, then, hold it back. For the Keepers of the Flame have the right to know and in knowing, to dare, to do, to be silent in the heart of God—and to know when and what message to shout from the housetops.

Economic debacle is foreseen. Prepare. Setbacks will be sudden. Be not lulled by the heyday. Many Band-Aids upon the economy, the money system, the banking houses. These will not prevent the collapse of nations and banking houses built on sands of human greed, ambition, and manipulation of the lifeblood of the people of God.

For they shall not prevail who have built their empires on the backs of the children of God who bear in their bodies the very Blood of Christ. The people, then, who bear that Light may no longer be used as foundation stones for the Cain civilization.

Beloved, you have known that this cannot be. The end must come that the beginning might begin. The judgment of the Lord Christ is at hand. Who shall stand in the hour of his coming? The Lord weeps not alone for his rejection by the good people but for their plight and predicament when they are found unprepared.

Beloved ones, the prophecies shall be fulfilled as God has decreed them. Where is the element of free will? It is present in ye all but alone in the divine spark. And those who think they are free are not free, for they are bound by karma and the karma of inordinate desire.

Seek ye first the kingdom of God and his

righteousness. Seek ye first to live, to endure, to survive the age. And know that it is possible to live through the worst of prophecy.

I may speak it, but I am not the origin of prophecy! Every living soul upon this earth and fallen angels and godless ones—all are harbingers of that which must descend. For the law of karma is inexorable, irrevocable, saving where the violet flame, the sacred fire, does consume it.

Thus, the LORD has said, "Be pillars of fire."

Go, then! Set your priority. For where there is economic debacle, there, as history records, are the conditions of war. Be not asleep. God is not mocked. Shall his people be mocked? I say, nay! Therefore, I have come this night to speak to my own.

Therefore, beloved, you have every reason to believe, to be concerned, and to be prepared for a first strike by the Soviet Union upon these United States. You have every reason to be alert. You have every reason to consider that the wilderness land [America] is indeed prepared for the Woman and her seed.

Therefore, secure the underground shelters, preserve the food, and prepare to survive. And if it be an exercise proven unneeded, then bless God that it did not go unheeded. For beloved, my word and your response, your very preparedness, is the one condition that can prevent the almost inevitable scenario of nuclear war.

Beloved ones, preparedness is the key. If you do not think and act in terms of survival, then surely, *surely*, I say, you will not survive!

Even as I speak, beloved, meetings unending take place. The enemy is prepared to survive a nuclear war—the United States is not. Unless there be a remnant, where, *where* shall the Everlasting Gospel and the one hundred forty and four thousand appear?

Beloved hearts, there are many called to make supreme sacrifices. Take, then, for example, the military establishment of this nation. Various groups of people upon earth have assignments to thwart the enemy's betrayal of the Light. Can you not understand, then, that though the troops be never used nor the armaments drawn, it is necessary in the hour of the judgment of the fallen angels and of the reapers who come to separate the tares from the wheat that some understand that survival and preparation is not for the ultimate doomsday but for the prevention thereof? And though it may never be needed, it must be accomplished.

Blessed ones, a great deal is at stake. Our first priority is to release such Light as to prevent the Darkness of the remainder of this century. But, beloved, I tell you frankly from our hearts, the hour is long past when there is opportunity for the many to respond.

When spirals of malintent begin to cycle into the physical, let the Keepers of the Flame watch and unite. The time comes when the avalanche cannot be turned back.

Seeds of unrest and betrayal, seeds of the profligate ones, seeds of those who are unalterably tied to a pleasure cult of materialism, who sleep already and know it not—these shall not be turned back [i.e., converted, to the Light].

Some have already awakened to the Light, and it has awakened in them their own evil. And thus, they are already in their everlasting contempt of the LORD. These will not be converted by the Holy Spirit.

Seek the Lightbearers and let them be galvanized to the very power of the Archangels, who know well how to achieve the victory.

What do you think is the karma of a nation? The sin of omission? When a nation allows Afghanistan to be devoured, when its members encourage the destruction of South Africa, leave alone the nest of serpents in the Caribbean, will not come to the aid of the freedom fighters appreciably, will not see the Panama Canal as the nexus of freedom, a territory to be claimed by the enemy if it does not act soon—when a nation of people turn their backs and allow millions to be aborted: what is the karma of that nation?

Can you understand, beloved, what is the priority in the heart of God? It is the survival of the soul. When God determines that the soul on its course of self-destruction shall indeed be destroyed for the neglect of Cosmic Law, then the intercessors are withdrawn, the Mediator may no longer mediate between a nation or an individual and his karma.

Think of what I have said and simply observe life. One is taken and another is left. Some pass from the screen of life, for they have outplayed the mercy of God and now must face that karma. Ungrateful they have been. Thus, the Law does descend. God desires to see the soul of a people survive. And for this, He has said, a whole civilization may be expendable.

Souls are being lost in this nation!—more so than in any other nation, beloved, because of the destruction of the body and the soul in hell through the subculture of drugs, allowing souls, then, to be deluded and to make their pacts with fallen angels and give to them all of their Light until there is nothing left.

Beloved hearts, these things ought not to be. Therefore, it is necessary and you must understand—one accident in Chernobyl and pollution of the environment that has not been told that has reached your own bodies. Another accident, the pollution of a river.

Beloved ones, how many "accidents" have the Archangels prevented? How many have they spared you because you have kept the light in the city? And how long will they hold back this karma?

Thus, get thee to the mountain of God, that the angels and the elementals might perform their work that is necessary for the cleansing of the elements polluted, not alone by nuclear fallout but by the hatred of men's hearts.

Yes, it is planned, it is a possibility, and it becomes expedient for the East to wage war upon the West for economic reasons, for reasons of survival, and for reasons of Evil. For Absolute

Evil will outplay itself that it may be no more.
Thus, the Assyrian and the Babylonian, each in
his own time, are the instrument of the judgment
of Israel.

If a remnant is to hold the balance and be, as
it were, the sacrifice of a nation, then let the
remnant know who they are and what is their
mission and reason for being. The mitigating
factor in economic debacle, in nuclear war, in
plague untold and death is the nucleus of Lightbearers and the quotient of sacred fire they invoke.

They who invoke it must know, then, that
they are as a star in the astral sea of the earth and
that as that star they, too, become—because their
physical bodies are precious—the target, then, of
the enemy. Thus, they must be, *above all people*,
prepared to meet the opposition to the very Light
they hold as the ensign of the people.

Understand, beloved, the unpredictability of
the carnal mind. There are no guarantees, even
from our level, else life should be a predestination
and all should sit and do nothing. Depending
upon the vigilance as never before of our Keepers
of the Flame, depending on the Light invoked, so
shall the protection be and so shall be the forestalling of cataclysm as well.

Each one of you in your own time has had
the experience of seeing burdens come upon you
for absence of prayer or dynamic decrees, and the
resolution of burdens by regular prayer and dynamic decrees. Thus the Law has taught you the

consequences of action and that for every action or nonaction there is fruit that is reaped—the bitter and the sweet.

Therefore, beloved, know this—that when the sinister force intensifies, it requires more Light and a closeness to Archangel Michael to consume it ere it cycle into the physical.

I tell you of a certainty that darkness in the land will increase beginning January 1, 1987. But, beloved, there are yet souls of Light to be rescued. I say know and find your right place in God and then defend it with your life.

Those of extraordinary Light—and I say ye all are counted in that number—must use extraordinary measures to defend that Light. And those who have children know that by the very nature of the dispensation for the next generation your children's Light [attainment, Christ consciousness] may be greater than your own, and therefore your need to defend it very great.

A more than ordinary number of you have had burdens of parents and family in growing-up years. Forgive them, beloved. It is your Light gainst which the force did wage war, and they were not able to withstand the hot heat of hell itself that came to prevent you from growing in the fullness of the Divine Wholeness.

Understanding, then, the burden upon your parents, forgive and let go, beloved, else you will carry with you the very forces of hell that worked through them that were designed to be your undoing. Let all of this go, as I am present with you, into my violet flame. Let the Holy Ghost come upon you and heal you because you understand the equation.

The records of the Book of Life so indicate, beloved, that your coming has been prophesied by your own I AM Presence for thousands of years, that you might be in this moment one who could keep a flame and keep it blazing in the physical chalice, in the mental body, in the spiritual body, in the memory of God which is yours, and in the desire body itself, which presents a number of challenges.

We have, then, a tripod of war, economic debacle, and cataclysm. Any one of these could be sprung at any time.

We are determined. You must be determined. When we do all in our power to assist you, you must appreciate how urgent is the moment and the hour—how great the need of response.

We place great emphasis upon your victory in the physical while many false preachers are gone about preaching the rapture and the Second Coming and all leaving the earth. See, then, how this defeats the very point of the victory of the Light in the earth and His kingdom come on earth, beloved.

Therefore, again the few see the whole and understand. Let the resurrection be a spiritual initiation which you receive from the heart of Jesus and the Archangel Uriel in the hour when thy soul becomes the bride of Christ. It is not necessary to equate the resurrection with the quitting of the physical temple! Instead, let the kingdom of heaven come down to earth rather than have escapees—all emigrating to the heaven world that they have not known or earned and then be required to return again, for they have allowed many points of the whole Law to escape them.

Do you see, beloved, it is a seductive force that causes people to desire to leave the body and find the rapture when the exact opposite is decreed by the LORD: to win the earth for Light, to bring in a golden age, and to see this sphere purified—to stand with Christ upon the mountain until Death and Hell are, literally, physically cast into the lake of sacred fire and consumed.

Here is the crossroads of Absolute Evil of the galaxies. Here on planet earth.

I tell you, beloved, angels attend as the words come out of your mouths. No sooner is the decree released than bands of angels rush forward to fulfill the fiat.

This is an age of a technological war in the physical octave. Beloved, those who win this battle cannot win it without reinforcement of spiritual fire, night and day, by those who understand the science of the spoken Word.

Beloved ones, the victory may be projected by the LORD God. But the outcome is not known until the victors fight the good fight and win.

You have seen what it has taken in decree power, hour after hour, to achieve your ends and our goals. May you equate that in an understanding of what it will take to endow the forces of Light of America and the West to defeat a very determined, ruthless, inhuman enemy.

If the third vision come to pass[18] because men have not heeded my call, because preachers have still cast me out as the devil, and because those in office, though they have known my name, have not called to me for aid—if there should be war upon this soil, it will be turned back only by divine intervention. This is the prophecy, beloved ones.

Where do you suppose this divine intervention will come from? Yea, *you* must be the answer to that prayer and, by the power of God, sustain heaven on earth in that Inner Retreat while the nation groans to regain a freedom and a purity and a standard that they allowed to be dragged through the streets.

I speak of the image of woman and of child and the desecration of the body and of the divine polarity of Alpha and Omega that has likewise been desecrated.[19]

I speak of the opening of the pits and of the vials of the last plagues and of what has come upon the earth because peoples have not challenged the diabolical actions of devils incarnate who have brought with them out of the pit these diseases. Knowing full well they went [were on their way] to the Last Judgment, they allowed themselves to be consumed by the plague that they might pass it into the mainstream of society to affect the children of the Light.

They never say die, beloved hearts, unless they can take one or a thousand with them. You must prevent them by your Body, by your Blood, as Christ did, as we all have done—our Life-essence magnified through the chakras seven, magnified by the power of the Great White Brotherhood.

Let the wrath of the Almighty fill your spirits this night as the anger of the LORD is upon those who destroy the people of Light, nation by nation. But I tell you, beloved, though the wrath of God be upon the Assyrian, the Babylonian, the Soviet— what do you think is upon those who could prevent it and have not but have joined them, having been enticed all over again by the Serpent in the garden?

O beloved, the wrath of God is indeed upon his own people, and they will know the meaning of wrath as a sacred fire descending and as a karma. They have forgotten to be their brother's keeper. And they have allowed themselves to be prevented and turned back by those in this very government and spies that are rampant in this nation.

Be fearless, beloved, but be watchful. Be bold, but decree.

I have entered this room wearing a white robe. A gold cross pattée in a circle is upon this garment. Beloved, it is the garment of those saints robed in white who march in the armies of heaven with the Faithful and True. I have added to this garment my purple cape of the Knight Commander. And this night it is a fiery blue-purple within and without—a piercing, chemical ray to dissolve that in you which is contamination. And my sword is a flaming sword, like unto Excalibur.

Thus, by my dress I reveal a habit that you ought to put on and wear—a ritual of knowing that the divine intervention that must come must come through those who elect to be the instruments of the divine intercessor on earth.

Now, then, you know. And you have understood the equation. There are others who will and can understand. To that end, beloved, your staff and mine have toiled to release the teachings that they might go forth, carried by you. For we have a twofold purpose and reason for being—survival and the preaching of the Word. Consider this your reason for being and determine how you can be cut free economically, karmically, and in every way.

Beloved ones, angels may knock but you may not hear if you are surfeited in noise, if you allow yourselves to be tossed and tumbled by responsibilities or interruptions. Therefore, listen. You must take fifteen minutes before retiring at night, establish the circle of fire round the place where you rest. Give certain decrees and let all the house be silent as you meditate without interruption upon Almighty God, your Mighty I AM Presence.

Then call to me. Let my angels deliver you to the Royal Teton Retreat, where you may be instructed. Then take note, upon awakening, of the first voices, the first messages that come into your mind. Try the spirits, of course, and always, but be attentive. For a thousand angels cannot alert you to your destiny if you are not tuned in, if you are not listening.

Let your aura be an electromagnetic field of the Seventh Ray. For in the Seventh Ray violet flame is the alchemy of communication between octaves. Let your aura be sealed by the tube of light and the action of Archangel Michael. Let your receptivity be pure because your heart is pure. Inordinate desire for money or things or other distractions clouds the reasoning of the Logos within you. Thus, the mind that is at peace with God, unattached to the consequences of the human and willing to follow when called, will surely hear my angels.

Beloved ones, cast out fear and doubt. Cast out whatever is the prevention of thy Godhood. Let God be your Guru. But remember this—that the I AM THAT I AM is self-revealed in the course of events.

The key, beloved, is the law of cycles. Thus Ecclesiastes wrote that there is a time to sow, a time to reap, a time to live and a time to die. There is a time to take up arms and a time to lay down arms, a time to marry and be with child and a time to remain in the holiness of God for a purpose. All things in their season will lead you to the harvest of a life that has been balanced in all equations.

Oh, to wish you had lived another day in the

past or the future—so many have thought this. Why are we here now? Why must we face this challenge and this oncoming calamity? Beloved ones, you volunteered, you raised your hand. You were chosen when the LORD called because you chose. You are able. You are capable.

And do not think that safety lies anywhere you may choose to have a retreat. If it is not cataclysm or water, it may be fire. If it is not fire, it may be nuclear contamination. If it is not nuclear contamination, it may be plague. Only for such reasons, beloved, could we have chosen such an inconvenient spot for our Camelot.

You have come, the land is a resource of God. Make the most of it, for, beloved, many of you will have plenty of opportunity beyond the year 2000 if you should desire another round. And others of you, by that time, for having gone the whole way, should find yourself ascended in the Light and free.

There is a purpose to every lifestream. And every lifestream—each one of you held in the heart of Jesus—may know that in his heart, the Lord has a dream for you, an opportunity, a love, a joy, a happiness, an assignment, and a battle to be fought and won.

If it must needs be, then I say, Let us get on with it, beloved, for Evil is far spent. Let not their cups be full of the blood of the Lamb's little ones. Let them be stopped, for the Light cometh.

I am Saint Germain. I remind you that I have tried in many ages to woo nations and peoples to the solution at hand. They would not. I do not weep, for the Lord has wept for me and thee this day. I say the hour is passed. Let us save the Lightbearers and look to the New Day.

Now, beloved, in view of my sayings and those sayings not said, I kneel before the altar of God, which you may do also.

Unto the Almighty, I dedicate my heart and to his Light in his own on the earth. I, Saint Germain, in this City of the Angels declare that the enemy of the LORD's host, of the Great White Brotherhood, and of the Messengers of freedom must go down.

Almighty God and the Father, let the judgments of the Lord Christ be upon them. And let every child of God's heart be delivered.

My legions are in the command of the Almighty and of my own. Be swift, O my souls, to answer, then be at peace.

In this moment of silence, beloved, through the electromagnetic field of my aura, now pour through me unto the Almighty all that your heart would speak to him in Christ's name. [one minute of silence observed]

The Shekinah glory descends from the Holy of Holies and it is the Divine Mother appearing. So the Divine Mother herself does descend in answer to the call of Keepers of the Flame. So the Divine Mother is the Mother of the Ruby Ray. And we see her face as the face of Kuan Yin,

Mother Mary, Portia, Pallas Athena, Liberty, and so many—even those of us who wear the masculine garb.

May the face of the Divine Mother, that is of the Holy of Holies of the Shekinah, appear through you, beloved. For the wrath of the Divine Mother in you will rescue God's children, and the love of the Divine Mother will comfort them.

In the name of the Father, the Son, the Holy Spirit, and this living presence of the Mother, I, Saint Germain, salute you, Keepers of the Flame! Rise and take the earth for God-freedom!

[standing ovation]

Thanksgiving Day
November 27, 1986
Los Angeles

Notes to Chap. 11:
16. The first recorded use of the word *freedom* occurs in a document written by Sumerian king Urakagina (c. 2350 B.C.) as *amargi* 'return to the mother'. S. Kramer, *The Sumerians* (Chicago: University of Chicago, 1963), p. 79.
17. **Jonas Savimbi,** founder of UNITA, fought for 8 years against Portuguese rule in Angola but when independence was granted in 1975 the Soviet-backed MPLA gained power. Today Savimbi leads anti-Communist guerrilla forces to free Angola from foreign oppression. Over 33,000 Cuban and Communist-bloc troops support the Marxist regime while U.S. industry and banks actively assist the economy, the banks through loans and credit. Gulf Oil paid $585 million in taxes and royalties to Angola in 1985. About 60 smaller U.S. companies are also involved in oil-related businesses there. Earnings from oil bring in 90% of Angola's foreign revenues, most of which go to Cuba and the USSR to pay for their war against Freedom and the Light.

Notes to Chap. 12:
18. See George Washington's third vision in *Saint Germain On Alchemy,* pocketbook, pp. 142-51, $5.95.
19. ...in pornography, on TV, in standard motion pictures as well as x-rated, and in advertising and rock video.

Picture Credits
(in order of page number)

NEW AGE CLASSICS ON THE ANCIENT WISDOM
by Mark L. Prophet and Elizabeth Clare Prophet

CLIMB THE HIGHEST MOUNTAIN / The Path of the Higher Self Discover the lost code of your Identity, of Nature, and of Life itself. The wisdom of the Ascended Masters clarifies the issues of Spirit and Matter, Good and Evil, and answers the fundamental questions concerning the psychology and the destiny of the soul. Practical and scientific explanations on how to make contact and maintain a relationship with the Higher Self. Examinations of Atlantis and Lemuria and their effect on society and planetary karma today. The chief cornerstone of a century of metaphysical literature. 8 full-color Nicholas Roerich art reproductions, 28 illustrations by Auriel Bessemer, charts, tables, comprehensive index. Softbound, 700 pp., #642, $16.95; hardbound, #100, $21.95. Beautiful gold-stamped blue leatherette.

CORONA CLASS LESSONS / For those who would teach men the Way Jesus and Kuthumi (Saint Francis) build with you precept by precept the pyramid of Divine Selfhood as they prepare you to deliver their teachings that illumine the scriptures and quicken hearts to the Inner Light. Every sentence in these 48 dictations from the World Teachers is a jewel of spiritual enlightenment opening the Christian mysteries for your sharing on the path of personal Christhood taught by our Lord. 500 pp., #1654, $12.95.

THE GREAT WHITE BROTHERHOOD in the Culture, History and Religion of America The Ascended Masters, their Messenger and chelas gathered at Mt. Shasta and the Inner Retreat to hear the word of the LORD. Here is their counsel—the violet flame, the Cosmic Clock, charting the daily astrology of your karma and self-mastery with color charts—every word of their lectures and dictations on freedom, America's destiny, prophecy. Special color section "The Flame of Freedom Speaks," a soul-stirring 4th of July message; photos of community life at the Royal Teton Ranch. 448 pp., #422, $10.95.

THE SCIENCE OF THE SPOKEN WORD From Saint Germain learn to summon the power of the violet flame through dynamic decrees. This spiritual fire cleanses your system of emotional and physical poisons, transmutes karma, erases the cause behind the effect of disease, helps deal with the long-term effect of drugs, and even clears the distressing records of past lives. Decrees, mantras, fiats, and affirmations with step-by-step instruction on how to apply the science of the spoken Word to everyday problems. 242 pp., #104, $7.95.

Saint Germain anointed Elizabeth Clare Prophet his Messenger in 1964. In Book One of this volume she tells you about the Master--his past lives and efforts in Earth's struggle for freedom. In Book Two she reinterprets Nostradamus and demonstrates *the* fundamental and dangerous error of other commentators. In Books Three and Four she publishes the most urgent of Saint Germain's prophecies dictated 1980 to 1986 on cataclysm, the economy, nuclear war, and the betrayers of the people in Church and State.

FOR MORE INFORMATION

For information about the Keepers of the Flame fraternity and monthly lessons; Pearls of Wisdom, dictations of the Ascended Masters sent to you weekly; Summit University three-month and weekend retreats; two-week summer seminars and quarterly conferences which convene at the Royal Teton Ranch, a 33,000-acre self-sufficient spiritual community-in-the-making, as well as the Summit University Service/Study Program with apprenticeship in all phases of organic farming, ranching, construction, publishing and related community services; Montessori International private school, preschool through twelfth grade for children of Keepers of the Flame; and the Ascended Masters' library and study center nearest you, call or write Summit University Press, Box A, Livingston, Montana 59047 (406) 222-8300.

Paperback books, audiocassettes and videotapes on the teachings of the Ascended Masters dictated to their Messengers, Mark L. Prophet and Elizabeth Clare Prophet--including a video series of Ascended Master dictations on "Prophecy in the New Age" and a Summit University Forum TV series with Mrs. Prophet interviewing outstanding experts in the field of health and Nature's alternatives to healing--are available through Summit University Press. Write for free catalogue and information packet.

Upon your request we are also happy to send you particulars on this summer's Summit University Retreat at the Royal Teton Ranch--survival seminars, wilderness treks, teachings of Saint Germain, dictations from the Ascended Masters, prophecy on political and social issues, initiation through the Messenger of the Great White Brotherhood, meditation, yoga, the science of the spoken Word, children's program, summer camping and RV accommodations, and homesteading at Glastonbury.

All at the ranch send you our hearts' love and a joyful welcome to the Inner Retreat!